COMPUTER SCHEDULING OF PUBLIC TRANSPORT
Urban Passenger
Vehicle and Crew Scheduling

COMPUTER SCHEDULING OF PUBLIC TRANSPORT

Urban Passenger Vehicle and Crew Scheduling

Papers based on presentations at the International Workshop held at the University of Leeds, 16-18 July, 1980

edited by

Anthony WREN

Head of the Operational Research Unit
Department of Computer Studies
The University of Leeds, England

NORTH-HOLLAND PUBLISHING COMPANY · AMSTERDAM · NEW YORK · OXFORD

ISBN: 0 444 86170 x

Publishers:

NORTH-HOLLAND PUBLISHING COMPANY
AMSTERDAM · NEW YORK · OXFORD

Sole distributors for the U.S.A. and Canada:

ELSEVIER NORTH-HOLLAND INC.
52 VANDERBILT AVENUE, NEW YORK, N.Y. 10017

PRINTED IN THE NETHERLANDS

FOREWORD

In 1975, a workshop was held in Chicago on Automated Techniques for Scheduling of Vehicle Operators for Urban Public Transportation Services. Under this title, a number of papers were presented on the subject of bus and bus crew scheduling, together with others on related topics. At that time a number of isolated successes were reported.

This same subject was treated in some presentations at the third European Operational Research Conference in Amsterdam in 1979, and during that conference the suggestion was made that there was a need for a further workshop to consider developments since the Chicago meeting. Subsequently, the Special Courses Division of the University of Leeds indicated its willingness to organise such a workshop, and an ad hoc planning committee was set up, with the following membership, in addition to myself:

Mlle. E. Heurgon, Regie Autonome des Transports Parisiens
M. M. Leprince, Societe des Transports Intercommunaux de Bruxelles
Drs. A.W. Roes, NV Nederlandse Spoorwegen
Professor R.E. Ward, West Virginia University
Mr. J.T. Gleave, University of Leeds (Special Courses Division)

with corresponding members:

Mr. L. Aligata, Ansaldo, Genoa
Dr. H.I. Stern, Ben-Gurion University of the Negev.

A meeting of this committee was held later in 1979, and as a result, a workshop was planned to be held in Leeds in July 1980. The workshop was organised by the University of Leeds Special Courses Division under the auspices of the International Union of Public Transport, the Association of European Operational Research Societies, and the Transportation Science Section of the Operations Research Society of America.

This volume constitutes the Proceedings of the Workshop, albeit in an order different from that of presentation. It includes revised copies of the papers presented; in one case the revision has taken the form of a substantial condensation. The papers have been arranged here according to subject areas. One paper is concerned with an underground railway; the others all treat bus operations, although in most cases the methods would be applicable to other modes.

Paper 1 consists of a review paper covering the whole field in brief. Papers 2 to 6 give the view of the bus management, or present general experience. Papers 7 to 11 deal with the scheduling of vehicles, while Papers 12 to 19 are concerned with scheduling of bus drivers. Paper 20 presents a method for scheduling vehicle and driver simultaneously. Papers 21 and 22 examine problems of assigning work to actual men, and of recording relevant information. Finally, I asked a colleague to compile a glossary of terms used in bus scheduling, and this forms Paper 23.

In the course of the Workshop, the question arose as to whether these should become regular events. It was felt that in two to three years there should have been sufficient further developments to merit another meeting, and that possibly the meetings should alternate between the eastern and western sides of the Atlantic. After some debate, it was agreed that three years was a suitable interval, and Professor J-M Rousseau kindly agreed to organise this in Montreal, probably in the Spring of 1983. Details will be available in due course from Professor Rousseau at:

    Centre de Recherche sur les Transports, Universite de Montreal,
    Case Postale 6128, Montreal, Quebec, H3C 3J7, Canada.
                    (Tel: 514-343-7575)

I am grateful to the staff of the Special Courses Division and of the Operational Research Unit for the organisation of the Workshop, and to the Planning Committee for much useful advice and help in publicity. I should like to thank Lynne and Trevor Hartley for the preparation and processing of the texts of this work. Without Trevor Hartley's assistance and monitoring of the progress of the papers, the volume could not have been completed in time. I also wish to thank Margaret Parker and Barbara Smith for proof-reading.

        Anthony Wren
        Operational Research Unit
        Department of Computer Studies
        University of Leeds

CONTENTS

Foreword   v

Surveys and Implementations

1. A. WREN

   General Review of the Use of Computers in Scheduling
   Buses and their Crews   3

2. J.W. SCHMIDT and R. KNIGHT

   The Status of Computer-Aided Scheduling in North America   17

3. R.R. DAVIES and D. WILLIAMS

   Service Optimisation and Route Costing and Associated
   Computer Programs   23

4. J. HOFFSTADT

   Computerized Vehicle and Driver Scheduling for the
   Hamburger Hochbahn Aktiengesellschaft   35

5. R.W. DICKINSON, W.F. DRYNAN and P.D. MANINGTON

   The Role of the Systems Department and the Role of Operations
   Management in Introducing Computer Assistance to Bus Scheduling   53

6. M.G. LANDIS

   A Perspective on Automated Bus Operator Scheduling:
   Five Years Experience in Portland, Oregon   61

Bus and Train Scheduling Methods

7. V. BRANDANI, G. CATAOLI, G. ORSI and P. TONI

   Bus Scheduling Program Development for A.T.A.F. Florence   71

8. H.I. STERN and A. CEDER

   A Deficit Function Approach for Bus Scheduling   85

9. B.M. SMITH and A. WREN

   VAMPIRES and TASC: Two Successfully Applied
   Bus Scheduling Programs   97

10. I.T. KEAVENY and S. BURBECK

    Automating Trip Scheduling and Optimal Vehicle Assignments   125

11. K.L.W. DEXTER

    Scheduling an Urban Railway   147

Bus Crew Scheduling Methods

12. P.M. HILDYARD and H.V. WALLIS

     Advances in Computer Assisted Runcutting in North America   183

13. M.E. PARKER and B.M. SMITH

     Two Approaches to Computer Crew Scheduling   193

14. C. PICCIONE, A. CHERICI, M. BIELLI and A. LA BELLA

     Practical Aspects in Automatic Crew Scheduling   223

15. J.M.J. BORRET and A.W. ROES

     Crew Scheduling by Computer: A Test on the Possibility of
     Designing Duties for a Certain Busline   237

16. R. LESSARD, J-M. ROUSSEAU and D. DUPUIS

     Hastus I: A Mathematical Programming Approach to the
     Bus Driver Scheduling Problem   255

17. D.M. RYAN and B.A. FOSTER

     An Integer Programming Approach to Scheduling   269

18. G. MITRA and A.P.G. WELSH

     A Computer Based Crew Scheduling System Using a
     Mathematical Programming Approach   281

19. R.E. WARD, P.A. DURANT and A.B. HALLMAN

     A Problem Decomposition Approach to Scheduling
     the Drivers and Crews of Mass Transit Systems   297

20. M.O. BALL, L.D. BODIN and R. DIAL

     Experimentation with a Computerized System for
     Scheduling Mass Transit Vehicles and Crews   313

Miscellaneous Papers

21. J.K. JACHNIK

     Attendance and Rostering System   337

22. J.W. SCHMIDT and R.J. FENNESSY

     Automating Extraboard Assignments and Coach Operator Timekeeping   345

23. T. HARTLEY

     A Glossary of Terms in Bus and Crew Scheduling   353

Surveys
and Implementations

Computer Scheduling of Public Transport
A. Wren (ed.)
© *North-Holland Publishing Company, 1981*

GENERAL REVIEW OF THE USE OF COMPUTERS
IN SCHEDULING BUSES AND THEIR CREWS

Anthony Wren

Operational Research Unit
Department of Computer Studies
University of Leeds
Leeds, UK

The use of computers in scheduling buses and their crews is
reviewed, drawing on sources available to the author from
private correspondence and from a previous Workshop in
Chicago, as well as from open literature and the present
Proceedings. A number of subject areas are identified, and
within some areas treatment is broken down by type of problem
and by type of approach. The review deals more with
methodology than with implementation, although comments are
made from time to time on the status of the systems described,
and a brief conclusion summarises the overall position with
regard to implementation.

1.0 INTRODUCTION

This paper outlines work on the applications of computers to bus and crew
scheduling as presented at the Workshop of whose proceedings this forms part, as
well as at an earlier Workshop in Chicago (C1-9), and in eighteen other sources.
It also makes use of the author's informal discussions with the originators of
some processes.

We shall examine each of a number of problem areas, and within the two major areas
we shall further subdivide the material under consideration. The treatment will
thus be by problem area, rather than by paper, and some papers may therefore be
mentioned more than once. The areas to be discussed are as follows:

1. Generate times of bus trips.

2. Construct a bus schedule. The treatment may depend on whether the problem
    falls most conveniently into the first or second class below:

    1. The schedule is route based, that is, buses are operating along one or
        more routes, at reasonably high frequencies. Often the routes involved
        here will be related in some way. The problem is usually to achieve
        efficient linking of arrivals and departures at terminals, and there may
        be little dead running involved.

    2. The schedule is network-based. Here the journeys to be scheduled may be on
        a wide variety of routes, and many of the routes may themselves have
        relatively few journeys. The problem is basically to arrange dead running
        between terminals where there are surplus arrivals and those where there
        are surplus departures.

3. Bus crew scheduling. Here we shall classify approaches by solution method:

    1. Heuristic approaches.

    2. Mathematical programming approaches.

    3. Interactive approaches.

4. Formation of rotating rosters.

5. Miscellaneous problems.

6. General papers

The references here are prefixed by one of the letters C, G or L. Those prefixed L are papers from this Workshop; those prefixed C were presented at the Chicago Workshop in 1975, while those prefixed G have appeared elsewhere (often only in informal reports).

2.0 GENERATION OF TRIP TIMES

In some parts of the world (not the United Kingdom), it is the practice to construct bus schedules based directly on counts of passengers on buses passing a peak loading point. The usual procedure is to form a cumulative count of passengers throughout the day, and to plan a journey every time the cumulative count passes a multiple of the notional bus capacity (allowing some spare capacity to cope with unexpected variations). There may be an over-riding maximum permitted headway so that a journey is planned after every so many minutes, even if the bus would not be full.

This process lends itself well to automation, although there may be problems in matching arrivals and departures at the termini which could be alleviated by slight variations in the planned times of journeys. Programs to generate times of journeys and to build schedules from them have been available, generally in the United States, since the early 1960s, although the earlier ones were often only of an experimental nature. Examples of such work were at the Philadelphia Transportation Company (G1) and the Los Angeles Metropolitan Transit Authority (G2). Other programs which included generation of trip times from passenger demand data as part of a larger process have been developed by Elias for the New York City Transit Authority and others (G3), and by Krotkov and Levin in Azerbaijan (G4). A similar program to that of Elias was incorporated within the RUCUS suite and was referred to in passing by Bennington and Rebibo (C1).

The TASC program developed at the University of Leeds and described by Smith and Wren (L9) includes automatic generation of times, but having been developed initially for British operators, the basic data consists only of times of the earliest journeys and of headways by time of day, although an extension to cater for passenger demand has been planned in outline. A pre-processor (not described in the paper) determines the times at which journeys should run in order to ensure even headways on common stretches of route where this can be achieved without adding to the number of buses.

Keaveny and Burbeck (L10) also refer to a process which generates trip times   from headway information.

3.0 CONSTRUCT A BUS SCHEDULE

As already stated, we shall differentiate here between two situations. To a certain extent these overlap, but perhaps the most obvious categorisation is between regular and irregular services. Regular services are those which operate up and down one or more routes at frequent intervals, such that buses turn round in a short time at each terminus, and where it is unlikely that any improvement may be made on manually produced schedules. Irregular services may include extra peak buses on what are otherwise regular services, together with odd journeys on infrequent services, where it is expected that there will have to be a considerable amount of dead running between terminals, and where considerable scope for savings may exist. Often because of the integrated working of an entire schedule, it may be convenient to include all services in this 'irregular' category, so that an overall good schedule may be obtained.

Catering for these two different categories, we obtain route-based and network-based methods, with some overlap.

3.1 Route-based Methods

We have already mentioned that programs to generate journey times have been written as part of a larger process, this generally being the process of scheduling individual routes (G1-4, C1, L9). The first four of these have already been discussed by Wren (G5). The Philadelphia program (G1) linked arrivals where possible with subsequent departures at individual terminals, and otherwise extended or inserted live journeys between terminals; where this could not be done, buses were brought out from the garage. The program was used for some years, but was subsequently abandoned, as it was found in some cases to use more buses than necessary.

The Los Angeles program (G2) also tied arrivals to departures at individual termini, subject to certain minimum and maximum layover conditions, but any unlinked trips after this process were printed by the computer and presented to the scheduler, together with the links already made. He was able to make any adjustments he required, and to complete the process manually. (His manual schedules were subsequently re-presented to the computer for analysis and preparation of documents.) This program was used successfully by the Southern California Rapid Transit District.

Elias's program (G3) was similar to the Philadelphia one, but was more sophisticated in a number of ways.

Several papers being presented at this Workshop deal with programs which are essentially route-based.

Keaveny and Burbeck (L10) describe, as an option within their Mini-scheduler system a process which is similar to many of the above, but which does cater for more than one route, and allows a considerable interaction between the scheduler and the machine at the schedule-building stage.

Smith and Wren (L9) describe a program which, while originally designed to operate on a single route, does deal successfully with several routes. In many ways the scheduling method is similar to the earlier programs, with arrivals and departures being linked at individual termini where reasonable, and journeys being inserted or extended otherwise. The inserted journeys are on service unless this would cost a bus or there is no linking service between the two points. There are facilities for several depots, and a heuristic is provided which attempts to ensure that buses which start their work near one depot finish near that depot. The program prints timetables and produces basic data for crew scheduling. It also provides an estimate of the number of crews required. This program is also mentioned by Davies and Williams (L3), who represent its major user to date.

Dexter (L11) describes a program written for the London underground system which has been modified to deal with bus operation. This first develops possible patterns of operation for a route structure, given the headways desired over each leg of the route. An interactive approach enables the scheduler to select that pattern which he wishes to operate, and the program proceeds to link the patterns over the whole day to provide a good transition from one period to another.

Brandani, Cataoli, Orsi and Toni (L7) describe a route-based program which in fact handles several complex patterns of forking and circular routes which are found in Florence. The program is said to be interactive in the sense that after inspecting intermediate results the user may stop the program if dissatisfied and re-run with modified data.

These route-based programs may be seen as aids to efficient production of schedules. It has not been claimed that any of them produce direct savings, but clearly their existence can allow the scheduler to experiment rapidly with many options, and therefore perhaps to arrive at a more efficient overall strategy than would otherwise be found.

4.0 NETWORK-BASED METHODS

At the Chicago Workshop, the only bus scheduling methods presented were of the network-based variety, and at that time (1975) it seemed that it was this type that would have most significant future impact, since these could hold out the promise of substantial savings. At this Workshop, however, the bus scheduling papers are fairly evenly divided between route-based and network-based programs, and this may reflect difficulties in the handling of network-wide approaches and of the large quantities of related data by the staff of bus companies.

At its simplest, the linking of trips to form work for individual buses is an assignment problem in which the rows of a cost matrix represent arrivals and the columns represent departures; the elements of the matrix are the costs of allocating the bus from a particular arrival to a particular departure, these costs often being expressed in terms of the amounts of dead running involved. In principle, an optimal solution to this problem may be obtained using the Hungarian method, but in practice the problems have often been too large, or there have been additional complicating features, so that it has been necessary to modify the method, thereby removing the guarantee of optimality.

We thus find in bus scheduling both heuristic methods, which are intended to produce good solutions in a reasonable amount of computer time, and mathematical programming based methods, which would in theory guarantee to produce optimal solutions, but have been modified by various heuristics to deal with practical problems.

One of the earliest network-based methods (STAMINA) was introduced by Kirkman (G6) in the United Kingdom and evolved gradually over the period 1961 to 1967. It was subsequently modified by a firm of consultants and marketed under a different name. This used the assignment problem approach, but divided the day into periods in order to reduce the size of the problem. The periods were then linked together in a special way, but the solution was then not necessarily optimal. This produced some good results when first introduced, but also some bad ones, often because of lack of understanding on the part of bus management about how to go about using a computer method, but sometimes because the method itself produced poor results. (The poor performance of this method, exaggerated by traditionalists within the industry, led to an unfortunate climate in which subsequent researchers had to work.)

Hoffstadt (L4) describes a method based on the Hungarian algorithm which is used in practice in Hamburg. Advances in computer power and in programming techniques since Kirkman's work have made the solution of problems of practical size feasible. A fuller description of the method is given by Ario, Bohringer and Mojsilovic (G7), who describe how the day is in fact broken into four periods which can then be linked in a manner which guarantees the optimal number of buses. The questions of several garages and different types of vehicle are dealt with by a heuristic modification.

Another method based on mathematical procedures is used in the RUCUS suite and was described by Bennington and Rebibo (C1). In this, bus trips are considered as arcs in a network, joining departure and arrival nodes. Permissible linkages between arrivals of trips and departures of other trips are considered as further arcs, as are potential journeys to and from the garage. The problem of finding the cheapest set of paths from the garage in the morning to the garage in the evening covering all nodes of the network is solved using the out-of-kilter algorithm. This would guarantee an optimal solution were the problem not too large to solve by this means. In order to reduce the problem size, the connections included from any node are restricted by a heuristic. The program as described handled only one garage and one type of vehicle. It is understood that it has since been adapted to deal with several garages.

A heuristic method originally developed for locomotive scheduling in the early 1960s was subsequently applied to bus operation, and in this form was first outlined by Wren in 1971 (G5) and subsequently elaborated by him (G8). Experiences with this method were presented by P.D. Manington and Wren in Chicago (C2), and enhancements to the methods and experiences are included in the present paper by Smith and Wren (L9). Use by over fifteen bus operators is claimed, with savings consistently in excess of five percent of peak vehicle numbers. The method handles many types of vehicle and many garages, and provides a facility for revising trip times where this would save buses.

Dickinson, Drynan and Manington (L5) describe the design and implementation of a data capture and bus scheduling system. This system is based on the University of Leeds program mentioned in the previous paragraph, and has now been implemented. The paper presents the problems which arose during the implementation process, and explains how they were overcome.

Stern and Ceder (L8) present an interactive procedure which incorporates heuristics based on deficit function theory, which provides bounds on the number of buses used. The version of their paper published in this volume is in fact an abbreviated version of their presentation, which will be published in full elsewhere. The computer displays to the scheduler information about when buses become available and when they are needed at the various terminals. The scheduler may select one of a number of automatic heuristics to insert dead runs between termini, or may choose to select these runs himself from a list of sensible possibilities presented by the computer. The program has been developed in the context of a national bus organisation, and is designed to investigate the problem of the peak.

5.0 BUS CREW SCHEDULING

We have already stated that we shall classify solution methods as heuristic, mathematical programming or interactive. It is desirable also to classify the problems tackled.

In some organisations it is possible for bus crews to work for up to about eight hours without a formal break. In these there is generally one of three situations:

1. there is no statutory break;

2. natural layover in the bus schedule is such that it totals sufficient over the whole duty to constitute the equivalent of a break;

3. a break is built during the bus scheduling process into the schedule of every bus following the morning and evening peaks.

In such circumstances one may form a substantial number of crew duties simply by cutting a portion as near to the maximum working time as possible from the beginning of every early bus which continues after the morning peak (forming complete early duties) and from the end of every late bus (forming late duties). The core of the scheduling problem is then the bringing together of the remaining pieces of work to form good duties. We shall call this type of scheduling problem a class-A problem, since it is generally the easier to solve. We shall then denote as class-B problems those in which it is necessary to take a crew off a bus to give a meal break, there being a statutory limit to the length of time a crew can work without a break (often between four and five hours).

> In parenthesis it may be remarked that it is generally simple to modify a bus scheduling program to include breaks after the peaks if the breaks can be taken at a terminus, provided that one accepts that some buses may then have no suitable breaks while others have two. (For example one may modify the costs of links at certain times of day.) In some heuristic methods it is even possible to ensure that every bus has a single break after each peak, and that the portions before the morning break and after the evening break are within the statutory limits. This could in theory reduce a complex class-B situation to the simpler class-A situation.

> However, many operating agreements do not permit breaks to be taken on the vehicle or the vehicle to be left unattended. The bus schedule then would have to have been constructed in such a way as to ensure that the breaks did not actually start until the vehicle could have been allocated another crew. The situation is more complex still where crews are normally changed in the course of a journey. Ball, Bodin and Dial (L20) present a method which will deal with this situation; we return to it later.

We shall now examine the three classes of solution method in turn, identifying the problems to which they have been applied as class-A or class-B.

5.1 Heuristic Approaches

The earliest known work on the scheduling of bus crews by computer was undertaken by Cooper, then of City of Oxford Motor Services, in the late 1950s, and is referred to in a feasibility study carried out in the University of Leeds (G9). Better known is some work by Deutsch in the early 1960s. Deutsch's work was initiated by London Transport and was later carried out under the auspices of an IBM research fellowship in the University of Oxford. This has not been published, but the method adopted was in effect an exhaustive tree-search, and not surprisingly it failed to produce good results even on small data sets (class-B) with the primitive equipment then available.

Elias (G10,11) started work about the same time as Deutsch and published a method for which he claimed fair success with a number of American organisations (class-B, but with high limits on the amount of time that could be worked without a break). The method consisted of a series of heuristics which developed a large number of different schedules quite quickly, of which the best was chosen. Subsequent work by Elias, which was not published, proceeded by subjecting the best of the above schedules to a series of refining heuristics. This work resulted in schedules being produced which were insignificantly different in cost from those obtained by manual schedulers. Ward and Deibel (G12) extended some of Elias's refining heuristics with considerable success.

Weaver and Wren also initiated an approach which consisted of producing an initial schedule and improving it by refining heuristics. The method of obtaining the initial solution was changed several times in the period 1967 to 1971, and has been gradually modified since then. Early variations were described chronologically in (G13), (G14) and (G5). An early version of the present approach is described by B. Manington and Wren (C3), while the current version is described by Parker and Smith (L13). The refining heuristics developed in this approach during the year 1967-8 bore a coincidental resemblence to the unpublished work of Elias, with whom there were later several exchanges of ideas. Other refining processes were added over a period up to about 1975. (Ward and Durant also experimented with the incorporation into this suite of some of the extended processes from (G12)). The suite has been used for a number of operators, sometimes experimentally, and sometimes leading to implementation (L13).

Another program suite developed along similar lines by the National Bus Company in the United Kingdom has not been published in detail. It appears to work better in class-A than in class-B situations.

Wilhelm (C4) describes the RUNS portion of the RUCUS suite as it was in 1975. This also then consisted of a program which produced an initial schedule and a series of refining techniques. The schedule was restricted to duties which contained work on no more than two buses, and the generation of the initial solution appeared rather crude. The refining techniques were similar to those developed by Elias and by the Leeds group. Hildyard and Wallis (L12) describe some of the difficulties inherent in the use of this system, along with some of the modifications which have been made in attempts to overcome these difficulties. Landis (L6) describes the implementation of RUCUS crew scheduling in Portland, Oregon and shows what may be achieved by using this system.

Another heuristic method was evolved by the Transport and Road Research Laboratory in conjunction with Manchester City Transport (later SELNEC). This was described by Edwards (G15) and was used experimentally in Manchester, but has since been abandoned.

5.2 Mathematical Programming Approaches

We have already met the assignment problem in scheduling vehicles. This same mathematical method has been used by a number of investigators for scheduling the crews. Here it is assumed that one has obtained partial duties by some process, and that one has to join the parts together in a matching process which will generally minimise the cost. This is a matter of forming two lists of the partial duties and finding the best overall matching so that every member of one list is paired with one member of the other list. While this may be solved by the well-known Hungarian method, some authors use another matching method.

An alternative approach consists in generating a large set of possible duties and using integer linear programming to select from that set a group of duties that cover all the work in the most efficient way. There are a number of variations of this approach. In one, a set of theoretical duties is generated, and one finds a group of these that fits the overall pattern of bus operation without necessarily providing realistic duties. This gives a pattern of theoretical duties, which may sometimes be bent to give practical duties. Young and Wilkinson are believed to have been the first to investigate this approach in the mid 1960s (G18).

The other variations are generally either 'set partitioning approaches', in which one imposes constraints which ensure that every bus has exactly one crew at any time, or 'set covering approaches', in which every bus must have at least one crew at all times. The advantage of the latter is that one need not generate so many duties; if any bus has two duties covering it at the same time, one may simply curtail one of the duties.

Both set partitioning and set covering approaches normally require that one is selective in the generation of duties, since the problem would be too large to handle if all possible duties were generated. Care needs to be taken in this selection of duties, so that the risk of not considering a duty which is essential to a good schedule is reduced.

5.2.1 Matching Methods –

Harris and Langsford (G19) described a process which, once it had been determined which portions of work would be used in split duties, matched these in an optimal fashion. This was used in Adelaide for a short time, but was subsequently abandoned, since it was felt that this process could not be treated in isolation. Bergmann (C5) later proposed a similar process which included treatment of overtime portions.

Hoffstadt (L4), in his description of the implemented Hamburg system, treats a class-A problem. Sensible straight duties are first cut from the beginning and end of buses, and the remaining pieces of work are matched together using the Hungarian method. Kregeloh and Mojsilovic (C7) described a predecessor of this approach, while fuller details are given in (G7).

Lessard, Rousseau and Dupuis (L16) describe a mathematical programming approach which does not appear to fit into any of the categories listed above, but which they say is nearly equivalent to that of Heurgon (C8). In order to reduce the problem to a practical size, however, they modify the process to become a matching process which is then refined by heuristics. One stage of the process involves a relaxation of the problem by a method similar to that of Young and Wilkinson.

Ball, Bodin and Dial (L20) also use a matching process, but here the bus schedule and crew schedule are built up simultaneously, and the matching is used continuously as the schedule is developed. By this method the bus schedule is designed to suit the requirements of the crew schedule. While the matching process is optimal whenever it is invoked, the decisions as to when the process should be invoked and what should be included in the sets to be matched follow a heuristic which may reduce the optimality. Good results are however claimed in comparison with a manual schedule in Baltimore. It is the intention of the authors to provide interactive facilities with this program.

We may also remark that two of the refining processes used in the Leeds University heuristic system described by Parker and Smith (L13) treat the matching of pieces of work to form complete duties as assignment problems.

5.2.2 Set Partioning –

Heurgon (C8) describes a method developed in Paris. This classifies relief opportunities into various grades of likelihood. The user selects the range of grades which he wishes to use, and duties are generated using the appropriate opportunities. He would normally select a limited range, thus restricting the amount of computer time needed, but would then increase the range if suitable results were not achieved. At the time of the Chicago Workshop good results were reported, treating bus routes one at a time (class-A). However, it is understood that the system is not in use at present, owing largely to the fact that every route in Paris is the responsibility of a different person, and that it is therefore difficult to obtain a unified policy.

Piccione, Cherici, Bielli and La Bella (L14) present a set partitioning method which is being developed in Rome for the public transportation system.

Borret and Roes (L15) present experiments based on Amsterdam schedules which are essentially class-B, with encouraging results.

Ward, Durant and Hallman (L19) describe a set partitioning method which treats the various types of duty sequentially. All possible duties of a chosen type (owl, late, middle, early or split) or group of types are constructed, and the best set of these is chosen, according to some criterion. Then duties of another type are generated from the remaining work, and the process continues until all work is covered. So far only owl, late and middle duties have been considered, but the results compare favourably with existing schedules on test data from both sides of the Atlantic (class-B).

5.2.3 Set Covering Approaches –

Mitra and Welsh (L18) present experience with a set covering approach on data originating from Dublin (class-B). In addition to normal constraints ensuring that every piece of work is covered at least once, ther are several global constraints limiting the number of duties of certain types and the average work content of duties of certain types. The results are reported as encouraging.

Mitra and Welsh also refer in passing to an approach based on that of Young and Wilkinson, and it is known that other consultants have experimented with such an approach. In this a good overall pattern of theoretical duties is formed, and an attempt is made heuristically to obtain a set of practical duties derived from the theoretical ones. The present author has been involved in a test of such a method, in which it was demonstrated that it worked well when relief opportunities were frequent (three or four per hour), but not when they were less frequent (hourly).

Parker and Smith (L13) present as their second method a set covering approach with restricted choice of duties being generated. The choice of generated duties is based on practical considerations for class-B problems. The method employs a device to obtain a good starting solution for the linear programming iterations, and good solutions are obtained in little computing time. As in all linear programming approaches it is necessary to obtain an integer solution. Experience to date indicates that such a solution can be readily obtained.

Ryan and Foster (L17) discuss approaches to mathematical programming problems related to bus crew scheduling, together with an application to bus crew scheduling problems in Auckland. The approach includes certain relaxations to the linear programming formulation, together with extensions to the solution process which enable one to broaden the set of duties considered in the light of the first solution.

5.3 Interactive Approaches

Although there would appear now to be a general movement towards interactive processes as a means of involving the scheduler more directly in the compiling function and of easing the task of data preparartion, there is relatively little written about such approaches to crew scheduling.

Hildyard and Wallis (L12) explain how their company has made the RUCUS concept more acceptable by replacing the automatic scheduling process by an interactive one, but do not describe this in any detail.

The method of Ball, Bodin and Dial (L20) has provision for the ultimate inclusion of interactive facilities, but is for the present fully automatic.

The present author and his associates had considered submitting a paper for the Workshop describing their TRICS interactive scheduling program, but withheld this in view of the pressure on space. Perhaps he may be forgiven therefore if he now devotes some space to an outline of it.

The system as it is at present is an aid to the scheduler in the compilation process. At its simplest it will determine whether a duty proposed by the scheduler is legal according to the constraints of the union agreement, and will present the cost of the duty. It will also determine whether any of the bus work in this duty is already covered by another duty, and if so it will present details of that other duty. The scheduler may then accept the new duty or the old one (or may reject them both).

At the next level of complexity, the scheduler may specify the details of all portions of a duty, except that the start or finish time of one portion is omitted. The computer will then supply details of the missing time such that the work content of the duty is maximised, and will supply the cost of the duty. Thus for example, the scheduler may specify that a duty will consist of work on bus number 35 from 0614 to 0935, and then on bus 16 from 1020; the computer will then supply the latest time the duty must finish on bus 16. The scheduler may again accept or reject the resultant duty.

At a higher level still, the scheduler may omit details of two start or finish times. For example, he may specify the first portion of a duty, and the computer will then supply details of all possible second portions which satisfy the condition that the meal break should not exceed a given length. (The scheduler supplies the meal break length in order to prevent the computer giving too many possibilities; if he does not like any of the possibilities given, he may lengthen the break.) The scheduler may then accept one of the suggested duties, or reject them all. Another possibility is for the scheduler to stipulate details of the start of the first portion of a split duty and the finish of the last portion. The computer will then give all possible breaks.

At any stage the scheduler may request a display of all the duties formed, or of those portions of bus work not yet covered. He may also at any stage delete duties already formed.

We see this partly as an aid to scheduling in its own right, and partly as a means of introducing the scheduler to the computer. We feel that once the scheduler has used this system for some time he will ask for the computer to do more for him. At that stage we would hope to incorporate automatic processes within the system. For example, the heuristic method described by Parker and Smith (L13) may be used to generate duties, but as each duty is generated it can be displayed to the scheduler, who may accept it or reject it, or use TRICS to explore other possibilities.

6.0 FORMATION OF ROTATING ROSTERS

In some countries bus crews work different duties on every day of the week, and then rotate their work through all the weeks of a roster. This poses the problem of how to group the days and weeks together so as to produce a roster which satisfies the local constraints. These may include specification of the type of duty to be operated in particular positions in the roster, and will usually include a minimum rest period between the end of one day and the start of the next.

Bennett and Potts (G16) describe a system developed in Adelaide. This consists of three stages, in the first of which a suitable pattern of rest days is found. The second stage is to fit an acceptable pattern of work into the remaining days, while the final stage is to use a combination of heuristics and mathematical processes to improve that pattern.

This method has been modified in the University of Leeds to suit British conditions, and is referred to as TRAM by Davies and Williams (L3). There have however been considerable difficulties in determining the conditions affecting roster patterns, and the method has not been applied.

Societe des Transports Intercommunaux de Bruxelles (G17) has been using an automatic method to construct rosters for about ten years. The method is heuristic and depends to a considerable extent on the particular conditions affecting Brussels rosters.

Guha and Browne (C9) described procedures for constructing rosters either manually or by computer.

Jachnik (L21) describes a system which constructs a roster eight days in advance, and modifies it on a day to day basis to take account of staff absences. The method is heuristic.

7.0 MISCELLANEOUS

An automatic scheduling system is complemented naturally by a system which will
assist in moving from the planned schedule to the daily operations which may be
affected by absences or extra work. Schmidt and Fennessy (L22) describe a system
which helps in progressing the drivers' pick and automates much of the work
necessary for day to day clerical processes, such as computing pay and assigning
extra cover.

8.0 GENERAL

We have been privileged to receive a number of papers which take a broad look at
the whole field of automation of scheduling.

Davies and Williams (L3) outline a number of processes which are in use or under
consideration by West Yorkshire Passenger Transport Executive. These include the
range of methods developed in the University of Leeds, together with one developed
by a firm of consultants and the National Bus Company's MAP system. They explain
the need for continuing review of the Executive's operations, and show how
automated processes will assist this review.

Hoffstadt (L4) describes the entire automatic scheduling system now in use in
Hamburg, and explains how the system was developed and the considerations which
had to be made in its implementation. Individual components of the system have
already been referred to above.

It will be appropriate to refer again here to the paper by Landis (L6) which,
while concerned primarily with crew scheduling, is of more general interest in its
treatment of problems of implementation.

Schmidt and Knight (L2) present a valuable review of North American experience,
principally with RUCUS and its derivatives. They review the historical background
and assess the achievements. A substantial number of American operators have
experimented with computer scheduling, and the number of successful
implementations has grown considerably in recent years. These implementations are
of on-going systems, and savings which more than justify the costs of
implementation are achieved.

An earlier general paper describing use of RUCUS as it was in 1975 was given by
Goeddel (C6).

9.0 CONCLUSIONS

A wide variety of methods have been applied to both bus and crew scheduling. Most
reported implementations have been achieved using heuristic methods, but there are
indications that mathematical programming will play an increasing role. It is also
likely that schedules in future will be compiled through an interactive process
involving the scheduler and the computer, each performing their most suitable
function.

One might have hoped for more implementations of systems which were now being used
in a continuing manner within the bus operating bodies. There would appear to be a
fair number of such implementations in North America, but only isolated ones, each
with different systems, in Europe. There have also, at least in the United
Kingdom, been several methods which have each been used successfully in a number

of locations, and whose results have been implemented, but often on a one-off basis.

10.0 REFERENCES

These are divided into three groups, and numbered within each group. The groups are identified in the text by use of the prefix letters G, C and L. Group L is not given here, as the numbers refer to chapters within the present volume.

10.1 Papers Published In General Sources (G)

1. Philadelphia Transportation Company. Electronic Transit Scheduling. Published jointly with IBM circa 1962.

2. Los Angeles Metropolitan Transit Authority. Mechanisation of schedules. 1964.

3. Elias, S.E.G. and Smith, N.S.Jr. The development and demonstration of an automatic passenger counter. West Virginia University Engineering Experiment Station Bulletin, no. 94, 1970 (two volumes).

4. Krotkov, Y.I. and Levin, V.S. Algorithmizatsia rascheta iskhodnykh dannykh dlya sostavlenia ratsionalnykh marshrutnykh raspisanii gorodskogo transporta. (An algorithm for the processing of initial data for use in the construction of rational route schedules for urban transport.) Za Tekhnicheski Progress, 1965, p.12.

5. Wren, A. Computers in transport planning and operation. Ian Allan, London. 1971.

6. Kirkman, F. Problems of innovation in the transport industry: a bus scheduling program. Proceedings of PTRC Public Transport Analysis Seminar. London, 1968, vol.2, p.23.

7. Ario, O., Bohringer, O. and Mojsilovic, M. Elektronische Bildung von Umlauf- und Dienstplanen bei der Hamburg Hochbahn Aktiengesellschaft. Hamburg-Consult. 1979.

8. Wren, A. Bus scheduling: an interactive computer method. Transportation Planning and Technology, vol.1, p.115, 1972.

9. The solution of large scale scheduling problems by computer: an appreciation of basic principles and future possibilities. Prepared at the request of the British Transport Commission by Leeds University Computing Laboratory. 1960.

10. Elias, S.E.G. The use of digital computers in the economic scheduling for both man and machine in public transportation. Kansas State University Bulletin, Special Report 49, 1964.

11. Elias, S.E.G. A mathematical model for optimising the assignment of man and machine in public transit run cutting. West Virginia University Engineering Experiment Station Research Bulletin 81, 1966.

12. Ward, R.E. and Deibel, L.E. The advancement of computerised assignment of transit operators to vehicles through programming techniques. Joint National Meeting of the Operations Research Society of America, Atlantic City, 1972.

13. Weaver, A. A crew scheduling program. Proceedings of PTRC Public Transport Analysis Seminar. London, 1968, vol.2, p.48.

14. Weaver, A. and Wren, A. The computer in bus and crew scheduling. Proceedings of PTRC Public Road Transport Analysis Symposium. London, 1970, p.58.

15. Bennett, B.T. and Potts, R.B. Rotating roster for a transit system. Transportation Science, vol.2, p.14, 1968.

16. Societe des Transports Intercommunaux de Bruxelles. Attribution previsionnelle des services au personnel (exploitation et technique). 1972.

17. Young, A. and Wilkinson, J.C. The scheduling of buses and crews by computer. Paper presented to the Public Transport Association annual conference, Scarborough, 1966.

18. Harris, F.R. and Langsford, P. The automation of duty rosters for traffic crews. UITP Revue no.4, vol.17, p.283, 1968.

10.2 Papers Presented At The Chicago Workshop (C)

The following papers relating directly to the subject of this Workshop were presented at the Workshop on Automated Techniques for Scheduling of Vehicle Operators for Urban Public Transportation Services held in Chicago in 1975. No proceedings were published.

1. Bennington, G.E. and Rebibo, K.K. Overview of the RUCUS vehicle scheduling program (BLOCKS).

2. Manington, P.D. and Wren, A. Experiences with a bus scheduling algorithm which saves vehicles.

3. Manington, B. and Wren, A. A general computer method for bus crew scheduling.

4. Wilhelm, E.B. Overview of the RUCUS package driver run cutting program (RUNS).

5. Bergmann, D.R. Minimal cost allocations of bus driving assignments between split runs and trippers.

6. Goeddel, D.L. An examination of the Run Cutting and Scheduling (RUCUS) system – a case analysis.

7. Kregeloh, H. and Mojsilovic, M. Automated formation of staff schedules and duty rosters.

8. Heurgon, E. Preparing duty rosters for bus routes by computer.

9. Guha, D. and Browne. J.J. Optimal scheduling of tours and days off.

Computer Scheduling of Public Transport
A. Wren (ed.)
© *North-Holland Publishing Company, 1981*

THE STATUS OF COMPUTER-AIDED SCHEDULING
IN NORTH AMERICA

James W. Schmidt and Robert L. Knight

SAGE Management Consultants
San Francisco
California
U.S.A.

This paper describes experience gained over the past decade in
computer-aided transit scheduling in North America. It begins
with a brief historical review, and then surveys the
experiences of North American transit properties which have
tested or installed computer-aided scheduling systems. This
survey is followed by a brief description of other emerging
and existing computer-aided systems related to scheduling.
The paper closes with general conclusions on the status of
this field of interest.

INTRODUCTION

During the past decade there has been substantial innovation and progress in
computer-aided transit scheduling in North America. This paper describes that
experience and outlines the present status of this important field. In so doing,
it updates earlier surveys by MITRE (3) and Hinds (2), among others. Hopefully
this review will make possible comparisons with similar efforts in Europe and
elsewhere, thereby speeding the identification and adoption of the more promising
innovations.

The paper begins with a brief historical review, and then surveys the experiences
of North American Transit properties which have tested or installed computer-aided
scheduling systems. This survey is followed by a brief discussion of other
emerging and existing computer-aided systems related to scheduling. The paper
closes with general conclusions on the status of this general field of interest.

This review relies principally on the personal experiences of the authors and
their colleagues at SAGE, who have been involved in computer-aided scheduling for
several years. Professional literature on this subject is also covered here,
although little exists. The personal experiences cited involve both participation
in actual development and installation projects (of which SAGE has done more than
any other organization) and contacts with other consultants and transit authority
staffs who have additional first-hand experience.

DEFINITIONS

A note on standard North American scheduling practices and terms is appropriate.
Most schedule adjustments are made at regular intervals averaging about three
months, and are based on historically-recognized seasonal demand changes as well
as on the findings of field checks of capacity utilization and schedule adherence.
Either concurrently or after this 'trip scheduling' step, an efficient allocation
of buses is sought by some manual or computer-aided method. The resulting
assignments of vehicles are typically referred to as 'blocks' or 'trains'.

Next a set of driver assignments is developed, again by various means including both manual and computer-aided techniques. This practice is termed 'run-cutting', and the resulting operator runs must meet both labor union contract requirements and vehicle schedule constraints while minimizing labor costs. This task may involve minor adjustments to the vehicle schedule in order to further decrease costs.

This whole process is loosely referred to as 'scheduling'. Other related functions include the 'bidding' process, in which operators pick daily or weekly assignments, usually based on their seniority; 'daily dispatching', including assignment of specific vehicles and recording and responding to all abnormal events in the daily service; 'extra board rostering', the daily assignment of reserve drivers to unscheduled driver absences or other needs; and 'traffic checking', the (usually manual) collection of wayside or on-board data on passenger activity and schedule adherence.

HISTORICAL REVIEW

Although there have been other attempts at computerization of the scheduling process, virtually all recent experience involves the so-called computerized 'RUCUS' (RUn CUtting and Scheduling) package and its derivatives. RUCUS was developed under sponsorship of the U.S. Department of Transportation's Urban Mass Transportation Administration (UMTA) and released to the industry in 1974 following a series of field tests in 1972-3 (Nussbaum et al (4)).

Since its introduction, RUCUS has undergone many modifications both by consulting firms and users at various transit authorities. As a result, several versions now exist under varying degrees of proprietary vs. public status. Technical operation and substantive capabilities differ markedly among these versions. Considering all of these variations and derivatives, formal tests or full installations of RUCUS-based computer-assisted scheduling systems have been undertaken by over forty transit properties in the U.S. and Canada.

Many of these properties are now using computer-aided methods, at least in part, in their routine scheduling operations. Some have also made decisions to cancel or delay full installation, pending further development of the techniques. More details on these experiences are presented in the next section.

Other recent computer-aided scheduling systems include BUS-SCHED, a private Canadian product, and an interactive run cutting system under development for the New York Metropolitan Transit Authority. Neither has yet achieved any significant market penetration. UMTA is also engaged in scheduling-related development work to expand the capabilities of its Urban Transportation Planning System (UTPS) package. UTPS, a general tool for multi-modal urban travel demand forecasting and assignment, has recently been augmented by addition of a capability to estimate the vehicle requirements of alternative transit services using relatively little special data development. This is intended mainly for future planning purposes, but may be refined eventually into a scheduling system. None of these are considered further in this paper. The new SAGE-developed 'Mini-Scheduler' and 'RUNCUTTER' packages are now winning wide acceptance but are technically RUCUS derivatives even though they differ radically from the parent in many important respects. Consequently this paper is focused specifically on the RUCUS family of computer-aided scheduling techniques.

EXPERIENCE WITH RUCUS-RELATED SYSTEMS

Market Penetration: As of mid-1980, about 45 U.S. and Canadian transit properties had at least begun formal tests of computer-aided scheduling (all RUCUS-related). About half of these were at least in partial use in the property's routine scheduling work, and only a few of the remainder had resulted in decisions against full installation. Thus nearly 40 authorities were either using RUCUS-related systems or moving toward their installation.

These 40 represent 40% of the U.S. and Canadian total of some 102 transit properties large enough to seriously consider use of such computer-aided systems. Most of the largest properties (over 500 peak-period vehicles) are included among present users, as are nearly half of those operating from 200 to 500 vehicles. The remaining 'non-user market' is somewhat skewed with smaller (75-200 vehicle) operations.

Vehicle and Operator Savings: It is difficult to estimate the degree of cost savings actually achieved via computer-aided scheduling, since in many cases no formal evaluations were conducted. However, it appears that savings in vehicle operating costs and driver labor have averaged about one per cent. Most but not all properties show indications of at least some savings; a few assert much larger cost reductions of as much as five per cent. Depending on the size of the property, the one per cent average may represent from about $40,000 to well over $1 million per year.

Technical Performance: Most current versions have many technical advancements beyond the capabilities of the original RUCUS package, such that the specific operational policies and constraints of virtually any transit property can be accommodated. However, many of the RUCUS-based scheduling systems now in use have not been able to meet the originally intended scope of the package. Most applications are essentially limited to run cutting, since the RUCUS trip and vehicle scheduling procedures have proved to be unsatisfactory both in ease of use and in quality of results. This necessitates large transfers of schedule data between manual and computerized forms, which has proved to be unacceptable in some properties. The card-image data base maintenance methods commonly used have also proven to be slow, costly and error-prone. In most systems, even the run cutting function is not adequately user-oriented and its results must often be modified extensively by hand.

These problems indicate considerable potential remaining for further operational savings through improved computer assistance. The only comprehensive solutions yet produced are SAGE's interactive 'Mini-Scheduler' and 'Runcutter' packages. The Mini-Scheduler encompasses trip and vehicle scheduling as well as data base management with automatic data-entry validation and system security. The Runcutter accepts vehicle assignments and related data directly from the Mini-Scheduler and produces optimal operator assignments with varying degrees of manual intervention at the user's discretion.

Both in the more conventional RUCUS and in the SAGE derivatives, the computerized data base has been highly effective for the economical production of scheduling documents (headway sheets, vehicle and driver paddles, assignment or bid sheets, etc.) as well as reports for many other uses. Attempts at standardization of such outputs, however, have so far met with only very limited success because of the insistence of many users on unique content and formats for their principal scheduling documents. In general, the standard computer-aided scheduling outputs must be linked to report programs especially created or heavily modified for each property.

Ease of Use: With the exception of the SAGE interactive Mini-scheduler and Runcutter derivatives, RUCUS is essentially a batch-mode package. This greatly limits the application of the scheduler's professional skills, particularly in run cutting. Also, as already noted, the inability of RUCUS to fulfil the trip and vehicle scheduling functions forces an awkward shifting between manual and computer-aided methods and data in order to complete the scheduling/run cutting sequence. Often the time saved by RUCUS in the run cutting step is offset by those difficulties in data transfer.

In some cases transit properties have found it necessary to add further personnel in data processing to assist schedulers in RUCUS use. This is attributable primarily to its batch-mode operation and the use of media such as punched cards and tapes. In addition, adjustments to the RUCUS parameters often require changes to the program code which are outside the competence of most scheduling personnel. The result is a sort of alienation, or a separation of the scheduler from the tools of scheduling. This limits the ability of the system to make full use of the scheduler's knowledge and judgment, and is a principal factor in the sometimes unacceptable quality of the resulting solutions. However, the new interactive approaches already described seem to solve these problems quite satisfactorily, and routinely produce fully acceptable vehicle schedules and operator run cuts with no need for manual adjustment.

Ease of Installation: In almost all cases consulting firms have been responsible for the installation of computer-aided scheduling systems, including any necessary programming enhancements and adaptations. Since the consultants active in this field have evolved their own versions of the original UMTA-supplied RUCUS package, there is no longer a standard software system. Thus the consultant is sought not only for installation services but for his product's capabilities as well.

The typical installation sequence includes an examination of the specific scheduling requirements and constraints; local operational test of the computer-aided system; specification and completion of any required system modifications, and finally a staged program of staff training and systemwide changeover from manual to computer-aided methods. Initial emphasis is often on run cutting, with trip and vehicle scheduling added in a second phase, or even as a separate project.

Installations require from six months to about two years, depending on factors such as property size, program changes needed, and local urgency. Typical installation costs range from $50,000 (U.S.) to over $500,000, primarily depending on property size. This translates to unit costs ranging from under $200 to more than $400 per vehicle. In addition to the consultant's effort, a fairly modest commitment of the property's senior scheduling staff is required. The major clerical tasks of one-time data base conversion can be handled either by consultant or property staff.

Net Benefit-Cost Results: Despite the technical deficiencies noted here, the net savings of RUCUS-based scheduling systems appear to be substantial. Annual operating costs (beyond those of conventional manual scheduling methods) tend to be small or negligible, since the additional computer processing costs are largely offset by reduced clerical labor. The average estimated (one per cent) annual savings in driver labor cost tend to repay the computer-aided system installation cost within one to two years, or less, with subsequent savings continuing to accrue as net benefits. In addition, other benefits such as increased data availability for other functions are recognized as valuable, although hard to quantify.

The improved performance of the new interactive scheduling systems should result in substantially greater cost savings, arising primarily from more efficient vehicle assignments. This is particularly promising since any vehicular-mile savings also include further operator labor savings. Results on this performance should be available within the next few months.

A LOOK AHEAD: THE NEXT STEPS

In the scheduling and run cutting functions, the use of emerging interactive, user-oriented computer techniques should expand rapidly. Within the present decade, most transit properties of moderate to large size will probably convert from manual or RUCUS batch-mode systems to these new methods. Similar methods, simplified and adapted to the special needs of smaller operators (e.g. under the 75 - 100 vehicle level) may also emerge as computer resources become more efficient and economical.

Greater attention is likely to be directed at several related functions, notably performance monitoring, service evaluation and planning, and the daily dispatching and extra-board rostering tasks. Major gains in economy and efficiency may be realized through improved computer-assistance in such areas. Potential benefits of automatic passenger counting, vehicle location and schedule adherence monitoring are now well established (see for example Bevilacqua et al, (1)) and improvements in data capture technology have removed earlier uncertainties regarding feasibility. The number of installations of such systems is already increasing rapidly, and by the end of this decade their widespread use can reasonably be expected. Similarly, software is now emerging with capabilities for the efficient handling of large volumes of data from such automated performance data collection systems. These data handling and analysis techniques will produce performance measures and identify specific route, time, location, and vehicle-specific needs for schedule adjustment or other managerial attention.

These emerging tools for performance monitoring and evaluation also offer opportunities for direct integration with interactive computer-aided scheduling techniques. Such integration would permit testing of various service options against the specifics of observed demand and performance data to develop schedules which are more cost-efficient and responsive to demand patterns. SAGE and others are already heavily involved in the development and application of such capabilities.

CONCLUSIONS

This paper's principal message is that computer-aided scheduling and related tools are developing rapidly in North America. The current second-generation RUCUS package has demonstrated some success despite some serious deficiencies, and is now being superceded by a new generation of interactive methods. These new methods hold great promise for furthur economies in transit operating costs, as well as greater ease of use and other benefits accruing from the convenient availability of a computerized schedule data base. The use of such methods will probably become standard within the coming decade.

More work needs to be done in development of improved computer aids for scheduling-related functions such as service performance monitoring, planning, and daily dispatching. However, the basic building blocks for such tools already exist and the required development work is moving rapidly. In addition, mounting cost pressures, coupled with increasing demands for transit service, are creating interest and support of many transit managers for modern cost-saving computer aids. There appear, therefore, to be no major obstacles, either technical or institutional, to the application and widespread adoption of these emerging techniques.

REFERENCES

1. Bevilacqua,O., Knight,R., Schmidt,J., et al., Evaluation of the Cincinnati Transit Information Systems (AVM/TIS), U.S.D.O.T. Transportation Systems Center (Cambridge, Massachusetts, 1978).

2. Hinds,David H., RUCUS: A Comparative Status Report and Assessment, Transit Journal (Winter,1979) 17-34.

3. Mitre Corporation, A Survey on the State of Research in Automated Scheduling for Urban Passenger Transportation, U.S. - U.S.S.R. Program for Scientific and Technical Cooperation on the Management of Large Cities (Washington D.C. 1977).

4. Nussbaum,E., Rebibo,K. and Wilhelm,E., RUCUS Implementation Manual, UMTA-VA-06-004-75-4, Urban Mass Transportation Administration (Washington D.C. 1975).

5. Schmidt,J.W. and Fennessy,R.J.W., Automating Extraboard Assignments and Coach Operator Timekeeping, appearing in this volume (1981).

Computer Scheduling of Public Transport
A. Wren (ed.)
© *North-Holland Publishing Company, 1981*

SERVICE OPTIMISATION AND ROUTE COSTING
AND ASSOCIATED COMPUTER PROGRAMS

R. R. Davies and D. Williams

West Yorkshire Passenger Transport Executive
Wakefield, U.K.

This paper places the use of computer programs for scheduling
and other functions in the context of the overall activities
of a Passenger Transport Executive. The role of the Executive
is set out, and its relationship with other bodies explained.
The financial processes are described, with regard both to
planning and to identification of costs. The need for service
optimisation is introduced, and the optimisation process is
set out. This leads to the need for computer programs which
can be used for speedy evaluation of options and for
preparation of final schedules. A number of programs are in
use or under investigation. These are set out, and their role
in the organisation is examined.

1. BACKGROUND TO PAPER

It is necessary to outline the reasons behind the operational strategy of the West
Yorkshire Transport Executive and its associated subsidiary companies before we
discuss the computer programs which are used by the Executive to assist in its
planning of Service Optimisation Programmes. The financial strategy provides for a
three-year rolling programme, which is a revenue forecast, and shows the
anticipated surplus or shortfall after all of the strategic options which are open
to the Executive have been introduced.

2. RESPONSIBILITIES OF THE COUNTY COUNCIL AND THE EXECUTIVE

In Britain, the concept of Passenger Transport Executives was introduced by the
Transport Act, 1968. There are eight such organisations throughout Britain,
centred on the major Metropolitan/Urban conurbations. The statutory duty of the
P.T.E.s is to break even each financial year. In this context, the P.T.E. Boards
must at least be seen to be taking the requisite action to achieve this end. As a
commercial operator, a P.T.E. must concern itself primarily with providing an
efficient, effective and viable transport service, consistent with overall current
financial constraints.

It is the P.T.E.'s general duty to exercise and perform its functions so 'as to
secure or promote the provision of a properly integrated and efficient system of
public passenger transport to meet the needs of the area with due regard to the
town planning and traffic and parking policies of the Local Authorities in West
Yorkshire and to economy and safety of operation' (Transport Act, 1968, Section
9(3)).

In view of the County Council's much wider responsibilities the factors actually
involved are considerably more comprehensive than town planning, traffic and
parking policies.

The general responsibility of the County Council is to determine policy in relation to the provision of public passenger transport, particularly on:-

(a) Levels of service to be provided on bus routes and passenger lines.

(b) Types of service.

(c) The overall financial approach.

(d) The fares to be charged.

The general responsibility of the Executive is to operate, or to arrange for the operation of, the public transport services within the policy guidelines laid down by the County Council, and to plan a system as a whole. Agreements have to be reached with other bus operators, particularly the subsidiaries of the National Bus Company, and the British Railways Board.

The financial duty of the Executive is to ensure, as far as possible, that it balances its books in each financial year.

The County Council has wide powers to make grants to the Executive, for example, for capital projects, or to cover any costs incurred, either as a matter of general policy, or for the provision of specific loss-making services. These payments are known as contractual payments.

Towards this end, it should be noted that the P.T.E., which normally operates approximately 1,500 public service vehicles, has control of a subsidiary, the West Yorkshire Metro National Transport Company Limited, which takes in another 1,000 vehicles which are operated by the National Bus Company. This company is a full subsidiary of the P.T.E., and now comprises some 2,500 vehicles and approximately 10,000 staff.

With regard to British Railways' services, the P.T.E. has now reached the stage where British Railways are a contractual partner of the P.T.E., and the P.T.E. now sets the level of service and the level of fares and the Conditions of Carriage associated with the operations of the railway network (i.e. some thirteen corridors within West Yorkshire). Operating arrangements are made with other subsidiary companies, and with independent operators, either inside or outside the boundaries of West Yorkshire. Corridors containing road and rail routes are the subject of Optimisation Programmes.

Some areas which have to be examined, partly as a result of our partnership with the National Bus Company, are:

   (i) Parity of Staff Conditions
      The parity of staff conditions as between P.T.E. and N.B.C. (West Yorkshire) employees is currently being investigated.

  (ii) Large scale economies of operation
      The need for these measures will be determined in the light of the statutory financial duty. Any such measures will be in addition to the service optimisation process.

(iii) Maximisation of use of resources
      This area will cover the use of depots, offices, staff, vehicles and the staff expertise contained within the new company. This will be a continuous process for many years to come.

3. FINANCIAL PROCEDURES

In order to comply with its statutory and commercial duties and responsibilities, the Executive has introduced a financial modelling/forecasting planning process, supported by a comprehensive route costing system. The financial model is regularly updated to reflect economic changes and any further Board policy directives. In addition, periodic financial statements and route costing information is provided to enable the Executive to monitor and control its overall financial performance.

3.1 Three-Year Financial Forecasts

More specifically, the procedure is that a current plus three year financial model/forecast is prepared. The basis on which the model is determined and re-aligned follows a comprehensive review by the Board in August/September of each year.

3.2 Main Features of Review

(a) Consideration of the current level of service provision operated at the financial model review point (mid-September). The model at this level will reflect trends to date and any revised Board policy directives since the last review point.
(b) Updating, taking into account any later view of the likely impact of inflation over the forecast period.
(c) Inclusion of any further or amended Board policy directives, e.g. service optimisation schemes as described later, variations to the Executive's five year capital programme plan, extension of one-person-operation, work study, productivity schemes etc. In this matter, it is vital that all such policy directives (whether relating to service optimisation, one-person-operation, work study etc.) are evaluated in detail, and their phased cost-reduction implications carefully computed prior to their insertion in the model. Evaluation must include both gross and cash flow effect.
(d) The projected level of contractual payments likely to be forthcoming from the Passenger Transport Authority (the County Council) in relation to its civic, social and any non-commercial service provision policies.
(e) Re-assessment of practical problems surrounding staff, vehicle and infrastructure availability.

Having placed all these factors or constraints into the financial model, the Executive is then left with the need to achieve its statutory duty of at least balancing its accounts (if still in deficit) in each of the years under consideration, by a combination of fare increases and/or further service optimisation schemes. In the matter of fare increases, market constraints are clearly all-important and, on the subject of service optimisation (i.e. cost reduction), bearing in mind that pay costs represent 75% of total costs, clearly, extensive trade union involvement is necessitated.

One of the major problems involved in the financial model process is the timing/phasing-in of the Executive's policy objectives, e.g. service optimisation, one-person-operation, work study schemes etc.

3.3 Action against the Plan

It is a fact that, as in the case of all medium/long term plans, the degree of accuracy and reliability decreases in the latter years of the Plan. The current year represents the budget against which the Executive monitors its Managers' financial performance, and, through them, the financial performance of all services provided by it.

In direct support of the financial model, the Executive has recently introduced a comprehensive route costing system, the second major financial input to the improvement of financial performance process.

The Executive has thus a clear indication of the financial performance and viability, or otherwise, of each of the routes, or group of routes, within the total service networks. The Executive considers the route costing outputs as vital indications of the base against which it will measure its overall intended policies in providing an efficient, effective and viable passenger transport network. This is particularly important in the case where improved financial performance is required, whether simply to eliminate waste/inefficiency/duplication of service provision, or for the general purpose of meeting statutory financial duty requirements. The route costing outputs pinpoint the contribution each route makes to variable, semi-variable, fixed and total costs. The route costing outputs are historical and can only be used as a base for predictive costing. In the predictive role, the financial model incomes and costs are allocated to routes based on all the factors inherent in it.

Both the financial modelling and the predictive element of route costing are currently undertaken manually. Computer application is, however, envisaged in the future, which will enable far more permutations of different options to be evaluated. The route costing information output has enabled us to classify all routes into nine financial performance categories, as follows.

(a) Frequency
Each route is classified into one of three frequency groups in terms of scheduled journeys per week, i.e.

Low	1 - 75	journeys per week (approx. less than hourly)
Medium	76 - 150	journeys per week (approx. hourly)
High	151 and above	journeys per week (approx. half-hourly or more)

(b) Financial Performance
Each route is classified into one of three groups in terms of the percentage of costs recovered by revenue. The cost and revenue figures used are derived from the P.T.E. and N.B.C. Route Costing Systems. The three groups are :-

High	- Service recovers 100% or more of costs
Medium	- Service recovers 80% - 99% of costs
Low	- Service recovers less than 80% of costs

It will be seen that by combining these groups there are nine classes of service; the financial information is obtained from the route costing system, and the frequency information is obtained from the service timetables. All routes are then identified by the route number, the route details, the operator, and then the frequency and financial performance classification, the latter being shown by a number from 1 to 9.

The routes are then examined to obtain the proportion of total revenue by service category, and the proportion of total costs by service category. From the ensuing charts, which display this information, it is possible to see which category of route should be attacked, and where the bulk of the losses are being made.

This information is regarded as a 'key indicator' in the process of assessing individual route viability and related management action required in terms of any service alteration. In this connection, the County Council, as the Passenger Transport Authority, is the Executive's major customer in the sense that it imposes its social, civic and political policies on the Executive, making contractual payments in support thereof. The services supported by County Council contractual payments at present are concessionary fares for old age pensioners, blind and disabled persons, infrastructure payments, prepayment schemes, rural bus support and fare policy payments. Clearly, however, it is vital for the Executive to ensure that it receives full contractual payments from all of its customers, and then to allocate all these incomes against specific routes, prior to taking any decisions in the area of service reductions.

In conclusion, it is now no longer acceptable to implement major policy changes, for whatever reasons, without a prior evaluation of the financial effects, both on current and future operation via the model. In this context, predictive individual route cost information is considered one of the key indicators.

4. ASSESSMENT OF ROUTE COSTING OUTPUT

In order to allow route costing to be seen as an integral part of the service optimisation process, it is necessary to consider its development and its use in all sectors of the industry.

4.1 Why was Route Costing Developed? General Background

For many years, the bus industry's rule of thumb measurement as to the financial performance of any particular service had been whether the revenue pence per mile statistic for that service had been greater, or less, than the average cost in pence per mile for the whole company. In effect, this provided a guide, but no more than this, as it did not take into account the financial effects of different types of crew, differing operating terrains, differing types and speeds of service.

At a time when the bus industry was making profits, detailed performance information, whilst considered useful, was not absolutely necessary - that was the Manager's job. The time came, however, when the financial viability of bus services was affected both by competition from other modes of transport and by rapid cost inflation. In large measure, the information requirement coincided with British legislation in the form of the Transport Act, 1968, which allowed County Councils, under Section 34, to support rural bus services, and required them to support identified non-profit-making services in Passenger Transport areas under Section 13. There was a greater need, therefore, to know which services were making the deficits, both in order that improvements in performance could be made which would allow operators to get back into a break-even situation, and also to identify loss-making services, both rural and urban, which could then be put forward to County Councils for financial support if they wished to retain them.

Further legislation in the form of the Local Government Act, 1972, included provision, under Section 203, for Shire County Councils to promote the co-ordination of passenger transport in their county, and to make grants, as necessary, to achieve this aim. As a result, it was essential to have a system which enabled operators to compare routes and monitor the effects of inflation. The system must also provide a consistent approach to all County Councils in order that all counties would know that the treatment received by them would be the same as that received by their neighbours, but, more important, that all counties would know the financial position of the whole network of stage carriage bus services in their area, from which the co-ordinated transport system required by the Transport Act could be developed.

4.2 Standardisation of the 'Route Costing' System

Recognising the need for standardisation, the Chartered Institute of Public Finance and Accountancy published, in April 1974, 'Recommendations on a Standard Financial Statement and a Route Costing System', and the costing principles included in that report, and the further developments of it, have now been accepted as the guide-lines by the industry as a whole.

The system operated by the West Yorkshire Passenger Transport Executive follows the recommendations of CIPFA, and, as such, is a full cost recovery system, rather than a marginal cost system.

4.3 Basis of System used locally in West Yorkshire

As mentioned earlier, the method of calculating costs on a per-mile basis will, at best, only produce average costs, as distinct from the actual costs attributable to a route, or group of routes. As approximately 50% of operators' costs are incurred on platform staff, and the total wage and salary bill of operators can approach 75% of total costs, time has been selected as the prime basis of allocation within the system.

There are specific items of costs which arise solely on a mileage basis. These items include tyre mileage, fuel and third party insurance premiums. These items are allocated to routes on a mileage basis.

In addition to the types of costs already mentioned, there are other costs which are primarily incurred because of the peak operations' requirement. The main example is vehicle depreciation. It is apparent that a method of allocation must be one which ensures that peak operation bears a weighted allocation of such costs. It will be appreciated that 'peak' will bear its correct portion of both time and mileage based costs due to the high incidence of time spent and mileage run during the peak. Other costs, such as non-payroll overheads, are allocated on a 'peak vehicle requirement' basis between routes.

4.3.1 Operation of the System

Treatment of costs: The cost heads on regular financial management information statements are identified as variable, semi-variable or fixed. All variable costs are allocated on a time or mileage basis; semi-variable costs on a time or peak-vehicle basis, and fixed costs (with certain exceptions such as welfare and medical) on a peak-vehicle basis.

   Treatment of revenue:
(a) Farebox income, by route, is taken from daily or weekly waybill route analyses (for the same period as the Financial Statement).
(b) Non-farebox income — the Executive allocates non-farebox income to routes on the basis of route survey information, which is updated with each change of fares policy. Adult pre-paid revenues are not allocated to school services; long distance pre-payments are not allocated to short routes; concessionary fare revenues are not allocated to routes where the concession does not apply.

   It should be noted that Authority contractual payments in respect of general fares or service support is not considered as income for route costing purposes, as one of the aims of the system is to determine profits or losses on routes, excluding general support, and thereby determine just where the support is being applied.

5. ROUTE COSTING AND ITS RELATIONSHIP WITH PURPOSEFUL PLANNING

Route costing, as presently operated by the Executive, is a historical full cost attribution system; that is to say, it always looks at events which have already happened, rather than predicting what might happen if a certain course of action were taken. Further, by being a full cost system, it might be said to lose some of the 'advantages' of a marginal cost system in decision-making. Why then adopt a full cost allocation technique? The CIPFA and the Executive's reasons are as follows:-

(a) General overheads/fixed costs have to be recovered from the revenue of the undertaking as a whole. This method of costing shows the contribution which each route makes towards fixed costs, and this can be compared with a reasonable pre-determined contribution which that route could be expected to make towards fixed costs.

(b) Although there is a case, in the short term, for providing services at a price which covers only their marginal costs, it is undesirable to base long-term strategy on such calculations, as in the long run (annually, in the Transport Act, 1968), fixed costs and general overheads have got to be paid for. In so far as the costing system proposed is designed to be a tool for long-term financial planning by operators, it is important that all costs are taken account of.

(c) The provision of services which fail to make their proper contribution to fixed costs is only possible if there are other routes, or other services, which contribute more than their proper contribution.

(d) In planning future alterations to levels of service provided, it is important that proper account is taken of all costs which may be involved, e.g. additional vehicles, additional garage accommodation. The bus industry uses scarce resources, and the cost of using these must be recognised if a true comparison is to be made with alternative strategies.

In making these comments, however, the need for an element of flexibility in approach must be recognised. Marginal costing is particularly useful in urgent short-term decision-making. For example, how much will it cost to increase the frequency of a particular bus service? The result can then be compared with the anticipated increase in revenue to see what the net effect of the decision may be. We have seen, however, that the main purpose of route costing, as originally devised, was not to meet such decisions, but to show the ongoing cost of operating services within an existing network of bus services for each county.

6. METHODS USED TO EFFECT A BALANCE IN THE REVENUE FORECAST

Normally, if the P.T.E. is effecting a reduction in operating expenses, or increasing revenue to balance a shortfall, the following methods are adopted:-

1. Reduce mileage operated (to reduce costs).

2. Increase revenue (to balance an anticipated shortfall).

3. Effect all operating economies (i.e. to increase operating efficiency).

4. Introduce a percentage each of 1, 2 and 3 in order to reduce the total impact on the passenger.

We may seek a long term improvement in the situation by investigating possible rationalisation of parts of the network.

We have already seen, in Section 3.3, that routes may be grouped into nine categories. Having determined the various categories of route, and decided broadly upon the categories to be attacked, the routes are identified on a large scale map of the operating area. A series of routes can be selected in a corridor, for example, and an identifying boundary be drawn; this then becomes the area selected for an Optimisation Scheme.

7. THE PROCESS OF SERVICE OPTIMISATION

7.1 Introduction

The Service Optimisation method has been adopted by the Metro National Company as a continual programme to optimise the level of service throughout West Yorkshire, in order to make the most efficient use of resources, and to tailor the use of those resources to meet identified passenger demand in the most effective way.

7.2 The Aims and Objectives of Service Optimisation

These are:-
(a) To rationalise the bus operating and routeing structure within West Yorkshire, so as to achieve the optimum use of resources, improve operational efficiency, and remove duplication.
(b) To bring the level of service into line with current identified demand, taking into account survey data, passenger comments, and comments from Elected Members, County Council Officers, members of staff and Trade Union representatives.
(c) To provide new links or facilities, where justified, wherever possible within existing resources (by the removal of duplication or excess capacity elsewhere).
(d) To implement the recommendations of the various Transportation Studies, where it is felt that these recommendations accord with Passenger Transport Authority Policy and the needs of the travelling public.
(e) To improve accessibility to, and thus enhance the attractiveness of, the MetroLink local rail network, where such improvements can be justified in cost benefit terms.

7.3 The Rationale of Service Optimisation

The whole Service Optimisation process is based on passenger survey data. The P.T.E. employs a 20-man HQ Survey Team to collect data on current and potential passenger demand, and this HQ Survey Team is supported by five Data Analysts, who use a computer program to prepare summarised information for management, and to build a data base.

The main types of surveys carried out are as follows:-
(a) Origin and destination surveys on each scheduled journey, or a cross-sectional sample of journeys, to collect information on precise passenger requirements.
(b) Static loading surveys (which are carried out at maximum demand points) measure corridor demand, to calibrate total demand against total corridor capacity, to ensure that the level of service operated along the corridor matches demand.
(c) House-to-house surveys, which are designed to collect detailed information on passenger travel habits, and to assess any potential or 'frustrated' demand.

7.4 The Mechanics of Service Optimisation

Each Optimisation Scheme requires careful planning, and requires input from several sources. Comments from Elected Members, Trade Unions, County Council Officers, the public and Metro National staff at all levels are fully considered at each stage. The implementation of the Optimisation Schemes is by means of a Working Party involving representatives of the Metro National Company at both headquarters and at local operating level, together with officers of the County Council and from British Rail where appropriate. In order to assist the processing of the Optimisation Schemes, the Metro National Company has drawn up a systematic critical stage programme for implementing revisions to service as smoothly as possible.

The programme, which takes the form of a flow chart, identifies the functions of all relevant parties involved and all critical points in the course of implementation.

This divides the implementation process into the following stages:-

(1) The Consideration Stage which determines the specific terms of reference and the implementation programme including critical dates and the target implementation date.

(2) The Consultation Stage during which there is full consultation with all parties, and during which passenger data is collected and analysed. At this stage the broad scope of the scheme is indicated to the Passenger Transport Authority, the travelling public, the Trade Unions and the Company's employees, and comments are invited.

(3) The Production Stage which produces the revised network and service levels, which are then submitted to the Passenger Transport Authority for comment and approval.

(4) The Scheduling/Licensing Stage during which the network is prepared for implementation, after any modifications arising from feedback from Elected Members, Trade Unions and the public.

(5) The Implementation Stage during which all the requirements for smooth implementation are checked and controlled.

(6) The Post-Implementation Stage during which there is detailed monitoring of the revised network to ensure it is meeting its objectives.

8. THE NEED FOR RAPID EVALUATION OF OPTIONS

Once an Optimisation Scheme has been selected a critical path immediately becomes operative as outlined previously. If all goes well, the critical path will take twelve months from start to finish and the duty schedule compilation will itself use up three months of that time.

It is abundantly clear, therefore, that if one option goes through the duty schedule compilation system, then three months will have been lost in the flow chart if the results are unacceptable at the end of the exercise.

It is necessary, therefore, to speed up the duty schedule compilation and evaluation systems by computer programs in order that the flow chart will not be held up, but still enabling the operator to evaluate several options before choosing one for processing.

Various computerised processes have been used to evaluate options and these are being constantly further developed.

9. FURTHER DEVELOPMENT

The service optimisation process is an evolving process, and as such, is modified and developed through experience, and through the search for improved cost-effectiveness. The Metro National Company is investigating and evaluating a wider use of computer programs and data handling techniques to assist in the optimisation process, and to enable a rapid cost assessment to be achieved by supplying information on the number of buses and the types of duty required to operate alternative timetables. The following systems are either under investigation or in use:-

A. RAPP

RAPP is a computer-based public transport modelling system using interactive graphic display techniques. It has been developed by Swiss Consultants W. and J. Rapp.

The system compares a base bus network with various revised alternative options for bus networks, and provides a rapid simulation through modelling techniques of the likely passenger and financial effects of the revised networks.

At present, the Executive is undertaking a pilot exercise with W. and J. Rapp for an optimisation scheme in Bradford, to assess the desirability of using the system on a regular basis.

B. TASC – Timetable and Schedule Compilation

This computer system has been developed by the University of Leeds, and has already been used by the Executive on a pilot basis; the results have been encouraging. The original concept was to provide the input data for a crew duty scheduling program, as it is very laborious and time-consuming to extract the necessary relief point data manually from the running boards. However, there appears to be very considerable scope for using this program for other purposes such as simulation and ancillary outputs, and the Executive has produced 155 schedules based on 41 networks for Leeds and Bradford Districts in order to show the effects of different options for different levels of service on a particular network.

Briefly, the system functions are:-

(1) Constructs running schedules, providing timetables with bus workings (optimal for the particular schedule only).
(2) Collates several services over specified common sections of routes.
(3) Can equalise headways of a particular service.
(4) Runs buses to and from garages as necessary.
(5) Runs buses 'dead' between terminals as necessary.
(6) Calculates the bus hours necessary to run the schedule.
(7) Estimates, by duty type, the number of crews necessary to run the schedule.

C. MAP – Marketing Analysis Project

This process utilises specially-written computer programs to analyse extensive data on existing passenger movement, with a view to reducing the number of buses required in service. To date, the system has been used only in areas of low intensity of public transport provision, and the technical processes are being investigated by the P.T.E. to establish their effectiveness, in particular in relation to the more rural areas of the county.

D. SMOOTH - Special Method Of Optimising Transport Headways, used in conjunction with TASC

A computer system to produce desired bus service headways over common stretches of routes for a number of services utilising the minimum number of vehicles, and making the overall service as regular as possible.

E. VAMPIRES - Vehicle And Mileage Pruning In Running Essential Services

This program produces bus schedules for a given number of journeys, indicating where vehicles can be saved. Experience has shown that the program consistently produces savings. It has been used by fifteen to twenty operators in the United Kingdom. The Executive has used VAMPIRES in Leeds.

F. TRACS - Techniques for Running Automatic Crew Scheduling

The crew scheduling suite which has been developed within the University of Leeds over a period since 1967 has been used quite extensively by the P.T.E., and it now consistently produces good schedules. The program has been developed in co-operation with the P.T.E. A list of possible future requirements was drawn up by the P.T.E. and parameters have been designed to cater for all these.

Recent use of the program has been for the production of holiday schedules and simulation of EEC regulations, and for the assessment of alternative proposals for Leeds District scheduling conditions.

G. TRICS - Techniques for Running Interactive Crew Scheduling

This program allows the scheduler to build up a crew schedule from a computer terminal, using the computer as a tool to check the legality of proposed duties, and as a means of proposing suitable pieces of work for combination together into duties.

H. TRAM - Transport Rostering Automatic Method

A program to fit a roster to a given pattern of duties.

I. RAFT - Revision Automatically of Fare Tables

A computer program for compiling new fare tables from given information about desired levels of revenue and passenger resistance. (This program is at the experimental stage.)

10. CONCLUSIONS

The need for computer programs covering a wide of the Executive's activities has been shown. Some programs are required to assist in the evaluation of options, for example, of different routeing structures, or different schedule proposals within routeing structures, or even different agreements with the Trade Union. Other programs may be used in the implementation of chosen options only, while many programs will be used in both contexts.

The Executive has examined a number of programs, in scheduling and in other areas. Some of these are in use, and have assisted the Executive in the performance of its duties. Others are in the process of evaluation.

Computer Scheduling of Public Transport
A. Wren (ed.)
© *North-Holland Publishing Company, 1981*

COMPUTERIZED VEHICLE AND DRIVER SCHEDULING
FOR THE HAMBURGER HOCHBAHN AKTIENGESELLSCHAFT

Dipl.-Volksw. Josef Hoffstadt

Hamburger Hochbahn Aktiengesellschaft
West Germany

A system is described which provides for the production of timetables, bus and driver schedules and driver rosters by computer. The system has been implemented in Hamburg, where it has produced all schedules since the summer of 1979. The paper sets out the background to the work, and describes the component parts of the system, outlining its mathematical basis. There follows a discussion of problems encountered in introducing the system, a description of the actual implementation, and a survey of the benefits already achieved and still to be achieved.

1. INTRODUCTION

1.1 Task setting for a program system designed to plan timetables, vehicle schedules, drivers' duties and duty rosters.

For every local transport company, the need to work out new vehicle and driver schedules prior to changes in the general timetable involves a vast amount of planning, most of which has to be done under the added stress caused by a strict deadline. Since the volume of data involved is so large, this would seem an ideal case for using electronic data processing.

The main objective in computerizing vehicle and driver scheduling must be to simplify and accelerate the process to such an extent as to reduce the workload for staff in the timetabling and scheduling offices and to allow faster and easier adaptation to meet the changing requirements of the transport situation. At the same time, electronic processing must take both government regulations and internal agreements into account and provide more economical planning without lowering the quality standard achieved before the computer system was introduced.

The Hamburger Hochbahn Aktiengesellschaft (HHA) has done a great deal of work on the problems connected with electronic processing in the bus sector. From the very outset, the aim was to develop a comprehensive integrated program system which would use electronic data files containing information on routes, timetables and schedules as a basis for a number of functions, ranging from printing bus-stop timetables to planning vehicle and driver schedules, determining operating performance (total number of kilometres) and compiling other statistical data. The aim was to design the vehicle and driver scheduling programs in such a way as to be able to provide the required service while keeping the number of buses, the number of journeys without passengers and the number of duty hours down to a minimum.

The system was also to be designed to take exactly the same internal peripheral factors into account as if planning were still being done on a non-automatic basis. Some of these factors were, for instance,

- the need to respect the rules governing working hours and work-breaks,

- the need for integrated processing of service data from different bus garages,

- the need to conform to given guidelines as to the number of vehicle and duty periods at the individual bus garages,

- the assignment of certain bus-types to predefined vehicle schedules,

- the need to process data of schedules operated by other companies, and

- the need to combine the rapid transit and city bus sectors so as to economise on vehicles.

At the same time, an amendment facility was to be provided so as to allow subsequent alterations to vehicle and driver schedules without unreasonable time and effort being involved.

1.2 General outline of the system

We were well aware from the start that previous experiments in using electronic data processing for timetabling and scheduling work had mostly proved sadly inadequate in practice. Frequent use of a heuristic approach led to unacceptably long computing times and failed to produce optimum results.

HHA has therefore developed a system whereby a mathematical model for the number of vehicles used and the number of duties - including paid idle-time - achieves optimal efficiency in terms of costs. The programs can be run on a UNIVAC 9400 computer with a working storage capacity of at least 192 Kilobytes and a magnetic disc. HHA itself possesses a UNIVAC 9060 with a working storage of 512 Kilobytes. As a consequence the tasks can be completed in a quicker and more optimal manner.

The design of the program system is such that it generally works on an integrated basis, i.e. the output from one subsystem acts as input for the next, although each subsystem can also be run in its own right. If no EDP-produced input data is available, the information must be suitably prepared in advance. Figure 1 shows the procedure for producing timetables, vehicle schedules, drivers' duties and duty rosters and determining operating performance using electronic data processing. All data on routes, journeys with passengers and possible routes for empty buses is stored in electronic master files for the computer's use and must always be updated before the programs are run. After this, preparations can be made for printing bus-stop timetables and timetable handbooks, while at the same time the required schedules are worked out. Thanks to the schedule amendment facility, the operator has a means of gaining access to the EDP-produced schedules and can thus make direct changes to the vehicle schedule file.

The vehicle schedules then serve as input data for the drivers' duty scheduling subsystem. If the latter is run in conjunction with the vehicle scheduling subsystem, the programs for duty scheduling exert influence on the vehicle schedules. These schedules can be taken apart and rearranged via the duty scheduling program in order to reduce the number of duties required and to improve the distribution of work-breaks.

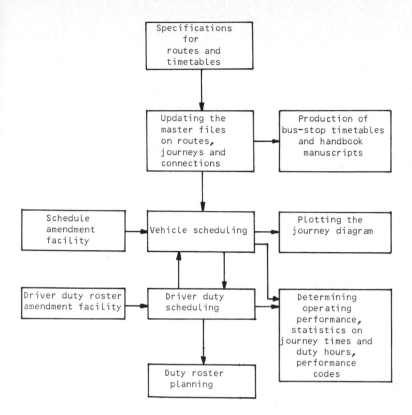

Figure 1: Procedure for timetable production, planning of vehicle
           schedules, drivers' duties and duty rosters and
           operating performance by electronic data processing at
           Hamburger Hochbahn Aktiengesellschaft (HHA).

After the vehicle schedules and duties have been drawn up, the journey diagrams
can be plotted. The advantage of the plotter over conventional drawing methods is
that it means the job can be completed in a much shorter time. A further advantage
of great importance is that automatically-drawn diagrams are much more easily
legible.

The duty schedule file then supplies the input data for the duty rostering
program.

2. THE MASTER FILES

2.1 Master file structures

The program system requires four electronic data files to act as master files. These consist of the following:
a) The master file of routes

   This file contains details of the routes used when carrying passengers. These are defined by the sequence of bus-stops, the journey times and the distance from the starting-point of the half-route.

b) The master file of connections

   The master file of connections contains information on the starting and finishing points of journeys without passengers, their duration and the distance covered.

c) The master file of journeys

   It contains information on one, two or more journeys carrying passengers.

d) The file of minimum turning time

   In order to prevent any delays which may build up during the course of a journey from affecting the punctuality of the next, a little extra time can be added to the time scheduled for each journey; the next journey may not then be started until this time allowance has elapsed. The necessary data can be taken from the file of minimum turning times.

Whenever the timetable is changed, the master files are up to date.

3. TIMETABLE MANUSCRIPTS AND BUS-STOP TIMETABLES

Given parameters dictate what transport sectors, routes or half-routes require their own timetables and manuscripts and how often. It is absolutely vital that the informtion stored in the master files of routes and journeys is correct before the schedules are planned and the timetables printed. The easiest way of making sure of this is by checking the timetable manuscripts. As soon as the data files have been changed to correct any errors which may have been discovered, the bus-stop timetables can be designed. The corrected originals are then stored, either on magnetic tape or magnetic disc, and printed or reprinted whenever necessary.

The master files are brought up to date by the staff in the timetabling and scheduling office not only as a preparatory measure for the production of bus-stop timetables and handbook manuscripts. On the contrary, the updating process is a vital preparation also for determining operational performance. The master files must be designed for easy handling by the operating staff and easy processing in subsequent programs.

4. VEHICLE SCHEDULING

During vehicle scheduling, a series of given journeys is connected to form a chain. These chains always begin and end at the same bus garage and are known as vehicle workings. They each have an identifying code number.

The Hamburger Hochbahn Aktiengesellschaft operates six bus garages and can allocate certain buses and services to these, depending on the number of parking spaces and the staff capacity they have available.

Before they can use the computer system to distribute capacity to the individual bus garages, the timetabling and scheduling staff must provide it with the following information:

a) Details of which routes belong to which bus garages. Each bus garage or group of bus garages will then supply vehicles for its own routes.

b) Details of services provided by other companies.

c) Internal restrictions,

for example: number of duties per bus garage, number of vehicles to be parked overnight at any particular bus garage, total parking facilities at starting points and destinations.

d) Program parameters

Weighting to avoid combining different types of vehicles (e.g. a vehicle on rapid transit service moving straight on to a city bus route). This type of combination is only permissible if it means that a whole bus can be saved.

Weighting to prevent unnecessary route changing.

Weighting to avoid combining express buses with city buses. These express buses have special identification markings which are only available in limited numbers.

4.1 The mathematical model

After due consideration it was established that, when considerably modified, the Hungarian method can provide a suitable mathematical model for the formation of schedules.

The problem can be formulated as follows. Journey j is allocated to journey i, as is journey k to j etc., meaning that from n number of journeys, chains are formed in the pattern i - j - k ....., whereby r, the number of chains is intended to be a minimum. The first chain is created from K_1 journeys, by means of K_1-1 linkages, the second from K_2 journeys by means of K_2-1 linkages,... the rth chain from K_r-1 linkages. The r chains thus consist of

$$\sum_{i=1}^{r} K_i = n \text{ journeys with } \sum_{i=1}^{r} K_i - r = m \text{ linkages} \qquad (1)$$

The formula r = n-m is thus obtained, which shows that r, the number of journeys, becomes a minimum when m, the number of linkages, becomes a maximum.

The question of finding a maximum number of linkages can be formulated as an assignment problem: the value of z, the objective function, is to be minimised.

$$z = \sum_{i=1}^{n} \sum_{j=1}^{n} c_{ij} \, x_{ij} \qquad (2)$$

subject to the following restrictions

$$\sum_{j=1}^{n} x_{ij} = 1 \quad (i = 1,2,\ldots,n) \qquad (3)$$

$$\sum_{i=1}^{n} x_{ij} = 1 \quad (j = 1,2,\ldots,n) \qquad (4)$$

$$x_{ij} = 0,1 \qquad (5)$$

Co-efficients c_{ij} contain the costs incurred when journey i is linked with journey j. Impossible linkages contain a large number M as costs. The variables x_{ij} can only take on the values 0 or 1. Minimizing the objective function (2) means the least number of elements with the value M enter the solution, and the maximum possible number of linkages can subsequently be attained.

The bus runs are assigned to the bus garages, taking vehicle and staff capacity into account. The transportation problem of linear programming ensures that the sum of pull-outs and pull-ins is kept to a minimum. Further programs use the bus run file and the master file of routes. These files are also the basic input for printing timetable diagrams on a plotter.

The vehicle shedules produced are then used as input data for the duty scheduling program. These - unlike the vehicle schedules - are planned individually for each bus garage.

5. DUTY SCHEDULING

5.1 Preconditions for duty scheduling

The purpose of duty scheduling is to split the various vehicle schedules up into duties and assign personnel to them. The ultimate objective is to reduce the number of duties to a minimum - always taking the official permitted length of a duty into account - and to achieve an optimal duty schedule, i.e. one in which the duration of duties matches the length of vehicle workings as efficiently as possible.

When a duty involves continuous work, the entire period between commencement and close of the duty is paid. In the case of a broken duty the time between the segments is unpaid. Duty scheduling has to take a large number of government, tariff and company regulations into account. Time regulations, for instance, have to be obeyed minutely.

All these quantifiable restrictions and the program parameters for strategy variations are stored in a data file. Apart from this parameter file for duty planning, other basic instruments used will be the master file of routes (for determining personnel relief points), the file of journey times (which is based on the master file of journeys and the master file of routes) and the master file of connections.

The following internal requirements must also be taken into account:

the average duty should be as nearly as possible identical with the nominal duty period;

continuous duties should always be given preference over broken ones.

Duty scheduling is divided into three parts. By cutting bus runs in the first part, duty segments are produced, which are then combined into duties in the second. The output of duties thus obtained ensues in the third part. One block of bus workings is processed at a time, for one bus garage and for one type of day (Figure 2).

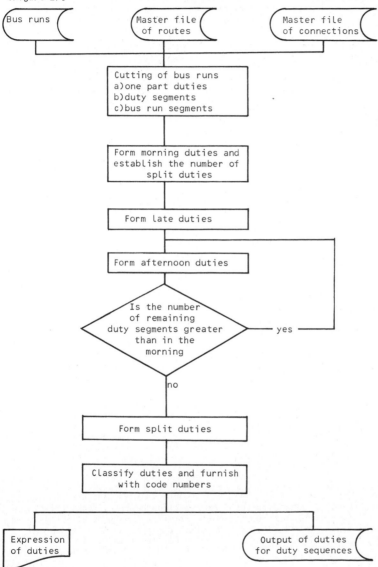

Figure 2: Survey of duty schedule planning

5.2 The formation of duty segments

Each duty begins and ends in the bus garage, as is the case with each bus working. The duration of the bus working, however, is often longer than the maximum duty permitted, necessitating two or more drivers to relieve one another during a run. The stops at which this procedure can take place are known as relief points, and the time required by the driver to get to a bus garage from a relief point as travel time. Since travel time forms part of working time, stops situated near the bus garage, or the garage itself, make especially suitable relief points.

Each bus working is analysed by a program, which ascertains whether it has to be cut or not. A bus working remains uncut if it complies with a duty, or if it proves too short to exist as a duty. Should a bus working be too short, it is combined at a later time. If a bus working has to be cut, this is done in such a way, that, when possible, the length of a duty segment can comply approximately with nominal manhours, taking those restrictions which must be observed into consideration. If this proves impossible, the duty segment is cut in succeeding programs. At the end of the program, we obtain different types of duty segments: segments which can exist as duty, small segments still to be combined, and bus working segments still to be cut.

5.3 The formation of morning duties

Considering the number of buses in operation on an average working day, it can be seen that F represents the number of morning duties which have to be created (Figure 3). If all morning duties have not been generated in the previously mentioned programs, a list A of still uncut bus schedule segments is formed, containing journeys from the first rush hour. There is also a list B containing all other morning duty segments left over from the formation of duty segments mentioned above.

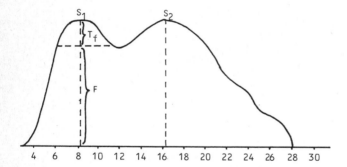

Figure 3:   Frequency of bus assignments

An assignment algorithm is applied to the elements of both lists, looking for the maximum number of assignments. Bus run segments from list A have to be split up in this process. Additionally the number of transition periods, a variable depending on costs, is minimized. The assignment problem can be formulated as follows:

List A contains m still uncut morning bus run segments. List B contains n morning duty segments. A number p of morning duty segments from list B is then allocated to p still uncut bus run segments of list A. In doing this, any part of a bus run segment still to be cut can only be combined with one duty segment.

c_{ij} is of a size corresponding to the cost function, with the value

$$c_{ij} = \begin{cases} K, \text{ when a combination is possible between the i-th bus run and the j-th bus run segment.} \\ M \text{ otherwise.} \end{cases}$$

The value of M is much greater than K. In programming, the value 9999 is used for this.

Furthermore

$$X_{ij} = \begin{cases} 1, \text{ when the j-th duty segment is allocated to the i-th segment.} \\ 0 \text{ otherwise.} \end{cases}$$

The objective function for the minimum of the costs now reads

$$D = \sum_{i=1}^{m} \sum_{j=1}^{n} c_{ij} \, X_{ij}$$

under the restrictions

$$\sum_{j=1}^{n} X_{ij} = 1 \quad (i = 1, 2, \ldots, m) \quad (6)$$

$$\sum_{i=1}^{m} X_{ij} = 1 \quad (j = 1, 2, \ldots, n) \quad (7)$$

The restrictions shown in (6) indicate that each bus run segment can only take over one duty segment, and those in (7) that only one bus run segment can be allocated to each duty segment.

The remaining morning segments are later processed into split duties.

Thus exactly $F = S_1 - T_f$ morning duties were formed.

5.4 The formation of late duties

In the formation of late duties, an attempt is made to arrange those elements still to be combined into 2 different lists. In doing so, the procedure followed in the formation of morning duties is reversed. List A includes all duty segments and still uncut bus run segments ending after a fixed point in time t_1 (e.g. 26.00 hours for night duties), whereas list B includes all duty segments and still uncut bus run segments after a fixed point in time t_2 (e.g. 21.00 hours). The matrix of costs is formed in the same way as for morning duties. The already described assignment algorithm is then applied.

The second and smaller peak discernible in Figure 3 is thus reduced. Constant changing of the parameters t_1 and t_2 enables the above mentioned process of co-ordination to be applied for the formation of the night duties, followed by the late, and then the afternoon duties. The peak in Figure 3 should consequently be reduced until the remaining number of duty segments is equal to the number of morning duty segments, from which the split duties are formed. This process is interrupted when no uncut bus run segments are left over and only small duty segments and already formed duties are remaining. List A then comprises all duty segments still to be combined, all the previously combined duty segments, and duty segments arising from the splitting up of one-part duty segments.

5.5 The formation of split duties

After all continuous duties have been formed, only the morning and afternoon duty segments remain. The morning segments appertain to a list A and the afternoon segments to a list B. With the aid of the assignment algorithm, the split duties can be obtained. For Saturday and Sunday no split duties will be formed but only continuous ones.

5.6 Identification of duties and schedule printing

Once defined, the duties are divided into categories, i.e. morning, afternoon, late and broken duty, and identified by means of a code number. The individual duties are then broken up into journeys and the details printed as required by the timetabling and scheduling office.

6. DUTY ROSTERING

6.1 Preconditions for duty rostering

During the duty rostering process, the duties arrived at by the duty scheduling program are arranged in a detailed pattern. Each duty is defined by its number, its starting and finishing times and its overall duration. Duties which can only be performed by a particular group of staff, e.g. driving instructors, are identified by a special code.

The following details are needed before a duty roster can be set up:

the number of duty weeks (cycles) required for each group, e.g. city bus drivers, rapid transit bus drivers, driving instructors, the number of weeks in reserve, i.e. duty cycles to which no particular service has been allocated, and their position within the sequences.

Duty rostering must again take government, tariff and company regulations, such as those governing noise emission at night, length of duty cycles etc., into account. The ultimate aim is to reduce the difference between nominal and actual cycle lengths to a minimum. Hamburger Hochbahn Aktiengesellschaft distinguishes between two types of duty cycle – one in which a driver works 6 days and then has 3 days off, and one in which he works 5 days (Monday to Friday) and then has 2 days off (Saturday and Sunday). All cycles belonging to the same type are planned at the same time.

The program also allows sequences to be planned using other cycles.

7. DETERMINATION OF PERFORMANCE CAPACITY

Overall performance capacity is calculated on the basis of the current vehicle schedule file. The system distinguishes between vehicle kilometres - with and without passengers - and vehicle kilometres which are paid for by the Hamburger Verkehrsverbund (Hamburg Transport Association).

Whenever the timetables are changed, any information likely to affect the performance capacity calculation must be passed on to the amendment facility for registration in the duty schedule file. This then provides the basis for a new vehicle schedule file, which in turn supplies the input data needed to calculate the nominal daily performance during the calculation period. The actual monthly operational performance can then be calculated with performance deviations registered by the control centres (MEMI = higher or lower performance rates). (Figure 4).

8. PLOTTING SCHEDULE DIAGRAMS

Journey diagrams are plotted using a 132 Benson plotter. The input data (vehicle runs with control commands) is read from magnetic tape. The speed of plotting is approximately 15 centimetres per second, so that it only takes about 40 hours to produce about 120 journey diagrams showing 1,600 Monday to Friday journeys.

The software needed for writing the magnetic tape consists of two parts:
a) Standard software, i.e. program routines for producing letters and numbers of various sizes as well as continuous or dotted straight lines and circles.
b) User software, which is used to draw the vehicle runs. This basically consists of three parts. First, there is a heading program, which is used to draw headings and captions. The columns representing starting points and destinations and the lines representing terminals and bus transfers from one journey to another are drawn in the plan program. The distances between the start and destination columns are in proportion to journey times as long as a certain minimum distance is reached. The time axis is extended in sections as a function of journey density.

Finally, the straight lines representing the individual journeys are drawn in the journey program.

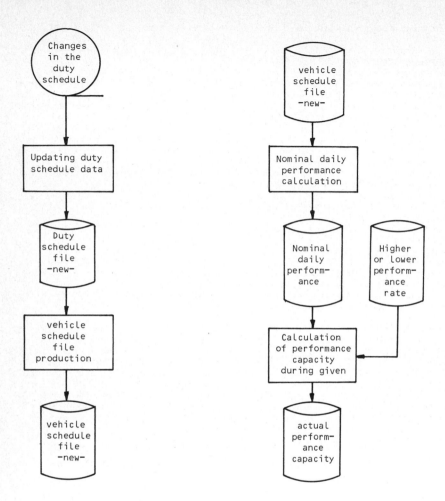

Figure 4:   Calculation of performance capacity

9. RESULTS AND EXPERIENCE IN PRACTICE

9.1 The original situation

At first, the staff in the timetabling and scheduling office were highly sceptical about using automatic vehicle and personnel scheduling. This was because they doubted whether it would ever be possible to convert the many and complicated tasks involved in planning timetables and duty rosters into a full program system without neglecting the diverse requirements of the company, the staff and the passengers using the service. From the company point of view, the most important objective apart from top-level economy is the achievement of absolutely comprehensive and correct results which take the interests of the company into consideration at every step. This is because the entire service system is based on the timetable and duty schedules and any mistakes at the planning stage automatically lead to breakdowns in the final service.

There were also doubts about how the personnel would react to computerized duty schedules. Day-to-day experience had made them all too aware of the problems involved. They were particularly worried that the kind of internal customs outside the framework provided by legislation and collective agreements which had always been taken into consideration during scheduling under the previous system would prove too complex to be included in the program and would thus be dropped.

Also - although this was never mentioned explicitly - the staff in the timetabling and scheduling office were afraid the introduction of the new system would endanger their jobs.

Furthermore, in the early sixties, when Hamburger Hochbahn Aktiengesellschaft started introducing computerized vehicle and personnel scheduling, there was no way of knowing what vast potential the future would bring for data processing in the planning and administration sectors. Nowadays, because of the huge technical progress made during the last few years, the possibilities are abundantly clear.

This is why arousing staff interest in the computer system and motivating them towards accepting it was one of the most important objectives during the initial stages of computerizing vehicle and personnel scheduling.

The first step towards motivation is always information - in this particular case, informing the staff about the ultimate purpose of the system and describing the working principles of data processing, its potential and its limitations.

9.2 Co-operation between timetabling and scheduling staff and data processing personnel

There was not the slightest doubt that although the task in question would have to be placed in the hands of expert computer personnel, we would be equally dependent on the assistance of experienced timetabling and scheduling staff. Unfortunately, there were no universally-trained staff available with sufficient knowledge of both sectors. It is possible - and indeed vital - to familiarize systems analysts and electronic data processing experts with the fringe elements involved in vehicle and personnel scheduling, but this can in no way replace the kind of experience gained in years of practical service within the company and in the timetabling and scheduling office. This was why the involvement of the works council was vitally necessary from the very start.

This type of problem can thus only be solved by teamwork, involving intensive effort both from the timetabling and scheduling staff and computer experts. This is not only true of the initial development phase leading up to the first computer-planned vehicle and personnel schedules. It also applies to all future work on the timetables, vehicle and duty schedules - all of which have to be reorganized at least twice a year when the timetables are changed.

9.3 The problems raised by internal company provisions

The first test results showing system analysis and the formulation of tariff conditions and agreements alongside internal company provisions were still not sufficient to dispel the fears of the timetabling and scheduling staff.

From the company point of view, the vehicle schedules and duty schedules drawn up by the computer were unsatisfactory in a number of ways. There are no complete lists of parameters for vehicle and personnel scheduling in the timetabling and scheduling office. Apart from those dictated by legislation and overall collective agreements, the formative provisions and restrictions are very largely governed by the timetabling and scheduling staff's knowledge of the company set-up, practical experience and efficiency (perceptive faculties, combinative skills).

When the poor results were analyzed, it transpired that - among other things - certain parameters and fringe provisions which had previously been taken into account by the timetabling and scheduling staff with their detailed knowledge of locations (e.g. minimum turning times, maximum parking facilities for vehicles at bus garages) or interconnected factors within the duty schedule (e.g. the distribution of work-breaks) had not been satisfactorily included in the formulation of internal company provisions or in program planning.

There then followed a long and reiterative programme of test runs, fault analyses and improvements until the system finally produced timetables, vehicle schedules, duty schedules and duty rosters which all satisfied company requirements.

9.4 The importance of the vehicle and duty schedule amendment facility

The achievement of an efficient vehicle and duty schedule amendment facility was an important milestone in the development of the program system. Understandably, one of the company's main arguments against using computer planning had been that they were afraid the necessary flexibility and ability to make vital - or merely useful - changes in vehicle or duty schedules, or to correct unsatisfactory results, would be lost if the only means of access to the system were via the basic programs and the total number of journeys. The timetabling and scheduling staff would then become far too dependent on program processing. Now, however, with the help of the amendment program, the staff can make desired modifications directly.

9.5 The introduction of the computer scheduling method

As company services and staff in Hamburg are spread over a total of six bus garages, it seemed best to start using computer-planned vehicle and personnel schedules at the bus garage whose route network has the least contact with others. The various programs were thus carefully tested, evaluated and improved at this one garage while planning at the others went on as before.

The computer-planned timetables and schedules were introduced step by step. The first task to be assigned to the computer was duty rostering. This was introduced when the previously-used 6 + 2 cycle was changed to 6 + 3 in the summer of 1975. The 1978/1979 winter timetable period saw the computer already producing schedule diagrams for the whole network, all schedules and timetables, including duty rosters, for one bus garage and the Saturday and Sunday timetables for the entire network. Since the 1979 summer timetable period, the computer has been doing all vehicle and personnel scheduling throughout the bus sector. The 1979/1980 winter timetable, which was introduced at the end of September last year, again demonstrates just how efficient the system is.

The results proved that we had been right to proceed so carefully in working out the programs and testing them one at a time before adopting the system for the whole company - even if this did cause rather a time lag.

9.6 Improved cost efficiency

One of the main reasons for introducing computerized vehicle and personnel scheduling was the need to achieve optimum results more economically than the previous system allowed. On the one hand, this means reducing the number of vehicles and duty staff needed to an efficient minimum and cutting the amount of journey time without passengers, and on the other hand, reducing the time and effort otherwise involved in drawing up timetables and schedules.

Just how far have we actually been able to economize by using the computer system? This question is impossible to answer in terms of statistics alone, since a whole range of influential factors must be taken into consideration if the results are to be properly evaluated.

The only way to produce exactly comparable results would be to draw up one set of vehicle and personnel schedules for the entire network using the original method and another using the computer - the information processed being identical in both cases. This, however, as we have already explained, was not possible in our case because we chose to introduce the computer programs gradually, bus garage by bus garage.

Furthermore, there have been considerable changes in the volume of timetable information and the network structure, caused by certain tram routes being switched to bus service and reorganization of the bus network after the opening of a new S-Bahn route (suburban railway) in the spring of 1979. The vehicle scheduling sector was also radically affected by the introduction of the first 25 articulated buses.

Another complicating factor was that certain changes were made in the overall tariff regulations, i.e. in the rules governing working hours, during the introductory period and these affected personnel scheduling.

As a result, the only way of quantifying the ultimate saving achieved is on the basis of test run results and comparison of the Hamburger Verkehrsverbund specifications with the final requirement figures. Evaluation on this basis indicates a saving of

> 20 vehicles and
> 35 bus drivers

in terms of the service volume provided by the 1979/1980 winter timetable.

There were also further savings which took the form of reductions in the number of personnel required to determine performance capacity, to run the timetabling and scheduling office and to produce and process statistical material on performance data. It must be remembered, that calculation and processing of performance data in Hamburg has to be done with a high degree of accuracy because they are the basis of revenue distribution among the members of the transport group (HVV). This will certainly also apply to companies in other transport group areas.

We must also remember that additonal expenses for data processing and program maintenance personnel must be set off against these savings.

We are not yet in a position to give details of the ultimate saving, since not all the functional areas affected by the system have been finally converted to it.

Investigation is currently going on into the possibility of making further savings in the collecting and processing of basic wage information. Every day, data affecting the payment of each driver has to be collected, processed and passed on to the data processing department for inclusion in the monthly wage account calculation.

This is a task which currently calls for several employees, both at the bus garages and in administration. Since the computer already has a range of basic duty schedule data (duration of duty, longer or shorter hours based on an average duty period, number of night duty hours, Saturday and Sunday duties and broken duties) stored in its memory, the logical conclusion would be to record only pay-affecting deviations using the current method and leave all the rest to the computer, thus making a considerable reduction in the amount of work involved in processing data of this type for about 2,300 drivers. At the same time, as a welcome side-effect, there would be a reduction in the number of errors of transcription, which are an inevitable hazard of the present system – no matter how careful the staff are: and we all know badly those affected react when mistakes are made in wage accounting – especially if a pay packet is short!

9.7 Further advantages from the company point of view

a) Reductions in time spent on timetabling and scheduling.

   As we have already demonstrated, another very important advantage of the system as far as the company is concerned is that far less time is spent on timetabling and scheduling – simply because the computer works faster.

   It is, however, vital that the basic data is closely monitored and brought up to date as often as necessary – especially the master file of connections, which is exceptionally important if the number of vehicles and drivers is to be reduced – and that any alterations are carefully recorded in the other files.

b) Plotting of journey diagrams.

c) Printing of duty schedules.

d) Examination of changes in timetables and duty schedules.

e) Production of statistics and other internal documentation.

9.8 The advantages of further use of the program system

Availability of the basic data for use in other computerized systems.

Transport companies everywhere are making more and more use of computers.

The Hamburger Hochbahn Aktiengesellschaft already uses computers in the commercial sector, for automatic vehicle and personnel scheduling and in two further areas: for the computerized bus control system (RBL) which monitors the entire bus service and for an automatic enquiry and information service (AFI).

This means that

- on the one hand, staff involved in recording data, building up software and designing computer programs must make even more intensive effort to think of other applications for these within the company,

- and on the other hand, that the overall effort and cost invested in data processing must be seen in relation to the whole range of its possible uses.

This basic data consists chiefly of information from the files of routes, connections and journeys relating to the routes and distances travelled and to the timetables. At Hamburger Hochbahn Aktiengesellschaft, any changes in this information which may affect timetables or vehicle schedules are passed on to the RBL direct.

It is also quite possible that we could make more use of basic duty schedule information in the driver performance and wage accounting field than we do at present. This is why the company requirement specification for the design of the computerized operational control system for the HHA bus service includes the requirement that it must be possible to use the system for driver information (e.g. staff code number). The idea is to carry out a comparison of nominal and actual driver service hours, using data drawn from the duty roster, and to pass the results straight to the wages department staff for their use. Obviously, the possibilities in this respect will have to be looked into in much more detail.

9.9 Internal surveys

It goes without saying that with the basic data available, we shall be able to carry out surveys of individual sectors much more quickly and easily than has been possible to date.

Such surveys could be carried out on individual routes, particular sections of the network or operating hours, for example. Alternatively, they could be designed to determine the best way of distributing the service over the available bus garages and cast more light on inter-connecting factors which - in the past - were either unknown or not quantifiable.

The same applies to the discovery and testing of internal company parameters with a negative influence on vehicle and staff requirements in vehicle and duty scheduling during the course of such surveys. Thorough investigation is necessary to determine whether changes are possible in order to achieve a higher productivity and what other effects these changes might have.

It would, for example, be possible to run a series of different vehicle and personnel scheduling programs, using different work-break points or altered turning times, to see which produce the most efficient results.

When planning vehicle and personnel schedules in the past, timetable and route networks have always been treated as fixed specifications, although staff did try to keep the number of vehicles required to a minimum as far as the non-automatic planning system would allow. In Hamburg, the timetable is dictated by the transport group and any reduction in the number of vehicles required is in the interest of all concerned since the maximum vehicle requirement is taken into account when distributing revenue. However, as long as timetable setting and route planning is still done on a non-automatic basis, it will be impossible to consider all vehicle and personnel scheduling aspects and thus achieve optimum efficiency.

Using the computer system, however, it should be possible to study the effect of the vehicle and personnel schedules on network and route planning and timetabling and thus achieve the most efficient overall result possible. Perhaps attention should be drawn at this point to such surveys as the McKinsey report on the effect of limiting operations and reducing non-productive personnel hours.

CONCLUSION

The introduction of computer-planned timetables, vehicle schedules, duty schedules and duty rosters was the climax of a long and difficult development process at Hamburger Hochbahn Aktiengesellschaft. However, we have not yet achieved full utilisation of all the potential economic and operational advantages a complex computer system of this kind has to offer. The program system described provides timetabling and scheduling staff with an ideal means of casting more light on the influence and direct result of vehicle and personnel scheduling elements and thus ultimately improving company efficiency on a lasting basis.

WHAT CONCRETE ADVANTAGES DOES THE SYSTEM OFFER?

a) You can provide the same service using fewer vehicles

b) You can provide the same service using fewer duties

c) All vehicle and personnel schedules are produced much more quickly

d) You need less staff capacity for vehicle and personnel scheduling

e) The system provides you with on-the-spot statistics on operating performance and efficiency rates - without errors and at no extra cost

f) You are in a position to assess the effect of alterations - both from a financial and from a staffing point of view - with absolute reliability and no loss of time (e.g. during tariff negotiations).

Computer Scheduling of Public Transport
A. Wren (ed.)
© *North-Holland Publishing Company, 1981*

THE ROLE OF THE SYSTEMS DEPARTMENT AND THE ROLE OF OPERATIONS MANAGEMENT
IN INTRODUCING COMPUTER ASSISTANCE TO BUS SCHEDULING

R.W.Dickinson, W.F.Drynan and P.D.Manington

Greater Manchester Transport
Manchester, U.K.

Obtaining the full benefits from an improved approach to
scheduling involves more than the necessary research and the
development of a good mathematical solution. Many problems
exist in the integration of the mathematical solution into our
business system. In order to obtain effective acceptance and
use of the new system, changes in staff and management
attitudes are required, and this presents further and more
difficult problems. GMT has recently completed the design and
commenced implementation of such a new scheduling system. The
problems encountered and lessons learned are considered and
some thoughts for the future generated.

1. INTRODUCTION

As a result of the Transport Act in 1968 the SELNEC Passenger Transport Executive
was established in 1969 to develop an efficient integrated passenger transport
system serving the needs of the Greater Manchester area. Since that time further
transport undertakings have been acquired, and in 1974 under the Local Government
Re-organisation, Greater Manchester Transport (GMT) was formed to provide a public
transport system for the whole of the Greater Manchester County area. Greater
Manchester Transport now operates over 2,300 buses at peak periods and employs
over 6,500 Drivers and Conductors.

It is obvious that operations on this scale involve very large costs (platform
staff wages alone exceed £40M per year) and even improvements of the order of two
or three per cent in bus scheduling efficiency are significant. Bus scheduling is
the day-to-day responsibility of Operating Management at Divisional and District
level. The methods used are still mainly manual, and vary from place to place,
although a certain amount of standardisation has been achieved by the introduction
of scheduling training supplied by Operations Headquarters management.

Bus schedules are in an almost constant state of change. Minor re-timings are
introduced weekly at many garages and more major re-scheduling changes occur
roughly twice a year for each District and Division. In the present economic
climate the public transport industry in Great Britain is facing the dual problems
of rising costs and falling passenger demand and the need for sizeable
re-scheduling exercises is increasing in frequency. The implementation of
Computer Assisted Bus Scheduling has only recently commenced in Greater Manchester
Transport. The computer method used is based on Leeds University's VAMPIRES suite
which GMT began to study in 1972 (1,2).

This very long period between the commencement of the study of VAMPIRES and the implementation now proceeding is the background against which the subject of the paper will be discussed. Many of those who have had a hand in the invention of bus scheduling programs are extremely puzzled and concerned that, although there have been many 'one-off' uses of bus scheduling programs there have been few, if any, permanent implementations of new systems. This paper is an attempt to account for this state of affairs. We have found it useful to discuss the matter in terms of the introduction of a new and unfamiliar entity into an existing environment.

Looked at from this point of view, it is obvious that the invention of the entity is not enough. Consideration has to be given to how the entity will be introduced into the environment in which it must operate. In most cases it is necessary to alter the environment to accommodate the new entity, and also to alter the entity to enable it to survive and operate in the environment. It is the work involved in fitting the entity to the environment and the environment to the entity that takes time.

2. NATURE OF THE ENVIRONMENT

Three aspects of the environment need consideration. These are:

    The existing systems (this word comprising both the activities and the people to conduct them)

    Staff (this refers to employees in general groups and as members of Trade Unions)

    Managers.

The existing systems present problems of two kinds. First there are the fairly mechanistic problems of the need for the new entity to relate (in terms of data exchange) with other activities both upstream and downstream of itself. For example, outputs from the bus scheduling system must be suitable for the crew scheduling process. There are more such relationships than might be thought. Second, there are the problems presented by the scheduling specialist staff. These include:

- natural feelings of loyalty to the familiar methods and the related resistance to any change (especially one involving computers, which have a bad press)

- widely varying working practices, all of which will not be retained in the computer-using method

- feelings of deprivation, arising in many cases from the fact that schedulers are not only experts but enthusiasts in scheduling skills

- hostility to outsiders presumptuous enough to suggest new approaches and methods, and

- some resistance to the degree of definition and separation of processes necessary for the introduction of computers.

Distinguished from the problems associated with scheduling specialist staff there are other problems general to all employees in the environment. These are fairly obvious. Resistance to change seems to be a natural component of human personality. Changes associated with computerisation are especially feared because of the assumption that all computerisation displaces clerical activity and jobs. Modern industrial relations thinking eliminates the possibility of simply imposing the change as a matter of discipline. The need to obtain an adequate level of acceptance of (or even resignation to) a change involves not only the individual members of staff involved in the activity being changed, but also the Trade Unions representing both them and larger groups of staff. Trade Union anxieties are not restricted to the protection of employment. They also have regard to other matters such as the de-skilling of jobs, the reduction in prospects for promotion, and aspirations to share in any benefit that comes from the implementation of changes.

In addition to these matters general to all staff, managers have further concerns. Among these are fairly strong feelings of resistance to external , and (perceived) amateurish, intervention in the industry in which they feel themselves to be expert; in many cases past experience of innovation involving computers has been unhappy; and in some cases managers feel that any innovation which tends to reduce the size of their management task or their familiarity with the way it is carried out beneath them must be resisted. A further concern specific to Greater Manchester Transport was the sensitive relationship between Operating Managers in the field and Headquarters management. As in any other sizeable business the emerging power and influence of Headquarters management is seen as a threat to the freedom of action of managers of individual operating units. To some extent innovations seen to be generated by Headquarters management suffer from this when the time comes to implement them in the field.

3. ACTIONS TAKEN BY GMT

The situation which presented itself to GMT, therfore, was an attractive entity called VAMPIRES and a highly complicated and resistant environment into which it would have to be introduced in order to obtain the benefits thought to be available from it. It would be gratifying to pretend that the following short account of the actions taken represented the realisation of a carefully laid plan of campaign to introduce VAMPIRES into GMT. This is not so. Much of the description of the environment given in section 2 above is hindsight. The existence of many of these problems was discovered by encounter rather than anticipation. Neither the Headquarters Operations management nor, to a lesser extent, the Systems management realised the extent and difficulty of the task in front of them.

GMT's actions are briefly described below together with comments upon whether the action was aimed at fitting the environment to the new entity or vice versa, and on which of the two partners in the innovation (Operations Headquarters management and Systems management) took the action.

Early work was done in investigating the available bus scheduling programs (3). The choice of VAMPIRES depended, not only on its ability to produce schedules of the requisite quality, but also on its flexibility. VAMPIRES employs an approach in which the objective function may be modifed to include secondary objectives, such as crew scheduling constraints and local agreements. This modification is easy and does not affect the power of the approach, unlike other techniques, where the methods are not as suitable for modification. This investigation was carried out by Operations Headquarters management and is essential in order to ensure that the entity is capable of being changed to fit the environment. There is little doubt that other scheduling programs were rejected mainly because they were too inflexible to change to fit the operating environment.

The emergence of the results of this study coincided with the creation of a more powerful systems and data processing department within GMT. It was at this stage that the necessary partnership between Operations Headquarters management as 'owners' of the scheduling system and Systems management as specialists was created. Further appraisal of VAMPIRES then took place but from a more technical point of view. The programming language, the processing hardware, and processing capacity required for VAMPIRES was appraised. This led to two actions: the decision to convert VAMPIRES from ALGOL to FORTRAN because of GMT's policy to support only one scientific programming language (altering the entity to fit the environment) and the decision to allow the VAMPIRES hardware nature and capacity needs to be a major influence on the selection of GMT's next mainframe computer (altering the environment to fit the entity). These actions were obviously taken by the Systems management.

Both Operations Headquarters management and Systems management were convinced that VAMPIRES was both functionally and technically the preferred bus scheduling program and that benefits were available from its use. It remained to quantify the costs and the benefits of implementation. Test were carried out on real data from two of GMT's operating centres. The results were satisfactory and indicated that substantial savings could be gained by the use of VAMPIRES. Both managements resolved that VAMPIRES would be introduced into GMT.

The next action is of extreme importance. Even at this stage it was obvious that the introduction of VAMPIRES would bring about major changes within GMT. It was therefore necessary to obtain not only agreement but commitment from the highest level of management. Explanatory presentations were made to the Senior Executives and Directors of GMT (the Executive Committee). These included both demonstrations of the internal logic of the VAMPIRES program, and descriptions of the results of the tests. The Executive Committee authorised the introduction of VAMPIRES into GMT and the then Director of Operations, J. B. Batty MBE, became sponsor of the project. This action, taken jointly by Operations Headquarters management and Systems management, was the first step in enabling the necessary changes to be brought about in the environment to fit the new entity and also the authorisation of funds to enable work to be done to alter the entity to fit the environment.

Whilst carrying out early work further explanatory presentations were given to Operations managers in the field. These presentations, to Divisional and District managers, concentrated on the benefits available from the introduction of VAMPIRES and the necessary costs, in terms of money and effort, which would be required to obtain the benefits. Although some brief explanation of the method was included the major intention of the presentations was not to make District and Divisional managers into scheduling experts but to draw their attention to the need for their own commitment to the effort to implement VAMPIRES.

Further presentations were then made to Traffic Superintendents and scheduling specialist staff. These altered the emphasis, concentrating a great deal on the scheduling logic rather than on the more general economics of the innovation. All these presentations were carried out jointly by Operations Headquarters management and Systems management. They were aimed at overcoming the reluctance to change on the part of both managers and specialists, and also at discovering at least in general terms where VAMPIRES departed undesirably from GMT scheduling practice. They were addressed, therefore, at changing both the environment and the entity to fit each other.

A formal Systems Project team was created to carry out design and implementation work. It is the policy of the Systems Department that all Systems projects teams contain both 'user' and technical staff. The Project Manager was assigned from the user management (in this case Operations Headquarters). The Systems

Department assigned a Project Leader to be technically responsible for the project.   The importance of this mechanism cannot be overstressed. It ensures that as work goes on, the functional requirements will not be sacrificed to technical novelty or, indeed, to technical difficulty. It also ensures that the right level of commitment is given.

It was the early work on the Project Team which led to two discoveries. Firstly, the method of supplying data to VAMPIRES was unsatisfactory for regular scheduling use. This consisted of manually entering data on to coding sheets and then keying the data for entry to the computer. The time and expense involved in collecting the data in this manner for every use of VAMPIRES was prohibitive. Secondly, the data required for VAMPIRES (with some minor additions) could also support many other applications, such as crew scheduling, service costing, garage location planning, working timetable production and running board production.

As a result of these discoveries, two decisions were taken - firstly, to modify the way in which data were supplied to VAMPIRES in order to fit it into the scheduler's job. This led to the design of a system entitled 'CABS' (Computer Assisted Bus Scheduling). The insertion of the word 'assisted' in the name was deliberate. The intention has never been to replace schedulers and their skills but to provide them with a tool to help them to do a better job. The second decision was to construct a data system, which would supply up-to-date information, not only for CABS but also for all other related systems in the Traffic function. This data supply and maintenance system is called TOPIC (Traffic Operations Information Capture) and is an extremely striking example of the need to alter the entity to fit the environment. The design and implementation costs of TOPIC are in excess of the total procurement and implementation costs of CABS itself.

The next step was to form a design study group of scheduling and Systems staff. The scheduling staff consisted of both Headquarters and field schedulers to ensure that the detailed design of CABS and TOPIC would be relevant to the scheduling needs of GMT and compatible with the working practices of schedulers. The work of this group proved invaluable and led to the design of a 'total bus scheduling system', which embraced TOPIC as a data supply sub-system and included both manual and computer scheduling options. This is yet another and extremely large scale example of the need to redefine perhaps rather than alter the environment to accommodate the new entity. Membership of the System Design Study Group was also extremely successful in overcoming the resistance and reluctance to change on the part of scheduling specialist staff. The difference between the attitude of those who worked on the Group and those who did not is most pronounced.

The design of TOPIC also brought about a change in the data processing strategy within GMT.   Early design work led to the proposal for a batch update version of TOPIC. After full consideration this was rejected as inadequate by Operations Headquarters management.   The fundamental problem was that no batch system could provide reaction times quickly enough to ensure that the Bus Workings data was always up-to-date and available for immediate use in the bus scheduling process. Accordingly it was decided that TOPIC should be designed as a real time, terminal using application and the distributed processing strategy which emerged from this has now been generalised for all of GMT. This also led to the procurement of the PDP 11/70 processor to support the implementation of TOPIC.

GMT now possesses a customised version of VAMPIRES, a fully designed and tested Computer Assisted Bus Scheduling system encasing VAMPIRES, and a bus scheduling data supply and update system called TOPIC. The implementation of these throughout GMT was considered and it was concluded that implementation would have to be conducted scheduling-centre by scheduling-centre rather than on an all-GMT basis. This was an obvious reaction to all that had gone before as the actual implementation of VAMPIRES was now seen as a major revision to the internal methods of the scheduling offices, not just as the making available of a computer program.

Rochdale and Bury Districts of GMT have changed to the new system and implementation for the remainder of GMT is planned to take place over the next nine months.

When this is complete, TOPIC and CABS will be available to all scheduling locations in GMT.

In future years, new systems (such as crew scheduling and garage location planning) will be developed and TOPIC will be expanded to include the extra data for each of these applications.

4. CONCLUSIONS

The brief conclusions of GMT's experience, which is recounted only in outline above, are these:

Innovations involving computer-using systems can only be successfully brought about by partnership of user managements and systems specialists. This has its dangers. Systems people tend to believe after a short time that they know the business activity better than the managers and must be dissuaded from either believing this or acting on it. On the other hand, many user managers and their staffs become very familiar with computer jargon and tend to develop into amateur data processing specialists. This also is to be avoided. However, it must be said that GMT's experience has been that so long as decision making is reserved to the correct side of the partnership, much good can come of the interactions. The systems specialists would agree that many extremely powerful design ideas came from managers on the business side and the managers would also agree that systems specialists produced some extremely useful insights into the business side of scheduling. This interaction is ideal as long as it remains on the opinion and advice basis. It must at all costs be prevented from contaminating the decision making process on either side.

GMT has not been entirely successful in handling the Industrial Relationships side of the introduction of VAMPIRES. We have now got to the point where CABS itself is acceptable to the Trade Union but not TOPIC. We expect to be able to obtain agreement for TOPIC quite soon and the reason for the problem seems more to be lack of understanding than lack of acceptability. We have learned the hard way to distinguish between three kinds of encounter with Trade Union institutions.

These are:-

- passing on information about what is going on

- entering into consultation about what is going on (both directly with individuals specifically involved and generally with Trade Union institutions) and

- negotiation of new terms and conditions of work.

Negotiation will be more effective if the earlier types of activity are done exhaustively. Although much time can be used in conducting both the informative and consultative encounters it is, in the end, worth it.

The amount of work done to introduce the new entity into its working environment compared to the amount of work done to create the new entity may surprise many people. GMT's estimate is that appraising and testing VAMPIRES involved only about 10% of the work done to introduce it into GMT. Even taking into account an estimate of how much work was done in creating the entity by Leeds University it would not be unreasonable to conclude that introducing VAMPIRES to GMT involved twice as much work as the creation of the entity by Leeds University. This suggests a message to those readers who are involved in the creation of computerised systems for use within business. It might, in the end, repay you to investigate the target environments into which you hope to introduce your product very early in its design stage. It might also repay you to think in terms of a highly adaptable system rather than one which assumes that all environments are the same and all environments are welcoming to a new entity.

5. REFERENCES

1. Manington, P.D. and Wren, A. Experience with a bus scheduling algorithm which saves vehicles. Presented at the Workshop on Automated Techniques for Scheduling of Vehicle Operators for Urban Public Transportation Services, Chicago (1975).

2. Smith, B.M. and Wren, A. VAMPIRES and TASC; two successfully applied bus scheduling programs. Appearing in this volume (1981).

3. Dickinson, R.W. A SELNEC view of computer scheduling, 5th Annual Seminar on Bus Operations Research, Paper 1, University of Leeds (1973).

Computer Scheduling of Public Transport
A. Wren (ed.)
© *North-Holland Publishing Company, 1981*

A PERSPECTIVE ON AUTOMATED BUS OPERATOR SCHEDULING —
FIVE YEARS' EXPERIENCE IN PORTLAND, OREGON

Mark Landis

Tri-Met Transit District
Portland, Oregon,
U.S.A.

The RUCUS run-cutting package has been in use in Portland
since 1975. This paper describes the process of implementation
and explains the difficulties encountered. Use of the package
is described, not only as part of the regular scheduling
process, but also as a tool for evaluating the consequences of
potential changes in operating patterns and in drivers'
agreements. Direct and indirect savings are reported for no
increase in scheduling staff.

The consultants and engineers who put automated scheduling programs together must
wonder what happens after their job is completed. Most likely, someone at the
transit operation is left with a commitment to use the new methods of driver
assignment in the real world environment of deadlines, budgets, staffing
constraints, and the everpresent pressure to deliver effective transit service.
The Tri-Met transit district has been using a computer to schedule drivers for
over five years. It is from this experience that we can provide answers to the
following questions:

How is computerized scheduling done? Not from a computer programmer's
perspective, but from the transit scheduler's perspective.

What are the steps to install a computerized scheduling package?

How long does it take to automate the system?

What expertise is required?

And, most important, what are the results?

Before I can answer these questions, we need to look at the present status of
computerized scheduling at Tri-Met. Constant improvement in the productivity of
the scheduling function characterizes our five years of experience. A 30% increase
in the hours of service operated has occurred while the staffing of the scheduling
function has remained constant. We found that it was not necessary to add staff
for the computerization function or for the expanded scheduling services. Because
of the automation, we found it possible to increase the productivity of our driver
work force, even in the face of increasingly restrictive labor agreements. We have
also found it possible to reserve enough staff time for an aggressive program of
research and development of improved computer techniques. All of this has been
done with a staff of six individuals, the same number required to maintain the old
manual scheduling function.

To put all this into context, I should mention that Tri-Met serves Portland, Oregon, with a fleet of 550 buses, and a complement of 1,000 drivers. There are three garages, 74 bus lines, and 70,000 miles of week-day vehicle service. The size of the Portland region is 3023 square miles; Portland ranks as the 26th largest city in the United States, and Tri-Met is the 23rd largest transit operation in the U.S. Tri-Met is characterized as a medium-size North American transit operation.

Tri-Met's computerized scheduling system uses the package of computer programs sponsored by the U.S. Department of Transportation. These programs are known as RUCUS (run-cutting and scheduling system)(1). We began with the basic RUCUS programs as vended by a consulting firm, and developed our own complex of day-to-day methods and procedures. Parallel to this process, we have methodologically replaced many of the original RUCUS programs with our own versions to meet our needs more closely. We have added new products to extend the utility of the transit operating data base into every possible practical application. Our philosophy is to allow the computer end-users, in this case the transit schedulers, the freedom to develop their own products. We found these products to be naturally user-oriented and exceedingly practical.

As a first step, Tri-Met implemented the RUCUS driver assignment component. The success of this effort soon went far beyond the mere assignment of drivers to vehicles. As the saying goes, 'Accurate data is limitless in its application'. Since the data-base which is used for the driver assignment accurately reflects the form and the function of the transit system, the utilization of this data is progressively seen in the emergence of scheduling systems, passenger information systems, and planning and development systems. Today, emerging at Tri-Met we see a system of performance analysis and management information that may, at last, allow us to apply objective cost criteria to the difficult area of service allocations and policy making.

The RUCUS story at Tri-Met began in 1974. We spent over a year capturing a machine-readable scheduling data base. The reason the data capture took so long was that transit schedules change constantly and in our data capturing process we lacked a mechanism to deal effectively with constant additions, deletions and changes. While we were automating we continued to do the manual scheduling function as always. The automated scheduling was done as a separate and parallel effort. The gap between the two resulted in constant discrepancies. Nevertheless, the computer run-cuts were showing substantial savings over the manual solutions. The inevitable outcome was that the decision was made to go ahead and implement the computerized run-cut. This is the point at which the difficulties culminated. The driver assignments came from the computer data base, and did not fully agree with the drivers' operating manifests, which came from the manual process. We were left in the embarrassing position of resolving disputes between operating documents, and ₂this adversity motivated us to rationalize the data capture process.

The scheduling and run-cutting data base essentially consists of machine-readable timetables. The most appropriate time to capture the machine-readable data is the time during which the timetables are being designed and built. It is essential to superimpose or integrate the data capture process and the service design process. If the machine-readable data is a natural by-product of procedures used to create service designs, then the entire problem of catching up with rapidly changing service goes away. Managers should be especially suspicious of an implementation strategy that calls for a parallel and separate effort. Perhaps the best outcome of all would be to let the automation effort be the handiwork of the craftsmen who are already fluent in manual scheduling. The computer then becomes a tool, to be welcomed, and does not become perceived as a weapon, which might be threatening. Perhaps the most advanced way to rationalize data capture is to provide on-line interactive computer terminals. These devices, when programmed with schedule designing functions, can certainly speed the scheduling work along, and the resulting data is virtually guaranteed to be accurate.

Another, slightly less efficient, method is to provide schedule writers with forms and procedures which are thoughtfully designed to meet the needs both of schedule designing and of the computer. Our procedures went through three distinct stages. Our first method was to have schedule writers code new service on forms which would be sent directly to a data entry station. This was satisfactory for the initial implementation. The second phase of evolution featured a technological solution to the data-entry problem. We used a shortcut or abbreviated service design form which could be translated directly into computer input by a special program which keeps track of time points and running times. Our third and present phase of rationalizing the data capture process involves two new principles. First, in the ongoing scheduling process, very few really new schedules are generated. The usual case is for new service to be some degree of modification to existing service. The second principle is that the modifications that are made to existing schedules are usually correlated to passenger loadings or to schedule adherence.

We developed a series of compatible and concurrent computer products which report on service performance, and which then allow adjustments to be made to the service without requiring undue data manipulation. This feedback process starts with data capture, proceeds to the driver assignment step, then to the production of operating documents, and then to a unique integrated evaluation step which causes a return back to the data capture step to modify the original data and to complete the circle.

The schedule designer is presented with a sequence of computer products. They are the following:

1. A special form of headway sheet which shows for each trip on each bus line: - the end point times; the maximum load point times; and the connection times for interline trips.

2. A compatible tabulation of passenger loadings at the maximum load point. This report matches the headway sheets and is programmed to average the last ten observations for each bus line.

3. A computerized diagram of the bus line. The diagram shows passenger activity at each bus stop as a histogram of passenger loading. The data is generated interchangeably by either on-board observers, or by automatic passenger counters.

4. A service design worksheet which tabulates running times and maximum load point arrival times. This worksheet is annotated by the schedule designer, and is key-entered into the data base to become the newly modifed schedule.

As you can see, the data capture step, which began during the initial implementation, has evolved into an effective and simple way to manage day-to-day service delivery. The end result, without a doubt, is better service for the people who use transit.

Before we move on to the mechanics of the driver assignment, a couple of postscripts need to be added to the discussion of the data capture. The first observation is that many larger transit operators have already taken advantage of computer methods to manage basic scheduling data. In this case the data capture step is probably already accomplished satisfactorily. All that is necessary is to proceed with appropriate vehicle assignment and driver assignment routines. A second observation on data capture is that particular attention must be given to the physical arrangement of the data within the available input format. The arrangement of the data must be thought out, keeping in mind all the eventual uses for the data. This is because the pattern of the data can be used later on in the computerized scheduling process to imply certain characteristics about the bus line. For example, one of the products that can be obtained downstream of the data capture is the automatic typesetting of the passenger timetable. If the initial data capture is arranged in a logical and consistent manner, then later on the timetable processing becomes very easy. To illustrate this principle, consider the problem of how to put footnotes on the passenger timetable to indicate express trips and to indicate local trips. If the initial data capture was thoughtfully done, the express trips will consistently follow an identifiable pattern, and can be identified by logic in the typeset routine which automatically highlights them for the passengers' convenience. The possibilities are endless, if the initial data capture is sound.

In addition to driver assignment and vehicle assignment, we have applied the basic timetable file to the following diverse areas:

> Mileage accounting for bus maintenance;
> Random selection of trips for surveying;
> Automatic coding of networks for computerized long range planning systems;
> Digital television displays of departure information;
> Automatic typesetting of timetables.

Tight procedure and thoughtful design during the data capture phase goes a long way toward facilitating the full use of the data.

During the course of our first implementation, the task immediately following the data-capture was to proceed toward an acceptable set of driver work assignments (or run-cuts). We made computerized run-cuts in parallel with the manual solutions of January, 1975 and of March, 1975. Then in June, 1975 the computer run-cut looked so good that the decision was made to put it into operation. The RUCUS software package was competent enough to produce a run-cut which so closely duplicated the style of the manual run-cut that no complaints were received from the drivers' collective bargaining union. The optimization that was done on the driver work assignments was not onerous or radical; the slight increase in productivity was largely unperceived by the workers. The computer program which actually prints out the drivers' version of the run-cut was also used to print out the March manual solution. So by the time the optimization arrived in June, the drivers were already familiar with the computer print-out.

The first computer run-cut required several hours of careful massaging by experienced schedulers before it was deemed ready for the street. However, the run-cut program has been fine-tuned over the course of several years to the extent that it now receives very little additional scrutiny. Management and labor have grown more comfortable with runs that are sometimes a bit unconventional, and at the same time, scheduling staff have become more fluent with the parameters that influence the style of the run-cut. The savings in driver pay experienced in the first computerized run-cut were calculated at over $100,000 annually. This more than pays for the entire implementation effort. The last time that we did a manual run-cut to check up on the validity of the computer solution was about two years ago, and the results were still in the same range, roughly a saving of six drivers, systemwide. This is perhaps a 1% direct saving in driver pay, but remember, driver pay is usually the largest cost component in the budget, and even small percentages represent substantial savings. And as we shall see shortly, there is an opportunity to use the automated run-cut as a catalyst for even larger savings in the area of service allocation and labour negotiations.

It is useful to back up a bit and identify the factors that have the greatest influence upon the run-cut. The three most important factors are:

1. The transit schedule to be manned.
2. The collective bargaining work rules.
3. The run-cut algorithm.

As a practical matter the run-cut algorithm is a very poor third place in influencing the composition of the run-cut. Since the easiest way to improve the run-cut is to change the service or to change the union agreement, the question becomes: 'What can be done to the run-cut to influence these two factors?'.

During the last round of labor negotiations, we made extensive use of the computer run-cut to establish the range of work-rule changes necessary to increase labor productivity. The interesting thing to note here is that the real change to the run-cut was not to the algorithm; the real change was in the union agreement itself. Incidentally, the change to the labor agreement that showed the most promise was to obtain the relaxation of the rule that requires a minimum of eight pay-hours daily. The relaxation of this rule has taken the form of a provision which permits part-time labour to be used. The effect was to make the run-cut much easier because the conditions of the union agreement fit more closely with the conditions imposed by the type of service we are committed to operate. In other words, the fit between the union agreement and the service design was closer. As a result of the relaxed work rules, we are now able to obtain a satisfactory run-cut after only one execution of the program. The entire process can be completed for all three divisions in less than one day, utilizing only one scheduling person. All in all, it is a satisfactory way to obtain work assignments, and it is difficult to imagine an easier way to do it, especially to one who has done manual run-cuts.

The scheduler must provide guidelines to the run-cut program in the form of parameters which are read into the program logic by the Fortran namelist function. As an example of how a parameter works, imagine a run-cut solution that required 310 drivers and a total of 2,371 pay-hours. By changing the parameter that regulates the maximum allowable length of straight runs, it is possible to increase the average amount of duty time per run. The result is that the driver requirement is reduced from 310 drivers to 301 drivers, a saving of 9. However, the driver pay increases from 2,371 hours to 2,393 hours, an increase of 22 hours. This actual example from our experience shows how it is possible to explore the relationships between the run-cut variables. Incidentally, there are about two dozen parameters available, but we seem to use only six with any regularity.

One of the difficulties experienced with implementing the run-cut is that only a limited amount of experience with the parameters can be exchanged from one transit operation to another. Again, the reason is that the service itself, within the context of the union agreement, really serves to shape the run-cut. It is probably necessary for each user to develop a methodology of experimentation with parameters in order to obtain good results. Another task that may have to be addressed is to make alterations to the subroutines of the run-cut source program. Certainly it will be necessary to make some slight alterations, at least to the costing subroutine, as the union work-rules are periodically changed. We feel that it is possible for astute schedulers to master some of the elementary logic in the Fortran code, and to make some minor modifications to the code. We have successfully done this without fully understanding much of the underlying mathematical theory. Designers of run-cut logic should be encouraged to document the program, and to make full use of subroutines and structured programming techniques to facilitate user interaction.

This brings us to the question of what is the level of training and expertise required to execute the automated crew scheduling package? The answer depends upon what is being done with the run-cut. In a day-to-day sense, it is our experience that it is possible to view the algorithm as a black box to produce run-cut solutions that are valid and operable. Once the programs and parameters are set, it is possible to produce run-cut solutions quickly, dependably, and repeatedly, without changing parameters, and without experimentation. As long as radical changes are not made to the style of the transit service, or to the rules of the union agreement, it is possible to deliver good run-cuts every time. The level of expertise required is that of a careful and accurate clerical person.

The initial implementation of the run-cut will require quite a different level of expertise. The run-cut logic will have to be tailored to represent accurately the union agreement. Unwritten customs and traditions that affect the composition of the runs will have to be identified and accommodated. The person designing this system needs to understand the labor agreement, the ramifications of the service policy, and the logic of the run-cut. This is in addition to understanding the program language and its compiler routine.

Our implementation strategy was to duplicate the style of the manual run-cut, while obtaining the benefits of a limited optimization. Later on, as we became more experienced with the mechanics of automated run-cutting, we found that there are some opportunities for benefits that go beyond the benefit of optimization. The automated run-cut technology presents the opportunity to experiment with changes in operating policy and to provide management with cost figures corresponding to the policy changes.

We have had two experiences with the concept of obtaining operating costs for proposed service policy decisions. The first experience occurred when a comprehensive plan for new transit service was being prepared. Of course, the first question that management asked was, 'How much will the new service cost?'. It was relatively simple to produce an input file containing the new service, and to submit the file to a run-cut. The driver costs were accurately determined, and the effect of the new service upon the labor force was ascertained. The second experience with experimental run-cuts came when management was faced with long range policy planning for rolling stock procurement and for labor negotiations. It was believed that the major opportunities for the future might be in expansion of peak-hour service, so the question was asked, 'What would happen to driver costs if the ratio of peak-hour service to base level service was advanced from two to one to a ratio of two-and-a-half to one?'. The methodology used to answer that question was again to produce an input file to represent the 'what if' situation, and to do a run-cut. The process of adding sixty rush hour trips to the existing schedules took one person about one-half day. Then a series of six run-cuts were made, each one of them testing a different approach to assigning drivers to the 'future network'. Then we carried the exercise a step further by using the statistics which are generated by the run-cut as input to a financial forecasting model which predicts all of the budgetary expense components such as tires, fuel, supervision, overhead, inflation, etc. The result of the exercise was a series of proposed annual budgets covering the five year period in which the new service was to be implemented. A comparison set of budgets was prepared to represent the null situation where the new service is not installed.

Essentially what we have developed is a tool that is able to predict transit budgets based upon assumptions about the service. The output of this process is a list of budget line items for five successive years. The figures for platform hours, driver pay, and the number of drivers are based upon an actual run-cut. The service assumptions are tangible enough to look at in the form of headway sheets. The imaginary network is capable of being put into service, right down to drivers' manifests and passenger timetables. This exercise is the one which showed the necessity of making changes to the drivers' working agreement in order economically to expand transit service. Consequently, management went into labor negotiations, and successfully obtained an agreement which provides for hiring of part-time drivers to operate peak hour runs.

The conclusion in Portland is that it is well within the ability of a traditional transit organization to adapt to automated scheduling, and that it makes a lot of sense to proceed aggressively. It is possible to produce scheduling deliverables that are more timely, more accurate and more effective than their manual counterparts. It is reasonable to expect computers to generate driver assignments that result in cost savings, and that can be operationalized without undue difficulty. An additional benefit in Portland has been the extension of automated scheduling tehniques into the areas of service planning, financial analysis, and labor negotiation. Perhaps the perception of automated scheduling as a significant movement toward rational alternatives analysis will give this useful technology new momentum.

REFERENCE

1. Wilhelm, E.B. Overview of the RUCUS package driver run cutting program (RUNS), Workshop on Automated Techniques for Scheduling of Vehicle Operators for Urban Public Transportation Services (Chicago, 1975).

Bus and Train
Scheduling Methods

Computer Scheduling of Public Transport
A. Wren (ed.)
© *North-Holland Publishing Company, 1981*

BUS SCHEDULING PROGRAM DEVELOPMENT
FOR A.T.A.F., FLORENCE

V. Brandani, G. Cataoli, G. Orsi and P. Toni

University of Florence
Italy

A computer program has been developed to provide bus schedules
for urban passenger transport routes. The program is based on
general criteria but has been adapted to the needs of A.T.A.F.
The program provides the required headways with the minimum
number of buses and the minimum amount of bus hours, and
minimizes also dead trips and lay-over time at termini. A
trial period having been completed, the program is now fully
operational and is providing bus schedules on all main bus
routes operated by A.T.A.F.; bus time-tables, bus departures
from the terminus or other places along the route,
comprehensive route schedules and statistical summaries are
part of the output.

1. INTRODUCTION

As shown by C.I.S.P.E.L. (the Italian Federation of Local Government Enterprises),
in Italian urban transport, passenger-miles amount approximately to 23% of total
seat-miles. This rather low figure (Italian railways achieve a ratio of about 56%)
shows a way, maybe an important one, to improve productivity: to adjust frequently
seat-miles offered to meet changing transport demands.

Schedule updating is comparatively slow and cumbersome if it is done 'by hand',
whereas scheduling can be prompt and efficient especially if all the different
stages can be computerized: processing of traffic surveys and running time
surveys; bus scheduling; crew scheduling in compliance with union agreements and
relevant regulations; rostering with even spreading of work loads, etc.

An increase in the passenger/seat ratio from 23% to 30%, which hopefully could be
achieved by computerization, would lead to better services being offered and to
savings in the order of 130 billion liras a year (approximately 65 million
pounds).

A.T.A.F., the local publicly owned bus company operating in the Florence area, can
be described as follows: employees: 1700; buses: 500; routes: 50; network, mostly
urban: 350 km; vehicle-km: 22 million a year; commercial speed: 17.12 km/h;
passengers carried per employee: 91000 a year; expenditure equals 2.88 times
revenue.

It is considered hardly possible to get better results in cities of comparable
size in Italy, and still the passenger/seat ratio for A.T.A.F. is about 24%.

In Figure 1, weekday passengers and buses operated throughout the day are shown on
a sample of 7 routes.

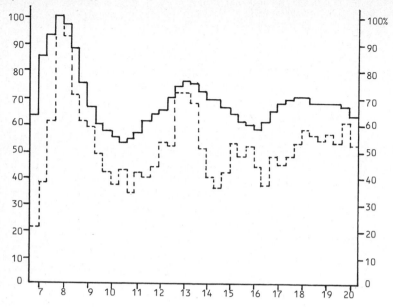

Figure 1 - Seats offered and passenger loads (broken line)
           at maximum load stop, on a weekday

Recent legislation, preventing any increase in the number of employees and
limiting expenditure increases below inflation level has made for increased
efforts to improve productivity, including a comprehensive transport plan being
formulated.

Seasonal variations in transport demand are matched by varying sets of schedules
(nine altogether), as shown in Figure 2.

The considerable amount of time required to provide a new set of schedules has led
A.T.A.F. to contract to the University of Pisa the development of a computer
program for crew scheduling and rostering.

A comprehensive computerization of bus scheduling should bring the desired savings
by making it possible to match more closely and timely the services offered to
transport demand.

As none of the available programs seemed fully to answer A.T.A.F. specific
requirements, it was decided to have an ad hoc program developed; a joint effort
was initiated in 1977, and the Institute of Mechanical Engineering of the
University of Florence developed a bus scheduling program which has already become
fully operational.

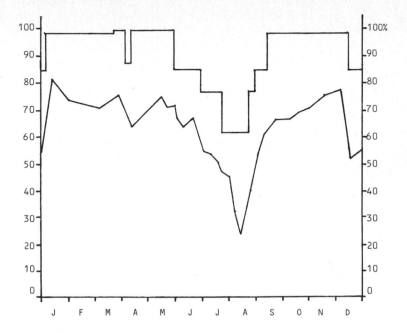

Figure 2 - Seats offered and passenger loads (lower line)
at maximum load stops, in a year

2. EARLY STAGES OF PROGRAM DEVELOPMENT

Several studies have been completed recently about bus scheduling problems
(1,2,3,4). Taking these experiences into account, an original scheduling program,
which provided bus board and graphical layout of trips for a simple route, was
implemented in 1977 by the Institute of Mechanical Engineering of the University
of Florence.

Encouraged by this favourable result, A.T.A.F. asked the Institute to develop a
new program which could handle all types of routes operated in Florence, most of
which are branched and would fall into any of the 7 graphs shown in Figure 3. A
program first completed along these lines (September 1979) is described in 5. A
two-month period of testing this first program and comparing with actual schedules
hand-produced by A.T.A.F. schedulers led to the conclusion that the program
required too much computer time, while it did not allow adequate control by the
schedulers, besides not being fully satisfactory in minimizing the number of
vehicles required.

The program was then completely revised, keeping some parts, and making it much more interactive by adopting different strategies in several stages.

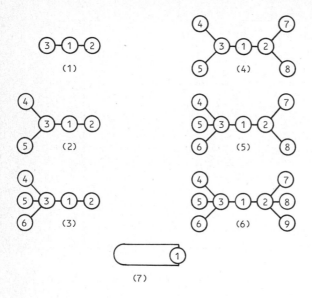

Figure 3 - Kinds of routes taken into consideration

3. THE MATHEMATICAL MODEL

We shall adopt the following notation:

A_{ij} - table of arrivals at point i from point j;

a_{ijk} - k-th element of A_{ij};

c_e - average cost of dead trips (lire/min);

c_l - average cost of layovers in route (lire/min);

c_g - average cost of layovers in garage (lire/min);

x - layover in an intermediate point (min);

x_s - standard layover in a terminus (min);

$h_{ij}(t)$ - required headway for trips from point i to point j at time t (direction i-j) (min);

H - set of headways;

$p_{ij}(t)$ - journey time from point i to point j at time t, (direction i-j) (min);

P - set of journey times;

I - set of points on a route;

n_i', n_i'' - beginning point and ending point of a chain of journeys;

D_{ij} - table of departures from point i for point j;

d_{ijk} - k-th element of D_{ij};

$\overline{t}_{ij}, \overline{\overline{t}}_{ij}$ - beginning time and ending time of bus service at point i (direction i-j) (min);

t_i', t_i'' - beginning time and ending time of chain of journeys i (min);

T_{ij} - table of dead transfer times from point i to point j.

The scheduling program has been subdivided into the following 3 subproblems:

3.1. A and D matrix

Data:

$h_{ij}(t)$, $p_{ij}(t)$, $\overline{t}_{ij}$, $\overline{\overline{t}}_{ij}$, $\forall(i,j) \in I$ $(i \neq j)$

being given, the algorithm, referring to route types shown in Figure 3, follows a logical path.

For a type 1, no-branch route (see Figure 3), the above-mentioned logical path is as follows:

a) D_{31} is produced complying with $\overline{t}_{31}$, $\overline{\overline{t}}_{31}$, and $h_{31}(t)$;

b) A_{13} is produced from D_{31} complying with journey times $p_{31}(t)$;

c) D_{12} is produced; obviously $D_{12} = A_{13}$ if in links (3,1) and (1,2) headways are the same for equal time intervals. If this is not the case there will be buses entering or leaving at point 1, and only adding or removing departures from table D_{12} would make $h_{13}(t)$ uneven, therefore a heuristic approach is followed and some elements in table D_{12} are adjusted to smooth headways. These adjustments modify some elements in tables A_{13} and D_{31};

d) A_{21} is produced from D_{12}, complying with journey times $p_{12}(t)$;

e) D_{21} is produced from A_{21}, by adding to the arrival time of each bus a given layover time x_s:

$$d_{21k} = a_{21k} + x_s \quad \forall k;$$

if bus entries or exits are needed, the same way mentioned at step (c) is followed;

f) A_{12} is produced from D_{21}, by adding journey times $p_{21}(t)$;

g) D_{13} is produced from A_{12} in the same above-mentioned way as D_{12} from A_{13} in (c). It should be noted that any adjustments in order to smooth $h_{13}(t)$ will modify tables A_{12}, D_{21} and also layover time in (e).

Branches make the program more complicated.

Conditions affecting branching are:

$$\text{I)} \quad \frac{1}{h_{1i}(t)} \geqslant \sum_{k=1}^{n_b} \frac{1}{h_{ik}(t)} \quad \forall\, t \quad (i=2,3)$$

n_b being the number of branches. (This condition means that buses arriving at a forking-point are in greater or equal number than required in branches);

II) headway requirements in the central parts of routes take priority over headway requirements in branches.

Under such conditions buses arriving at points 2 and 3 are simply sent on to the branches, unless it becomes possible to turn-round a bus and send it on a return journey.

For links (3,4), (3,5), (3,6), there will not be any changes in the tables produced earlier, while when links (2,7), (2,8) and (2,9) are concerned, modifications may occur.

3.2 Joining arrivals and departures at termini

As shown in 3.1, layover time at terminus 2 (no-branch route) or 7,8,9 (routes forking at right-hand side) is equal to x_s or slightly modified because of adjustment.

Joining of arrivals and departures at terminus 3 (no branches) or 4,5,6 is affected by an algorithm based on the 'Hungarian method'.

An arrival at time t* may be joined to a departure if the following condition is satisfied:

$$x_{min} \leqslant d_{ijk} - a_{ijk} \leqslant h_{ij}(t*) + \bar{h},$$

x_{min} and $\bar{h}$ being chosen in advance and h(t*) the required departure headway. Costs arising from matching an arrival to a departure are defined by:

$$c_{kr} = (d_{ijk} - a_{ijr} - x_s)^2$$

The 'Hungarian method' ensures that the maximum number of journeys are joined with minimum costs.

It may be noted:

a) by imposing $\bar{h} = 0$ 'first-in, first-out' principle is used;

b) high $\bar{h}$ to join a great number of journeys may lead to high costs (because of high layover time);

c) $x_{min} < x_s$ may lead to layover times less than required.

3.3. Production of schedules

At the end of steps 3.1 and 3.2 a number of chains S have been produced, consisting of journeys, giving layover times at right-hand termini, and different layover times at left-hand termini, as determined by the 'Hungarian method'.

Data:

$$t_k', \ n_k', \ t_k'', \ n_k'' \qquad \forall \ k \in S,$$

are known for each chain, i.e. point and time of beginning and end of each chain.

Final boards (the combination of journeys operated by each bus for the day) are produced joining different chains together, under condition that:

$$t_j' - t_i'' \geqslant T'_{n_i' n_j''} + \Delta T$$

where ΔT is a given minimum extra time. In final boards therefore more layover time than provided by steps 3.1 and 3.2 may appear, as chains ending and beginning at the same terminus or point are linked or dead journeys are introduced. The algorithm chosen for this step, based upon a 'branch and bound' method, will minimize a function which is directly related to operating costs.

It is important to note that some layovers at termini of less than the standard x_s may result, as is explained at step 3.1 or, if a value $x_{min} \leqslant x_s$ is chosen at step 3.2. In this case a final step may be necessary to adjust some journey times; in this way only layovers greater than or equal to the standard x_s appear on the running board. These small variations in journey times are allowed only if statistical conditions and union agreements are satisfied.

4. MAIN FEATURES OF THE SOFTWARE PACKAGE

To solve the problem, we did not produce a single computer program. Instead a software package based on five main applications was designed, built up and verified.

Each program runs in an interactive way and the operator can see some intermediate results on the console-display. In this way it is possible to stop the computer run, modify some data then restart the program in order to check for the effects of the improved modification.

This package is now running on a Digital PDP 11/34 computer in the 'Mechanical Engineering Institute' of the University of Florence; as soon as possible the programs will be run on a suitable computer of A.T.A.F. that will directly manage this application.

Five main procedures are as follows;

LETT   – With this program it is possible to store the input data in a data file on the disk-unit or, if required, to up-date previously stored data;
GEST   – This program builds A_{ij} and D_{ij} tables following the algorithm described in Section 3.1.
UNGHER – This procedure, using the method described in Section 3.2, connects at the left-hand terminus (i) the arriving trips with departing ones;
TREN   – This program, according with the method reported in Section 3.3, produces the final running boards;
ORARIO – After checking final results on the display, with this program the

operator can print, via a line-printer, the following documents:

1) running boards;

2) full timetables;

3) list of entry/exit from the garage with histogram of buses on the route and of bus hours required during the service;

4) times at any point with starting and destination termini;

5) summary of relevant data, in order to appreciate various features of the computer schedule.

Figure 4 shows a general flow-chart of the package; we can note that all the programs are connected by data stored on some data files.

The quality of a bus schedule depends not only on the computer program, but on the quality of data input too, and on the scheduler's decisions at the different stages.

It is worth noting that it would be difficult to leave certain decisions to a computer, as in this type of problem it is usually very difficult to estimate the results of even minor changes in input data. A scheduler's experience usually leads to intuition that would be impossible to implement in a computer; and on a computer, the scheduler can develop and compare different results. We would therefore stress that there are many points where scheduler intervention is allowed.

Computer times are around 5 minutes overall, and typing-in times are around 15 minutes. Several tests indicate that, leaving aside first entry and printing, it takes from one to two hours to check displayed data, compare results and modify them as required, especially to minimize vehicles needed.

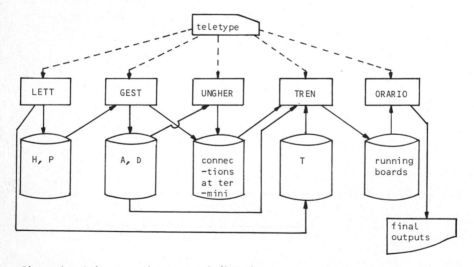

Figure 4 — Software package general flow-chart

5. AN EXAMPLE

The route considered is a complex one in the network operated by A.T.A.F.. This route connects two city suburbs to the centre of the city and the Railway Station; in one of the suburbs there are a hospital and several university schools; therefore, they need a more frequent bus service at some hours not necessarily coinciding with peak hours. With reference to Figure 3 the route is a type (4). Actually, point 8 and point 2 coincide; which we describe by giving the running time:

$$p_{28}(t) = p_{82}(t) = 0 \quad V \, t.$$

We can see that the types of routes shown in Figure 3 may really become more than seven, by manipulating in an appropriate way the input data. In this example the Railway Station is at point 1 and the Hospital is at point 4.

In Figure 5 the required headways are shown for input. There are three peak periods: the highest about 8.00 a.m.; the others about 12.00 noon and 5.30 p.m.. About 11.00 a.m. and 2.00 p.m. we have (shown with broken line) an increased service in the route half 1-4.

We can now examine the outputs of the program. Figures 6 and 7 show two timetable extracts: particularly in Figure 6 we can note short trips to and from the Hospital; in Figure 7 we can note a situation in which the small headways and the great difference between the running times on the two branches cause bus 14 to overtake bus 18.

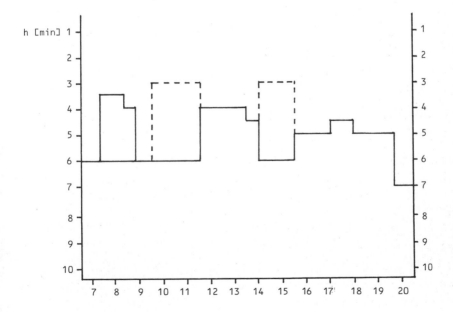

Figure 5 - Required headways

```
            16      18       2      23      4       1      12
U.DEP
CAP2     15.00A          15.03B 15.06A       15.09A 15.12A
PATO     15.05           15.08  15.11        15.14  15.17
STAZ     15.20           15.23  15.26        15.29  15.32
BRIV                     15.39               15.45
CAP1                     15.39B              15.50A
CAP1             15.08A                15.19B
BRIV             15.13                 15.19
STAZ     15.25   15.28           15.31 15.34        15.37
PATO     15.39   15.42           15.45 15.48        15.51
CAP2     15.43A  15.46B          15.49A 15.52A      15.55B
E.DEP                            16.09


CAP2  A = CARE                            CAP1  A = RIPA
      B = TOLE                                  B = BRVP
```

Figure 6 — An extract of timetables

```
             3      14      18      14     16     12      4
U.DEP
CAP2             17.05A 17.09B         17.14A 17.18B 17.23A
PATO             17.09  17.13          17.18  17.22  17.27
STAZ             17.25  17.29          17.34  17.38  17.43
BRIV             17.45  17.49          17.54  17.58  18.03
CAP1             17.50A 17.49B         17.59A 17.58B 18.08A
CAP1     17.45A         17.54B 17.54A         18.03B
BRIV     17.50          17.54  17.59          18.03
STAZ     18.06          18.10  18.15          18.19
PATO     18.20          18.24  18.29          18.33
CAP2     18.24A         18.28B 18.33A         18.37B
E.DEP                                                18.13


CAP2  A = CARE                            CAP1  A = RIPA
      B = TOLE                                  B = BRVP
```

Figure 7 — Another extract of timetables.

Figure 8 shows a running board as given to the bus driver, with entry/exit from the garage, short trips directions, etc.

Figure 9 is a diagram showing the number of buses scheduled (the required buses for increasing service in route half 1-4 drawn in broken line).

```
LINEA N. 14                               TRENO N. 12
  CAP2  PATO  STAZ  BRIV      CAP1      BRIV  STAZ  PATO  CAP2

**U.DEP.  **  7.45 **
                            7.53A  7.58  8.14  8.30  8.34A

**E.DEP.  **  8.54 ************  U.DEP.  **  14.01 **

14.25A 14.29 14.44+                   14.49 15.03 15.07A
15.12A 15.17 15.32+                   15.37 15.51 15.55B
16.00B 16.05 16.21 16.39 16.39B 16.41B 16.41 16.57 17.11 17.15B
17.18B 17.22 17.38 17.58 17.58B 18.03B 18.03 18.19 18.33 18.37B
18.44B 18.48 19.04 19.22 19.22B 19.28B 19.28 19.43 19.57 20.01A
** E.DEP.  **  20.21 **

CAP2                                           CAP1
A = CARE                                    A = RIPA
B = TOLE                                    B = BRVP

CARTELLI
 + LIMITATA A STAZ
```

Figure 8 - An example of running boards

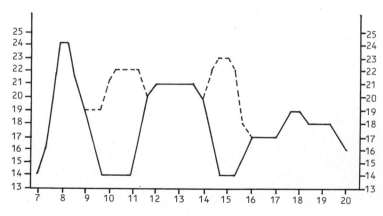

Figure 9 - Required buses at different times.

Figure 10 is a summary of statistical data of the route; from the left we have:

- running board number;
- total layover at termini;
- total dead trips time
- layover time because of dead trips;
- transfer time from/to the garage;
- total manned hours;
- total layover time / total running time ratio;
- time spent at the garage;
- total trips number (direction 3-2);
- total trips number (direction 2-3).

Other prints are possible as shown at the preceding paragraph.

RIEPILOGHI FINALI LINEA   14

TR.	T.COR	S.CAP	TR.VT	S.VTO	TR.DP	T.TOT	C.UT.	S.DEP	C.3-2	C.2-3
1	1051	144	0	0	20	1215	0.865	0	13	14
2	767	84	0	0	10	861	0.891	0	10	10
3	759	83	17	17	20	896	0.847	0	9	9
4	653	69	3	3	13	741	0.881	0	9	9
5	755	72	3	0	22	852	0.886	0	10	9
6	404	60	0	0	72	536	0.754	39	4	5
7	954	108	21	15	13	1111	0.859	0	13	12
8	815	89	24	14	13	955	0.853	0	10	11
9	469	54	0	0	28	551	0.851	0	6	7
10	357	51	0	0	13	421	0.848	0	3	3
11	640	56	15	2	57	770	0.831	34	7	8
12	334	43	0	0	72	449	0.744	307	3	4
13	705	75	0	0	7	787	0.896	0	9	9
14	743	93	29	5	10	880	0.844	0	8	7
15	353	34	33	18	17	455	0.776	0	4	4
16	621	66	4	1	68	760	0.817	109	7	6
17	701	94	0	0	27	822	0.853	0	10	9
18	653	75	4	28	34	794	0.822	0	8	8
19	641	65	0	0	44	750	0.855	102	8	8
20	680	94	19	31	24	848	0.802	0	9	9
21	721	102	4	7	80	914	0.789	161	10	8
22	428	60	4	8	42	542	0.790	0	5	5
23	550	124	0	0	59	733	0.750	55	5	5
24	547	57	0	0	34	638	0.857	187	8	7

TOTALI

T.COR	S.CAP	TR.VT	S.VTO	TR.DP	T.TOT	C.UT.	S.DEP	C.3-2	C.2-3
255.01	30.52	3.00	2.29	13.19	304.01	0.84	16.34	188	186

Figure 10 - Summary of statistical data of route '14'

6. CONCLUSIONS

Such timetables need at least three to four days of work by an experienced scheduler.

At a computer desk, these timetables are made in a morning of work at the most.

After considerable testing, A.T.A.F. management considered the program profitable, and now most timetables are generated by this program.

Developments are expected in the future to consider many routes at the same time, with the goal of minimizing the number of buses needed, and to produce a crew scheduling program in cooperation with the University of Pisa.

7. REFERENCES

1. Piccione, C., Un algoritmo per la determinazione meccanografica degli orari delle linee urbane di trasporto, Ingegneria Ferroviaria, 6 (1974).

2. Servizio Studi ATM, Milano, Determinazione automatica degli orari delle linee urbane di superficie (appunti), (Dic. 1975).

3. Heurgon, E., Present, M., and Tarim, G., Construction automatique des horaires d'une ligne d'autobus, 7e Conf. IFIP sur les techniques d'optimization, Nice, (Sept. 1975).

4. Manington, P.D. and Wren, A. Experiences with a Bus Scheduling Algorithm which saves Vehicles, Operational Research Unit, Centre for Computer Studies, University of Leeds, (1975).

5. Brandani, V., Cataoli, G. and Toni, P. Formazione automatica degli orari di servizio delle linee di trasporto urbane, XXVII Giornate Colombiane, Genova, (1979).

Computer Scheduling of Public Transport
A. Wren (ed.)
© *North-Holland Publishing Company, 1981*

A DEFICIT FUNCTION APPROACH
FOR BUS SCHEDULING

Helman I. Stern and Avishai Ceder

Ben Gurion University of the Negev
and
Technion - Israel Institute of Technology
Israel

This paper begins with a description of the operational
aspects of bus-scheduling at Egged - the Israel National Bus
Carrier - and their experience with attempts to fully
computerize the scheduling of buses to trips. Due to the
limitations of this procedure an investigation of a
semi-automatic computer system was initiated. The man-machine
algorithm described in this paper is a result of this
investigation. The algorithm employs a highly informative
graphical technique based on deficit function theory. The
approach provides immediate feedback on the value of inserting
deadheading trips in order to reduce the fleet-size
requirements for a given timetable of required services. A
preliminary technique provides potential users with bounds on
the greatest savings possible for the operation in question.

1. INTRODUCTION

Bus scheduling may be thought of as a multistep process. Due to the complexity of
this process, each step is normally conducted separately, and sequentially fed
into the other. The process steps are: (1) determining demand for bus service, (2)
planning bus stops and routes, (3) constructing timetables, (4) scheduling buses
to trips, and (5) driver scheduling. In this paper we will describe a new approach
to the problem of scheduling buses to trips. The approach assumes the existence of
a timetable of trips which has been purged of any existing deadheading trips. Trip
times are assumed to include enough slack to cover any start-up or trip-end
delays. The main goal of the approach is to reduce the number of buses required -
the fleet size - through the introduction of deadheading trips. The algorithm is
most useful for scheduling buses during the major peak period of a normal day's
bus operation. Reducing the bus requirements during the morning or evening peak
periods reflects the real savings possible in capital costs. In the process,
operating costs may also be reduced and are considered through the incorporation
of a man-machine process designed to allow experienced schedulers to evaluate the
results of their own suggestions. Before embarking on the main thrust of this
paper, it is of interest to review the situation at Egged - the Israel National
Bus Carrier - which motivated this endeavour. This will be followed by a
description of deficit functions, and the effect of deadheading trip insertions on
fleet size. This provides the theoretical basis of the fleet reduction deadheading
trip insertion algorithm, which is described immediately before the concluding
remarks.

2. BACKGROUND

Egged's bus fleet is presently comprised of 5,070 buses and is expected to expand
to 5,500 by 1981. Of this total, 1,700 are used exclusively for relatively short
urban runs, 900 are relegated to long intra-urban runs, and 2,470 are used
interchangeably as the need arises. Egged's fleet amounts to 97% of the public
transportation buses in Israel. The remaining 3% belong to the city fleets of
Beersheva and Nazareth. Egged's fleet operates over a widely spread network of
about 4000 lines. Table 1 shows a breakdown of the work load for an average
weekday schedule.

TABLE 1. BUS ACTIVITIES ON A DAILY BASIS

TYPE	NUMBER OF TRIPS	VEHICLE-KM.
Service	36,000	754,000
Deadheading	14,000	81,000
Special (Routine)	4,000	91,000
Special (Others)	400	70,000
Total	54,400	996,000

Daily travel amounts to 996,000 vehicle-kilometres for 54,400 passenger trips. The
majority of these trips are regularly scheduled and provide service to the general
public. This accounts for almost 75% of the total travel and provides daily
service to almost every city, town and village in the country. In addition, a
number of trips of a more specialized nature are carried out, four thousand of
them on a regular basis to provide transportation to and from places of work and
for planned organizational activities. On the average, 400 daily trips are devoted
to accommodating the irregular requirements of schools, tour groups, funerals and
special charter events. Due to the dispersed nature of the service, an additional
14,000 deadheading trips are employed for travel to and from bus depots, and to
relocate buses where they are most needed throughout the day. Among the more
volatile demands are those which occur on special days such as the holidays of
different religions and days of national celebration. Due to the ad hoc nature of
these latter demands, new daily plans must be drawn up on a one-time custom basis.
On the other hand, the normal workday or weekend demands for travel may be planned
for in a systematic way, usually updated 3 or 4 times a year. Recent growth,
however, has resulted in frequent changes in the timetable and increased pressure
on the planning staff. Bus schedules are currently produced manually by a team of
60 schedulers using a trial and error Gantt chart approach. Years of experience
have led to a large degree of confidence in the resultant schedules. However, the
need to respond more quickly to timetable changes led management to embark on an
investigation of a fully-computerized system.

The computerized system is based on a technique reported in Gavish et al. (1)   The technique is carried out in two stages. In the first stage, bus trips are grouped in sequential order, interspersed with idle time and deadheading trips. In the second stage, buses are assigned from depots to the bus schedules generated in the first stage. The first stage is formulated and solved as a large-scale assignment problem, designed to minimize a combination of fleet-size, deadheading, and idle time costs. The second stage is formulated as a transportation problem. Figure 1 shows a comparison between the results of this technique and those obtained manually by the scheduling team. Further details of this experiment may be found in Ceder and Gonen (2). The program has a 190 K-byte memory requirement and is capable of solving problems of up to 2,500 bus trips. All of the examples were for peak-hour bus schedules and management was quite excited with the results until implementation was attempted. At that point it was discovered   that   the computer-generated schedule had to be considerably modified to meet a number of necessary constraints imposed by practical considerations. Among the major limitations was the model's inability to include driver constraints such as meal-breaks and driver relocations. In addition, the program could not include the constraints imposed by vehicles of different types. Finally, the real problems requiring solution exceeded the 2,500 size limitation of the   comuterized technique. Once the computerized solution was modified to satisfy the constraints it bore no resemblance to the original solution. Normally, during the manual scheduling of buses to trips these considerations were included by the scheduling team, and it was felt that the need to manually redevelop the optimal schedule provided no advantage over the traditional methods.

Other computer procedures were also examined and found to possess similar disadvantages. Moreover, the schedulers had no idea of how these techniques worked, felt uncomfortable using them, and therefore lacked confidence in them. It was decided that what was needed was a technique which would take advantage of automated computer technology and at the same time allow the operator to guide and advise the steps of the evaluation. It was therefore decided to look in the direction of a man-machine scheduling system. This would satisfy two important requirements needed for implementation. It would avoid the fait accompli result coughed up by one-pass computer run procedures, and it would allow the operator to be in control of the steps of the evaluation and to 'feel' the improvements in the schedule as they are made. It would also allow direct inclusion of the more practical constraints that experienced schedulers wished to insert into the schedule. Due to its visual nature, the deficit function (Gertsbakh and Gurevich (3), Gertsbakh and Stern (4)) was selected as a natural vehicle to form the basis of such a man-machine procedure.

3. DEFICIT FUNCTIONS

A deficit function is simply a step function which increases by one at the time of a trip departure, and decreases by one at the time of a trip arrival. For a multiterminal bus system, such a function may be constructed for each terminal. The only information needed to construct a set of deficit functions is a timetable of required trips. Consider the timetable shown in Table 2. We shall refer to such a timetable as a fixed schedule of trips - fixed because at this point we do not allow departure times to be varied. Such a schedule may be displayed graphically over the time axis as illustrated at the top of Figure 2. More formally, let $d(k,t)$ represent the deficit function of terminal k. Its value at time t represents the total number of trips that have departed from k, less the total number of trips that have arrived at k, up to and inluding time t. Deficit functions for the three-terminal example are shown at the bottom of Figure 2. Note that these functions provide a decomposition of the more familiar function showing the number of trips in simultaneous operation. Let this latter function be represented by $g(t)$. We shall refer to it as the overall deficit function, as it

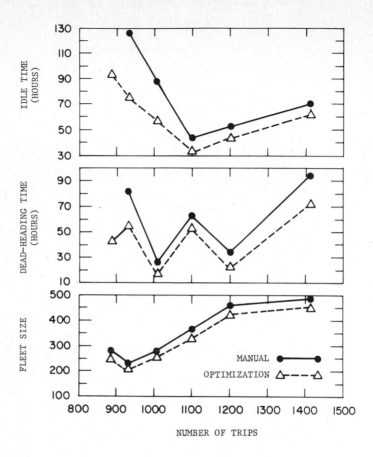

Figure 1:   A comparison between manual & optimization
            (programmable) planning.

$$t_{ab} = t_{ac} = t_{cb} = 2_{DH} \, (4_{service})$$

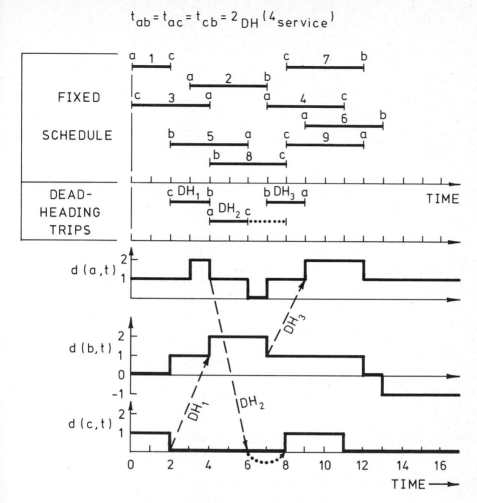

Before (5 chains): [1-7], [2], [3-4], [5-6], [8-9].

After (4 chains): [1-DH$_1$-8-9], [2-DH$_3$-6], [3-DH$_2$-7], [5-6].

Figure 2: Example of a Fixed Schedule of Trips and
Associated Deficit Functions

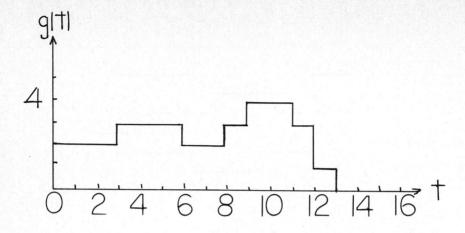

Figure 3: Overall Deficit Function for the Example of Figure 2

may be constructed by summing up all the deficit functions for each point t,

$$i.e. \quad g(t) = \sum_{k \in T} d(k,t)$$

where the set of terminals in the system is represented by T. Figure 3 shows the overall deficit function for the three-terminal example. Note that the area under the curve represents the total amount of work (34 vehicle hours) to be done in the system. It is often thought that the peak value of this function sets the value for the required fleet size. This is in general not true, and although it does indicate the maximum number of buses on the road at any one point in time throughout the day, we shall see that the total number of buses required to carry out the schedule may exceed this value.

TABLE 2. TIMETABLE OF REQUIRED BUS TRIPS

Trip Number	Departure Terminal	Departure Time	Arrival Terminal	Arrival Time
1	a	0	c	2
2	a	3	b	7
3	c	0	a	4
4	a	7	c	11
5	b	2	a	6
6	a	9	b	13
7	c	8	b	12
8	b	4	c	8
9	c	8	a	12

For the example in question, the maximal number of buses required to be in simultaneous operation is 4, while a quick application of the first-in-first-out rule indicates that 5 buses are needed. The 5 chains or sequences of trips assigned to individual buses are shown at the bottom of Figure 2. The chain [1-7] indicates that some bus must start its schedule from terminal a on service trip number 1, which ends at terminal c, and thereafter do service trip number 7, completing its work at terminal b. Further examination determines that 2 buses must initiate their schedules from each of terminals a and b, and one bus is required to start from terminal c. Interestingly enough, these initial bus requirements at the respective terminals may be found by examining the maximal values of the respective deficit functions, and the sum of these maximal values yields the number of required buses. This is not merely a coincidence and has been known for some time as the fleet size formula or the fleet size theorem. To appreciate this result it helps to interpret the value of the deficit function, $d(k,t)$, at time t, as the number of trips departing from k at or before time t which cannot be served by buses arriving from some other terminal in the system. Hence, these trips must be serviced by buses originating at terminal k. The maximal value of the deficit function represents the least number of buses that must be initially available (produced) at the terminal in order to service all the required departures from that terminal. Let this maximum be defined as $D(k)$ – the deficit at k. Taking the sum of the deficits over all terminals yields the total number of buses required to service all of the trips in the schedule.

The Fleet Size Theorem

For a given set of terminals, T, and a fixed schedule of trips, the minimal number of buses required to service all the trips in the schedule is:

$$N = \sum_{k \in T} D(k) = \sum_{k \in T} \underset{t}{Max}\ d(k,t)$$

As previously alluded to, the value of N may be greater than the maximal number of buses simultaneously in operation throughout the day. If G is selected to represent this latter number, then the following can be proved:

The Fleet Size Lower Bound Theorem:

Let G = Max g(t). The minimal number of buses required to service the given fixed schedule of trips must be at least as large as G (G $\leqslant$ N).

4. DEADHEADING TRIP INSERTION

A deadheading (DH) trip is an empty trip not appearing in the original bus timetable, but inserted into the schedule for one of the following reasons: (i) to ensure that the schedule is balanced, i.e. the number of buses located at the start of the day at a depot (garage) must be the same set of buses that return to the depot at the end of the day, (ii) for refuelling, maintenance or driver-transfer purposes, or (iii) for transferring a bus during the day from one terminal where it is not needed to another terminal where it is needed to service a required trip. Let us consider DH trips of the third type. Suppose a bus becomes available at some terminal, say p, at time t_1, and is needed at some other terminal q at a later time t_2. The demand at q can only be satisfied if an empty bus can travel from p to q in time t_2-t_1 or less. That is to say, a feasible insertion of a DH trip requires that $t_1 + t_{pq} \leqslant t_2$, where t_{pq} is the DH travel time from p to q.

To show the effect of a DH trip insertion on the deficit functions themselves, and the resultant fleet size, consider the two deficit functions displayed on the left side of Figure 4. According to the fleet size theorem, a total of 7 buses are required to carry out the underlying schedule. Four buses are required at terminal 1, and 3 are required at terminal 2. Suppose a DH trip of unit length departs from terminal 2 at time 2 and arrives at terminal 3 at time 3. This will have the effect of increasing deficit function d(2,t) by one unit at and after time 2, and decreasing d(1,t) by one unit at and after time 3. Upon insertion of this trip, the deficit functions are transformed to those shown on the right hand side of Figure 4. Notice that the addition of this DH trip has had the effect of reducing the maximal deficit at terminal 1 by one unit, while that of terminal 2 remains unchanged. The bus fleet has now been reduced by one unit to 6. Note also that the lower bound remains at 6. From the lower bound theorem, this implies that the fleet size can no longer be reduced. It is to be understood that this new bound applies to the new fixed schedule of trips which includes the newly added DH trip. This result may now be stated as the following theorem:

The DH Trip Fleet Reduction Theorem:

If G = N, it is impossible to reduce the fleet size N through insertion of additional DH trips.

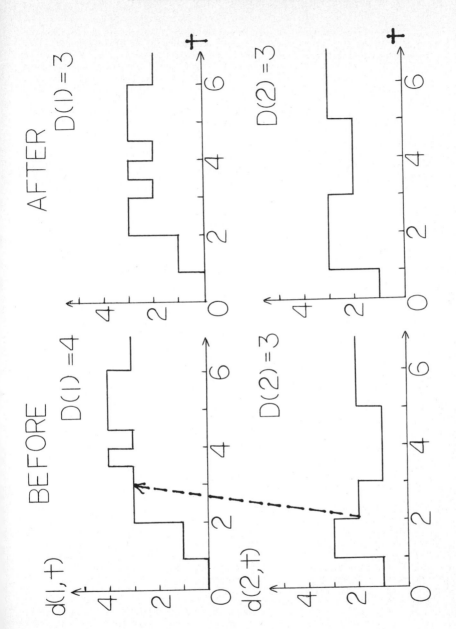

Figure 4: The Effect of Dead-Heading Trip Insertions on Deficit Functions

Returning to the three-terminal example of Figure 2, the dashed lines indicate the insertion of a 'string' of three DH trips each of length 2. After the insertion of this string, the bus fleet size requirements are reduced from 5 to 4. The schedule of each of these buses, which now include the newly-added DH trips, are shown at the bottom of the Figure. Since the overall deficit had a maximal value of G=4, this must be the minimal fleet size and no further reductions are possible. When the above theorem is combined with the fleet size lower bound theorem, an indication of how much one can expect, in the most successful case, to reduce the fleet size is obtained. This is stated in the following proposition:

Maximal Possible Reduction Proposition:

For a given fixed schedule of trips, the maximal possible number of buses that can be saved through the ·insertion of DH trips is:

$$N - G \geqslant 0$$

This proposition can be quite useful as it provides a measure of the potential of the DH insertion technique for fleet size reduction.

5. THE FLEET REDUCTION DEADHEADING TRIP INSERTION ALGORITHM

All of the above provides the basis for two very important practical applications: (i) a quick method for determining the potential value of embarking on the deficit function approach, and (ii) a heuristic method for actually carrying out the DH trip insertions and resultant bus schedules. To assess the potential for fleet size reduction, it is sufficient to perform a number of easily computerized calculations. These computations lead to the construction of a deficit function for each terminal in the schedule, as well as the overall deficit function which shows the number of trips in simultaneous operation throughout the day. If the potential saving is deemed worthwhile, a heuristic procedure based on the insertion of DH trips should be used to reduce the fleet requirements. Such a procedure has been developed and programmed for the CDC Cyber 170/720 computer in Fortran IV. This procedure is designed to operate in a conversational man-machine mode. This implementation of the algorithm allows the practical considerations of experienced schedulers to be brought into the process. As much freedom of choice exists in the selection of DH trips during DH trip string construction, the operator may select among a number of computer-suggested DH trips the one he deems most appropriate. The algorithm can also be operated in purely automatic mode to give a solution for comparison purposes. In addition, the algorithm has been programmed for use with a PDP 11/40 video screen and light pen. This allows the operator to insert and delete DH trips (and required trips as well) quickly, and immediately see the effect on fleet size through the modified deficit function display. Figure 5 shows a typical PDP display of deficit function information. The pointer (arrow) may be repositioned by the light pen to the starting and ending points of the trip to be inserted or deleted. Once the trip has been inserted or deleted the deficit functions are immediately updated. In this manner, the operator may also investigate the effect of varying the departure time of required trips. Moreover, insertions of trips during meal-breaks can be avoided. Deadheading trips that can be used for other purposes can be given priority. The only inputs required for the algorithm are the fixed schedule of trips, and the deadheading trip travel matrix. The output of the algorithm is a table of trips including the newly inserted DH trips, and the fleet size required at each terminal. In order to construct the schedule of trips assigned to each bus, a second phase is required. This can be done using the first-in-first-out rule. At this point, trips from and to the depots may be inserted to balance the schedule if required. The consideration of various types of buses may also be introduced here through a modified version of the first-in-first-out rule.

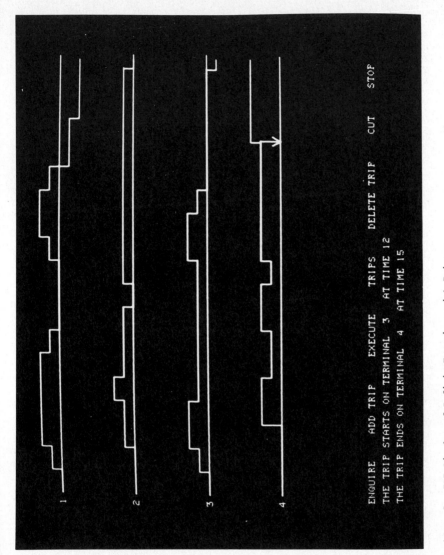

Figure 5: PDP Display of Deficit Functions with Pointer
at Dead-Heading Trip End Point

6. CONCLUSION

In this paper we have described some of the highlights of a new approach to semi-automated bus scheduling. This approach employs highly informative graphical displays in the form of deficit functions. The approach is based upon reductions of bus fleet size through the introduction of deadheading trips. It is suggested that potential users of this or other more sophisticated deadheading insertion techniques perform a short investigation of potential savings. For this purpose, a pre-analysis technique has been developed to assess the maximal possible savings for a given bus timetable of trips. The value of embarking on such a technique should be enhanced if any of the following conditions are present:

1. A substantial number of the trips in the schedule are now deadheading trips (for the case discussed in this paper, one in four trips were deadheading trips).

2. The bus route network is dispersed over a large network with many different end point trip locations.

3. A large number of irregular services are present.

The deficit function bus scheduling algorithm is currently in the 'breaking in' process. Work is continually progressing to provide the algorithm with an enhanced flexibility to incorporate a large number of practical considerations. Among these are:

1. the ability to handle large numbers of terminals,

2. the evaluation of candidate schedules using multi-objective criteria,

3. interaction with other components of the planning process,

4. flexible trip travel and trip departure times,

5. improved methods for handling garage limitations, non-identical bus types, driver meal and location restrictions.

A more detailed description of the algorithm appears in Ceder and Stern (5).

REFERENCES

1. Gavish,B., Schweitzer,P. and Shlifer,E. Assigning buses to schedules in a Metropolitan area, Computers and Operations Research 5 (1978) 129-138.

2. Ceder,A. and Gonen,D. The operational planning process of a bus company, Internal Technical Report, Transport and Operation Department, Egged, Israel (1979).

3. Gertsbakh,I. and Gurevich,Y. Constructing an optimal fleet for a tranportation schedule, Transportation Science, 11 (1977) 20-36.

4. Gertsbakh,I. and Stern,H. Minimal resources for fixed and variable job schedules, Operations Research, 26 (1978) 68-85.

5. Ceder,A. and Stern,H. A deficit function procedure with deadheading trip insertions for fleet size reduction. Submitted for publication and available from the authors.

Computer Scheduling of Public Transport
A. Wren (ed.)
© *North-Holland Publishing Company, 1981*

VAMPIRES AND TASC:
TWO SUCCESSFULLY APPLIED BUS SCHEDULING PROGRAMS

Barbara M. Smith and Anthony Wren

Operational Research Unit
Department of Computer Studies
University of Leeds
Leeds, U.K.

Two bus scheduling programs are described; both have been
used in practical situations. The earlier and more powerful
program, VAMPIRES, consistently leads to savings of five per
cent or more in vehicle numbers. TASC is a simpler program,
easier to understand and use, which does not apparently
achieve as much. Recent experience is that the simpler
program is more acceptable to bus operators.

1.0 INTRODUCTION

Let us be clear from the outset what we mean by bus scheduling. We are dealing
here with the situation where the operator has already decided the times at which
he provisionally wants his journeys to run, although these times may be modified
in the light of the computer results, either as an automatic process, or after
inspection by management of proposals the computer may have made for revising
journeys.

We are not considering here the problem of deciding when journeys should run,
since in the United Kingdom it is not the practice to derive the journey times
directly from passenger demand. The manager rather builds up a pattern of timings
from his general knowledge of passenger demand, bearing in mind his desire to
provide a good overall level of service. It is of course possible to develop
programs which will compute journey timings based on directly observed demand, and
such programs have been written, here and elsewhere. The output from these
programs can serve as input to the type of program being described here.

We are thus concerned now with the provision of buses operating on fixed routes at
times which have been defined. The definition of times may have been explicit, or
may have been implicit, in that the time of a first journey has been given,
together with a service interval.

The fixed routes with which we deal may be regular public services, or may be
special services of one form or another (contract journeys, school or hospital
services with one or two trips per day, or irregularly operated public services).
Normally in scheduling we have to deal with a mixture of various types of service,
and the opportunities for improvement lie mainly in the efficient integration of
irregular services of one form or another. We may in fact differentiate between
the scheduling of individual routes or groups of related routes, and the
integration of the schedules of different services implied in scheduling total
systems. In this paper, two programs are described, one to deal with each of the
above different problems.

The first of these programs to be developed, the one described in the next section, deals with the integration of the schedules of different services which may be spread across a whole bus network or a substantial portion of such a network. This program takes advantage of possibilities of switching vehicles between services, and indicates to the user how savings can be made by revising the times of services. This program consistently enables management to achieve significant savings in vehicle numbers.

The second program is more suitable for situations in which a single route or group of related routes (perhaps operating along a single corridor) is to be scheduled. It enables the user to develop schedules and public timetables rapidly, either in an experimental or in a live situation. It will not normally produce savings in vehicle numbers, but may occasionally do so if used over an entire network. However, it takes much less computer time than the first program.

2.0 VAMPIRES

VAMPIRES (Vehicle And Mileage Pruning In Running Essential Services) was developed from a railway locomotive scheduling program described by Wolfenden and Wren (1). It was first used for bus scheduling in 1970, in a small pilot study, and was used in earnest in 1971, when dramatic savings of 24% and 20% in vehicle numbers were achieved in two exercises for one company. The total saving in these exercises amounted to 23 buses out of 107. (Some of this saving was attributable to the fact that the company in question had recently taken over the operations of a smaller company and had not integrated the operations.)

The basic algorithm used in the primitive version of the program has been described by Wren (2), but very significant developments have taken place since then. Some of these developments were described by Manington and Wren (3) at the Chicago Workshop, and while the program has remained relatively static since then, there has been one important change, and further experience has been gained in the application of the program.

The opportunity is therefore being taken here to describe the program and its use since its inception in a single text. This does of course make use of some portions of the papers already mentioned and of other descriptive material issued from time to time.

2.1 Data Requirements

It will be easier to follow the descriptions of the algorithms used if we describe first the data required. This falls into two classes, in addition to a set of parameters which need not be explained here.

An essential feature of a bus scheduling program is that it should be able to send vehicles from a terminal where there is a surplus to other points in the system as required. It is therefore necessary to specify the amount of time needed to make such a journey, which will normally be without passengers. Such an empty journey is known as a 'dead journey' and the minimum time necessary for the journey is known as the 'dead running time'.

In theory it is necessary to specify the dead running times between any pair of termini, but it is tedious to have to do this (up to about 150 terminals have been involved in a single exercise). The program therefore provides for the user to specify dead running times only between selected points, generally points close together; other times are then calculated using a shortest path algorithm. The program will print a warning if it finds a path between two points which is shorter than that specified by the user. In order to provide for situations where there is a route between two distant points which is considerably faster than the sum of the components specified to the computer, the user is advised to specify times to a number of selected important points in the system from the majority of other points.

Experience shows that it is normally appropriate to specify times between about five per cent of the possible point pairs, thus saving a considerable amount of user effort.

This part of the data thus consists of a list of terminal names, associated with each of which are dead running times to a selection of other points.

The other principal set of data consists of details of the journeys to be scheduled. The description of each journey consists of four essential items, plus a number of options. The essential items are:

        DEPARTURE PT.   (time)   ARRIVAL PT.   (time)

The optional items appear only if their use has been specified in the parameter list. Any optional item therefore appears either in none or in all of the journey specifications. They are as follows:

1. This specifies whether this journey is followed on an existing schedule by the journey immediately following in the data. This assists in data checking, since the computer can determine whether the existing schedule violates any of the given constraints. The user may then correct the data, or may proceed, in which case the computer will allow the violation only in the exact circumstances in which it occurs in the existing schedule. This allows, for example, a schedule to be retained if it contains a feature which would not be accepted by the drivers if it were to appear elsewhere, but has been accepted by tradition in the existing situation. The computer also uses this item of data in order to minimise the deviations of the new schedule from the old one, since it often occurs that there are many possible ways of covering the work at the same cost; it will cause less disruption if the existing way is chosen in these circumstances. A figure '1' in this item indicates that the next journey does follow this one, while a figure '0' indicates that it does not.

2. Pre-layover. There are circumstances where a bus is required to arrive at a point a stipulated time before its scheduled departure, this time being in excess of the normally specified layover (which is defined in the earlier set of data as the journey time from a point to itself). An example of this is where a bus is to pick up children from a school and must be waiting outside the school before the children come out, even if it does not depart until several minutes afterwards. The number specified here is the number of minutes of pre-layover required.

3. Post-layover. This allows for situations where there is a high probability of the bus arriving late due to traffic conditions. The figure specified here is the number of minutes which must elapse before the bus is next used.

4. Retiming. An optional feature of the program is that it may revise the times of journeys if this enables vehicles to be saved. It is necessary to specify limits on the amount of such retiming, which will generally differ from one journey to the next.

1. The maximum number of minutes by which the journey may be retimed to run earlier.

2. The maximum number of minutes by which the journey may be retimed to run later.

5. There is an option whereby the computer allows for several types of vehicle. For each type, one of the digits 0-9 is used to indicate its suitability for the journey being specified. When this option is used there are therefore as many entries here as there are types of vehicle, the ith entry referring to the ith type. The digit 0 is used to indicate that this is an ideal type of vehicle for the journey. The digits 1 to 8 are used to indicate degrees of suitability, while the digit 9 is used to show that a vehicle of this type cannot be used on the journey.

2.2 The Basic VAMPIRES Algorithm

2.2.1 Preamble –

The objectives of any bus scheduling exercise may appear to vary slightly from one undertaking to another, but two goals are common to all cases, although they themselves may appear to be contradictory.

1. Minimise the number of buses used.

2. Minimise a function of dead running time and total time away from the garage.

In practice, the first goal will normally take precedence, the costs being such that saving a vehicle (and hence implicitly a crew) will be of paramount importance.

Other objectives which have been met include:

1. Buses which only work over the peak should be away from the garage for a period as near to a given target as possible. (A target of three hours has proved useful for crew scheduling.)

2. School work should be assigned to buses which are about to return to the garage or which have just left the garage, so that in the school holidays there will be minimum disruption of the schedule.

3. Where a morning peak bus starts its work far from the city centre and finishes at the city centre, it should be allocated to a garage near its starting point rather than to one near the city centre, so that the slack time in running dead to or from the garage occurs later in the day. This means that the bus would not start so early in the morning. The reverse should operate in the evening.

4. The final schedule should be as close to the previous schedule as possible to minimise disruption when the schedule is changed.

In practice, all these objectives may be combined with appropriate weights and added to the second goal above. The dual objective of the program therefore becomes:

1. Minimise the number of buses used.

2. Within this minimum, determine the schedule which best satisfies a given combination of the various other objectives.

This is of course a simplification of the problem, since the user will normally be prepared to make concessions in his requirements for journeys if this would reduce the number of buses. Such concessions may be in the form of retiming of journeys, which can be handled automatically if required, but may also involve curtailing or cancelling journeys. It is our experience that users seldom want to let the computer make revisions to times automatically, since it is then necessary for them to think carefully in advance about every journey, to determine whether, and by how much, it may be retimed. They prefer to have the computer indicate which journeys are critical, and then to investigate these journeys in depth.

The mode of operation which seems best to reflect the needs of users is as follows.

1. Determine a target number of vehicles. We often suggest to users that this should be five per cent fewer than the number in an existing schedule. Where there is no appropriate existing schedule, the computer can determine a good starting number by determining the maximum number of simultaneous 'extended' journeys, where an extended journey has had its arrival time amended to equal the departure time of the next journey which may be done by the same bus.

2. Produce a schedule with this number of vehicles. If no feasible schedule can be produced, this schedule can indicate which journeys would have to be revised in order to make it feasible.

3. If the above schedule is feasible, or if any infeasibilities can be removed by revision of journeys, select a lower target and repeat.

4. If infeasibilities cannot all be removed, select a higher target and repeat.

In practice, it is generally easy to select a good target for repetitions of the process, and three passes through the system have always been sufficient.

We may now see what is required of a basic algorithm. It should be capable of producing a schedule for any given number of buses which minimises the extent of any infeasibilities, and satisfies well a stipulated objective which may be a combination of various factors. The algorithm to be described does just this. It cannot guarantee optimality, but has been tested against known optimal solutions on many occasions and has always produced an equally good solution.

2.2.2 The VAMPIRES Algorithm Explained -

We shall illustrate the algorithm by reference to Figure 1, in which the horizontal lines represent four terminals, T1 to T4, and there is a horizontal time scale. The continuous diagonal lines represent journeys to be scheduled, while the dotted lines represent links between journeys. We shall suppose that Bus 1 after leaving a garage does a portion of work (A) followed by trip i from T1

to T2;   it then runs dead to T3 to work trip j followed by portion (C), before
returning to its garage. Meanwhile Bus 2 after leaving its garage does portion
(B) followed by trip r from T3 to T4, then runs dead to T2 to work trip s, which
is followed by portion (D) before it returns to its garage. The portions of work
(A-D) may in general include several trips and dead runs each, or may be empty.

Clearly, we may consider the possibility of switching Bus 1 to take trip s
followed by portion (D) after working trip i, while Bus 2 would run dead from T4
to T3 to take trip j followed by portion (C). This may well be a better solution,
since it will reduce the dead running involved in these two links. However, other
factors may have to be borne in mind in assessing the cost of such a change.
These are basically those already listed, but there is an added complication if
more than one garage is involved.

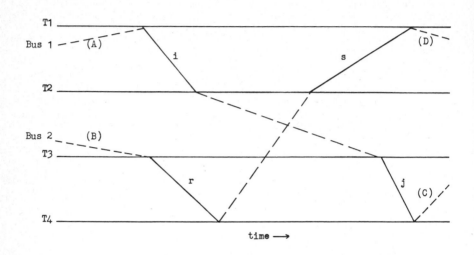

FIGURE 1

Portions (A) and (C) may respectively start and finish near one garage, while (B)
and (D) are more suited to another, in which case a switch may result in an
increase in dead running to and from the garage.   The algorithm therefore
considers which would be the best garage for each of the revised bus workings if
the change were made, and determines the overall change in dead running, both in
the links being switched and in the garage journeys. Other costs are also taken
into account with relevant weightings, and a switch is made if there is no
worsening in the total cost.

The simple heuristic is therefore to examine every pair of links in turn and to
switch them if the cost is not worsened. Note that the switch is made if the cost
is unaffected, since this perturbs the situation and may lead to the heuristic
finding a better solution in a later pass. Switches are also considered where
journey r does not exist, i.e. where trip s is the first trip for Bus 2.   A
solution in which journey i is followed on Bus 1 by journey s and journey j is the

first journey for Bus 2 may be better.

A pass through the heuristic therefore consists of examining all possible pairs of links, and the process continues until two successive passes produce no positive improvement.

The program next enters a tidying-up phase which consists of further passes through the heuristic in which switches are made to satisfy the following.

1. A link is restored which was present in the original schedule, if this does not increase other costs.

2. A first-in/last-out (FILO) rule is adopted where this does not increase the costs. This leaves long gaps in the workings of some buses, and consideration is given (using a fairly complex algorithm which will not be discussed here) to returning buses to garages during these gaps. This may involve switching buses between garages since there may be a garage close to where the gaps occur which is not the original home garage for the bus, but which may now be better as a base.

A further pass takes place in which journeys which were not linked to the garage after the above FILO process are re-linked on a first-in/first-out (FIFO) basis.

While no guarantee can be given regarding the optimality of the results, the method has been tested against optimal schedules produced by mathematical programming in cases where the number of trips was sufficiently small to allow solution of the associated assignment problem in a reasonable amount of computer time. In these comparisons the heuristic has always produced an optimal solution. Such tests have of course only been made when the costs depended only on the individual links between trips, since the overall problem of examining the total work of a bus (for example to account for garage allocation) cannot be treated as an assignment problem.

While no solution has ever been found to be better than the VAMPIRES solution in these simple cases, it has been possible with some effort to construct better solutions than the VAMPIRES ones in some situations with more complex objectives. The deviation of VAMPIRES from the better solution has however been very slight (of the order of two or three minutes dead running out of several hundred bus-hours). No schedule actually in operation has ever been found to be superior to a VAMPIRES produced schedule in terms of the objective specified.

2.2.3 The Starting Solution –

We have assumed until now that we have had a schedule to which we have applied a cost reducing technique. We shall now explain how we obtain a starting schedule, which may not be feasible, and in the next section we shall extend the algorithm just described to deal with infeasibilities.

We have already explained that the process starts with a target number of buses. It is in fact easy to construct a schedule with any given number of buses, provided one allows the buses to travel backwards in time if necessary!

Experiments with a number of methods for constructing a starting solution have shown that the quality of the final solution and the time taken to converge do not depend significantly on the quality of the initial solution, unless one happens to obtain a very good starting solution, in which case computer time may be reduced.

An algorithm which ensured a good starting solution would itself be complex and time-consuming, and we therefore use a very simple method to obtain a crude starting solution. We shall explain this by reference to Figure 2.

Initially only the continuous lines representing journeys to be scheduled are present. These represent twelve journeys between four terminals, and we number them in chronological order of departure time. We shall assume a target of three buses.

We start by assigning the first three trips, one to each bus. (We do this even where it is obvious that two may be done by the same vehicle, since we do not wish to waste time on a search.) We now work through the trips in order, checking first that the trip has been allocated to a bus, then linking it to its earliest possible unallocated successor.

Thus trip 1 is linked to trip 4 (Bus 1), and other immediate linkings are 2-5 (Bus 2), 3-7 (Bus 3), 4-6 (Bus 1), 5-9 (Bus 2), 6-10 (Bus 1), 7-12 (Bus 3). We now come to trip 8 which has not been allocated to a bus. The rule we follow is that any unallocated trip is assigned to Bus 1 after its current last trip, even though this is infeasible.

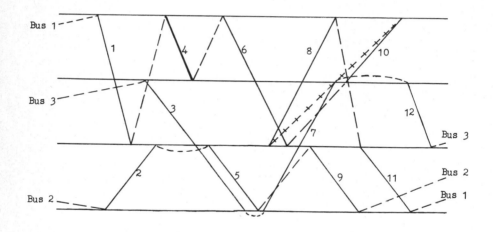

FIGURE 2

Thus we link 10-8 (Bus 1); this link is marked as impossible by the use of crosses in Figure 2. We may now proceed to find a successor to trip 8, and we link 8-11 (Bus 1). We now seek a successor to trip 9, but there is none, so the bus is returned to the garage. Trip 10 has already been assigned a successor, and trips 11 and 12 are followed by journeys to the garage.

At this stage we have a schedule with three buses, but the schedule is unworkable.

2.2.4   Reducing And Removing Infeasibilities -

We now follow the normal switching procedure already described, but we assign penalty costs to infeasible links, and the prime consideration in making a switch becomes whether it reduces the penalty.

A switch is made if the penalty is reduced, even if other costs are increased, but at the same time normal switches are made where there is no change in penalty.

The penalty is defined as zero for a feasible link, and the difference between the time necessary to make a link and the time available, for infeasible links. Since the time available may be negative, the penalty may be greater than the time necessary (and would be greater in the above example). The penalty is in fact the number of minutes by which one of the trips involved would have to be retimed in order to make the link feasible.

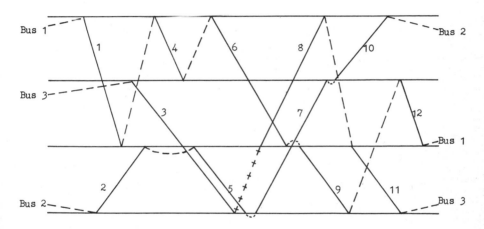

FIGURE 3

Under this switching procedure we might, for example, consider the linkings 10-8 and 6-10. A switch now would result in the links 10-10 and 6-8. The total penalty is reduced, and the fact that trip 10 is now linked to itself is for the present immaterial (it does not have a bus allocated, but the links may be reassigned in later stages). The ultimate linking may well be (see Figure 3):

    Bus 1:   1-4-6-9-12
    Bus 2:   2-5-7-10
    Bus 3:   3-8-11 (link 3-8 infeasible)

The penalty involved in the link 3-8 may well be small, and this solution could be presented to management. Consideration may then be given to whether this link could be made feasible by manual adjustment of the times of one or both of the trips involved. Such retiming may well be acceptable to management, bearing in mind that the alternative is the cost of an additional bus and associated crews. In some cases the correct decision may be to cancel a trip that is costing an additional vehicle, where a trip has been identified by the program as critical.

When the program was first used for bus scheduling (in 1971) our practice was to determine first the maximum number of simultaneous trips, and to use this as the number of buses, getting the computer to add buses automatically one at a time, printing out each 'solution' until a fully feasible one was found. One of our early experiences, however, was a case where the operator used 41 buses, and the computer, having calculated that the maximum number of simultaneous trips was 33, produced a series of solutions with from 33 up to 39 buses, the first six being infeasible, and the last feasible. Management having inspected these and having found the 33-bus solution to be operable after suitable adjustments of the timetable, asked us to try again with even fewer buses, and finally accepted a solution with thirtyone.

The above, and similar experiences in which several solutions were produced unnecessarily, led us to modify the practice. On being faced with a new problem, we now normally discuss with management the number of buses to be used in the first computer run, suggesting five per cent fewer than the number currently used unless there is good reason to believe that another figure would be more appropriate. If the solution contains no infeasibilities, or if all the infeasibilities can be accepted, we then undertake a second run with fewer buses still. If, however, there are infeasibilities which cannot be accepted, the second run will be given more buses.

Our experience in inspecting the results of first runs has put us in a position where we can normally estimate fairly well, after discussions with management, how many buses will ultimately be required. The second run is undertaken with a number of buses slightly below this estimate, and it is always possible from the results of this second run to obtain a very good assessment of the (slightly greater) number of buses actually required. A third run is then undertaken with this revised estimate. No more than three computer runs have ever been required.

2.2.5 Refinements To The Algorithm -

Several variations on the objectives have already been listed. These and other similar ones have been met by appropriate adjustments to the costs of the schedules as assessed by the switching process. In some cases the program has been adapted so that such adjustments have been made only after the solution has stabilised following a series of normal iterations; a series of modified iterations has then been followed.

Three major additional facilities have been: the automatic return of buses to the garage during idle periods of the day; provision for retiming trips automatically to remove infeasibilities; handling of different types of vehicle.

2.2.5.1 Returning Buses To Garage During Idle Periods –

This feature is more complex than may at first appear. After gaps have been created in the schedule because of the FILO principle, one expects to be able to return many buses to the garage for substantial portions of the day, especially between the peaks. This would be easy if only one garage were involved, or if a bus were sent to the nearest garage (not necessarily its home garage) during an idle period. In practice a bus often has to return to its home garage during an idle period, and this raises problems.

We have chosen to determine the best garage for any bus, bearing in mind its positions at the beginning and end of the day, and at the beginning and end of any gap, and to bear the effect on the choice of best garage in mind when considering switches. This does make the switching algorithm rather complicated, especially when we are considering breaking a link representing a gap on a bus which has other gaps elsewhere in its schedule. We have therefore been forced to compromise on the amount of searching we can do. Our compromise has been reached only after extensive experiments, and we are confident that very little, if anything, has been sacrificed.

2.2.5.2 Automatic Retiming Of Trips –

It is of course possible for the computer, having found an irreducible infeasibility, to retime trips automatically, provided that the user can specify the limits between which this can be done.

While some programs have been made available where retiming can be done within global limits, we have felt that the amount of possible retiming should normally vary from trip to trip, since some are more severely constrained by operating objectives than others. There is therefore an option whereby the user may specify, for any trip, the maximum numbers of minutes by which it may be moved earlier or later.

This facility was included at the request of one company, but in practice it has proved tedious for users to examine closely every trip in order to determine the amount of retiming possible, in the absence of any knowledge of which particular trips will prove critical. In practice therefore the facility has not been used often, it being preferred to concentrate on determining whether individual trips may be retimed once the program has identified them as critical.

2.2.5.3 Vehicle Types –

We have encountered situations where there have been up to nine different types of vehicle, with types being classified for any trip in categories ranging from ideal to impossible. Coping with such circumstances did not prove easy, but the program has been adapted for this purpose.

Within the context of the algorithm being used, we had to choose between an approach in which we first produced a schedule independent of vehicle type and subsequently modified it, and one in which we produced separate schedules for each type and then amalgamated and modified them. We chose the first approach, on the grounds that we should obtain after the first phase a schedule which could be regarded as an ideal. The manager could then see how much consideration of type of vehicle was costing.

In line with this approach, we decided to produce first the ideal schedule without considering type of vehicle, then an 'ideal' schedule taking into account vehicle types, but assuming an unlimited supply of any type, and finally a schedule in which the numbers of buses of certain types were restricted to the numbers available. The second schedule could then serve to the manager as an indication of what the ideal fleet mix should be.

Obtaining the second schedule is relatively straightforward. Once a schedule is obtained ignoring the types of vehicle, it is possible to assign the 'best' type to every bus working, according to a two-tier costing system. If there are trips in a particular bus working which cannot be operated by a particular type of bus, then the cost of that type being allocated to that working is taken as a first tier cost, equal to the total number of minutes for which the type would be infeasible. If there are no such trips, then the cost is taken as a second tier cost obtained by summing the products of the numbers indicated in option 5 of section 2.1 with the durations of the associated trips.

The normal VAMPIRES switching process then proceeds, taking the overall cost as a weighted sum of the penalty cost of infeasibilities and the first tier cost of infeasible types, if there are either sort of infeasibility, and as a weighted sum of the normal VAMPIRES cost and the second tier cost of vehicle types otherwise. This leads to a schedule which is feasible by type of vehicle, after the usual consideration of the consequences of infeasibilities, and the addition of buses if necessary.

The next stage is to restrict the numbers of vehicles of any type to those specified in the data. Clearly the schedule already obtained may be feasible in this respect, in which case the process is complete. If the schedule is not feasible, an attempt is made to assign bus workings to feasible types in a manner which is optimal according to second tier costs. This is a standard transportation problem. If this is successful, the switching process continues, but now we do not allow any switches which would lead to the consequential workings being such as to violate the limits on the numbers available of any type.

If the solution to the transportation problem contains infeasible allocations, critical types of vehicles and critical bus workings are identified by reference to the shadow costs, and the switching continues with ever increasing costs attached to workings associated with these types of vehicle.

After every iteration the transportation problem is solved again with the modified bus workings, and the process continues until no further improvement results.

This process was successful, in that it obtained results which could not be bettered on problems tackled over a number of years. However, in two more recent exercises situations have arisen where feasible schedules in terms of vehicle types were not obtained, despite a simple visual scan of the resulting infeasible schedules showing how they should be modified to obtain feasibility. As a result of this, the algorithm is being modified to incorporate a simple three-way switching process in a single pass after convergence of the normal two-way switches; if this produces an improvement we revert to the two-way switching.

2.2.6   Results -

It is not possible to present the precise savings achieved on every application of
the program.   In some cases the results are confidential to the client.   In
others, savings were agreed by management, but could not be implemented directly
because of changing circumstances.   In such cases the savings were generally
achieved over a long term by virtue of the schedulers working gradually towards
the schedule indicated by the computer.   It can however be categorically stated
that wherever a manually produced schedule existed before the application of
VAMPIRES to the same set of data, a better schedule has always been created by
VAMPIRES.   The savings have always been at least five per cent of vehicle numbers.

These figures have always been either agreed by management or presented to
management and not refuted.   (In a few cases no response was received from the
organisation after presentation of results, and it is in these that the results
have been presented and not refuted.)

The cost of the exercise has always been insignificant in comparison with the
savings made.   The most expensive VAMPIRES project cost between five and six
thousand pounds in 1980 values; that showed how six buses could be saved.

Notes on work for individual clients (and on one unsponsored demonstration
project) follow.

1.   Aberdeen City Transport.   Work previously done by 32 buses operating over the
     evening peak only was presented to the program.   In collecting data, the
     schedulers discovered how to make do with only 26 vehicles.   VAMPIRES produced
     a feasible solution with 26 buses, and also an acceptable infeasible solution
     with 24 vehicles.

2.   W.Alexander and Sons (Fife) Ltd.   The manual schedule had 71 buses at the
     busiest time.   The program produced an acceptable schedule with 67 buses, and
     one which might have been operable with 66.

3.   W.Alexander and Sons (Midland) Ltd.   Five buses were saved out of 65 from one
     depot.

4.   Coventry City Transport.   An exercise was undertaken to reschedule the school
     transport following a reorganisation of the City's education system in 1973.
     VAMPIRES was run in a proving exercise on the previous year's requirements,
     and showed how, without retiming, two buses could be saved out of 72.   The
     program was then run on the new year's requirements, where there was no
     previous schedule for comparison, and the results were accepted and
     implemented.

5.   Edinburgh City Transport.   About fifty evening peak special buses were
     examined.   VAMPIRES produced a solution acceptable to management (after
     suitable retimings) with four buses fewer, but an urgent need for more drastic
     economies led to much of the work covered by this schedule being abandoned.

6.   Greater Manchester Transport.   Many exercises have been undertaken for this
     body, who sponsored comparisons between the results produced by VAMPIRES and
     those produced by two other programs.   GMT have purchased rights to use
     VAMPIRES on their own machine, and have incorporated it within a more global
     system.   See Dickinson, Drynan and Manington (4).

7. Kingston-upon-Hull Corporation Transport. Seven buses were saved out of 114. The figure of 114 had already been reduced from 120 as a result of applying a rival program. The schedule was implemented.

8. Merseyside Passenger Transport Executive. Two exercises have been undertaken, both indicating savings in excess of five per cent.

9. Societe des Transports Intercommunaux de Bruxelles. An exercise was undertaken to assess the suitability of the program for scheduling buses in Brussels. This was carried out on a single route with one branch, which is not an ideal situation for VAMPIRES (we should probably now have recommended the more recent TASC program). One bus was saved out of 39 (by running empty from the terminus on one branch to that on another branch). The STIB assessment was that the program was suitable for their requirements, but a moratorium was then placed on computer scheduling developments.

10. Stadtwerke Wien. An unsponsored demonstration exercise was carried out on three tram routes (separately). The program produced savings based on the data submitted to us, but no response was received after results were sent to Vienna.

11. Trent Motor Traction Company Ltd. An exercise was undertaken covering six depots of and the Midland General Company, to determine whether savings could be produced by integrating the work. The exercise was not completed owing to other pressures on the staff of the Company, but acceptable results were produced saving eight buses out of 120. There were indications that further savings could be achieved.

12. Ulsterbus Ltd. An exercise was undertaken covering nine depots and two types of vehicle. A full assessment of the results is not available, owing to the management having to spend their time dealing with problems arising from the political situation. Substantial savings were however indicated.

13. West Yorkshire PTE. An exercise was undertaken using two of the Leeds depots. Savings in excess of five per cent out of about 120 buses were shown, but implementation was not possible because of crew scheduling problems at that time.

14. Yorkshire Traction Company Ltd. This was the first undertaking to use VAMPIRES; they sponsored the initial conversion of the program from a rail scheduling program, as well as the addition of facilities to deal with several garages, several vehicle types and automatic retiming of trips. Several exercises were undertaken:

    1. A saving of ten buses in 41 was agreed by management, but not directly implemented, because they preferred to await further program developments which they were sponsoring. The schedulers did however work towards obtaining the schedules produced by the computer.

    2. A saving of thirteen buses in 66 was agreed by management, with the same outcome as above.

    3. A saving of six buses in 32 was achieved in the first test run of the program after it was adapted to handle more than one garage. This was implemented.

4. A saving of two buses in 18 was achieved, and the schedule was implemented.

5. At least two buses were saved out of 43 in the prototype run of the version of the program to handle more than one type of vehicle, but change in management led to the company losing interest in the program.

15. <u>National Bus Company</u>. The program has been used by NBC on two occasions to assess the consequences of possible service alterations.

16. <u>R.Travers Morgan and Partners Ltd.</u> The program was used in the course of the Bradford Bus Study.

17. <u>Overseas operator</u>. A feasibility study has recently been undertaken in an overseas city, and it has been shown that savings could be achieved through use of VAMPIRES in conjunction with the University's bus crew scheduling programs. It is hoped that a full scale implementation of a specifically designed system will be commissioned shortly.

3.0 TASC

TASC (Timetable And Schedule Compilation) is, as its name suggests, a bus scheduling program which also produces output in the form of a public timetable. However, as a bus scheduling program TASC is not as powerful as VAMPIRES and is more suited to smaller-scale problems.

The data for TASC is in the form of a network of routes with the times of journeys along each route. This makes TASC particularly suitable for scheduling regular public services, and it is commonly used to schedule regular journeys along a single route or small group of routes.

The advantage of TASC over VAMPIRES as a bus scheduling program is that it is both easier and quicker to use. It can be run in batch mode, but this is done only for very large problems, which are outside the normal use of TASC; usually, the program is run from a terminal and the bus schedule is immediately available. The program is also simple to use, so that bus operators can run it themselves with very little help. A typical use of TASC is in re-designing the regular public services on a small portion of the route network, where the bus operator wishes to try out several different ideas quickly.

3.1 Data Requirements

The data required for TASC fall into two parts: the description of the route network and the list of journeys to be scheduled. All this information can be input interactively via the terminal; at the opposite extreme, the information can be set up beforehand in two files, called the network file and the headway file, and there are several intermediate options.

3.1.1 The Network File –

The information given here describes the routes on which journeys are to be scheduled. A network diagram is often used as a basis for gathering together this information, although this is simply to help the operator, and is not required by the program.

Example. Figure 4 shows how the various points in a network are connected by bus routes. It bears no relation to their geographical position.

Fazakerley is represented by two points with different numbers and the same name because this is the easiest way to deal with a complicated pattern of routes between Fazakerley and Field Lane. These points will be considered as a special group of points, equivalent for some purposes, and distinct for others.

The running time in minutes is shown on each link of the network. In fact, the running time is specified separately for each route at present, even though in most cases all routes using a particular link in the network will have the same running time along it. The input will shortly be modified so that individual links need be described only once.

The running times from point 7 to points 6 and 13 are shown as 21/18 and 7/4 respectively. This is to indicate differential running times along these sections of the network. The longer time operates after 0700; before then, the running time is 3 minutes shorter. If differential running times are being used, the time-bands over which the different times operate must be described in the network file.

The program must also be given sufficient information to construct a dead-running matrix. A fraction (say 0.75) is specified and the program calculates the dead-running time as this fraction of the live-running time, for any pair of points in the network which are connected by a route or sequence of routes. In most cases, this is sufficient, except possibly for a few points; in the example, it is also necessary to give the dead-running time from the garage to Spellow Lane, since no route goes to the garage, and to link points 2 and 3 by specifying 0 minutes dead-running time between them.

Finally, the routes which operate on this network must be described. In fact, each route in the bus operator's sense, normally consists of several route-variants as far as TASC is concerned: the variants are the different directions of the route, as well as short workings and other deviations from the standard route. For instance, in the example, route 20 runs between Fazakerley and Aigburth Vale via Whitechapel. There are two route-variants, 20.1 and 20.2, for the two directions of travel, and two more which are short workings from Spellow Lane to the ends of the route, to cater for journeys to and from the garage.

The route variants are defined by the points along the route, and the running times between them. It is also possible (as an option) to specify the mileage along each section of the route. TASC also needs to know the layover (number of minutes waiting-time) to be allowed at the end of the route, and whether a crew can be relieved along the route.

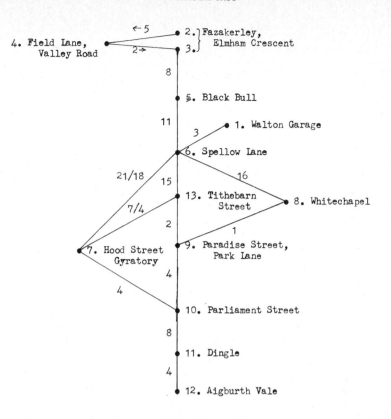

FIGURE 4

For example, for route-variant 20.1, the network file contains a line of data as
follows:

```
20.1                   (name of route-variant)
8                      (8 points on this route)
3 5 6 8 9 10 11 12     (the points in order)
8 11 16 1 4 8 4        (running time along each section)
4                      (minutes layover)
1 6                    (one crew relief point, at Spellow Lane)
```

To summarise, the network file contains:

1. Some dimensioning information.

2. Definitions of differential running time bands.

3. The fraction to be used to calculate dead-running time.

4. A list of points in the network, with any additional dead-running information.

5. Definitions of groups of equivalent points.

6. A list of route-variant definitions.

3.1.2 The Headway File -

Having defined the route network, we can now specify journey-times on the various routes. Since TASC is designed particularly for regular services, this is done by specifying the time of the first journey, the service interval (or headway), the time until which this service interval applies, and so on to the end of the day.

For example, the journey-times on route-variant 20.1 might be given as:

                0526 60 0726 30 0826 20 1046 40 2246

which means: '0526 and every hour until 0726, then at 0756 and 0826, then every 20 minutes until 1046, then every 40 minutes until 2246'. If there is no regular service, the service interval is entered as 0, e.g. '0726 30 0826' is equivalent to '0726 0 0756 0 0826'. The default is that the times specified are departure times from the first point on the route, but by specifying the number of another point in brackets before the first time, we may construct the timetable based on times at any selected point.

Secondly, details of how buses are to travel from the garage to other points of the network are required (although this should logically be part of the network information). The standard options are (a) buses run dead to every point of the network, (b) buses run dead to the nearest point of the network (in the example, Spellow Lane) and then in service. It is also possible to specify garage journeys exactly for any or all of the points. There may be more than one garage in the network, in which case this information is required separately for each.

Finally, the timetables to be printed for this run are specified. For each timetable, TASC needs to know which services to include, which points to include, and whether to add running-board numbers and layovers from the bus schedule. It also needs to know at which point the journeys are to be consecutive, since in many timetables journeys do not appear in the same order at every point.

Normally, at least two timetables would be required, one for each direction of travel, but it is often useful to print more than this. For instance, if several routes are being scheduled together, there could be individual timetables for each route and one or more summary timetables showing journeys along common stretches of route.

This completes the data requirements for TASC. Each network file can often be used with several headway files; for instance, if services are being re-designed and different options are being tested, then only the journey times will change from one run to the next, and the route network will be unchanged. Even if TASC is being applied to an existing situation, there will probably be separate schedules for Monday-Friday, Saturday and Sunday, with the same network file being used for all three schedules.

3.2 Method

The program first generates all the trips specified in the data. It then denotes every arrival and departure as an event, and sorts these in chronological order by point.

The progam next links arrivals with subsequent departures from the same point, provided that this does not result in a bus being idle for more than a specified time. Any events which are not linked by this process are put into a separate list, and such events are linked according to a fairly complex algorithm. Such a link is either between an arrival and a departure from another terminal of the same group, or is a journey from a terminal with a surplus arrival to one with a surplus departure.

The algorithm allows for journeys being inserted live (i.e. as advertised passenger-carrying journeys), if there is a route linking the terminals, and if this can be done without the necessity for an additional vehicle. If an additional vehicle would be needed for such live journeys, or if no live journey is possible, dead journeys are inserted if possible, provided that it would not be better to return the bus to a garage.

Where a bus has to move from one terminal group to another, and this can be done as an extension to an existing journey, such an extension is given priority over the use of additional live or dead journeys. Thus, if a bus arrives at point A at 1000, and is not required again at A, while a vehicle is required at B at 1015 to make a journey to C, the order in which possibilities are considered is:

1. See whether A and B are members of the same terminal group.

2. See whether there is a route which goes from A to C via B; if so replace the journey from B to C by one from A to C, if there is sufficient time for the bus to do this, leaving B at the predefined time.

3. See whether there is a route which includes A and B in that order, and whether there is time to make a journey on that route in time to be ready to leave B at 1015.

4. See whether there is enough time for a bus to run out of service from A to B.

In practice there will usually be several departures which may be linked with the arrival at A. The computer will choose a suitable departure according to the above order of priority, giving preference to earlier departures within the same priority level.

As a result of this process in which additional passenger carrying journeys may be inserted, the headways on some routes may become irregular. An option exists whereby headways may be smoothed out as far as possible over specified periods on given routes.

Journeys are next inserted provisionally to and from garages, and a simplified version of the VAMPIRES heuristic (see earlier) is then used to adjust the workings of buses where possible, so that they start and finish near the same garage.

A complete bus schedule now exists within the computer, and all the information necessary to compile running boards and timetables is present. It is possible to instruct the computer to prepare any number of timetables to show services over any specified portions of route.

3.3 Output

Examples of output from TASC are shown at the end of the paper.

Figure 5 shows a timetable for the route network described earlier. (In order to fit the whole timetable on to one page, the number of journeys scheduled is very small.) As can be seen, the form of the timetable is very similar to most public timetables, with the addition of some bus scheduling information which is optional.

The timetable indicates where journeys have been extended or inserted in order to balance the schedule, by printing E or I next to the layover. It also gives the layover at the end of each journey, unless the bus next returns to the garage, or runs dead to another point, or the end of the journey does not appear in the timetable.

If required, the 'running no.' of each journey is given, that is, the number of the running board it has been allocated to; a running board is a list of the journeys operated by one bus. A code letter is sometimes printed alongside the running board number: this is explained at the end of the timetable, and indicates for instance that this is the first journey done by the bus after leaving the garage. Using this information, it is possible to follow the journeys operated by each bus through the timetables. As an option, notes may be printed below the timetable, specifying that a journey begins or ends at a point not on the timetable (see Figure 5A).

After the timetables, are the running boards, as shown in Figure 6. These, in effect, give the bus schedule constructed by TASC; they consist for each bus of a list of the start and finish times of each journey, together with dead runs and the journeys to and from the garage. If mileages have been specified in the route variant descriptions, the running boards give the mileage for each journey and the total mileage for each bus.

The output also contains a histogram showing how many buses are on the road at any time of day (Figure 7: this does not correspond to schedule shown in Figures 5 and 6, which required only three buses). From the information used to construct the histogram, together with information supplied by the bus operator, an estimate is made of the number of crews which would be required to operate the schedule (Figure 8): this is useful when the costs of different options are being compared.

Finally, for each running board, the times at which the bus passes a crew relief point are printed out. This information can also be output to a file, so that it can be passed on directly to a crew-scheduling program, but this option has so far been used only for demonstration purposes.

3.4 Uses Of TASC

The major user of TASC, as of many of our other programs, has been West Yorkshire Passenger Transport Executive. The first exercise in which the P.T.E. made use of TASC took place in August, 1978. The program was used to help in the evaluation of different operating policies on a large number of routes throughout the county. The costs of different options were compared using the bus schedule and the estimate of crew requirements produced by TASC. The timetables printed for each option were also useful as a means of presenting the different policies to laymen.

For that exercise, the program was run on the University's DEC-10 computer, and the work of data collection, input and running the program was shared by the O.R. Unit's staff and P.T.E. staff. Since then, the P.T.E. staff have used the program on several occasions and are now able to use the program with very little help from the O.R. Unit. The program has been mounted for them at a bureau in Leeds which has a DEC-10 machine, and so the P.T.E. can use the program completely independently.

Currently, a feasibility study is under way, in which output from the program is presented directly to computer type-setting equipment, in order to print the public timetable.

TASC has been used by one county council in order to check that claims presented by a bus operator in respect of costs of providing certain services were reasonable.

The program has been demonstrated to a number of operators, and negotiations are now in hand for further applications.

4.0 COMPARISON OF VAMPIRES AND TASC

Since the TASC program was introduced two years ago, bus operators have shown much more interest in TASC than in VAMPIRES. It may be instructive to consider why TASC appears to be more popular than VAMPIRES, and the following are some of the reasons which we have identified.

1. It is difficult to describe the two programs simply without giving the impression that TASC is a more useful program than VAMPIRES, since it does timetabling as well as bus scheduling. For a bus operator, it may be hard to grasp the idea that different bus scheduling programs are not equally good bus scheduling programs, and still harder to decide whether his particular problems can be dealt with adequately by TASC. The danger is that an operator will choose TASC rather than VAMPIRES for its ease of use and later begin to ask for additional facilities, such as the capability to deal with diferent vehicle-types, which are in fact already available in VAMPIRES. This is something which we have to resist, because as TASC is made more powerful and more like VAMPIRES, it may simultaneously lose its advantage of speed.

2. The data for VAMPIRES is more difficult and tedious to gather than the data for TASC. This is unavoidable, because of the different ways in which the programs are used, but may still be seen as a disadvantage of VAMPIRES. VAMPIRES is the more suitable program when a large proportion of the journeys to be scheduled are odd trips outside the normal route network, such as school and works journeys, or irregular services. In this case, it is appropriate to list each trip separately. TASC on the other hand, is most suitable for regular services on a route network; although the program can cope with odd

trips the data format then becomes tedious, since the route description and
journey time have to be specified separately.

VAMPIRES also requires more data to set up the dead-running matrix; in many
cases, TASC can construct most of the dead-running matrix using a fraction of
the live-running time, with only a few times actually specified. Again,
however, this is a consequence of the different uses of the two programs:
VAMPIRES is most powerful where dead runs are important in constructing an
efficient schedule, whereas TASC is usually applied to small sections of a
route network where very little dead-running between outer termini is
required.

3. Bus operators seem to find the timetables produced by TASC particularly
    attractive. This is probably because a large amount of output, which would
    normally have to be written out by hand, can be produced from a small amount
    of input. The usefulness of this part of the program, even if the bus
    scheduling part of the program is ignored, is therefore immediately apparent,
    although from the computing point of view, this is a very simple part of the
    program and was initially thought of as a by-product of bus scheduling.

4. To date, the TASC program has been used mainly as an aid when groups of bus
    routes have been re-organized. This means that the decision to implement a
    new bus schedule and a new crew schedule has already been taken. If TASC is
    not used, the bus schedules must be constructed manually by the bus operator's
    scheduling staff, and for a large-scale re-organisation this may take a long
    time. Hence, TASC can be used to save time, so that the scheduling staff can
    concentrate on designing the options to be tested, and the scheme can be
    implemented much more quickly.

    On the other hand, VAMPIRES is an independent exercise, the aim being to run
    the existing services with fewer buses. The work involved in such an exercise
    is considerable: a large amount of data must be collected, a completely new
    crew schedule must be constructed, and since the savings from VAMPIRES are
    likely to be greatest when a large bus schedule is being dealt with, it may
    not be a trivial task to implement the new schedules.

    Hence, a decision to use TASC generally means choosing between computer
    scheduling and manual scheduling, at a time when choosing manual scheduling
    may overload the available staff. A decision to use VAMPIRES means
    undertaking a large amount of additional work, for a benefit (saving buses)
    which must be taken on trust.

5. The TASC program is much more accessible to bus operators than VAMPIRES can
    be. The program can be run either on an operator's own computer, or via a
    telephone link to our consulting partners, Wootton, Jeffreys. After a short
    period of instruction, users can easily input data themselves directly from
    terminals in their own offices. The results can be sent back to the user very
    quickly. Users of VAMPIRES on the other hand usually require help from the
    O.R. Unit in collecting the data and there is usually a considerable delay
    before sensible results can be obtained.

It may be useful to bear in mind, then, that although a powerful bus scheduling
program such as VAMPIRES may be able to reduce the costs of bus operation
significantly, the difficulties involved in using the program may mean that it is
not used very much. Bus operators may prefer a simpler program, such as TASC,
which can be used as an aid in the work of the scheduling staff, even though the
benefits offered may be less.

5.0 REFERENCES

1. Wolfenden, K. and Wren, A. Locomotive scheduling by computer. Proceedings of the British Joint Computer Conference. Institution of Electrical Engineers, Conference Publication no.19 (Eastbourne, 1966) p.31.

2. Wren, A. Bus scheduling: an interactive computer method. Transportation Planning and Technology 1 (1972) p.115.

3. Manington, P.D. and Wren, A. Experiences with a bus scheduling algorithm which saves vehicles. Presented at the Workshop on Automated Techniques for Scheduling of Vehicle Operators for Urban Public Transportation Services (Chicago, 1975).

4. Dickinson, R.W., Drynan, W.F. and Manington, P.D. The role of the systems department and the role of the operations management in introducing computer assistance to bus scheduling. Appearing in this volume (1981).

SERVICE 20   Fazakerley, Elmham Crescent – Aigburth Vale   via Black Bull, Spellow Lane, Whitechapel, Paradise Street, Parliament Street, Dingle

SERVICE 20B   Spellow Lane – Dingle   via Whitechapel, Paradise Street, Parliament Street

SERVICE 20E   Fazakerley, Elmham Crescent – Spellow Lane   via Black Bull

Service	20B	20B	20B	20	20	20	20	20	20	20	20	20	20E	20E
Fazakerley, Elmham Crescent	....	....	....	....	0826	1026	1226	1426	1626	1826	2026	2126	2129	2329
Black Bull	....	....	0618	0718	0834	1034	1234	1434	1634	1834	2034	2134	2137	2337
Spellow Lane	0513	0618	0718	0723	0845	1045	1245	1445	1645	1845	2045	2145	2148	2348
Whitechapel	0529	0634	0734	0739	0901	1101	1301	1501	1701	1901	2101	2201	....	....
Paradise Street, Park Lane	0530	0635	0735	0740	0902	1102	1302	1502	1702	1902	2102	2202	....	....
Parliament Street	0534	0639	0739	0744	0906	1106	1306	1506	1706	1906	2106	2206	....	....
Dingle	0542	0647	0747	0752	0914	1114	1314	1514	1714	1914	2114	2214	....	....
Aigburth Vale	....	....	....	0756	0918	1118	1318	1518	1718	1918	2118	2218	....	....
LAYOVER OR SLACK	3	3	3	26	4	4	4	4	4	4	4	4	OI	OI
RUNNING NO.	1X	1	2X	1	3	3	3	3	3	3	3	3	1G	4G

CODE:

G = BUS RETURNS TO GARAGE
I = JOURNEY HAS BEEN INSERTED BY THE COMPUTER
X = FIRST JOURNEY FOR THIS BUS

FIGURE 5. TIMETABLE.

SERVICE 264   YEOVIL, Bus Station - TAUNTON, Bus station   via Halfway House, Langfoot, Wrantage, Henlade

Including journeys on between

SERVICE 261   LANGFOOT   & TAUNTON, Bus station   via North Curry, Henlade

Service	264	261	264	264	261	264	264	264	264
		a			a				
YEOVIL, Bus Station...	0616	....	0900	1010	....	1230	1430	1630	....
YEOVIL, Kingston Bus Sh	0620	....	0904	1014	....	1234	1434	1634	....
MUDFORD ROAD...	0627	....	0911	1021	....	1241	1441	1641	....
HALFWAY HOUSE...	....	....	....	....	....	....	....	....	....
MONKTON ELMS...	....	....	....	....	....	....	....	....	....
LANGFOOT...	0726	0750	1010	1120	1115	1340	1540	1740	1840
NORTH CURRY...	....	0818	....	....	1143	....	....	....	....
WRANTAGE...	0748	....	1032	1142	....	1402	1602	1802	1902
HENLADE...	0754	0833	1038	1148	1158	1408	1608	1808	1908
TAUNTON, Bus station..	0806	0845	1050	1200	1210	1420	1620	1820	1920
LAYOVER OR SLACK	9	20	10	5	5	85	10	0	0
RUNNING NO.	1X	19X	5	12	22	34Z	19	1G	14G

CODE:

G = BUS RETURNS TO GARAGE
X = FIRST JOURNEY FOR THIS BUS
Z = FIRST JOURNEY FOR BUS WHICH NEXT RUNS DEAD
a = Starts from South Petherton, departing 30 minutes earlier

FIGURE 5A. TIMETABLE.

```
BUS    3
                    DEPARTS FROM  WALTON GARAGE              0804

Spellow Lane                0807I Fazakerley, Elmham Crescent 0826I 20.8
Fazakerley, Elmham Crescent 0826  Aigburth Vale               0918  20.1
Aigburth Vale               0922  Fazakerley, Elmham Crescent 1014  20A.2
Fazakerley, Elmham Crescent 1026  Aigburth Vale               1118  20.1
Aigburth Vale               1122  Fazakerley, Elmham Crescent 1214  20A.2
Fazakerley, Elmham Crescent 1226  Aigburth Vale               1318  20.1
Aigburth Vale               1322  Fazakerley, Elmham Crescent 1414  20A.2
Fazakerley, Elmham Crescent 1426  Aigburth Vale               1518  20.1
Aigburth Vale               1522  Fazakerley, Elmham Crescent 1614  20A.2
Fazakerley, Elmham Crescent 1626  Aigburth Vale               1718  20.1
Aigburth Vale               1722  Fazakerley, Elmham Crescent 1814  20A.2
Fazakerley, Elmham Crescent 1826  Aigburth Vale               1918  20.1
Aigburth Vale               1922  Fazakerley, Elmham Crescent 2014  20A.2
Fazakerley, Elmham Crescent 2026  Aigburth Vale               2118  20.1
Aigburth Vale               2122I Spellow Lane                2155I 20E.4

                    RETURNS TO   WALTON GARAGE               2158


BUS    4

                    DEPARTS FROM  WALTON GARAGE              2104

Spellow Lane                2107I Fazakerley, Elmham Crescent 2126I 20.8
Fazakerley, Elmham Crescent 2126  Aigburth Vale               2218  20.1
Aigburth Vale               2222I Field Lane, Valley Road     2319I 20A.2
DEAD RUN
Fazakerley, Elmham Crescent 2329I Spellow Lane                2348I 20E.5

                    RETURNS TO   WALTON GARAGE               2351
```

FIGURE 6. RUNNING BOARDS.

```
32F                 -FF
31E                E-EE                             -      E-
30D                D-DD                            D-DDD-DDD-
29C                C-CC                       C  CCC-CCC-CCC-C
28B                B-BB                      BBB-BBB-BBB-BBB-B
27A                A-AAA         AAA-     AA-AAA-AAA-AAA-AAA-A
26Z                Z-ZZZ-Z       ZZZ-ZZZ-ZZZ-ZZZ-ZZZ-ZZZ-ZZZ-ZZ
25Y               YY-YYY-YYY-YYY-YYY-YYY-YYY-YYY-YYY-YYY-YYY-YYY
24X               XX-XXX-XXX-XXX-XXX-XXX-XXX-XXX-XXX-XXX-XXX-XXX
23W               WW-WWW-WWW-WWW-WWW-WWW-WWW-WWW-WWW-WWW-WWW-WWW-
22V               VV-VVV-VVV-VVV-VVV-VVV-VVV-VVV-VVV-VVV-VVV-VVV-
21U              UUU-UUU-UUU-UUU-UUU-UUU-UUU-UUU-UUU-UUU-UUU-UUU-
20T              TTT-TTT-TTT-TTT-TTT-TTT-TTT-TTT-TTT-TTT-TTT-TTT-
19S              SSS-SSS-SSS-SSS-SSS-SSS-SSS-SSS-SSS-SSS-SSS-SSS-
18R              RRR-RRR-RRR-RRR-RRR-RRR-RRR-RRR-RRR-RRR-RRR-RRR-
17Q             -QQQ-QQQ-QQQ-QQQ-QQQ-QQQ-QQQ-QQQ-QQQ-QQQ-QQQ-QQQ-Q
16P             -PPP-PPP-PPP-PPP-PPP-PPP-PPP-PPP-PPP-PPP-PPP-PPP-P
15O             -OOO-OOO-OOO-OOO-OOO-OOO-OOO-OOO-OOO-OOO-OOO-OOO-O
14N             -NNN-NNN-NNN-NNN-NNN-NNN-NNN-NNN-NNN-NNN-NNN-NNN-N
13M             -MMM-MMM-MMM-MMM-MMM-MMM-MMM-MMM-MMM-MMM-MMM-MMM-MM
12L            L-LLL-LLL-LLL-LLL-LLL-LLL-LLL-LLL-LLL-LLL-LLL-LLL-LL
11K            K-KKK-KKK-KKK-KKK-KKK-KKK-KKK-KKK-KKK-KKK-KKK-KKK-KK
10J            J-JJJ-JJJ-JJJ-JJJ-JJJ-JJJ-JJJ-JJJ-JJJ-JJJ-JJJ-JJJ-JJJ
 9I            I-III-III-III-III-III-III-III-III-III-III-III-III-III-
 8H            H-HHH-HHH-HHH-HHH-HHH-HHH-HHH-HHH-HHH-HHH-HHH-HHH-HHH-
 7G           GG-GGG-GGG-GGG-GGG-GGG-GGG-GGG-GGG-GGG-GGG-GGG-GGG-GGG-GGG-
 6F           FF-FFF-FFF-FFF-FFF-FFF-FFF-FFF-FFF-FFF-FFF-FFF-FFF-FFF-FFF-FFF-
 5E          EEE-EEE-EEE-EEE-EEE-EEE-EEE-EEE-EEE-EEE-EEE-EEE-EEE-EEE-EEE-EEE-EEE
 4D          DDD-DDD-DDD-DDD-DDD-DDD-DDD-DDD-DDD-DDD-DDD-DDD-DDD-DDD-DDD-DDD-DDD-
 3C          CCC-CCC-CCC-CCC-CCC-CCC-CCC-CCC-CCC-CCC-CCC-CCC-CCC-CCC-CCC-CCC-CCC-
 2B        B-BBB-BBB-BBB-BBB-BBB-BBB-BBB-BBB-BBB-BBB-BBB-BBB-BBB-BBB-BBB-BBB-BBB-B
 1A     A-AAA-AAA-AAA-AAA-AAA-AAA-AAA-AAA-AAA-AAA-AAA-AAA-AAA-AAA-AAA-AAA-AAA-AAA-AA
    4.  5.  6.  7.  8.  9. 10. 11. 12. 13. 14. 15. 16. 17. 18. 19. 20. 21. 22. 23. 24.  1.
```

THE FIRST PORTION OF EVERY HOUR IS REPRESENTED BY A DASH

FIGURE 7. BUS HISTOGRAM.

TOTAL BUS TIME: 364 HOURS, 12 MINUTES

USING THE GIVEN INFORMATION:
MAXIMUM AVERAGE PLATFORM TIME =   7.00
MAX. LENGTH OF FIRST STRETCH OF EARLY DUTY =   4.30
MAX. LENGTH OF LAST STRETCH OF LATE DUTY =   4.30
LATEST TIME OFF BUS FOR SPLIT DUTIES = 1930
LATEST TIME OFF BUS FOR MIDDLE DUTIES = 2030
NUMBER OF MIDDLE DUTIES WHICH CAN BE SAVED BY CHAINING =   1

THE FOLLOWING IS AN INDICATION OF THE DUTIES REQUIRED:
   14   EARLY DUTIES
    7   LATE DUTIES
   18   SPLIT DUTIES
    6   MIDDLE DUTIES
    1   DAY DUTIES
    7   ADDITIONAL DUTIES ARE REQUIRED TO BRING THE AVERAGE PLATFORM TIME
          TO AN ACCEPTABLE LEVEL — IT WOULD OTHERWISE HAVE BEEN 7.55

THE TOTAL NUMBER OF DUTIES IS THUS LIKELY TO BE   53
  WITH AN AVERAGE PLATFORM TIME OF 6.52

FIGURE 8.   CREW ESTIMATE.

Computer Scheduling of Public Transport
A. Wren (ed.)
© *North-Holland Publishing Company, 1981*

AUTOMATING TRIP SCHEDULING
AND OPTIMAL VEHICLE ASSIGNMENTS

Dr. Ian T. Keaveny and Dr. Stephen Burbeck

SAGE Management Consultants
Toronto, Canada and
San Francisco, California

An interactive trip and vehicle scheduling system which has
been used successfully at a number of transit properties in
North America is described. The user may converse with the
computer in a personalized manner by selecting from a large
number of available commands. Vehicle assignment may be
performed either optimally, or by a sequential process similar
to that conventionally performed manually. The immediate
response of the on-line feature together with the system
versatility permit the scheduler readily to examine a large
variety of options.

OVERVIEW

The application of computers to the scheduling process has received a great deal
of attention in recent years. This is not surprising since a large portion of the
scheduler's work involves time consuming and repetitive tasks that lend themselves
to computer application. The generation of trips according to a constant headway
or frequency, and the summary of statistical schedule information are typical
examples of this laborious work. However, an equally important aspect of the
scheduler's function does not lend itself to any automated procedure and comes
only from years of experience. For example, the personalized knowledge of a route
and the feasible variance in the running times often enable the scheduler to
selectively alter the scheduled trip in order to optimize vehicle requirements.

With these criteria in mind, a fully interactive, on-line, trip and vehicle
scheduling system called the MINI-SCHEDULER has been developed and applied by SAGE
Management Consultants. Since many schedulers have little or no computer
background, any successful computerized system must be easy to use and communicate
in a language that is familiar to the scheduler.

The Mini-Scheduler permits the user to converse with the computer in a
personalized manner by selecting from a large number of available commands. These
commands not only facilitate schedule generation but also provide all the tools
necessary for vehicle assignment. The vehicle assignments may be performed
optimally with or without user intervention and according to various constraints
including any layover and deadhead restrictions. In addition, the immediate
response of the 'on-line' feature, together with the system versatility, permit
the scheduler readily to examine a large variety of 'what if' questions with the
capability of creating responsive and efficient schedules.

This paper describes the conceptual and operational features of the system.

BACKGROUND

Early efforts to computerize the scheduling process were often frustrated. This frustration was primarily due to the unfamiliarity with transit scheduling operations by the data processing industry, and the absence of computer sophistication among skilled schedulers. As the data processing specialist became more familiar with the scheduling process and the scheduler began to appreciate the potential benefit of the use of computers, there resulted an increasing number of software packages for transit scheduling.

In order to determine those scheduling activities that are best suited for computer application, it is important to have an appreciation of the overall process.

There are, in general, five major scheduling activities:

- Planning
- Schedule writing / Vehicle assignment
- Run-cutting
- Off-day assignment
- Sign-up

MANUAL SCHEDULING

The first stage in the scheduling process is the planning of new or revised service. Typically the transit planning activities include such tasks as passenger count checks and running time checks. The resulting analyses are then usually translated into service requirements.

The service requirements are designed to meet passenger demand or expectations. However, each transit operation has real constraints in the form of equipment, manpower, and money. In addition, the property must respond to social needs so that it is necessary to make policy decisions as to what the actual level of service will be. This service definition is in the form of routes, headways and hours of service.

The next stage of the scheduling process, schedule writing, is to construct trip schedules which will provide, as closely as possible, the required level of service. The scheduler uses skill and experience to construct even headways as well as realistic running and recovery times. In the manual process, these schedules are generally created in such a manner that one trip connects to the next. The process results in the creation of the vehicle assignment simultaneously with the schedule generation. The assignment of vehicle blocks to trips is thus often an integral part of the scheduling task. The trips are generated based upon the movement of a vehicle throughout the day and the vehicle's activity is completely determined as the trips are generated.

Run-cutting essentially consists of determining driver workloads from the previously determined vehicle workloads. The assignment of drivers' work to the vehicles, according to the constraints of the union contract, is perhaps the most complex of the scheduling tasks, and requires considerable skill and expertise on the part of the scheduler.

Having produced daily crews to cover the schedules, it is necessary to allocate days-off to each man's weekly work so that as many five-day crews are produced as possible whilst catering to preferences such as weekends off.

The final activity is the signing up of individual drivers to the crews, usually on the basis of seniority. In general, the resulting sign-up is used as input to the payroll system.

This completes the primary sequence of activities in the transit scheduling process, from planning through to implementation. Other related activities include providing timetables (headway sheets), producing vehicle paddles, preparing pull-out logs, mileage reports and public timetables, rostering of the actual buses to the vehicle schedules, monitoring the system to provide input to the analysis of existing and future service, and the preparation of management summaries.

COMPUTERIZED SCHEDULING

As may be appreciated from the above, a large portion of the scheduler's work is involved in time-consuming, laborious tasks. This detracts from the scheduler's primary goal: namely, to create, review and optimize a schedule. In addition, the large volume of standard reports and analyses that must be routinely prepared at each stage of the process places very real yet unfortunate time constraints on the scheduler. Consequently, one of the first aims of any computerized system must be to remove the drudgery from the scheduling process.

Historically, there are two approaches to computerized scheduling. In the first approach, which is widely adopted, the scheduler does not access the computer directly. Instead, the finished hand-written schedule is presented to the data processing personnel for input to the computer. The reason for this appears to be that the time and effort required to train the schedulers to operate the system with all that is involved in the way of punched cards and job control language, precludes their use of the system directly. The problem of encoding the schedule, even by trained personnel, should not, however, be diminished. Not only is it time consuming and laborious but often leads to data transposition errors which may result in even more delays.

Once the schedule is input, the various reports and statistical summaries may readily be produced and this does constitute a definite time saving. Dependent on the state of the input schedule data, a number of available software products may now be used to perform the vehicle and/or driver assignment.

Whereas overall time savings may be realized by such an approach, the scheduler is isolated from the actual operation and receives the results in a series of printed outputs. Furthermore, as schedule modifications occur these too must be converted from the scheduler's format into a form that can be used by the computer system. In many cases, although the actual schedule change is trivial, the resultant impact on the schedule data file may be extensive.

The whole problem of data file maintenance is especially critical for larger properties. Maintaining the schedule data base for a small transit system cannot be compared to the task of maintaining one for a transit system with say, 1000 or more vehicles. However, this encoding advantage is somewhat offset by the fact that the smaller properties do not generally have the depth of data processing personnel.

A recent survey of a number of North American transit properties in the use of the batch-oriented scheduling package RUCUS perhaps provides the best insight into the stated needs of the scheduler. The table below shows the outcome of the ranking of the identified problem areas by the transit properties. The difference in the relative importance as expressed by the two groups clearly shows that the user of RUCUS views the data input and maintenance as an important deficiency, whereas the scheduler with no computerized scheduling experience, and hence no awareness of the problems, sees the schedule generation as one of the areas of most benefit.

PRIORITY RANKING OF IMPROVEMENTS

ITEM	OPERATORS WITH RUCUS EXPERIENCE		OPERATORS WITHOUT RUCUS EXPERIENCE	
	Rank	Score	Rank	Score
1. Data handling and file control tools	1	31.5	3	18
2. Program Maint. support	2	29	4	18
3. Run-cutting	3	28.5	11	2
4. Vehicle assignment editing	4	15	7	7
5. Multiple garage capability	5	14	8	6
6. Comprehensive reporting	6	13	9	4
7. Schedule generation	7	12	2	19
8. Interfaces to other components	8	6	5	15
9. Personnel planning	9	3	6	9
10. Aid in data processing orientation	10	2	10	3
11. Pre-implementation analysis	11	1	1	44

NOTE: Score is derived by summing the rank numbers assigned by each operator.

CONCLUSIONS

Based upon this and other analyses it was felt that for any computerized system to be accepted by the scheduling personnel the following criteria must be met.

The system must :

- converse with the scheduler in a free-form, English-like language which uses familiar scheduling concepts and terminology,
- accept schedule data and modifications simply and quickly,
- manipulate schedules faster than can be done manually,
- display schedule data in a number of ways (headway sheets, vehicle blocks, and driver shifts),
- provide data overlap with other scheduling components - run-cutting, report generators, etc.,
- accept data from other systems,
- perform edit and syntactical checks on all user transactions to ensure total data integrity,
- be a multi-user system,
- provide all the necessary security controls,
- provide extensive data file maintenance.

As a consequence, it was felt that a more responsive approach to the scheduling needs would best be provided by an on-line interactive system rather than the batch-orientated approach discussed above. It is the purpose of this paper to present this approach by describing the main features of the Mini-Scheduler.

MINI-SCHEDULER

Specifically, the Mini-Scheduler, which was designed primarily to aid the scheduler in the writing and vehicle assignment aspect of the scheduling process, was developed over a period of three years. It is the result of an exhaustive analysis of the scheduling practices in a number of large and small transit properties.

One of the most frustrating problems encountered in this analysis was the lack of commonality in the scheduling terminology. For this reason an alphabetical glossary of all the schedule-related terms appearing in this paper is presented in Appendix A. These terms were taken, in part, from a report sponsored by the Urban Mass Transportation Administration of the U.S. Department of Transportation (UMTA-WA-11-0005-76-1).

BASIC MINI-SCHEDULER CONCEPTS

The Mini-Scheduler is a unique software tool designed for building and maintaining schedules and other related transit data. It permits the user to develop accurate and efficient schedules quickly and perform the optimal vehicle assignment. It provides extensive error checking that ensures the schedules will be consistent with the established criteria for running times, deadhead times, layover times and other operating policies. Typing, edit checking and re-typing are virtually eliminated, thereby reducing clerical and scheduling costs. Because of the in-built database handling techniques, the generated schedule data is made readily accessible to other applications.

As mentioned earlier one of the basic premises in the development of the Mini-Scheduler was to provide the user with all the capabilities necessary to duplicate the scheduling techniques. This duplication is in the form of <u>commands</u> and <u>documents</u>.

COMMANDS

The commands are easy to learn and in free form. Each command must begin with a valid command word and may be followed by one or more keywords and/or data values. Connective words may be used to make the command seem more natural.

Each command is thoroughly checked for syntactical errors and the keyword data values are checked for validity and consistency. If an error is detected, that portion of the command is highlighted and an error message results. The user now has the option of dynamically correcting the problem or aborting the command.

Analogous to the manual procedure, information maintained by the Mini-Scheduler system is presented to the user in the form of a document. Each document consists of rows and columns of data and may be viewed on a video display unit (screen). The Mini-Scheduler screen is divided into three distinct areas — STATUS, COMMUNICATION and DOCUMENT.

The <u>status</u> area provides the user with all the information necessary to categorize completely the currently displayed document — number of document rows, number of document columns, the document name and any associated document keywords. A document keyword is that label or index that is used to identify the document uniquely. For example, asking the system to display a headway sheet is not sufficient. The user must specify the line and service of the headway sheet that is desired. Here, line and service would be the keywords for the schedule document.

The <u>communication</u> area is used to display the user command that was typed on the
keyboard.   It is also used to display any system messages (error, warning and
information).

The <u>document</u> area is used to display the document itself. The first three rows of
the document area give the column number and the column heading and the remaining
rows contain the document data. Because of the variable size of a document and
the limited size of a screen, it is not possible, in general, to display on one
screen the complete contents of a document. For this reason the user is provided
with a number of 'display commands'.   These commands are used to control the
presentation of the document data on the screen. They are:

```
UP     - to move the screen up the document
DOWN   - to move the screen down the document
LEFT   - to move the screen to the left on the document
RIGHT  - to move the screen to the right on the document
TOP    - to move the screen to the top of a document
BOTTOM - to move the screen to the bottom of a document
SET    - select specific rows and/or columns to be displayed
FIND   - to select specific rows based on certain data criteria
PRINT  - to print the contents of a document on a printer
```

With these commands the user has the ability to change the screen contents to a
more convenient and familiar format.

DOCUMENTS

All the user transactions take place on a document.   In order to display a
document, the user inputs the GET command followed by the document name and any
associated keywords. If any data necesary to categorize the required document is
missing from the command, the system will automatically ask the user for the
missing values.

The Mini-Scheduler documents fall into one of three categories:

>   - System
>   - Supporting
>   - Scheduling

The <u>system</u> documents, which are not normally available to the scheduler, contain
all the information necessary to translate the input commands, define the user's
security profile, and retrieve and display a document.   It is on the system
documents that any property-dependent customization is achieved.   Here the
commands and keywords can be made more meaningful; the document names can be
altered to duplicate the standard nomenclature and the interrelationship of the
scheduling documents and their associated keywords defined. In addition to these
cosmetic changes, a more far reaching and important flexibility is provided by the
system documents. For each document available to the user there is an associated
data file and <u>document description.</u> The data file contains all the document data
and the document description describes how each data record is to be displayed on
the screen.

One of the most important aspects of the scheduling system is the ability to
dynamically change both the format and the content of a user document. This is
achieved via the document description.   Each row of the document description
completely defines each column on a document. It contains such information as the
column heading, the data type, the width of the column, the output format of the

data and the field in the data file where the column information is stored. It is possible, therefore, by editing the contents of a document description to re-define completely a user document. The only restriction is that any data that is to be displayed on the document must be contained in the associated file. In some cases, for example, the data file will contain elements that would not normally be displayed and thus have not been included in the document description. However, by judiciously adding a row to this document description to include the characteristics of this additional data, the extra column may now be included in the displayed document.

It is the schedule <u>supporting</u> documents that contain all the auxiliary information necessary to perform the edit checks that guarantee schedule integrity. There are four major supporting documents - NODES, PATTERNS, RUNTIMES and DEADHEAD. The Nodes document defines for each line all the time points. Each time point or node is represented by a description, a node label and a node direction. The label permits the user to provide specific significance to a particular node. For example, a node may be labelled 'T' for terminal, 'R' for relief and 'M' for the maximum load point.

Based upon the content of the Nodes document, the next logical step is to define all the permitted patterns. Each unique pattern in contained on the <u>Patterns</u> document and is assigned a unique label or name. The <u>Runtimes</u> document contains all the revenue node-to-node running times (broken down by time of day) and the <u>Deadhead</u> document contains all the non-revenue node-to-node running times (broken down by time of day). The creation of the Nodes document is essential to schedule generation. However, the Patterns, Runtimes and Deadhead documents are optional. Their presence, which does represent an initial investment, guarantees full schedule integrity since no trip can be introduced into the system which is in violation of their content.

Finally, there are two documents on which the user may schedule trips - TRIPS and BLOCKS. These documents represent alternative ways of looking at the same data. The Trips document displays the scheduled trips sorted by the time at the maximum load point, whereas the Blocks document displays the scheduled trips sorted by time at the first revenue node within block number. The Trips document is essentially the Headway sheet or timetable and the Blocks document shows, in sequential document rows those trips that are serviced by the same vehicle.

Each user of the scheduling system is assigned a security profile. It is this profile that determines exactly the functions that can be performed. The profile determines not only the commands accessible to each user but also the documents that may be obtained.

SCHEDULE GENERATION

Assuming a schedule is to be generated with full trip integrity, the minimum information required to add a trip to the Trips or Blocks document is a pattern identification code and the time at a trip node (generally maximum load point). For example, a command of the type:

                    ADD PATTERN X-6 MLP 700A

initiates the following process.

The pattern number (X-6) is matched against all the valid patterns appearing on the Patterns document. If successful, this match will result in a complete definition of the nodes comprising pattern X-6. A similar search of the Runtimes document is made matching the pattern code and the time at which the trip is to be

created (700A). This results in all the component node-to-node running times and
hence a complete trip description. The created trip then appears on the screen
sorted into any previously existing trips by the time at the maximum load point.

If there is any inconsistency found either in the command syntax or in the
appropriate supporting information, an error message will be displayed enabling
the user to correct the mistake or abort the command. Thus, for example, if an
illegal pattern is requested or the time at the maximum load point does not
correspond to a valid running time range, an error message results to indicate
this.

The simple 'ADD' command does, therefore, initiate an intensive 'behind the
scenes' edit check. (In the case where full trip integrity is not required and
the Patterns and Routes are not present, the user must specify all the component
trip times).

By now using the BUILD, SHIFT, CHANGE and DELETE commands, a normal schedule may
be generated rapidly. The BUILD command will automatically create a specified
number of trips with a defined headway at a particular node. Here the user simply
specifies the base trip to be used together with the required headway. The number
of trips to be created is either input explicitly or using a 'time of last trip'
value. As the time at the headway node changes from one running-time period to
another, any changes in the composite node-to-node running times are automatically
reflected. The SHIFT command may be used to shift either complete or partial
trips and/or blocks forward or backward in time; the CHANGE command performs any
necessary editing; and the DELETE command removes unwanted document rows (trips).

VEHICLE ASSIGNMENT

Once the schedule has been built, the problem now reduces to one of forming the
trips into vehicle blocks. This is achieved by using the SOLVE command.
Associated with each generated trip is a maximum and minimum layover value. These
specify respectively the maximum and minimum layover (recovery) time that must be
applied in order to make a valid vehicle connection (hook). In addition to these
restrictions, other constraints of deadhead and interlining may be dynamically
entered on the command itself. Below is presented a list of all the available
options:

1. Target layover - used to specify the desired layover per trip
    connection. If this value is not input, the minimum layover value is
    assumed.

2. Weight Option - when two equivalent hooks have been formed the user may
    specify the system to take either the one that is above or the one that
    is below the target layover value.

3. Intermixing - the amount of interlining and/or deadheading, and/or the
    permissible node-to-node connections may be specified.

4. Vehicle Requirements - the user may specify the maximum number of
    vehicles permitted. If this number is insufficient the unhooked trips
    will be flagged.

A typical SOLVE command would take the form:

                      SOLVE TLO 10, LINE 1,2

Here, the user is asking the system to determine the vehicle requirements permitting the scheduled trips for lines 1 and 2 to intermix as required subject to a target layover (TLO) of 10 minutes. The system will automatically solve the problem and display, for the scheduler's approval, the vehicle requirements and solution statistics (total layover, total deadhead, average layover per hook). If the solution is acceptable to the scheduler, the document will be updated and displayed on the screen, reflecting the created blocks. The user now has the ability to intervene manually and make any necessary adjustments to the solution. Alternatively, preferred hooks may be specified manually prior to an automatic solve and will be retained in the blocking process. It is important to remember that at any stage in the scheduling process the user may obtain a hard copy of any document. This provides the user with the ability to study any schedule at leisure before proceeding.

So far we have only dealt with the general form of the SOLVE command. The actual mechanism used in obtaining the solution has not been discussed. There are two distinct mechanisms in which the hooks can be obtained - consecutive and optimal. The consecutive solution is perhaps more naive yet in many respects more closely resembles the manual process. Here the first scheduled trip is chosen and all the potential hooking mates for this trip are found. Each potential hook is assigned a cost based on the input command parameters and the one with the least cost is chosen. The chosen trip now becomes the source of a similar search for its mate. This process is continued until there are no connections found for the last trip. The process is now repeated for the next block and so on until all the trips have been assigned a vehicle. The important point to note in this mechanism is that once a connection (hook) has been made it will never be undone. For most schedules, this does not represent a problem since the trips were generated by the scheduler with a particular blocking scheme in mind.

The optimum procedure is very different. Here, a number of 'arcs' are created between all the possible connecting trips. Each arc is assigned a cost, based on its desirability or otherwise as determined by the input SOLVE parameters. The whole network is now solved optimally, guaranteeing a minimum <u>total</u> system cost. The algorithm used to solve the network and incorporated in the Mini-Scheduler was developed by Gordon Bradley, Gerald Brown and Glenn Graves (Management Science, Vol 24, No. 1, Sept. 1977).

According to these authors:

- The solutions produced are absolutely free of rounding error.
- As of copyright date, it is the world's fastest known code for large minimum cost network problems.
- The algorithm cannot cycle in the presence of primal degeneracy - terminal solution is guaranteed.
- The algorithm uses much less memory for execution than any known competing method.

The ease with which the scheduler can generate and modify schedules and determine the resultant vehicle requirements on the Mini-Scheduler provides a whole new dimension to scheduling. It is now possible for many hooking schemes to be examined readily and to obtain the answer to a large variety of 'what if' questions. The effect of layover, deadheading and interlining on the vehicle requirements may be answered almost instantaneously and the possibility of schedule optimization becomes a reality.

In addition to the schedule commands that have been presented so far, there are a number of other commands that may be used (see Appendix B). The GENERATE command permits the user automatically to create a series of connected trips to form a vehicle block. Here the composite patterns together with any required layover are input and the trips comprising the block will be generated and displayed according to the trip times (and deadhead) specified in the relevant supporting documents.

The REGEN command will automatically update (regenerate) a schedule according to any updates in the supporting documents. Thus the deletion and insertion of nodes or the redefinition of a pattern or running time does not necessarily mean that the schedule has to be re-written.

The EXTRACT command is used to extract from a schedule all the unique running times and patterns. In addition, the data required to perform the run cut, namely the relief point nodes and times, may be extracted for input into any required run cutting module.

Finally, the LOAD and UNLOAD commands permit the scheduling document to be loaded or unloaded respectively from an external data file. A sample run of the Mini-Scheduler is illustrated in Appendix C.

SUMMARY

The Mini-Scheduler has been used successfully at a number of transit properties in North America. Not only does it result in substantial time savings in the overall schedule data flow, but the ability readily to examine numerous vehicle assignments results in a much more critical schedule analysis. An obvious extension to the capabilities described in this paper would be the incorporation of schedule planning and run-cutting modules. In fact this process is already under development.

As more user commands are identified, they may be readily incorporated because of the modular nature of the software. Finally, since all the Mini-Scheduler software was written in ANSI Fortran and uses few machine-dependent routines, it may be readily converted to operate on almost any computer.

APPENDIX A

Glossary of Terms

ARC: A possible connection (Hook) between the end of one revenue-producing trip and the beginning of another trip.

BLOCK: A collection of scheduled trips serviced by a single vehicle.

BLOCK NUMBER: A number assigned to each block.

DEADHEAD: Also known as non-revenue or out-of-service time/miles. The vehicle travel time/miles between time points when not in service.

DIRECTION: Specific one-way movement along a line.

DIVISION: A group of lines that operate out of a common depot or garage.

HOOK: The association of one revenue trip to another revenue trip in the formation of a vehicle block.

LAYOVER TIME: The time a vehicle has between the completion of one trip and the beginning of another within the same block. Sometimes called recovery time and allows for any tightness in the schedule.

LINE: A series of time points delineating the movement of vehicles in service. A line may have several variations, or patterns.

LINK: An arc existing between any two nodes.

MAX LOAD PT.: The stop on a transit line at which the passenger volume is the greatest.

NODE: A unique location in space which may or may not be located on a transit line.

PATTERN: Specific time point to time point route along a line which a vehicle follows on a particular trip.

RECOVERY: See layover time.

RUNTIME: The time required to travel from one timing point to another. It generally varies dependent on the time of day.

ROUTE: See line.

SCHEDULE: A chronological listing of transit services on one line which shows service provided at various timing points along the line.

SERVICE: A type of schedule operation - i.e., weekday, weekend.

TIMING POINT: A specific location along a transit line at which vehicle departure/arrival times are recorded.

TRANSIT STOP: A specific location along a transit line at which the vehicle stops for passengers.

TRIP: A one-way movement of a vehicle in service along a line between terminal points (end points).

APPENDIX B

List of Mini-Scheduler Commands

COMMAND   DESCRIPTION

HELP   Obtain help in the use of a specific command

ASSIGN   Used to create user synonym

ADD   Add a row to a document

CHANGE   Change a data element(s)

DELETE   Delete a row from a document

GET   Display a document on the screen

FIND   Find a data element in the specified row(s) or column(s)

SET   Set specific rows and columns on a document

LEFT   Move the screen to the left of the document

RIGHT   Move the screen to the right of the document

UP   Move the screen up the document

DOWN   Move the screen down the document

TOP   Display the top row of the document on the top row
           of the screen

BOTTOM   Display the bottom row of the document on the top row
           of the screen

LOAD   Load a document from an external file

PURGE   Purge a document

BUILD   Build a series of trips from a base trip

SHIFT   Shift a trip or block

TIME   Change the time display (APX/seconds, military)

GENERATE   Generate a complete block according to specified patterns

VALIDATE   Do not check the current command against the contents
           of the supporting documents

PRINT   Print the contents of a document

SOLVE   Create vehicle blocks

UNHOOK   Unhook a block (total or partially)

HOOK   Manually hook trips

EXTRACT   Extract from the trips document the composite pattern
            running times and data required for run cutting

REGEN   Regenerate a complete schedule based on updated
            supporting information

UNLOAD   Unload a document into an external file

TRACE   Produce a trace of the current scheduling session

DUPE   Duplicate one row of a document into another

LOCK   Lock a document preventing update

FILL   Facilitates the input of the running times

INPUT   Used to create all the time periods for the run times
            document

APPENDIX C

SAMPLE SCHEDULING SESSION

In the following pages, there is presented a sample scheduling session.   Because
of size constraints, it is by necessity brief and obviously does not show all the
capabilities.   Furthermore, the simplicity of the schedule should not distract the
user from the concepts that are presented.

The output for this session was obtained using the TRACE feature of the
Mini-Scheduler.   Here all screen transactions are automatically directed to an
associated line printer.


```
SAGE MINI-SCHEDULER    DOCUMENT : NODES    SIZE :  8  8    USER : SAGE01
LINE:DOWNTOWN  SER  SATURDAY
--------------------------------------------------------------------------
?  GET DOCUMENT NODES LINE DOWNTOWN


--------------------------------------------------------------------------
 01   -02-   -03-   -04-   -06-   -07-
ROW   NODE   NODE   NODE   DIR    NAME
      NUM    ABBR   LABL          ABBR
0001 1001   1ST    T         0    1ST LANE
0002 1002   2ND    M         0    2ND LANE
0003 1003   3RD              0    3RD LANE
0004 1004   4TH    T         0    4TH LANE
0005 1004   4TH    T         1    LANE 4TH
0006 1003   3RD              1    LANE 3RD
0007 1002   2ND    M         1    LANE 2ND
0008 1001   1ST    T         1    LANE 1ST
```


The user (SAGE01) asks the system to display the current contents of the
Nodes document.   There are 8 rows (nodes) and 8 columns in this document as
indicated by the two values associated with the SIZE keyword.   As may be
seen, not all the columns are displayed (5 and 8 are missing).   The actual
default columns that will be displayed are pre-determined by the user.

The second row in the status area of the screen displays the current keyword
values as input in the user's last session — the active keywords are
identified by a colon (:).

For each node (row) there is defined a node number, an abbreviated node
description (see Blocks document), a node label, a node direction, and a node
name.   The rows of this document would be input using the ADD, DUPE, and
CHANGE commands.

```
SAGE MINI-SCHEDULER    DOCUMENT : PATTERNS      SIZE :  4  14    USER : SAGE01
LINE:DOWNTOWN  SER  SATURDAY
-------------------------------------------------------------------------------
?  GET DOCUMENT PATTERNS

-------------------------------------------------------------------------------
```

01 ROW	-02- PAT NUM	-05- DIR	-06- MILE AGE	-07- 1ST LANE	-08- 2ND LANE	-09- 3RD LANE	-10- 4TH LANE	-11- LANE 4TH	-12- LANE 3RD	-13- LANE 2ND	-14- LANE 1ST
0001	101	0	12	1	1	1	1				
0002	102	0	12	1	1		1				
0003	1101	1	12					1	1	1	1
0004	1102	1	12					1		1	1

There are four patterns. Note the column headings (7 - 14) are taken directly from the Nodes document. A '1' under a timing point signifies that the pattern goes through that node. Each pattern is assigned a unique number or name and will be identified by this label in the trip generation.

```
SAGE MINI-SCHEDULER    DOCUMENT : RUNTIMES      SIZE : 12  16    USER : SAGE01
LINE:DOWNTOWN  SER :SATURDAY
-------------------------------------------------------------------------------
?  GET DOCUMENT RUNTIMES SER SATURDAY

-------------------------------------------------------------------------------
```

01 ROW	-02- FROM TIME	-03- TO TIME	-04- PAT- NUM	-09- 1ST LANE	-10- 2ND LANE	-11- 3RD LANE	-12- 4TH LANE	-13- LANE 4TH	-14- LANE 3RD	-15- LANE 2ND	-16- LANE 1ST
0001	100A	700A	101	10	14	36	-1				
0002	700A	900A	101	12	16	35	-1				
0003	900A	100X	101	10	14	36	-1				
0004	100A	700A	102	10	48		-1				
0005	700A	900A	102	12	49		-1				
0006	900A	100X	102	10	48		-1				
0007	100A	700A	1101					36	14	10	-1
0008	700A	900A	1101					35	16	12	-1
0009	900A	100X	1101					36	14	10	-1
0010	100A	700A	1102					48		10	-1
0011	700A	900A	1102					49		12	-1
0012	900A	100X	1102					48		10	-1

For each pattern there is provision on this document to input, for as many time periods as necessary, the individual node-to-node running times. In this example there are three time breakdowns for each pattern (100A-700A, 700A-900A, 900A-100X). Referring to row 1, between 100A and 700A any trip generated for pattern 101 takes 10 minutes to travel from 1ST LANE to 2ND LANE, 14 minutes to travel from 2ND LANE to 3RD LANE, and 36 minutes to travel from 3RD LANE to 4TH LANE.

```
SAGE MINI-SCHEDULER      DOCUMENT : TRIPS          SIZE :  1  20     USER : SAGE01
LINE:DOWNTOWN   SER :SATURDAY
--------------------------------------------------------------------------------
?  ADD 101 MLP  530A


--------------------------------------------------------------------------------
 01   -05-  -13-  -14-  -15-  -16-  -17-  -18-  -19-  -20-
ROW   PAT-  1ST   2ND   3RD   4TH   LANE  LANE  LANE  LANE
      NUM   LANE  LANE  LANE  LANE  4TH   3RD   2ND   1ST
0001   101  520A  530A  544A  620A
```

The first trip is added to the Trips document. The pattern is 101 and the
time at the maximum load point (MLP) is 530A. The maximum load point was
defined by the label 'M' in column 4 of the Nodes document.   The previously
defined routeing for pattern 101 together with the running times is
sufficient to define the trip. This trip is added to the document and
displayed on the screen.


```
SAGE MINI-SCHEDULER      DOCUMENT : TRIPS          SIZE : 20  20     USER : SAGE01
LINE:DOWNTOWN   SER :SATURDAY
--------------------------------------------------------------------------------
?  BUILD HEADWAY 60  NUM  19  COL  14


--------------------------------------------------------------------------------
 01   -05-   -13-   -14-   -15-   -16-  -17-  -18-  -19-  -20-
ROW   PAT-   1ST    2ND    3RD    4TH   LANE  LANE  LANE  LANE
      NUM    LANE   LANE   LANE   LANE  4TH   3RD   2ND   1ST
0001   101   520A   530A   544A   620A
0002   101   620A   630A   644A   720A
0003   101   718A   730A   746A   821A
0004   101   818A   830A   846A   921A
0005   101   920A   930A   944A  1020A
0006   101  1020A  1030A  1044A  1120A
0007   101  1120A  1130A  1144A  1220P
0008   101  1220P  1230P  1244P   120P
0009   101   120P   130P   144P   220P
0010   101   220P   230P   244P   320P
0011   101   320P   330P   344P   420P
0012   101   420P   430P   444P   520P
0013   101   520P   530P   544P   620P
0014   101   620P   630P   644P   720P
```

Using the previously added trip, the user wishes to add 19 more related trips
separated by a headway of 60 minutes. This headway is to be maintained at
2nd lane. Note as the headway node passes the running time boundary (700A)
the trip times are automatically adjusted.

```
SAGE MINI-SCHEDULER    DOCUMENT : TRIPS        SIZE : 21  20    USER : SAGE01
LINE:DOWNTOWN  SER :SATURDAY
-------------------------------------------------------------------------------
?  ADD 102 * 600A

-------------------------------------------------------------------------------
 01   -05-  -13-  -14-  -15-  -16-  -17-  -18-  -19-  -20-
ROW   PAT-  1ST   2ND   3RD   4TH   LANE  LANE  LANE  LANE
      NUM   LANE  LANE  LANE  LANE  4TH   3RD   2ND   1ST
0001  101   520A  530A  544A  620A
0002  102   550A  600A        648A
0003  101   620A  630A  644A  720A
0004  101   718A  730A  746A  821A
0005  101   818A  830A  846A  921A
0006  101   920A  930A  944A 1020A
0007  101  1020A 1030A 1044A 1120A
0008  101  1120A 1130A 1144A 1220P
0009  101  1220P 1230P 1244P  120P
0010  101   120P  130P  144P  220P
0011  101   220P  230P  244P  320P
0012  101   320P  330P  344P  420P
0013  101   420P  430P  444P  520P
0014  101   520P  530P  544P  620P
```

A trip for pattern 102 is now added and displayed. Note that this trip is automatically added in the correct headway sequence, sorted by the time at the maximum load point. The user would now build the requisite number of trips by specifying row 2 as the base trip.

```
SAGE MINI-SCHEDULER    DOCUMENT : TRIPS          SIZE : 78  20     USER : SAGE01
LINE:DOWNTOWN   SER :SATURDAY
--------------------------------------------------------------------------------
?

--------------------------------------------------------------------------------
 01   -05-   -13-   -14-   -15-   -16-   -17-   -18-   -19-   -20-
ROW   PAT-   1ST    2ND    3RD    4TH    LANE   LANE   LANE   LANE
      NUM    LANE   LANE   LANE   LANE   4TH    3RD    2ND    1ST
0001  101    520A   530A   544A   620A
0002 1101                                440A   516A   530A   540A
0003  102    550A   600A          648A
0004 1102                                512A          600A   610A
0005  101    620A   630A   644A   720A
0006 1101                                540A   616A   630A   640A
0007  102    648A   700A          749A
0008 1102                                611A          700A   712A
0009  101    718A   730A   746A   821A
0010 1101                                639A   714A   730A   742A
0011  102    748A   800A          849A
0012 1102                                711A          800A   812A
0013  101    818A   830A   846A   921A
0014 1101                                739A   814A   830A   842A
```

In a manner similar to the previous two screens, the entire schedule is built. By using the SHIFT and CHANGE commands the trip times can be feathered as desired.

By using the FIND and SET commands, virtually any required format changes to the contents of this document can be accomplished. For example, all the trips corresponding to only one direction can be displayed; alternatively, only those trips that pass through a particular node at a particular time of day can be displayed, and so on.

```
SAGE MINI-SCHEDULER    DOCUMENT : BLOCKS        SIZE : 78  26    USER : SAGE01
LINE DOWNTOWN  SER : SATURDAY
-------------------------------------------------------------------------------
?  GET DOCUMENT BLOCKS

-------------------------------------------------------------------------------


  01    02    03   -05-  -09-  10    -11-  -12-  13    -18-  -19-  -20-
  ROW   TRIP BLOK LINE  PAT-  NODE  LV    AR    NODE  LOVR  LOVR  LOVR
        HOOK NUM       NUM   1     1     2     2     TIME  MAX   MIN
  0001  U          2 1101 4TH   440A  540A 1ST
  0002  U          2 1102 4TH   512A  610A 1ST
  0003  U          2  101 1ST   520A  620A 4TH
  0004  U          2 1101 4TH   540A  640A 1ST
  0005  U          2  102 1ST   550A  648A 4TH
  0006  U          2 1102 4TH   611A  712A 1ST
  0007  U          2  101 1ST   620A  720A 4TH
  0008  U          2 1101 4TH   639A  742A 1ST
  0009  U          2  102 1ST   648A  749A 4TH
  0010  U          2 1102 4TH   711A  812A 1ST
  0011  U          2  101 1ST   718A  821A 4TH
  0012  U          2 1101 4TH   739A  842A 1ST
  0013  U          2  102 1ST   748A  849A 4TH
  0014  U          2 1102 4TH   812A  910A 1ST
```

The Blocks document is simply an alternative way of looking at the trips. Here for each generated trip, the first and last revenue times are displayed. The order of the rows on this document is by block number and the time at the first revenue node. Accompanying each time value is the abbreviated node description (see Nodes document). The 'U' in column 2 signifies that the trip is unhooked - has not been assigned to a vehicle (no block number).

```
SAGE MINI-SCHEDULER      DOCUMENT : BLOCKS        SIZE : 78  26     USER : SAGE01
LINE DOWNTOWN   SER :SATURDAY
--------------------------------------------------------------------------------
? CHANGE ALL COL 19 TO 20,5


--------------------------------------------------------------------------------
 01    02    03  -05- -09-  10   -11-  -12-  13   -18-  -19-  -20-
ROW   TRIP BLOK LINE PAT- NODE   LV    AR   NODE  LOVR  LOVR  LOVR
      HOOK NUM       NUM   1     1     2     2    TIME  MAX   MIN
0001 U              2 1101 4TH   440A  540A 1ST          20    5
0002 U              2 1102 4TH   512A  610A 1ST          20    5
0003 U              2  101 1ST   520A  620A 4TH          20    5
0004 U              2 1101 4TH   540A  640A 1ST          20    5
0005 U              2  102 1ST   550A  648A 4TH          20    5
0006 U              2 1102 4TH   611A  712A 1ST          20    5
0007 U              2  101 1ST   620A  720A 4TH          20    5
0008 U              2 1101 4TH   639A  742A 1ST          20    5
0009 U              2  102 1ST   648A  749A 4TH          20    5
0010 U              2 1102 4TH   711A  812A 1ST          20    5
0011 U              2  101 1ST   718A  821A 4TH          20    5
0012 U              2 1101 4TH   739A  842A 1ST          20    5
0013 U              2  102 1ST   748A  849A 4TH          20    5
0014 U              2 1102 4TH   812A  910A 1ST          20    5
```

In order to block the trips, the user applies, to all the trips, a maximum
and minimum layover (recovery) of 20 and 5 minutes respectively. This means,
for example, that the 440A-540A trip (row 1) can hook to any other trip that
has a first node time between 545A and 600A. If deadheading is involved,
these times will be adjusted accordingly.

```
SAGE MINI-SCHEDULER      DOCUMENT : BLOCKS        SIZE :  78  26     USER : SAGE01
LINE DOWNTOWN   SER :SATURDAY
--------------------------------------------------------------------------------
? SOLVE OPTIMUM LO 13
---> OPTIMAL SOLUTION   NUMBER OF BLOCKS = 22      OK(Y/N) ? N
--------------------------------------------------------------------------------
 01    02    03  -05- -09-  10   -11-  -12-  13   -18-  -19-  -20-
ROW   TRIP BLOK LINE PAT- NODE  LV    AR   NODE  LOVR  LOVR  LOVR
      HOOK NUM       NUM   1     1     2     2    TIME  MAX   MIN
0001 U              2 1101 4TH   440A  540A 1ST          20    5
0002 U              2 1102 4TH   512A  610A 1ST          20    5
0003 U              2  101 1ST   520A  620A 4TH          20    5
0004 U              2 1101 4TH   540A  640A 1ST          20    5
0005 U              2  102 1ST   550A  648A 4TH          20    5
0006 U              2 1102 4TH   611A  712A 1ST          20    5
0007 U              2  101 1ST   620A  720A 4TH          20    5
0008 U              2 1101 4TH   639A  742A 1ST          20    5
0009 U              2  102 1ST   648A  749A 4TH          20    5
0010 U              2 1102 4TH   711A  812A 1ST          20    5
0011 U              2  101 1ST   718A  821A 4TH          20    5
0012 U              2 1101 4TH   739A  842A 1ST          20    5
0013 U              2  102 1ST   748A  849A 4TH          20    5
0014 U              2 1102 4TH   812A  910A 1ST          20    5
```

The optimum solve, with a target layover of 13 minutes, produces 22 blocks.
This is not acceptable.

```
SAGE MINI-SCHEDULER    DOCUMENT : BLOCKS        SIZE : 78  26    USER : SAGE01
LINE DOWNTOWN   SER :SATURDAY
-------------------------------------------------------------------------------
? SOLVE OPTIMUM LO 13
---> NBLK = 5       TREV = 462     TLOV = 112     TDHD = 0      AL/H = 15.3
-------------------------------------------------------------------------------
 01    02   03  -05- -09-  10   -11-  -12-  13    -18-  -19-  -20-
ROW   TRIP BLOK LINE PAT- NODE   LV    AR  NODE   LOVR  LOVR  LOVR
      HOOK NUM            NUM  1    1     2     2   TIME   MAX   MIN
0001 S       1    2 1101 4TH   440A  540A 1ST    10    30    5
0002 +       1    2  102 1ST   550A  648A 4TH    23    30    5
0003 +       1    2 1102 4TH   711A  812A 1ST     6    30    5
0004 +       1    2  101 1ST   818A  921A 4TH    19    30    5
0005 +       1    2 1101 4TH   940A 1040A 1ST    10    30    5
0006 +       1    2  102 1ST  1050A 1148A 4TH    24    30    5
0007 +       1    2 1102 4TH  1212P  110P 1ST    10    30    5
0008 +       1    2  101 1ST   120P  220P 4TH    20    30    5
0009 +       1    2 1101 4TH   240P  340P 1ST    10    30    5
0010 +       1    2  102 1ST   350P  448P 4TH    24    30    5
0011 +       1    2 1102 4TH   512P  610P 1ST    10    30    5
0012 +       1    2  101 1ST   620P  720P 4TH    20    30    5
0013 +       1    2 1101 4TH   740P  840P 1ST    10    30    5
0014 +       1    2  102 1ST   850P  948P 4TH    24    30    5
```

By changing the layover maximum to 30 minutes, and hence increasing the hooking possibilities, 5 blocks were obtained. The total revenue time is 4620 minutes, the total layover is 1120 minutes, there is no deadhead and the average layover per hook is 13 minutes. The trip hook code and layover time columns are automatically updated. A trip hook code of 'S' signifies the start of a block, a '+' is an intermediate trip in a block and an 'E' (not shown) the end of a block. The block numbers of the created blocks are automatically assigned unless overridden by the user.

Computer Scheduling of Public Transport
A. Wren (ed.)
© *North-Holland Publishing Company, 1981*

SCHEDULING AN URBAN RAILWAY

Kenneth L. W. Dexter

Data Processing Railway Systems
London Transport
London, U.K.

High-capacity urban railway systems demand an operational plan
which optimises the use and control of trains and crews.
Creation of the plan, or timetable, is a highly complex,
protracted and labour intensive task. Investigation into the
application of computer technology to compiling work led to
the successful development within London Transport of the
Computer Aided Railway Timetabling system. This has already
proved to be a powerful tool for achieving most of the tasks
tackled from timetable conception to completion. As a
conversational system, CART in fact enables the compiler to
determine the best service pattern options more quickly and to
enhance his productivity and skills in the art of compilation.
The package is destined to become integral with the total
system for processing time and duty schedules.

THE LT COMPILATION TASK

Fundamental to the management and operation of a public transport system is its
timetable. It is more than a marketing tool. Rather, it is the operator's plan for
the optimum use and control of resources which produce the services. These
resources are principally rolling stock and manpower.

In this paper I propose to define the timetable compilation task in the context of
the London Transport Underground network and show how that task has changed as a
result of new technologies. A full description of the Computer Aided Railway
Timetabling system will follow, using a typical compilation exercise. Finally
reference to its use will be given and how it is expected to be integrated with
other LT railway based computer systems will be explained.

To begin with, I do not intend to imply that compilation and production of
timetables is more difficult for LT Underground railways than for other comparable
high-capacity metro systems of the world. Each system has its own scheduling
problems and methods of dealing with them. But the problems are there and
overcoming them within the compilation phase of the timetable production lengthens
that phase. As a result, timetables are either implemented at a point in time
remote from the circumstances which demanded the change, or the lead time
available for compilation is insufficient. Moreover, the more intensive the
service the greater the effect the operation of uneconomic, inadequate or
ill-planned services has on running costs and revenue - certainly out of all
proportion to compiling costs!

The solution to timetable production timescales is not to be found in the
employment of additional compilers or paying the existing ones to work harder! In
any case it is common for an urban railway timetable to be the brain child of one
highly experienced compiler who receives clerical assistance from a 'probationer'.

The compilation task could be eased by elimination or reduction of a number of factors which complicate operation. However, this is easier said than done. Complex interworking together with extensive 'short-working' and multi-branch operation are longstanding features of the LT Railway network. This is not necessarily by historical accident, for the practice of scheduled reversing of trains at a multiplicity of intermediate timing points has been carried over to the Victoria and Jubilee Lines opened since 1968. It must be remembered, too, that much of London's Underground caters simultaneously for central area traffic movement, British Rail 'feeder' traffic and considerable commuter movement between the central area and outer suburbs. A variety of operational patterns are both necessary and economic common sense.

Another factor complicating the compiling task is the need for graduated increments and decrements of additional running time over central area sections of Line. This is to help maintain schedules at times of peak traffic demand when station dwell times become extended. This requirement is not peculiar to London Transport; wherever intensive services are operated over lengthy routes, inaccurate determination of the boundaries of peak service headways and different running allowances can so easily affect the number of trains and crews required for the service.

Looking more closely at the task, there are seen to be many other constraints peculiar to the task of scheduling an urban railway. For example, it does matter that a compiler avoids timing two trains to cross a track intersection simultaneously or reach a junction in less than the permitted safety signalling headway! It also matters that the rolling stock 'balances' by depot within each operational day and that trains by stock type 'rotate' between major overhaul depots and subsidiary stabling points to ensure stock maintenance can be fully programmed. Furthermore, LT operates a system of disseminating de-icing fluid by suitably equipped trains over non-tunnel sections of the network during winter months. For this the compiler must devise schedules which ensure adequate coverage at the required intervals utilising trains to the best advantage.

In another area specific to LT, programme machine signalling was introduced in 1958 to promote train regularity and overcome the problem of signalman recruitment. These electro-mechanical machines have since been installed at scores of local unmanned signal interlockings. Each of the 150 or so machines is 'programmed' to do one or several things, e.g. call for routes, hold trains and check Train Description. Machines maintain trains to time without supervision unless the service is late or deviates from the timetable, when supervisory and over-riding control is assumed by a remotely situated central control room.

Each programme machine requires a version of the timetable specific to its supervisory role. The timetable is in fact punched on a plastic roll! These developments in automated signalling have emphasised the importance of timetable workability, placing a stricter discipline upon compilation. Any tight workings or unscheduled platform road working on many Lines can no longer be left to the signalman to 'iron out'. He has in fact been progressively replaced by the programme machine or, more lately, the mini-computer.

Centralised railway control is not being overlooked in the advances being made in the use of computer technology. An On-Line Computer control system is being developed to supervise the operation of the Northern and Victoria Lines. Like computers for local interlockings, the central control installation requires the full working timetable, but reformatted and continually updated in a finer and more precise form. This emphasises the importance of timetable precision and workability which the skilled compiler must achieve however complex his task, by reason of other factors referred to earlier in this paper.

THE BIRTH OF CART

Faced with the need to ease the compilation task and reduce production lead times, London Transport in 1974 commissioned an investigation into the application of computing techniques to timetable production. This was prompted by the recognition of the fact that the work proceeded in broadly definable stages and that, in particular, it included the evaluation and selection of service options and their integration into the intended timetable.

The availabiliy of interactive computing techniques supporting the development of 'conversational' programs gave impetus to the success of this investigation, conducted by London Transport's Director of Operational Research. Within two years programs had been developed which on command could

>   i) generate service patterns ('Standards') at minutes past the hour based upon basic requirements entered through a computer terminal
>
>   ii) expand a Standard into real times of the day
>
>   iii) calculate a rough transition between two differing Standards
>
>   iv) permit individual trips generated on the train trip file to be edited.

The programs were designed to accept commands and parameters and apply them to a previously entered description of the Line, consisting basically of timing points, their capacity for reversing trains and station to station running allowances.

With this promising start, it was clear there was a case to develop further the basic algorithms into a comprehensive computer assistance package. Responsibility for the development was assumed by the Data Processing Manager in April 1976, a timetable compiler was seconded to the programming team and the package was given a name - CART which is an acronym for Computer Aided Railway Timetabling. There is also a daughter system, CABS (Computer Aided Bus Scheduling) which is a bus route orientated version of CART.

CART TO-DAY

Today, after four years DP development, CART, a 60K FORTRAN (26K Overlaid) program, is a very powerful tool having in 1979 been implemented in the timetable compiling section of London Transport's Railway Operations department. All compilers have been trained to use the system which, it is emphasised, is not intended to replace compilers but rather enhance their skills and productivity. Considerable use of the system has been made in research, in producing solutions to current operational service problems and in determining rolling stock replacement programmes. Fuller reference to these are given at the end of the paper.

The generation of the best service options from variable operating criteria, the powerful facility to expand by direction of travel service standards respectively over many hours of the traffic day and the ability to link and form differing levels of service leaving finesse to be carried out by the compiler - these attributes emphasise the value of CART. I propose to illustrate many of the system's capabilities in the following exercise.

CART IN ACTION

Let us assume the need has arisen to improve the morning peak service on the
Piccadilly Line. Figure 1 shows that the Line, over 40 route miles long, crosses
London in an east/west direction serving suburbs in north-east London, Piccadilly
and the West End and, in west London bifurcates at Acton Town. Separate branches
then serve London Airport (Heathrow Central) and the Ruislip and Uxbridge area of
north-west London.

In order to determine the number of trains required to provide the desired level
of service, the CART system is to be used to generate a number of service pattern
options. If one is found that is acceptable, a detailed service specification will
be prepared by the Train Services Manager. The CART system will be used to
generate an early morning service building up to the new peak service and to
compile a Transition between the latter and the existing mid-day off-peak service.

Using a computer terminal, the compiler 'logs on' to the ICL MAXIMOP time-sharing
system run on a remotely situated 1900 mainframe computer. The CART program is
called and the Line required to be processed is selected. Communication between
the compiler and the program is strictly controlled by MAXIMOP and there are
several commands available to provide assistance in the use of the system.

Having selected the Line Description for the Piccadilly Line from a file of
Descriptions for several Lines, the compiler is at liberty to use it, amend it or,
alternatively, he may enter an entirely new one.

Each Line Description consists of two parts as shown in Figure 2. The first part
contains each timing point on the Line in a similar way to those portrayed in the
namebank of the working timetable. For each point, which is also commonly one at
which trains can be reversed, minimum and optimum lay-over values are held. In the
creation of service patterns, 'Standards', CART will aim at providing optimum
lay-overs wherever possible.

The Line Description also contains, for each timing point, Conflict Period values,
used to describe the type of reversing facilities available. The values in minutes
and half-minutes are the clearance allowances that must be honoured between trains
reversing in platforms or sidings. Finally, against each terminal point the
reversing capability is held in terms of the number of platform roads or sidings
available. The second part of the Line Description holds, under individual section
numbers, the timing point to timing point distances and basic directional running
time allowances.

When satisfied with the Line Description, the compiler proceeds to enter the
'level of service' parameters. This entails the use of the 'PATTern' command (all
ninety commands are recognised by the first four characters) to enter the number
of trains per hour or fraction of hour that are intended to run over each section
of the Line.

The compiler has been directed to provide a two-and-a-quarter minute headway
service in the central trunk section of the Piccadilly Line. This is equivalent to
32 trains in 72 minutes or 16 in 36, so, by entering the command PATTern 36, the
CART system recognises 36 minutes as the basic cycle time. The system then asks
the compiler to specify the number of trains per cycle time required to serve each
section of the Line. In this example it is assumed the compiler will specify the
maximum number (16) of trains to operate between Wood Green and Acton Town (the
service trunk section). Other parameters indicate that 4 trains in every cycle
(every 9 minutes) will reverse at Wood Green, leaving the balance of 12 trains
every 36 minutes to be worked to the ultimate terminus - Cockfosters. For the west
end of the Line, the compiler enters 8 trains per cycle each from Acton Town to

LONDON TRANSPORT PICCADILLY LINE   FIGURE 1

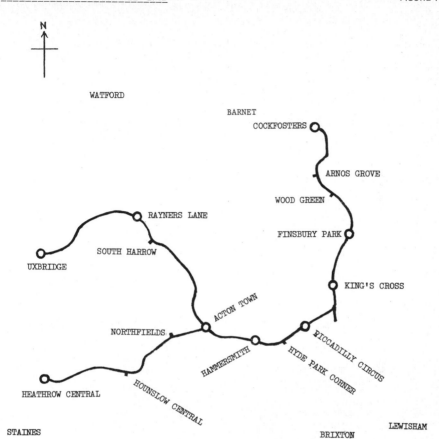

FIGURE 2

```
        TYPE COMMAND (W/B)_DESC

C.A.R.T. LINE DESCRIPTION FOR THE PICCADILLY  LINE

CREATED ON 28/07/80 IN SUBFILE KLWD
PRINTED ON 29/07/80 AT 12:46

LIST OF TIMING POINTS:-

NUMBER     NAME      MINIMUM   OPTIMUM   CONFLICT   TERMINAL
                     LAYOVER   LAYOVER   PERIOD     CAPACITY
    1    COCKFOST      5          7        1+        3 PFM
    2    ARNOS GR      4+         8        1+        2 PFM
    3    WOOD GRN      7         11        3         1 SDG
    4    KINGS X       7         11        2         1 PFM
    5    HYDE PRK      4+         8+       1+        1 PFM
    6    ACTON TN      7+        11        3         1 SDG
    7    NORTHFDS      7         11        3         1 SDG
    8    HEATHROW      4+         6        2         2 PFM
    9    S HARROW      4+         8        2         1 PFM
   10    RAYNERS       7         11        3         1 SDG
   11    UXBRIDGE      4+         8        3         3 PFM

THE DIRECTIONS ARE:-
  1 - WEST BOUND       2 - EAST BOUND

TRAINS WILL NORMALLY BE MADE UP OF 6 CARS

LIST OF SECTIONS:-                         BASIC
                                                          PEAK
SECTION         SECTION        MILES  RUNNING TIME   R.T.   VARIATIONS
NUMBER                                W/B    E/B     W/B      E/B
   1    COCKFOST TO ARNOS GR   3.21    7      8
   2    ARNOS GR TO WOOD GRN   1.73    4+     5
   3    WOOD GRN TO KINGS X    5.18   13+    14     + 1
   4    KINGS X  TO HYDE PRK   2.87   11     11     + 2      + 1
   5    HYDE PRK TO ACTON TN   6.19   16+    15+    + 1      + 1+
   6    ACTON TN TO NORTHFDS   1.61    4      4
   7    NORTHFDS TO HEATHROW   7.28   16+    17              + 1+
   8    ACTON TN TO S HARROW   5.99   16     15
   9    S HARROW TO RAYNERS    1.18    3      3+
  10    RAYNERS  TO UXBRIDGE   5.36   14     13

        TYPE COMMAND (W/B)_
```

OPTIONAL ENTRY
DURING RUN

Heathrow and Acton Town to Rayners Lane, 4 of which latter 8 are to be projected to Uxbridge. The 'conversational' interaction between compiler and computer is shown below:

PATT 36

GIVE THE NUMBER OF TRAINS PASSING OVER EACH SECTION EVERY 36 MINUTES:-

COCKFOST TO ?-<u>WOOD GRN 12</u>
WOOD GRN TO ?-<u>ACTON TN 16</u>
ACTON TN TO ?-<u>HEATHROW 8</u>
ACTON TN TO ?-<u>RAYNERS 8</u>
RAYNERS TO UXBRIDGE ?-<u>4</u>
ARE THERE ANY R.T.V.S ?-<u>YES</u>

The next prompt from the CART system asks if there are any variations to the basic running time allowances. The compiler has the choice of answering 'yes' or 'no'. Because a peak service is to be compiled, additional running time allowances will be required, and, by indicating accordingly to CART, it will invite the compiler to give the section numbers and the required additional running time allowances in minutes and half-minutes. This procedure is carried out for each direction of travel as shown in Figure 3.

FIGURE 3

```
SPECIFY THE RUNNING TIME CHANGES IN MINUTES
TYPE "END" WHEN EACH DIRECTION IS CORRECT

TYPE SECTION NUMBER (W/B)_3
      AND RTV_1

TYPE SECTION NUMBER (W/B)_4
      AND RTV_2

TYPE SECTION NUMBER (W/B)_5
      AND RTV_1

TYPE SECTION NUMBER (W/B)_END

TYPE SECTION NUMBER (E/B)_7
      AND RTV_1

TYPE SECTION NUMBER (E/B)_5
      AND RTV_1+

TYPE SECTION NUMBER (E/B)_4
      AND RTV_1+

TYPE SECTION NUMBER (E/B)_END

THIS SERVICE REQUIRES 1456.80 TRAIN-MILES PER HOUR
```

CART now has all that is necessary in order, firstly, to tell the compiler how many train miles per hour this service will incur and secondly, list a number of suggested destination/headway patterns for each end of the Line. For example, at the eastern end where one train in four is to reverse at Wood Green and where headways between trains range between two and two-and-a-half minutes, one pattern presented can show a headway of two minutes between the Wood Green reverser and the following train to or from Cockfosters whereas another pattern can portray this headway as being two-and-a-half minutes. The compiler has the option of accepting or rejecting any of these patterns, which are portrayed by the use of asterisks plotted against a namebank (see Figure 4).

FIGURE 4

```
SUGGESTED DESTINATION/HEADWAY PATTERNS FOR THE EAST   END:-

P A T T E R N    1

COCKFOST  *          *    *
WOOD GRN  *    *     *    *
HEADWAYS  :  2+:  2  :  2+:  2
   9   MINUTE CYCLE  -  IS THIS ACCEPTABLE ?_YES

P A T T E R N    2

COCKFOST  *    *          *
WOOD GRN  *    *     *    *
HEADWAYS  :  2+:  2  :  2+:  2
   9   MINUTE CYCLE  -  IS THIS ACCEPTABLE ?_YES

SUGGESTED DESTINATION/HEADWAY PATTERNS FOR THE WEST   END:-

P A T T E R N    3

HEADWAYS  :  2+:  2  :  2+:  2
ACTON TN  *    *     *    *
HEATHROW  *          *
RAYNERS        *          *
UXBRIDGE       *
   9   MINUTE CYCLE  -  IS THIS ACCEPTABLE ?_YES

P A T T E R N    4

HEADWAYS  :  2+:  2  :  2+:  2
ACTON TN  *    *     *    *
HEATHROW       *          *
RAYNERS   *          *
UXBRIDGE  *
   9   MINUTE CYCLE  -  IS THIS ACCEPTABLE ?_YES

ARE THERE ANY MANDATORY TRIPS ?_NO
```

CART is now set to portray a list of directional services comprising combinations of each of the individual destination/headway patterns which have not been rejected by the compiler. However, before CART produces this list it requires to know if any mandatory trips must be considered during the Standard compilation phase. This facility enables regard to be paid to operational practice such that trips originating from a terminus at one end of the Line must only be scheduled to one specific timing point/terminus at the other end of the Line. This has a strait-jacket effect upon the results that CART may produce and, in the case being described, it is assumed that the compiler answers 'no' to this question.

The List of Directional Services is portrayed in the same way as the patterns, i.e. by use of asterisks against the namebank, and will, in this case, total 8 by reason of the combination of alternative patterns of reversing and the uneven trunk section headway (see Figure 5). The compiler has the option of accepting or rejecting any of the Directional Services listed by the system. In next to no time CART combines each of the 8 Directional Services for one direction with those of the opposite direction to create up to 64 combinations. Some of these may be totally unacceptable for a variety of operating reasons, others may be devoid of any tight clearances or conflicting movements.

CART uses an iterative process to deduce the six best options, applying weights to each option based upon the number of conflictions and terminal platform capacity violations there are and their extent in terms of minutes and half-minutes.

The six best options are automatically tabulated (Figure 6), each giving the Directional Service number used for each direction, the number of trains required and the numbers of conflictions, clearance and capacity problems. For example, one option might indicate 16 conflictions in the 36 minute cycle, 4 of which are clearance problems at one terminus, that is to say it is attempting to schedule trains into that terminus without sufficient clearance time following the previous departing train. The same or another option might show the presence of capacity problems, that is, there are instances when the number of trains to be reversed, within a certain time period, is greater than the number of platform roads or sidings that will become available during that period.

It should be noted that attempting to schedule an intensive service such as that proposed is likely to produce these problems. It is also very likely that these problems can be overcome with the minimum of effort and adjustment by the compiler. Using the command 'COMBine', the compiler obtains a list of all combinations of the services (see again Figure 6).

Using the 'SELEct' command enables the compiler to take a closer look at each option. This command, of course, expects an option number. For each option selected, CART immediately portrays the 'Train Self-containment Cycles' and the 'Confliction Analyses' (Figure 7). The first set of information serves to tell the compiler how many of the total number of trains required work to a specific cycle. For example, this could mean that of the 75 trains required, 28 may work repetitively from Cockfosters to Heathrow to Wood Green to Heathrow and back to Cockfosters. This is an important aid to the compiler, and indeed Railway Management, to determine the type of service desirable. The confliction analysis serves to identify at which timing points conflictions or tight clearances occur and their degree, represented by multiples of minutes and half-minutes. In addition, the 'Self-containment Cycle' list gives the lay-overs for each train at each reversing point.

The compiler has the option of keeping each service combination as a Standard for use at a future date. He is also at liberty to examine in the same close way all the other options portrayed earlier. Compiling experience will enable the compiler, at this stage, to know which is the best option. On the other hand, to determine the best of, say two, or at the most three close contenders, the compiler may wish to examine them even more closely. This is done by using the command 'DISPLay'. CART responds by portraying a 'minutes past the hour' tabulated 'Standard' set against the full station namebank for each direction (Figure 8).

FIGURE 5

```
LIST OF DIRECTIONAL SERVICES:-


COCKFOST  *      *   *   *        *   *   *      *   *   *      *   *
WOOD GRN  *   *  *   *   *   *  *  *   *   *  *  *   *   *  *   *   *
HEADWAYS  : 2+: 2 : 2+: 2 : 2+: 2 : 2+: 2 : 2+: 2 : 2+: 2 : 2+: 2 : 2+: 2
ACTON TN  *   *  *   *   *   *  *  *   *   *  *  *   *   *  *   *   *
HEATHROW  *      *       *       *       *       *       *       *
RAYNERS       *       *       *       *       *       *       *       *
UXBRIDGE      *               *               *               *
DO YOU WANT TO KEEP THIS SERVICE ?_YES
SERVICE ASSIGNED NUMBER  1


COCKFOST  *      *   *   *        *   *   *      *   *   *      *   *
WOOD GRN  *   *  *   *   *   *  *  *   *   *  *  *   *   *  *   *   *
HEADWAYS  : 2+: 2 : 2+: 2 : 2+: 2 : 2+: 2 : 2+: 2 : 2+: 2 : 2+: 2 : 2+: 2
ACTON TN  *   *  *   *   *   *  *  *   *   *  *  *   *   *  *   *   *
HEATHROW  *      *       *       *       *       *       *       *
RAYNERS       *       *       *       *       *       *       *       *
UXBRIDGE              *               *               *               *
DO YOU WANT TO KEEP THIS SERVICE ?_YES
SERVICE ASSIGNED NUMBER  2


COCKFOST  *   *      *   *   *        *   *   *      *   *   *      *
WOOD GRN  *   *  *   *   *   *  *  *   *   *  *  *   *   *  *   *   *
HEADWAYS  : 2+: 2 : 2+: 2 : 2+: 2 : 2+: 2 : 2+: 2 : 2+: 2 : 2+: 2 : 2+: 2
ACTON TN  *   *  *   *   *   *  *  *   *   *  *  *   *   *  *   *   *
HEATHROW  *      *       *       *       *       *       *       *
RAYNERS       *       *       *       *       *       *       *       *
UXBRIDGE      *               *               *               *
DO YOU WANT TO KEEP THIS SERVICE ?_YES
SERVICE ASSIGNED NUMBER  3


COCKFOST  *   *      *   *   *        *   *   *      *   *   *      *
WOOD GRN  *   *  *   *   *   *  *  *   *   *  *  *   *   *  *   *   *
HEADWAYS  : 2+: 2 : 2+: 2 : 2+: 2 : 2+: 2 : 2+: 2 : 2+: 2 : 2+: 2 : 2+: 2
ACTON TN  *   *  *   *   *   *  *  *   *   *  *  *   *   *  *   *   *
HEATHROW  *      *       *       *       *       *       *       *
RAYNERS       *       *       *       *       *       *       *       *
UXBRIDGE              *               *               *               *
DO YOU WANT TO KEEP THIS SERVICE ?_YES
SERVICE ASSIGNED NUMBER   4
```

```
COCKFOST  *   *      *   *   *        *   *   *      *   *   *      *
WOOD GRN  *   *  *   *   *   *  *  *   *   *  *  *   *   *  *   *   *
HEADWAYS  : 2+: 2 : 2+: 2 : 2+: 2 : 2+: 2 : 2+: 2 : 2+: 2 : 2+: 2 : 2+: 2
ACTON TN  *   *  *   *   *   *  *  *   *   *  *  *   *   *  *   *   *
HEATHROW      *       *       *       *       *       *       *       *
RAYNERS   *      *       *       *       *       *       *       *
UXBRIDGE      *               *               *               *
DO YOU WANT TO KEEP THIS SERVICE ?_YES
SERVICE ASSIGNED NUMBER  8
```

FIGURE 6

SUGGESTED COMBINATIONS OF THE SERVICES:-

OPTION NUMBER	WEST BOUND SERVICE	EAST BOUND SERVICE	NO. OF TRAINS	NUMBER OF CONFLICTIONS	CLEARANCE PROBLEMS			CAPACITY PROBLEMS		
					NUMBER	WORST	TOTAL	NUMBER	WORST	TOTAL
1	7	4	75	16	4	1 M	4 M	12	0+M	6 M
2	1	8	75	12	0	0 M	0 M	12	1 M	8 M
3	8	3	75	16	4	1 M	4 M	12	0+M	6 M
4	2	7	75	12	0	0 M	0 M	12	1 M	8 M
5	5	2	75	16	4	1 M	4 M	12	0+M	6 M
6	6	1	75	16	4	1 M	4 M	12	0+M	6 M

TYPE COMMAND (W/B)_ COMB

LIST OF ALL COMBINATIONS OF THE SERVICES:-

WEST BOUND SERVICE	EAST BOUND SERVICE	NO. OF TRAINS	NUMBER OF CONFLICTIONS	CLEARANCE PROBLEMS			CAPACITY PROBLEMS		
				NUMBER	WORST	TOTAL	NUMBER	WORST	TOTAL
1	1	75	8	0	0 M	0 M	8	1+M	8 M
1	2	75	8	0	0 M	0 M	8	2+M	18 M
1	3	75	20	4	1+M	6 M	16	0+M	8 M
1	4	75	8	0	0 M	0 M	8	1+M	10 M
1	5	75	20	4	1+M	6 M	16	1 M	10 M
1	6	75	16	4	0+M	2 M	12	1 M	10 M
1	7	75	8	0	0 M	0 M	8	3 M	18 M
1	8	75	12	0	0 M	0 M	12	1 M	8 M
2	1	75	8	0	0 M	0 M	8	2+M	18 M
2	2	75	8	0	0 M	0 M	8	1+M	8 M
2	3	75	8	0	0 M	0 M	8	1+M	10 M
2	4	75	20	4	1+M	6 M	16	0+M	8 M
2	5	75	16	4	0+M	2 M	12	1 M	10 M
2	6	75	20	4	1+M	6 M	16	1 M	10 M
2	7	75	12	0	0 M	0 M	12	1 M	8 M
2	8	75	8	0	0 M	0 M	8	3 M	18 M
3	1	75	16	4	0+M	2 M	12	1+M	10 M
3	2	75	20	4	1+M	6 M	16	0+M	8 M
3	3	75	8	0	0 M	0 M	8	1+M	8 M
3	4	75	8	0	0 M	0 M	8	2+M	18 M
3	5	75	12	0	0 M	0 M	12	1 M	8 M
3	6	75	8	0	0 M	0 M	8	2+M	16 M
3	7	75	20	4	1+M	6 M	16	1 M	10 M
3	8	75	16	4	0+M	2 M	12	1 M	10 M
4	1	75	20	4	1+M	6 M	16	0+M	8 M
4	2	75	16	4	0+M	2 M	12	1+M	10 M
4	3	75	8	0	0 M	0 M	8	2+M	18 M
4	4	75	8	0	0 M	0 M	8	1+M	8 M
4	5	75	8	0	0 M	0 M	8	2+M	16 M
4	6	75	12	0	0 M	0 M	12	1 M	8 M
4	7	75	16	4	0+M	2 M	12	1 M	10 M
4	8	75	20	4	1+M	6 M	16	1 M	10 M
5	1	75	16	4	0+M	2 M	12	1+M	12 M
5	2	75	16	4	1 M	4 M	12	0+M	6 M
5	3	75	16	4	1 M	4 M	12	1 M	8 M
5	4	75	8	0	0 M	0 M	8	3 M	20 M
5	5	75	8	0	0 M	0 M	8	1+M	8 M
5	6	75	8	0	0 M	0 M	8	2+M	18 M
5	7	75	20	4	1+M	6 M	16	0+M	8 M
5	8	75	8	0	0 M	0 M	8	1+M	10 M
6	1	75	16	4	1 M	4 M	12	0+M	6 M
6	2	75	16	4	0+M	2 M	12	1+M	12 M
6	3	75	8	0	0 M	0 M	8	3 M	20 M
6	4	75	16	4	1 M	4 M	12	1 M	8 M
6	5	75	8	0	0 M	0 M	8	2+M	18 M
6	6	75	8	0	0 M	0 M	8	1+M	8 M
6	7	75	8	0	0 M	0 M	8	1+M	10 M
6	8	75	20	4	1+M	6 M	16	0+M	8 M
7	1	75	8	0	0 M	0 M	8	2+M	18 M

FIGURE 7

TRAIN SELF-CONTAINMENT AND CONFLICTION ANALYSIS

```
                        SELE 2

SELF-CONTAINMENT CYCLES FOR OPTION NO. 2        CONFLICTION ANALYSES

      A R R I V A L S                    CONFLICT  ARR.  DEP.  CAPACITY    MINUTES
  TRIP TERMINUS LAYOVER                  LOCATION  TRIP  TRIP  VIOLATED ?  PROBLEM

   1W  HEATHROW    5+
   4E  COCKFOST    8               COCKFOST   4E    8W      YES        0+
  12W  RAYNERS    10               RAYNERS   12W   11E      YES        1
  15E  COCKFOST    8               COCKFOST  15E    3W      YES        0+
   7W  HEATHROW    5+
  10E  COCKFOST    5+

  14 TRAINS FOLLOW THIS CYCLE


      A R R I V A L S                    CONFLICT  ARR.  DEP.  CAPACITY    MINUTES
  TRIP TERMINUS LAYOVER                  LOCATION  TRIP  TRIP  VIOLATED ?  PROBLEM

   2W  UXBRIDGE   10
   1E  WOOD GRN    8
  14W  UXBRIDGE   10
  13E  WOOD GRN    8
  10W  UXBRIDGE   10
   9E  WOOD GRN    8
   6W  UXBRIDGE   10
   5E  WOOD GRN    8

  19 TRAINS FOLLOW THIS CYCLE


      A R R I V A L S                    CONFLICT  ARR.  DEP.  CAPACITY    MINUTES
  TRIP TERMINUS LAYOVER                  LOCATION  TRIP  TRIP  VIOLATED ?  PROBLEM

   3W  HEATHROW    5+
   6E  COCKFOST    5+
  13W  HEATHROW    5+
  16E  COCKFOST    8               COCKFOST  16E    4W      YES        0+
   8W  RAYNERS    10               RAYNERS    8W    7E      YES        1
  11E  COCKFOST    8               COCKFOST  11E   15W      YES        0+

  14 TRAINS FOLLOW THIS CYCLE


      A R R I V A L S                    CONFLICT  ARR.  DEP.  CAPACITY    MINUTES
  TRIP TERMINUS LAYOVER                  LOCATION  TRIP  TRIP  VIOLATED ?  PROBLEM

   4W  RAYNERS    10               RAYNERS    4W    3E      YES        1
   7E  COCKFOST    8               COCKFOST   7E   11W      YES        0+
  15W  HEATHROW    5+
   2E  COCKFOST    5+
   9W  HEATHROW    5+
  12E  COCKFOST    8               COCKFOST  12E   16W      YES        0+

  14 TRAINS FOLLOW THIS CYCLE


      A R R I V A L S                    CONFLICT  ARR.  DEP.  CAPACITY    MINUTES
  TRIP TERMINUS LAYOVER                  LOCATION  TRIP  TRIP  VIOLATED ?  PROBLEM
```

FIGURE 8

SAMPLE PEAK STANDARD

TYPE COMMAND (W/B)_DISP

TRIP NO:	1	2	3	4	5	6	7	8	9	10	11	12	13	14	15	16
COCKFOST	23		27+	30	32		36+	39	41		45+	48	50		54+	57
ARNOS GR	30		34+	37	39		43+	46	48		52+	55	57		01+	04
WOOD GRN	34+	37	39	41+	43+	46	48	50+	52+	55	57	59+	01+	04	06	08+
KINGS X	49	51+	53+	56	58	00+	02+	05	07	09+	11+	14	16	18+	20+	23
HYDE PRK	02	04+	06+	09	11	13+	15+	18	20	22+	24+	27	29	31+	33+	36
ACTON TN	19+	22	24	26+	28+	31	33	35+	37+	40	42	44+	46+	49	51	53+
NORTHFDS	23+		28		32+		37		41+		46		50+		55	-
HEATHROW	40		44+		49		53+		58		02+		07		11+	-
S.HARROW		38		42+		47		51+		56		00+		05		09+
RAYNERS		41		45+		50		54+		59		03+		08		12+
UXBRIDGE		55				04				13				22		
LAYOVER:	5+	10	5+	10	5+	10	5+	10	5+	10	5+	10	5+	10	5+	10
NEXT TRP	4	1	6	7	8	5	10	11	12	9	14	15	16	13	2	3

TRIP NO:	1	2	3	4	5	6	7	8	9	10	11	12	13	14	15	16
UXBRIDGE	17				26				35				44			
RAYNERS	30		34+		39		43+		48		52+		57		01+	
S HARROW	33+		38		42+		47		51+		56		00+		05	
HEATHROW	-	29		33+		38		42+		47		51+		56		00+
NORTHFDS		47		51+		56		00+		05		09+		14		18+
ACTON TN	48+	51	53	55+	57+	00	02	04+	06+	09	11	13+	15+	18	20	22+
HYDE PRK	05+	08	10	12+	14+	17	19	21+	23+	26	28	30+	32+	35	37	39+
KINGS X	18	20+	22+	25	27	29+	31+	34	36	38+	40+	43	45	47+	49+	52
WOOD GRN	32	34+	36+	39	41	43+	45+	48	50	52+	54+	57	59	01+	03+	06
ARNOS GR		39+	41+	44		48+	50+	53		57+	59+	02		06+	08+	11
COCKFOST		47+	49+	52		56+	58+	01		05+	07+	10		14+	16+	19
LAYOVER:	8	5+	8	8	8	5+	8	8	8	5+	8	8	8	5+	8	8
NEXT TRP	14	9	11	12	2	13	15	16	6	1	3	4	10	5	7	8

THIS STANDARD REQUIRES 75 TRAINS
AND WILL GENERATE 1456.80 TRAIN-MILES PER HOUR

TYPE COMMAND (W/B)_STAN 4 9 1

O.K.

At this stage the compiler is able readily to see the embryo peak timetable showing the trip pattern of operation, lay-overs and the number of the next trip formed in the opposite direction. This display also affords a clearer visual presentation of the clearance or capacity violation problems which were forewarned in the first place. By judicious adjustment it is highly likely that these problems can be obviated by the compiler. For example, there may be 4 instances in every 36 minute cycle, where one train entering Cockfosters terminus appears to conflict with another when entering the terminus. Yet by scheduling a half-minute or a one-minute wait or 'stand' at an intermediate timing point such as Wood Green, the confliction problem can be avoided. In so doing the compiler will ensure the avoidance of breaking the minimum headway rule over the sections of Line concerned. To implement this action the compiler uses the command 'STANd'.

Alternatively, there is another command called 'BEND' which has the effect of re-timing the first· section of one or many specified trips earlier to a specified point at which a 'stand' indication will be inserted by CART and from which point the remaining timings of the trip will be unaltered. During all interactive work to do with timetable portrayal and editing, the computer informs the compiler in what direction of travel it is set, whereas the compiler is free to command CART to change direction at any time.

Having edited the preferred standard to eliminate the clearance/confliction problems, the compiler can command the 'Standard' to be displayed again if thought desirable. The choice now presents itself of either storing this Standard in a Standards Library for use at a later session, or alternatively, proceeding to expand the Standard into real times of the day. The compiler takes the first course of action because it is intended to create a timetable covering the traffic day from about 0600 hours through the period of maximum peak service to well into the mid-day off peak period.

The next action to take is the development of what can be known as a pre-peak service. Basically this comprises a 6 minute interval trunk service between Arnos Grove and Heathrow Central, alternate trains having originated from Cockfosters. In this Standard, the compiler proposes to exclude the Uxbridge branch because it is intended later to generate and introduce a Shuttle service between Acton Town and Uxbridge. Commands are available for this purpose. Very quickly the compiler will develop this pre-peak Standard which inevitably produces only one directional pattern service. CART informs the compiler that to operate this Standard requires 26 trains. Using the command 'KEEP', the compiler will, following a suitable prompt, name this Standard and cause it to be filed away in his Standards Library.

The compiler now proceeds to create a mid-day off-peak service which is based upon a trunk section interval of 3 trains in 10 minutes: namely, 18 trains per hour. Rather than call for a Pattern Cycle based upon 60 minutes, one of 10 minutes is chosen which produces perfectly adequate results and minimises the amount of data to be listed and examined. The trains-per-section parameters provide for one train in three at the East End to be reversed at Wood Green and, of the projected trains, every alternate train extended to the ultimate terminus at Cockfosters. At the West End of the Line the compiler opts for the provision of 2 trains in every 10 minutes to Heathrow Central, and the third train to Rayners Lane. CART next prompts the compiler to indicate whether mandatory trip working is required. Parameters are then entered instructing that all Cockfosters trains must work to and from Rayners Lane only.

For the off-peak service, CART produces 36 service combinations, the best six of which utilise 44 trains each and provide no confliction problems. However, in each of these pattern options, lay-overs are seen to be at a minimum. The compiler, therefore, uses a command called COMBine, which in effect combines two independently numbered Directional Services for each end of the Line. This option indicates that one additional train will be required. Further information reveals that lay-overs for this option are more satisfactory. Having displayed and inspected the Standard (Figure 9) as "minutes past the hour", the compiler, using the command 'ADVAnce', re-times the westbound direction service by half a minute to ease working at the single reversing siding site – Wood Green. Adjustments are also made on westbound trains at South Harrow to ease the working at Rayners Lane.

At this stage the compiler has, over an hour and a half period, generated and filed three acceptable Standards which will form the basis of generating a complete timetable from, say, 0615 to 1515 hours. All is ready to proceed with the generation of the timetable. The first action to take is to RETRieve the pre-peak Standard and use the command 'EXPAnd' which causes CART to generate train trips at real times. Before the system can do this it must be given more information by the compiler. A short question and answer session enables the compiler to specify when the peak service is to begin, at what timing point it will start and with which trip type the service will commence. Additional details of what time and at what timing point the service will end are also entered. These parameters are entered independently for each direction of travel. The compiler decides to operate this first Standard for the duration of one hour from 0615 to 0715 hours based on Hyde Park Corner in each direction. The compiler is immediately advised by the system that it has generated this portion of timetable, and in doing so has allocated each trip its own individual trip number. (Figure 10 illustrates this action and the time taken.)

Next, the compiler RETRieves the peak service Standard and immediately enters the command 'TRAN 45' for the westbound direction. This instructs CART to generate 45 minutes' worth of trips starting with the last of the pre-peak service trips. The command used is 'TRANsition' and is one of the most useful in the CART system. By it, trunk section headways between trips will progress geometrically from the pre-peak six minute interval to the peak two-and-a-quarter minute interval. The program provides for trip origins to follow the pattern at the end of the existing timetable whilst the destinations follow the pattern of the next (peak) Standard.

Expansion of the peak Standard for as long as it is required to operate is the next task which, clerically, is normally a lengthy, boring one. The compiler chooses the trip type from the Standard which the peak service is required to start from, and enters the time at which this level of service must end before it is widened into the off-peak Standard. These parameters have to be entered for each direction in turn, which enables the compiler to prolong the operation of a service for a longer period in one direction than for the other if desired, say, for traffic reasons (Figure 11).

Finally, the mid-day off-peak Standard is retrieved and a <u>Directional Transition</u> for 35 minutes is chosen and requested. The TRANsition command produces a result (Figure 12) whereby the first trip incorporates the 'outgoing' running time allowances and the following trips will be generated using the 'incoming' or next stipulated allowances. In this case there is a total of 4 minutes additional running time allowed for peak trains through the trunk section. The effect will be to show the first train overtaking the second at a point somewhere in the latter half of the trunk section. There is a command to overcome this but before using it the compiler will EXPAnd the off-peak Standard from the end of this Transition to the mid-afternoon, giving, say, 5 hours' worth of timetable. The time taken to generate this block of timetable, including keyboard work, totals no more than 1 minute.

With regard to the incidence of two consecutive trains running with differing running allowances, the compiler uses the command 'SMOOth' which takes the difference in trunk section running time between the two trips concerned and spreads out the change over the intervening trips making up the period of

FIGURE 9

ADJUSTING THE OFF—PEAK STANDARD .

TYPE COMMAND (E/B)_DISP

TRIP NO:	1	2	3
COCKFOST	27		
ARNOS GR	34		41
WOOD GRN	38+	42	45+
KINGS X	52	55+	59
HYDE PRK	03	06+	10
ACTON TN	19+	23	26+
NORTHFDS	–	27	30+
HEATHROW	–	43+	47
S HARROW	35+		
RAYNERS	38+		
LAYOVER:	10+	6+	6+
NEXT TRP	1	2	3

TRIP NO:	1	2	3
RAYNERS	39		
S HARROW	42+		
HEATHROW	–	40	43+
NORTHFDS	–	57	00+
ACTON TN	57+	01	04+
HYDE PRK	13	16+	20
KINGS X	24	27+	31
WOOD GRN	38	41+	45
ARNOS GR	43		50
COCKFOST	51		
LAYOVER:	6	10+	11
NEXT TRP	1	2	3

TYPE COMMAND (W/B)_ADVA 1 3 0+

O.K.

TYPE COMMAND (W/B)_DISP 1 3

TRIP NO:	1	2	3
COCKFOST	26+		
ARNOS GR	33+		40+
WOOD GRN	38	41+	45
KINGS X	51+	55	58+
HYDE PRK	02+	06	09+
ACTON TN	19	22+	26
NORTHFDS	–	26+	30
HEATHROW	–	43	46+
S HARROW	35		
RAYNERS	38		
LAYOVER:	11	7	7
NEXT TRP	1	2	3

TYPE COMMAND (W/B)_STAN 1 9 1

O.K.

TYPE COMMAND (W/B)_

DISP

TRIP NO:	1	2	3
COCKFOST	26+		
ARNOS GR	33+		40+
WOOD GRN	38	41+	45
KINGS X	51+	55	58+
HYDE PRK	02+	06	09+
ACTON TN	19	22+	26
NORTHFDS	–	26+	30
HEATHROW	–	43	46+
S HARROW	B36		
RAYNERS	39		
LAYOVER:	10	7	7
NEXT TRP	1	2	3

TRIP NO:	1	2	3
RAYNERS	39		
S HARROW	42+		
HEATHROW	–	40	43+
NORTHFDS	–	57	00+
ACTON TN	57+	01	04+
HYDE PRK	13	16+	20
KINGS X	24	27+	31
WOOD GRN	38	41+	45
ARNOS GR	43		50
COCKFOST	51		
LAYOVER:	5+	10	10+
NEXT TRP	1	2	3

THIS STANDARD REQUIRES 45 TRAINS
AND WILL GENERATE 892.08 TRAIN—MILES
PER HOUR

TYPE COMMAND (W/B)_

FIGURE 10

GENERATION OF PRE-PEAK SERVICE

```
16:44. TYPE COMMAND (W/B)_RETR
WHAT IS THE NAME OF THE STANDARD ?_MJZ PP12

O.K.

16:44. TYPE COMMAND (W/B)_EXPA

WHEN IS THE W/B EXPANSION TO BEGIN ?_0615
AT WHICH TIMING POINT ?_HYDE PRK
WHICH TRIP IN THE STANDARD IS TO BE USED FIRST ?_1
WHEN IS THE W/B EXPANSION TO END ?_0715
AT WHICH TIMING POINT ?_HYDE PRK

W/B STANDARD EXPANDED - TRIPS ALLOCATED NUMBERS  21 TO  31

WHEN IS THE E/B EXPANSION TO BEGIN ?_0615
AT WHICH TIMING POINT ?_HYDE PRK
WHEN IS THE E/B EXPANSION TO END ?_0715
AT WHICH TIMING POINT ?_HYDE PRK

EXPANSION ACTUALLY BEGINS AT 06 17+ AT HYDE PRK

E/B STANDARD EXPANDED - TRIPS ALLOCATED NUMBERS  21 TO  30

EXPANSION ACTUALLY ENDS AT 07 11+ AT HYDE PRK

        TYPE COMMAND (W/B)_PRIN
```

TRIP NO:	21	22	23	24	25	26	27	28	29	30
COCKFOST	05 39		05 51		06 03		06 15		06 27	
ARNOS GR	05 46	05 52	05 58	06 04	06 10	06 16	06 22	06 28	06 34	06 40
WOOD GRN	05 50+	05 56+	06 02+	06 08+	06 14+	06 20+	06 26+	06 32+	06 38+	06 44+
KINGS X	06 04	06 10	06 16	06 22	06 28	06 34	06 40	06 46	06 52	06 58
HYDE PRK	06 15	06 21	06 27	06 33	06 39	06 45	06 51	06 57	07 03	07 09
ACTON TN	06 31+	06 37+	06 43+	06 49+	06 55+	07 01+	07 07+	07 13+	07 19+	07 25+
NORTHFDS	06 35+	06 41+	06 47+	06 53+	06 59+	07 05+	07 11+	07 17+	07 23+	07 29+
HEATHROW	06 52	06 58	07 04	07 10	07 16	07 22	07 28	07 34	07 40	07 46

```
        TYPE COMMAND (W/B)_EAST

O.K.

        TYPE COMMAND (E/B)_PRIN
```

TRIP NO:	21	22	23	24	25	26	27	28	29	30
HEATHROW	05 41	05 47	05 53	05 59	06 05	06 11	06 17	06 23	06 29	06 35
NORTHFDS	05 58	06 04	06 10	06 16	06 22	06 28	06 34	06 40	06 46	06 52
ACTON TN	06 02	06 08	06 14	06 20	06 26	06 32	06 38	06 44	06 50	06 56
HYDE PRK	06 17+	06 23+	06 29+	06 35+	06 41+	06 47+	06 53+	06 59+	07 05+	07 11+
KINGS X	06 28+	06 34+	06 40+	06 46+	06 52+	06 58+	07 04+	07 10+	07 16+	07 22+
WOOD GRN	06 42+	06 48+	06 54+	07 00+	07 06+	07 12+	07 18+	07 24+	07 30+	07 36+
ARNOS GR	06 47+	06 53+	06 59+	07 05+	07 11+	07 17+	07 23+	07 29+	07 35+	07 41+
COCKFOST	06 55+		07 07+		07 19+		07 31+		07 43+	

FIGURE 11

PART OF EXPANDED PEAK

TYPE COMMAND (E/B) _PRIN 68 83

TRIP NO:	68	69	70	71	72	73	74	75	76	77	78	79	80
UXBRIDGE				08 13				08 22				08 31	
RAYNERS		08 21+		08 26		08 30+		08 35		08 39+		08 44	
S HARROW		08 25		08 29+		08 34		08 38+		08 43		08 47+	
HEATHROW	08 16		08 20+		08 25		08 29+		08 34		08 38+		08 43
NORTHFDS	08 34		08 38+		08 43		08 47+		08 52		08 56+		09 01
ACTON TN	08 38	08 40	08 42+	08 44+	08 47	08 49	08 51+	08 53+	08 56	08 58	09 00+	09 02+	09 05
HYDE PRK	08 55	08 57	08 59+	09 01+	09 04	09 06	09 08+	09 10+	09 13	09 15	09 17+	09 19+	09 22
KINGS X	09 07+	09 09+	09 12	09 14	09 16+	09 18+	09 21	09 23	09 25+	09 27+	09 30	09 32	09 34+
WOOD GRN	09 21+	09 23+	09 26	09 28	09 30+	09 32+	09 35	09 37	09 39+	09 41+	09 44	09 46	09 48+
ARNOS GR	09 26+	09A29	09A31+		09 35+	09A38	09A40+		09 44	09A47	09A49+		09 53+
COCKFOST	09 34+	09 37	09 39+		09 43+	09 46	09 48+		09 52	09 55	09 57+		10 01+

TYPE COMMAND (W/B) _PRIN 78 93

TRIP NO:	78	79	80	81	82	83	84	85	86	87	88	89	90
COCKFOST	08 41+	08 44	08 46		08 50+	08 53	08 55		08 59+	09 02	09 04		09 08+
ARNOS GR	08 48+	08 51	08 53		08 57+	09 00	09 02		09 06+	09 09	09 11		09 15+
WOOD GRN	08 53	08 55+	08 57+	09 00	09 02	09 04+	09 06+	09 09	09 11	09 13+	09 15+	09 18	09 20
KINGS X	09 07+	09 10	09 12	09 14+	09 16+	09 19	09 21	09 23+	09 25+	09 28	09 30	09 32+	09 34+
HYDE PRK	09 20+	09 23	09 25	09 27+	09 29+	09 32	09 34	09 36+	09 38+	09 41	09 43	09 45+	09 47+
ACTON TN	09 38	09 40+	09 42+	09 45	09 47	09 49+	09 51+	09 54	09 56	09 58+	10 00+	10 03	10 05
NORTHFDS	09 42		09 46+		09 51		09 55+		10 00		10 04+		10 09
HEATHROW			10 03		10 07+		10 12		10 16+		10 21		10 25+
S HARROW		09P57+		10 01		10B06+		10 10		10B15+		10 19	
RAYNERS		10 00+		10 04		10 09+		10 13		10 18+		10 22	
UXBRIDGE				10 18				10 27				10 36	

TYPE COMMAND (W/B) _EAST

O.K.

FIGURE 12

```
16:49. TYPE COMMAND (W/B)._TRAN

HOW MANY MINUTES SHOULD THE W/B TRANSITION LAST FOR ?_35

SUGGESTED HEADWAY TRANSITION IS:-
```

TRIP NO:	93	94	95	96	97	98	99	100	101	102	103	104	105	106
COCKFOST		09 19	09 21+	09 24		09 29	09 31+	09 34		09 40	09 43	09 46		09 52
ARNOS GR		09 26	09 28+	09 31		09 36	09 38+	09 41		09 47	09 50	09 53		09 59
WOOD GRN	09 27	09 30+	09 33	09 35+	09 38	09 40+	09 43	09 45+	09 48+	09 51+	09 54+	09 57+	10 00+	10 03+
KINGS X	09 41+	09 44	09 46+	09 49	09 51+	09 54	09 56+	09 59	10 02	10 05	10 08	10 11	10 14	10 17
HYDE PRK	09 54+	09 55	09 57+	10 00	10 02+	10 05	10 07+	10 10	10 13	10 16	10 19	10 22	10 25	10 28
ACTON TN	10 12	10 11+	10 14	10 16+	10 19	10 21+	10 24	10 26+	10 29+	10 32+	10 35+	10 38+	10 41+	10 44+
NORTHFDS	-	10 15+		10 20+	10 23		10 28	10 30+		10 36+	10 39+		10 45+	10 48+
HEATHROW		10 32		10 37	10 39+		10 44+	10 47		10 53	10 56		11 02	11 05
S HARROW	10 28		10B31			10B38+			10B46+			10B55+		
RAYNERS	10 31		10 34			10 41+			10 49+			10 58+		
UXBRIDGE	10 45													

```
TRANSITION ACTUALLY LASTS FOR 35+ MINUTES

THE E/B TRANSITION SHOULD LAST FOR 37 MINUTES TO GIVE THE CORRECT STANDARD LAYOVERS

HOW MANY MINUTES SHOULD THE E/B TRANSITION LAST FOR ?_30

SUGGESTED HEADWAY TRANSITION IS:-
```

TRIP NO:	83	84	85	86	87	88	89	90	91	92	93	94
UXBRIDGE	08 40											
RAYNERS	08 53		08 59+		09 04+		09 09+		09 15+		09 21+	
S HARROW	08 56+		09 03		09 08		09 13		09 19		09 25	
HEATHROW		08 54+		08 59+		09 04+		09 10		09 16		09 22
NORTHFDS		09 11+		09 16+		09 21+		09 27		09 33		09 39
ACTON TN	09 28+	09 31	09 33+	09 36	09 38+	09 41	09 43+	09 46	09 49+	09 52+	09 55+	09 58+
HYDE PRK	09 41	09 42	09 44+	09 47	09 49+	09 52	09 54+	09 57	10 00+	10 03+	10 06+	10 09+
KINGS X	09 55	09 56	09 58+	10 01	10 03+	10 06	10 08+	10 11	10 14+	10 17+	10 20+	10 23+
WOOD GRN												
ARNOS GR												
COCKFOST	10 14											

```
16:51. TYPE COMMAND (W/B)._          EXPA

WHICH TRIP IN THE STANDARD IS TO BE USED FIRST ?_1
WHEN IS THE W/B EXPANSION TO END ?_1500
AT WHICH TIMING POINT ?_HYDE PRK

W/B STANDARD EXPANDED - TRIPS ALLOCATED NUMBERS 107 TO 187

EXPANSION ACTUALLY ENDS AT 14 58 AT HYDE PRK


WHEN IS THE E/B EXPANSION TO END ?_1500
AT WHICH TIMING POINT ?_HYDE PRK

E/B STANDARD EXPANDED - TRIPS ALLOCATED NUMBERS 95 TO 184

EXPANSION ACTUALLY ENDS AT 14 58+ AT HYDE PRK

16:53. TYPE COMMAND (W/B)._
```

HEADWAY TRANSITION — UNSMOOTHED

Transition. The 'SMOOth' command ensures that the maximum running time variation from one trip to the next will be half a minute. (Figure 13).

Let us summarise what the compiler has achieved so far:
A pre-peak service at basic running times with no trains to the Uxbridge branch has been generated; a peak service with maximum additional running time allowances exists and a mid-day off-peak service at basic running time allowances has been appended. Each of these three services has been expanded over discrete parts of the day and each have been 'joined' together by the TRANsition command. However, services for each direction of travel are still held separately.

By using the command 'FORM', CART immediately links, for each reversing point in turn, train arrivals with train departures so as to form lay-overs as near to the optimum as possible, but without violating the minimum. An attempt is also made by the system to link any remaining spare arrivals with later spare departures on a first-in, first-out basis. In using this command, no account is taken of terminal capacities or conflicts, as these were considered during the Standard compilation phase. If required, CART can validate the timetable, giving a warning of any clearance problems, trip paths closer than the minimum headway or any trips overtaking an adjacent trip, any of which may have arisen resulting from the compiler's adjustments. Trains not formed into a following trip are shown to 'stop'; trains not formed by a previous trip are annotated with the legend 'start'. In compiling parlance, this command 'forms up the service' and in so doing allocates train set numbers. These are allocated in octal range by Line Description 'depot', but can be altered to the requirements of the Railway Operations Manager (Figure 14 - pre-edited timetable in 'short' format).

At this stage in the development of the timetable, the compiler will want to take action in three areas. Firstly, to examine the whole span of timetable to determine what adjustments need to be made to improve the train service to and from outer termini. This of course will include the provision of a shuttle service over the Acton Town/Uxbridge branch before 0715 hours. Secondly, to decide what re-timings are thought desirable to give smoother operation without detriment to lay-overs or terminal capacity. Thirdly, the compiler will want to know how many trains have been utilised from each 'starting' (pseudo depot) point. Note should here be made that details about depots and storage sidings have not yet been incorporated into the Line Description, but facilities are to be provided for the compiler to edit these into the file.

Examination of the timetable for the first two items is facilitated by use of the command 'PRINt all trips'. This formats and prints the contents of the timetable file in the traditional style of galley pages of trips set against a station namebank. It is appropriate at this point to describe the method of storing individual trip records. Each record contains:

         Trip Number
         Train Set Number
         Trip Mode ('Empty', 'Staff', etc.)
         Miscellaneous Notes (Connections; non-stopping)
         Trip Starting Point and Time
         Trip Finishing Point (and Time after 'forming-up')
         Location and value of Hesitations ('Stands')
         Location and value of RTVs

CART is programmed to apply these data to the Line Description in order to format and print a trip.

FIGURE 13

SMOO 93 106

SUGGESTED RTV TRANSITION IS:-

TRIP NO:	93	94	95	96	97	98	99	100	101	102	103	104	105	106
COCKFOST		09 19	09 21+	09 24		09 29	09 31+	09 34		09 40	09 43	09 46		09 52
ARNOS GR		09 26	09 28+	09 31		09 36	09 38+	09 41		09 47	09 50	09 53		09 59
WOOD GRN	09 27	09 30+	09 33	09 35+	09 38	09 40+	09 43	09 45+	09 48+	09 51+	09 54+	09 57+	10 00+	10 03+
KINGS X	09 41+	09 44+	09 46+	09 49	09 51+	09 54	09 56+	09 59	10 02	10 05	10 08	10 11	10 14	10 17
HYDE PRK	09 54+	09 57+	09 59+	10 02	10 04	10 06+	10 08+	10 10+	10 13+	10 16	10 19	10 22	10 25	10 28
ACTON TN	10 12	10 15	10 17	10 19+	10 21+	10 24	10 26	10 28	10 31	10 33+	10 36+	10 39	10 42	10 44+
NORTHFDS	-	10 19	-	10 23+	10 25+	-	10 30	10 32	-	10 37+	10 40+	-	10 46	10 48+
HEATHROW	-	-				10B41	10 46+	10 48+	10B48	10 54	10 57	10B56	11 02+	11 05
S HARROW	10 28	10 35+	10B34	10 40	10 42	10 44			10 51			10 59		
RAYNERS	10 31		10 37											
UXBRIDGE	10 45													

16:54. TYPE COMMAND (W/B)_EAST

O.K.

16:55. TYPE COMMAND (E/B)_SMOO 83 94
WARNING - ONLY RTVS COMMON TO ALL TRIPS WILL BE SMOOTHED

SUGGESTED RTV TRANSITION IS:-

TRIP NO:	83	84	85	86	87	88	89	90	91	92	93	94
UXBRIDGE	08 40				08 51+		09 09+		09 02+		09 21+	
RAYNERS	08 53		08 59+		09 04+		09 13		09 15+		09 25	
S HARROW	08 56+		09 03		09 08				09 19			
HEATHROW	-	08 54+		08 59+		09 04+		09 10		09 16		09 22
NORTHFDS	-	09 11+		09 16+		09 21+		09 27		09 33		09 39
ACTON TN	09 11+	09 15+	09 18	09 20+	09 23	09 25+	09 28	09 31	09 34	09 37	09 40	09 43
HYDE PRK	09 28+	09 32	09 34+	09 36+	09 39	09 41	09 43+	09 46+	09 49+	09 52+	09 55+	09 58+
KINGS X	09 41	09 44+	09 47	09 49	09 51+	09 53+	09 56	09 58+	10 01+	10 04	10 07	10 09+
WOOD GRN	09 55	09 58+	10 01	10 03	10 05+	10 07+	10 10	10 12+	10 15+	10 18	10 21	10 23+
ARNOS GR			10 06	10 08		10 12+	10 15		10 20+	10 23		10 28+
COCKFOST				10 16			10 23			10 31		

16:55. TYPE COMMAND (E/B)_

SMOOTHED TRANSITION

K.L.W. DEXTER

FIGURE 14

TRIP NO:	85	86	87	88	89	90	91	92	93	94	95	96	97	98	99	100
TRAIN NO	22	1	60	23	24	73	61	72	25	67	30	66	26	122	2	74
ARRIVED:	START	STOP	08 00+	START	START	08 14	08 05+	08 10	START	08 25	08 17+	08 21	START	08 34	08 24	08 29+
COCKFOST	08 01		08 05+	08 08	08 10		08 14+	08 17	08 19		08 23+	08 26	08 28		08 32+	08 35
ARNOS GR	08 08		08 12+	08 15	08 17		08 21+	08 24	08 26		08 30+	08 33	08 35		08 39+	08 42
WOOD GRN	08 12+	08B15	08 17	08 19+	08 21+	08 24	08 26	08 28+	08 30+	08 33	08 35	08 37+	08 39+	08 42	08 44	08 46+
ACTON TN	08 57+	09 00	09 02	09 04+	09 06+	09 09	09 11	09 13+	09 15+	09 18	09 20	09 22+	09 24+	09 27	09 29	09 31+
NORTHFDS	09 01+	-	09 06	-	09 10+	-	09 15	-	09 19+	-	09 24	-	09 28+	-	09 33	-
HEATHROW	-		09 22+		09 27		09 31+		09 36		09 40+		09 45		09 49+	
S HARROW		09 16				09 25										
RAYNERS		09 19		09B21+		09 28		09 29+		09 34		09 38+				09 47+
UXBRIDGE		09 33				09 42		09 32+				09 41+				09 50+
TO FORM:	STOP	STOP	09 28+	STOP	09 32	STOP	09 38+	09 37+	09 42	STOP	09 48+	09 47+	09 52	STOP	09 58+	09 57+

TRIP NO:	101	102	103	104	105	106	107	108	109	110	111	112	113	114	115	116
TRAIN NO	31	120	75	27	3	121	110	32	76	123	111	4	33	63	112	5
ARRIVED:	08 32	08 43	08 34+	START	08 40+	08 52	08 43	08 45+	08 49+	09 01	08 52	08 54+	08 58+	09 10	09 01	09 03+
COCKFOST	08 37	08 44	08 41+	08 44	08 46		08 50+	08 53	08 55		08 59+	09 02	09 04		09 08+	09 11
ARNOS GR	08 44		08 48+	08 51	08 53		08 57+	09 00	09 02		09 06+	09 09	09 11		09 15+	09 18
WOOD GRN	08 48+	08 51	08 53	08 55+	08 57+	09 00	09 02	09 04+	09 06+	09 09	09 11	09 13+	09 15+	09 18	09 20	09 22+
ACTON TN	09 33+	09 36	09 38	09 40+	09 42+	09 45	09 47	09 49+	09 51+	09 54	09 56	09 58+	10 00+	10 03	10 05	10 07+
NORTHFDS	09 37+		09 42		09 46		09 51		09 55+		10 00		10 04+		10 09	
HEATHROW					10 03		10 07		10 12		10 16+		10 21		10 25+	
S HARROW						09 49										
RAYNERS				09B57+				10B06+				10B15+				10B24+
UXBRIDGE				10 00+				10 09+				10 18+				10 27+
TO FORM:	10 02	STOP	STOP	10 07+	10 08+	STOP	10 12	10 17+	10 18+	STOP	10 22	10 27+	10 28+	STOP	10 32	10 37+

SECTION OF PRE-EDITED TIMETABLE

Apart from the need to plan carefully the generation and grafting in of the Uxbridge Branch shuttle service, the compiler anticipates the necessity to make several other adjustments to the timetable generated so far. Using the command 'SAVE' enables the current timetable to be preserved, so that, in a future CART session, work can be resumed from where the compiler left off. The compiler is free to leave the terminal, carrying away the results so far produced and can give undivided attention to deciding what alterations should be made. The terminal is now free to be used by another compiler and here it is pointed out that, with the exception of disc accessing commands, the system is capable of being used by more than one compiler at a time.

Having skilfully planned what adjustments are to be made, the compiler proceeds to implement them. Firstly, the provision of the Uxbridge Branch Shuttle service to work in with the 'main line' service at Acton Town. Using the command 'SHUTtle', the system is ready to produce a self-contained regular interval service over any part of a Line. While using this command, the compiler is required to enter the starting point and time of the first trip, the destination, the service frequency and the start time of the last trip. If varied running time allowances and/or 'stands' (hesitations) are required these may also be entered. The rest of the task is borne by CART and it will quite happily show its work on request by the compiler! Again, a shuttle service can be further edited if required (see Figure 15 for part of the integrated shuttle service).

Secondly, the compiler proceeds to manipulate individual or blocks of trips using many of the powerful commands available. Use of 'RTV' causes the running time of selected trips to be altered over a specified section of Line – a facility particularly useful at the 'shoulders' of the peak. Other commands enable the compiler to delay a trip by x minutes ('DELAy'), to re-time the first or second part of a trip ('STANd' or 'BEND'), to cause a trip to run earlier ('ADVAnce') or to 'straighten out' a trip at a specified timing point or over a nominated section ('NO Bend' or 'NO Rtv'). Following any adjustment, the option is available to print the whole trip or series of trips or, alternatively, timings of one or several trips at nominated sections only.

Thirdly, to ascertain the situation with regard to how many trains have 'entered service' from various sections of the Line, the compiler uses the command 'STOCk' which causes a list of the Start and Finish details plus a Depot Summary to be printed. This summary does not include real Depots, but termini at which trains are regarded as 'starting' because there are no previous trips for such trains, or 'stabling' because there are no following trips.

Very quickly the compiler can use the Stock Analysis to determine from which depots the 'starting' trains shall emanate or at what depots 'finishing' trains shall be stabled. For example, it may be seen in Figure 16 that in this exercise two dozen trains are entering service at Heathrow Central. This terminus has no facilities for stabling that number of trains. The nearest depot on this section of the Piccadilly Line is Northfields. The compiler has therefore the choice of three actions. One to use the command 'EXTRa' to generate a number of additional trips from Northfields depot to Heathrow Central. Another, to use the command 'STARt' to start a selected number of these Heathrow 'starters' eastbound from Northfields, which is a double-ended depot. Usually both of these lines of action are adopted in order to produce the most satisfactory result, but in this case the compiler made use of the 'SHUTtle' command facility.

Similarly, after the peak period, the compiler can use the commands 'TERMinate' and 'CANCeL' in order to correct the distribution of stabling trains not required during the off-peak. Facilities are also available to the compiler to form one specified trip into another by using the command 'LINK', to 'REFOrm' the whole service or to annotate trips with alphabetic column notes, day restriction codes,

FIGURE 15

INTEGRATED SHUTTLE

13:46. TYPE COMMAND (W/B)_PRIN

TRIP NO:	21	22	23	24	25	26	27	28	29	30	31	32	33
TRAIN NO	50	51	52	53	63	54	55	64	56	57	66	60	61
ARRIVED:	START	START	START	START	05 34	START	START	05 49	START	START	06 04	START	START
NOTES...	STAFF	EMPTY	EMPTY										
COCKFOST													
ARNOS GR													
WOOD GRN													
ACTON TN					05 42			05 57			06 12		
NORTHFDS	05 22	05 29+	05 37	05 44+	−	05 52	05 59+	−	06 07	06 14+	−	06 22	06 29+
HEATHROW	05 38+	05 46	05 53+	06 01	05 58	06 08+	06 16	06 13	06 23+	06 31	06 28	06 38+	06 46
S HARROW					06 01			06 16			06 31		
RAYNERS					06 15			06 30			06 45		
UXBRIDGE													
TO FORM:	05 47	05 53	05 59	06 11	06 27	06 17	06 23	06 42	06 29	06 40+	06 56	06 46	06 51

TRIP NO:	34	35	36	37	38	39	40	41	42	43	44	45	46
TRAIN NO	67	1	30	120	2	31	3	121	110	32	4	111	63
ARRIVED:	06 17	START	START	06 28+	START	START	START	06 43+	START	START	START	START	06 58+
NOTES...		PT			PT					PT			
COCKFOST		05 39	05 52		05 51	06 03	06 03					06 15	
ARNOS GR		05 46	05 56+		05 58	06 10	06 10		06 16			06 22	
WOOD GRN		05 50+	06 37+		06 02+	06 08+	06 14+		06 20+			06 26+	
ACTON TN	06 27	06 31+	06 41+	06 42	06 43+	06 49+	06 55+	06 57	07 01+	07 07+			07 12
NORTHFDS	−	06 35+	06 58	−	06 47+	06 53+	06 59+		07 05+	07 11+			−
HEATHROW	−	06 52		06 58		07 04	07 10	07 16			−	07 22	07 28
S HARROW	06 43		06 58		07 13	07 16		07 13	07 16+			07 25+	07 28
RAYNERS	06 46		07 01		07 16	07 19+		07 16	07 19+			07 28+	07 31
UXBRIDGE	07 00		07 15		07 30			07 30				07 45	
TO FORM:	07 10	06 59+	07 03	07 28	07 09+	07 16	07 22	07 37	07 27+	07 26+	07 35+	07 36+	07 55

FIGURE 16

STOCK BALANCE ANALYSIS

DO YOU WANT TO ASSIGN REAL TRAIN NUMBERS ?_NO

STOCK BALANCE ANALYSIS:-

TIMING POINT	MORNING STARTS	MORNING FINISHES	AFTERNOON STARTS	EVENING FINISHES	EVENING STARTS	NIGHT FINISHES	BALANCE
COCKFOST	25	8	0	8	0	0	-9
UXBRIDGE	9	12	0	0	0	0	3
HEATHROW	24	5	0	16	0	0	-3
RAYNERS	7	2	0	8	0	0	3
ARNOS GR	8	3	1	7	0	0	1
WOOD GRN	3	2	0	6	0	0	5
TOTALS	76	32	1	45	0	0	
TRAINS IN USE	76	44	45	0	0	0	

THIS TIMETABLE REQUIRES 76 TRAINS
AND WILL GENERATE 8546.94 TRAIN-MILES

e.g. SO, and mode codes 'empty', 'staff', etc. by appropriate commands. Figure 17 portrays a section of the timetable as completed to the current point of development covered in the exercise.

It is not possible, within the scope of the paper, to describe the many other facilities available to the compiler in CART. Suffice it to say there are comprehensive library facilities for storage, naming and retrieval of Standards and Timetables; also numerous aids to help the compiler trace information held in a timetable file. Above all, provided the compiler has properly analysed and drafted a plan of action, and that there is no problem regarding keyboard work or system response, timetable manipulation through CART facilities is outstandingly faster than the pencil and rubber method. There is also reason to believe the introduction of Visual Display Units, supplementary to the existing hard-copy terminal printers, will further aid the compiler in his or her work.

In this exercise it will have been seen that CART is quite capable of giving great assistance to the compiler in the production of a timetable for most of the operational day. Indeed for a full day's service on file it enables a compiler to request a Rolling Stock Balance, in order to determine what depot working adjustments need to be made to satisfy, for example, the Rolling Stock Engineer's maintenance schedule requirements. Also, use of the command 'SCHEdules' causes CART to print the complete running schedule for each individual train on file – a facility which has many uses, including providing the basic data upon which crew duty schedule compilation can proceed (see Figure 18 for an example).

EARNING RECOGNITION

By this exercise, the discerning expert in compiling will doubtless have noted that CART has certain deficiencies both in scope and as to absolute validity of the finished product. Much has yet to be done to enhance the capability and use of the system in accord with a development programme which has been jointly agreed with the users. However, as early as 1977, CART development was sufficiently advanced for the system to be reliably used in the production of results urgently required by Railway Senior Management.

One case concerned late running of the Victoria Line Monday-to-Friday service which by 1977 had so deteriorated that the matter was causing operating staff discontent. Source of the problem was insufficient recovery time in the off-peak timetable, which service was barely adequate to cater for the tremendous growth in usage of the Line continuously throughout the day. This was forcing station dwell times to be longer than originally allowed for, thus causing late running. The solution was to provide additional running time during peak periods at the expense of widening intervals from two to two-and-a-quarter minutes and to run 3 trains in 10 rather than 3 trains in 9 minutes during the off-peak period – a deceptively simple revision. But, as subsequently reported in the Computer Press, a revision that demonstrated the speed and flexibility of CART.

A large number of service options, based on differing running time allowances, was generated on a terminal during an October meeting of Railway Managers concerned to resolve the problem of late running. The remit was to effect a minimum reduction in service and to avoid the use of additional trains. Within a few weeks, a new Victoria Line timetable was introduced based entirely on the results produced by CART.

More recently, CART has been instrumental in determining the rolling stock replacement programme for the Jubilee Line in the mid-eighties. Here, the number of factors involved precluded the production of a satisfactory clerically-produced solution in the time and with the resources available. The factors involved

FIGURE 17

	47	48	49	50	51	52	53	54	55	56
TRIP NO:	47	48	49	50	51	52	53	54	55	56
TRAIN NO	33	112	5	34	64	113	6	114	35	7
ARRIVED:	START	START	START	START	07 13+	START	START	START	START	START
COCKFOST	06 28		06 27	06 40			06 39		06 51+	06 50
ARNOS GR	06 32+		06 34	06 44+			06 46		06 56	06 57
WOOD GRN	07 13+		06 38+		07 27		06 50+		07 37	07 01+
ACTON TN	07 17+		07 19+	07 25+			07 31+		07 41	07 42+
NORTHFDS	07 34		07 23+	07 29+			07 35+		07 57+	
HEATHROW			07 40	07 46	--		07 52			
S HARROW		07 34+			07 43	07 43+		07 52+		07 58+
RAYNERS		07 37+			07 46	07 46+		07 55+		08 01+
UXBRIDGE					08 00					08 15+
TO FORM:	07 40	07 45+	07 44+	07 53+	08 13	07 54+	07 58	08 03+	08 02+	08 22

(Annotation in the left columns: AS SHOWN IN FIGURE 16 UNTIL)

	57	58	59	60	61	62	63	64	65	66	67	68
TRIP NO:	57	58	59	60	61	62	63	64	65	66	67	68
TRAIN NO	62	115	50	10	52	65	36	51	53	11	37	12
ARRIVED:	START	START	06 53+	START	07 05+	06 55+	START	07 07+	07 17+	START	START	START
COCKFOST			07 02	06 59+	07 10+	07 07		07 13+	07 23+	07 19	07 28	07 23
ARNOS GR			07 06+	07 06+	07 15	07 14	07 17+	07 20+	07 28	07 26	07 32+	07 30
WOOD GRN				07 11		07 18+	07 22	07 25	08 09	07 30+		07 34+
ACTON TN			07 47+	07 52	07 56	07 59+	08 03	08 06	08 13	08 12	08 15	08 18+
NORTHFDS			07 51+		08 00		08 07		08 29+		08 19	
HEATHROW	07 47		08 08	--	08 16+		08 23+			--	08 35+	
S HARROW	08 03+	08 01+		08 08		08 15+		08 22		08 28		08 34+
RAYNERS		08 04+		08B12		08 18+		08 25		08 31		08B38+
UXBRIDGE						08 32+				08 45		
TO FORM:	08 11+	08A12+	08 16	08 21+	08 25	08 40	08 29+	08B39+	08 34	08 51+	08 43	08 48+

SECTION OF CART GENERATED TIMETABLE

FIGURE 17

	21	22	23	24	25	26	27	28	29	30	31	32
TRIP NO:	21	22	23	24	25	26	27	28	29	30	31	32
TRAIN NO	63	64	65	66	50	51	67	52	70	120	53	54
ARRIVED:	START	START	START	START	05 38+	05 46	START	05 53+	START	START	06 01	06 08+
NOTES...	STAFF	EMPTY	PT	EMPTY	PT	PT	EMPTY	PT	PT	START	PT	PT
UXBRIDGE										05 57		
RAYNERS										06 10		
S HARROW										06 13+		
HEATHROW	05 30	05 45	05 58	06 00	05 47	05 53		05 59				
NORTHFDS	05 34	05 49	06 02	06 04	06 04	06 10	06 13	06 16	06 22	–	06 28	06 34
ACTON TN			06 42+		06 08	06 14	06 17	06 20	06 26	–	06 32	06 38
WOOD GRN					06 48+	06 54+		07 00+	07 06+	06 28+	07 12+	07 18+
ARNOS GR			06 47+		06 53+	06 59+		07 05+	07 11+		07 17+	07 23+
COCKFOST			06 55+			07 07+			07 19+			07 31+
TO FORM:	05 42	05 57	07 07	06 12	07 02	07 13+	06 27	07 10+	07 25	06 42	07 23+	07 38+

	33	34	35	36	37	38	39	40	41	42	43	44
TRIP NO:	33	34	35	36	37	38	39	40	41	42	43	44
TRAIN NO	121	55	56	71	63	57	60	61	64	72	1	30
ARRIVED:	START	06 16	06 23+	START	06 15	06 31	06 38+	06 46	06 30	START	06 52	06 58
UXBRIDGE	06 12			06 27						06 42		
RAYNERS	06 25			06 40						06 55		
S HARROW	06 28+			06 43+						06 58+		
HEATHROW	–			–						–		
NORTHFDS	06 43+	06 23	06 29	06 58+						07 12+		
ACTON TN		06 44	06 50		06 46	06 52	07 03	07 07	07 12	07 13+		07 16+
WOOD GRN				06 58+		07 01+	07 07	07 12				
ARNOS GR		07 24+	07 30+	07 36+	07 41+	07 47+	07 52+	07 57+	08 01	08 02	08 09+	08 17+
COCKFOST		07 37+	07 43+	07 49+		07 52+	08 00+	08 05+		08 10		08 17+
TO FORM:	06 57	07 43	07 50	07 56+	07 12	07 57	08 05+	08 14+	07 27	08 17	08B15	08 23+

FIGURE 17

TRIP NO:	45	46	47	48	49	50	51	52	53	54	55	56
TRAIN NO	66	2	73	74	31	75	67	3	110	32	122	76
ARRIVED:	06 45	07 04	START	START	07 10	START	07 00	07 16	07 19+	07 22	START	START
UXBRIDGE	06 56						07 10				07 19	
RAYNERS	07 09						07 23		07 27+		07 32	
S HARROW	07 12+						07 26+		07 31		07 35+	
HEATHROW	--	07 09+			07 16		--	07 22		07 26+	--	
NORTHFDS		07 26+	07 29	07 31	07 33	07 35		07 40		07 44+		07 49
ACTON TN	07 27+	07 30+	07 33	07 35	07 37	07 39	07 41+	07 44	07 46	07 48+	07 50+	07 53
WOOD GRN	08 08	08 11	08 14	08 16+	08 19	08 21+	08 25	08 27+	08 29+	08 32	08 34	08 36+
ARNOS GR	08 13	08 16		08 21+	08 24	08 26+		08 32+	08A35	08A37+		08 41+
COCKFOST	08 21	08 24		08 29+	08 32	08 34+		08 40+	08 43	08 45+		08 49+
TO FORM:	08 26	08 32+	08 24	08 35	08 37	08 41+	08 33	08 46	08 50+	08 53	08 42	08 55

TRIP NO:	57	58	59	60	61	62	63	64	65	66	67	68
TRAIN NO	111	4	120	33	112	5	121	77	113	34	123	6
ARRIVED:	07 28+	07 28	07 15	07 34	07 37+	07 40	07 30	START	07 46+	07 46	START	07 52
UXBRIDGE			07 28				07 37			07 46		
RAYNERS	07 36+		07 41		07 45+		07 50		07 54+	07 59		
S HARROW	07 40		07 44+		07 49		07 53+		07 58	08 02+		
HEATHROW	--	07 35+	--	07 40	--	07 44+	--		--	--		07 58
NORTHFDS		07 53+		07 58		08 02+		08 07				08 16
ACTON TN	07 55	07 57+	07 59+	08 02	08 04	08 06+	08 08+	08 11	08 13	08 15+	08 17+	08 20
WOOD GRN	08 38+	08 41	08 43	08 45+	08 47+	08 50	08 52	08 54+	08 56+	08 59	09 01	09 03+
ARNOS GR	08A44	08A46+		08 50+	08A53	08A55+		08 59+	09A02	09A04+		09 08+
COCKFOST	08 52	08 54+		08 58+	09 01	09 03+		09 07+	09 10	09 12+		09 16+
TO FORM:	08 59+	09 02	08 51	09 04	09 08+	09 11	09 00	09 13	STOP	09 19	09 09	09 21+

FIGURE 18

C.A.R.T. TRAIN RUNNING SCHEDULE   PICCADILLY LINE
PRODUCED ON 30/05/80 AT 15:00   ==================

TIMETABLE NUMBER LEEDS 1   TRAIN NO. 64
OPERATING ON 15-18 JULY 1980   6 CARS

TRAIN STARTING FROM NORTHFDS AT 05 45

```
COCKFOST
ARNOS GR                      0938   12 00   14 20
WOOD GRN                      09 51+ 12 13+  14 33+
KINGS X                       10 04  12 24+  14 44+
HYDE PRK                      10 21+ 12 41   15 01
ACTON TN   05 57 07 27        10 25+ 12 45   15 05
NORTHFDS     -                10 42  13 01+  15 21+
HEATHROW     -
S HARROW   06 13 07 43
RAYNERS    06 16 07 46
UXBRIDGE   06 30 08 00

NOTES... EMPTY

UXBRIDGE   06 42 08 13
RAYNERS    06 55 08 26
S HARROW   06 58+ 08 29+
HEATHROW                      10 48+ 13 08+
NORTHFDS   05 45              11 05+ 13 25+
ACTON TN   05 49 07 13+ 08 44+ 11 09+ 13 29+
HYDE PRK         09 01+       11 25  13 45
KINGS X          09 14        11 36  13 56
WOOD GRN         09 28        11 50  14 10
ARNOS GR
COCKFOST
```

TRAIN TO FINISH AT HEATHROW AT 15 21+

TRAIN IS IN SERVICE FOR 09 HRS 36+ MINS AND COVERS 181.62 MILES

WHEEL-TURNING TIME = 08 HRS 07+ MINS
      TERMINAL TIME = 00 HRS 46 MINS
           LAYOVER = 00 HRS 43 MINS

included:

a) Trunk section service levels ranging by fractions of a minute from 2 to 3 minutes

b) Three intermediate reversing points where either one, two or three could be used

c) Three types of driving and braking characteristics either on plain track or in reversing sidings or in both

d) Three sets of running allowances as a result of (c)

e) Minimum or standard lay-over allowances at one or both extremities of the Line.

It is quite understandable why some 12,000 timetable options were possible! Use was made of Service Value Factors to assist in the production of the final Which?-type report, which formed the basis of placing the contract for rolling stock.

CART IN THE FUTURE

It will be realised from these examples that as a research tool CART is second to none. As a compiling aid it is of significant benefit to the compiler, but present capability is confined to Lines or routes with single central trunk sections. The system has yet to be enhanced to handle more complex Lines epitomised by the Northern which divides into two central area routes both of which converge to serve one route to South London and two branches to North London suburbs.

The system is currently being developed to calculate scheduled train working at multi-platform termini and intermediate alternative platform routeing points. It is hoped this will obviate the need for compilers both to compile this working and to key it into the timetable file. Coincident with the calculation of platform working at termini is the scheduling of timing paths for trains required to enter service from, or stable at, depots or sidings adjacent to each terminus.

Finally, it is planned to link CART with the existing long established computer system run in the Central DP Computer Installation of London Transport. It is this system (diagrammatically described in Figure 19) which supports the automatic production of programme machine rolls and which accepts, exhaustively validates and processes manually-compiled timetables, at present entered on a trip input record basis through Direct Data Entry terminals. It is planned to tailor CART to produce timetable files acceptable to the established system and thus obviate or reduce data preparation.

The established timetable processing system comprises several suites of programs, each dedicated to the production of widely differing outputs. These range from the production of train registers used, for example, in the booking of the train service by control regulators and signalmen, to the production of duty cards for traincrew, train and duty analyses for Station Management and, more dramatically, the generation of magnetic drive tapes for use on a photo-typesetter. The latter facilitates the speedier and cheaper production of printed timetables, the fully formatted, correctly justified and properly type-faced pages having been generated by our own application software using basic randomly input train trip data without timing point detail. (A sample photo-typeset page is shown in Figure 20.) Current development foresees the production of timetable posters and other passenger train and bus information by the same technology.

FIGURE 19

RAILWAY OPERATIONAL PLANNING

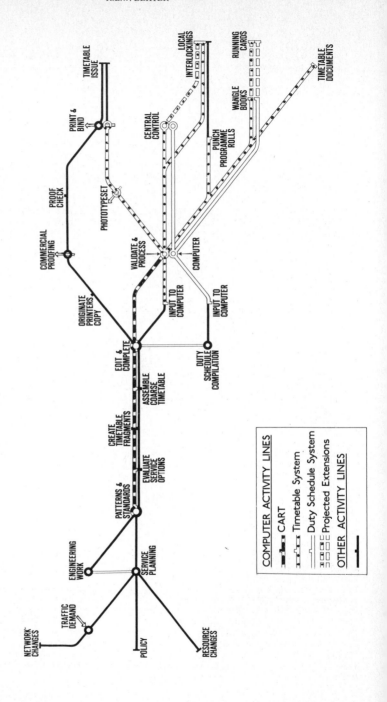

COMPUTER ACTIVITY LINES

CART

Timetable System

Duty Schedule System

Projected Extensions

OTHER ACTIVITY LINES

FIGURE 20

-14

MONDAYS TO FRIDAYS **WESTBOUND**

Train No.	251D	252D	253	D105	254		256D	316D	D106	330D	251D		D43	253	431	431	251
Notes	Start Staff	Start Ety	Staff	Start Ety	Start Staff		Ety	PL ZX		PT				Ety	Start RR XA	RR XA	Start
Cockfosters Pfm. No.	...	...	...	...	...	...	...	...	...	1	1	...	...	4	...	...	...
COCKFOSTERS	...	...	...	...	...	...	...	...	...	05 53	06 31	...	...	06 46	...	...	...
Cockfosters Depot	...	...	...	...	...	...	...	...	...	—	—	...	...	06 49	...	...	...
Oakwood	...	...	...	...	...	...	...	...	...	05 55	06 33	...	...	...	...	...	...
Arnos Grove Pfm. No.	...	...	...	...	...	...	...	...	...	4	4	...	...	...	...	...	...
ARNOS GROVE	...	...	...	...	...	...	...	...	...	06 00	06 38	...	...	...	...	...	...
Arnos Grove Sidings	...	...	...	...	...	...	...	...	...	—	—	...	...	...	...	ex EB Pfm 14 12 to Northern Line	...
WOOD GREEN	...	...	...	...	...	...	...	05 11 ex	...	06 04½	06 42½	...	...	...	...		...
King's Cross	...	...	...	...	...	...	...	West	...	06 18	06 56	...	...	...	...		...
HYDE PARK CORNER	...	...	...	...	...	...	...	Ken	...	06 29	07 07	...	...	...	...		...
Barons Court	...	...	...	...	...	...	...	05 12½	...	06 39	07 17	...	...	...	...		...
HAMMERSMITH No. 2 Pfm.	...	...	...	...	...	...	...	LL	...	06 40½	07 18½	...	...	...	...		...
HAMMERSMITH No. 1 Pfm.	...	...	...	...	...	...	...	05d16	ex	—	—	...	...	...	13 17		...
Turnham Green	ex 21 Sdg	ex 23 Sdg	ex 21 Sdg	...	ex 21 Sdg	...	...	05 20	Earl's Court	06 44	—	...	ex T Hill	...	ex Acton Works	...	...
ACTON TOWN No. 1 Pfm.	04 37	...	...	...	...	...	ex WB	05 24	06 32	—	—	...	07 35	...	13 19	...	...
ACTON TOWN No. 2 Pfm.	LL	04 42	04 55	...	05 09	...	fast Pfm	LL	—	06 47	07 23½	...	—	...	LL	...	...
Northfields	04 41	—	—	05 08 ex	—	...	05 13	05 28	—	06 51	07c29	...	—	...	13 23	...	...
Northfields Depot	—	—	—	Depot	—	...	—	—	—	—	07 34	...	—	...	to	...	17 02
Osterley	04 46	—	—	...	—	...	05 18	05 33	—	06 56	...	...	—	...	Depot	...	17 07
HEATHROW CENTRAL	04 57½	—	—	...	—	...	05 29½	05 44½	—	07 07½	...	...	—	...	Recep	...	17 18½
Heathrow Central Pfm. No.	2	—	—	...	—	...	2	2	—	2	...	...	—	...	Road	...	2
Ealing Common	...	04 44	04 57	05 10	05 11	...	...	...	06 34	...	...	...	07 37	...	...	...	...
EALING BROADWAY	...	—	—	rev in EB Pfm	—	...	...	...	06 36½	...	...	...	07 39½	...	...	...	...
South Harrow Sidings	...	—	—		—	...	...	...	...	...	...	...	...	...	...	...	...
South Harrow	...	04 58	05 11	...	05 25	...	...	...	...	...	...	...	...	...	...	...	...
RAYNERS LANE	...	rev in EB Pfm	rev in EB Pfm	...	05 28	...	...	...	...	...	...	...	...	...	...	...	...
Ruislip	...	...	...	...	...	...	...	...	...	...	...	...	...	...	...	...	...
Ruislip Siding	...	...	...	...	...	...	...	...	...	...	...	...	...	...	...	...	...
Hillingdon	...	...	...	...	...	...	...	...	...	...	...	...	...	...	...	...	...
UXBRIDGE	...	...	...	...	...	...	...	...	...	...	...	...	...	...	...	...	...
Uxbridge Pfm. No.	...	...	...	...	...	...	...	...	...	...	...	...	...	...	...	...	...
To form	05 07	05 05	05 26	05 14½	Stop	...	Stop 23 38½	Stop	Stop	Stop	Stop 1702W	...	Stop	Stop 18 16E	13 38½	...	Stop

Train No.	350	D16	259	469	362D		355	365D	366	D32	342		342	344	344	D52	353D
Notes	Start		Ety (3cars)	RR TWO	Start PT		Start Ety	Start PT	Start AR PT	AB	Start		Ety	Start AS PT	Ety	Ety	Start Staff
Cockfosters Pfm. No.	...	...	...	...	...	...	...	...	...	...	...	...	...	2	...	...	...
COCKFOSTERS	...	...	...	ex	...	...	...	...	...	...	...	...	...	23 49	...	...	...
Cockfosters Depot	17 03	...	...	Vic	...	...	...	...	...	...	...	...	...	—	...	...	...
Oakwood	17 08	...	...	Line	...	...	...	...	...	...	...	...	...	23 51	...	...	...
Arnos Grove Pfm. No.	4	...	...	20 06	3	...	...	3	3	...	...	...	...	4	...	...	...
ARNOS GROVE	17 13	...	...	ex	22 31	...	...	23 06	23 34	...	...	...	...	23 56	...	...	...
Arnos Grove Sidings	—	...	...	Fins Park	—	...	...	—	—	...	...	...	...	—	...	...	...
WOOD GREEN	17 17½	...	19 07½	...	22 35½	...	...	23 10½	23 38½	...	...	...	...	00 00½	...	...	...
King's Cross	17 31	...	19 20½	20 13	22 48½	...	...	23 23½	23 51½	...	...	...	...	00 13½	...	...	...
HYDE PARK CORNER	17 43	...	19 31	20 23½	22 59	...	...	23 34	00 02	...	...	...	...	00 25½	...	...	...
Barons Court	17 54	...	19 40½	20 33	23 08½	...	...	23 43½	00 11½	...	...	...	...	00 35	...	...	...
HAMMERSMITH No. 2 Pfm.	17 55½	...	19 42	20 34½	23 10	...	...	23 45	00d15	...	...	...	...	00a37	...	...	...
HAMMERSMITH No. 1 Pfm.	—	...	—	...	—	...	...	—	—	...	...	...	...	—	...	ex	...
Turnham Green	—	ex Upstr	—	...	23 13½	...	ex 21 Sdg	23 48½	00 18½	ex Upstr	ex 21 Sdg	...	...	00 40½	...	Mans House	ex 23 Sdg
ACTON TOWN No. 1 Pfm.	—	18c06½	—	...	—	...	...	—	—	00 23½	...	...	...	—	ex EB	01 07	...
ACTON TOWN No. 2 Pfm.	18 01	—	19 47	...	23 16½	...	23 18½	23 51½	00 21½	—	00 24	...	←	00 43½	Local Pfm	—	01 50
Northfields	—	—	19 51	...	23 20½	...	23 22½	23 55½	—	—	00 28	...	00 28	00 47½	01 02	—	—
Northfields Depot	—	—	19 56	...	—	...	—	—	—	—	→	...	—	to 7 Sdg	01 07	—	—
Osterley	—	—	...	...	23 25½	...	23 27½	00 00½	—	—	...	...	00 33	...	...	—	—
HEATHROW CENTRAL	—	—	...	...	23 37	...	...	00 12	—	—	...	...	to	...	...	—	—
Heathrow Central Pfm. No.	—	—	...	...	1	...	to H'slow Cent arr 23 30½	2	—	—	...	...	Hatton Cross Pfm 1 arr 00 42	...	...	—	—
Ealing Common	18 03	18 08½	...	...	...	...		...	00 23½	00 25½	...	...		...	...	01 09	01 52
EALING BROADWAY	—	18 11	...	...	...	...		...	—	00 28	...	...		...	...	rev in WB Pfm	—
South Harrow Sidings	—	...	...	...	...	...	...	...	—	...	...	...	...	...	...		—
South Harrow	18 17	...	...	...	...	...	...	...	00 37½	...	...	...	...	...	...	...	02 06
RAYNERS LANE	18 20	...	...	...	...	...	...	...	00 40½	...	...	...	...	...	...	...	02 09
Ruislip	...	...	...	...	...	...	...	...	...	...	...	...	...	...	...	...	02 14½
Ruislip Siding	...	...	...	...	...	...	...	...	...	...	...	...	...	...	...	...	—
Hillingdon	...	...	...	...	...	...	...	...	...	...	...	...	...	...	...	...	02 18½
UXBRIDGE	...	...	...	...	...	...	...	...	...	...	...	...	...	...	...	...	to Sdgs
Uxbridge Pfm. No.	...	...	...	...	...	...	...	...	...	...	...	...	...	...	...	...	arr 02 25
To form	Stop	Stop	Stop	Stop	23 50	...	23 36	00 18	00 51	Stop	→	...	00 47	00 57	Stop	01 13	Stop

CART, although at present a stand-alone package, will, in the longer term, play an increasingly important role linked with other systems. It will be an integral part of the total system for the support of a fully automatic urban railway, inclusive of unmanned operation. Nevertheless, at the end of the day, it must always be remembered that a public transport system is as good as its timetable, or as bad as its inability to keep to it.

I would like to conclude by thanking London Transport Data Processing and Railway Managements for permission to present this paper, and to thank Marek Ziemba and David Miall for their assistance in its preparation.

Bus Crew
Scheduling Methods

Computer Scheduling of Public Transport
A. Wren (ed.)
© *North-Holland Publishing Company, 1981*

ADVANCES IN COMPUTER-ASSISTED RUNCUTTING
IN NORTH AMERICA

Peter M. Hildyard and Hugh V. Wallis

SAGE Management Consultants
Toronto
Canada

The history of the use of the RUCUS runcutting system is traced, and lessons are drawn from the difficulties encountered in achieving regular use by scheduling staff. It is concluded that the original system had no provision for user feed-back, and that its commands were difficult for personnel to understand. The need for an interactive system is presented, and the development of such a system is described. The outlook for scheduling in the future with the aid of microprocessors is examined.

INTRODUCTION

Before preparing this paper, we looked at the proceedings of the international workshop on computer scheduling that was held in Chicago in 1975, and scanned through the papers. Very few of those papers indicated real implementation experience. Five years later, reviewing the list of papers for this conference, there are a significant number of papers reflecting real implementations of computer scheduling techniques in transit. Much has been achieved in the past five years, in bringing the state-of-the-art in the research field to the transit scheduling department.

Our experiences in computer-assisted runcutting should be of great interest, since SAGE Management Consultants is the largest consulting firm in North America working in the area of computer-assisted scheduling. Perhaps the biggest lesson that we have learned from this experience is that making a system work technically is only part of the problem. Developing something that the end-users will accept as part of their daily working environment is by far the larger task.

This paper describes the types of experience that we have gone through in the past five years, how the computer-assisted runcutting has developed in North America, the lessons we have learned and where we stand today.

THE ORIGINAL 'RUCUS' RUNCUTTING SYSTEM

The RUCUS (RUnCUtting and Scheduling) system was developed by the Urban Mass Transportation Administration in the late 1960s, and was field tested in the early 1970s. The first version was made available for general industry-wide transit use in 1973 (1).

The overall structure of RUCUS runcutting in its original form is shown in Figure 1. The first step reads in the data that describes the vehicles to which the drivers are to be assigned. Once the data has been fully edited, the program proceeds to execute a number of optional predefined runcutting steps. The first step cuts one-piece runs, typically eight hours of work without the driver getting off the vehicle. The second step cuts the morning straight runs (either one piece of work approximately eight hours long, or two pieces of work with a fairly small meal break between the pieces). The program proceeds to cut the evening straight runs followed by swing runs (two pieces of work with an extended break between the two pieces). What remains at this point is loose-ends or tripper pieces.

After making this rough cut of all the vehicle blocks, the system executes a number of 'tripper elimination' routines which try to construct desirable runs out of the loose-end pieces. They do this by breaking up and restructuring some of the runs that had been created earlier.

When all tripper elimination routines have been executed, the next step is a first level cost optimization. This step tries to improve the overall cost and quality of the runs through various techniques of switching pieces of work and shifting end points, making sure that the resultant runs conform to the union contract. Beyond the first level of cost optimization, a second level of cost optimization is available for the user. This attempts to reduce pay-hours by switching and shifting pieces, but allowing runs to be created which violate the union contract. The third and final level cost optimization attempts to legalize the invalid runs that were created in the second level, by switching and shifting the pieces around to create valid runs.

Central to the whole runcutting logic is a single routine called the 'cost routine'. This incorporates the provisions of the union contract for the particular transit system. The cost routine serves two purposes. Whenever the runcutting algorithms determine a candidate run, the starting and ending time for each piece of work, together with the vehicles from which the work is to be cut, are passed to the cost routine. The cost routine is required to indicate whether this candidate run conforms to the union contract, and to compute the pay-hour cost of the run.

EARLY EXPERIENCES WITH 'RUCUS' RUNCUTTING

Consultants from SAGE were among the first to try to implement these computer programs in transit properties, specifically for the Toronto Transit Commission. The scope of the project was to demonstrate the feasibility of computer-assisted runcutting in one division (garage) of the Toronto Transit Commission system.

It was soon realized that the programs had both software and logic problems, and would require significant modifications to make them meet the requirements of the Toronto Transit Commission. After the modifications were undertaken, it was shown that, using the computer techniques, operator pay-hour savings in the order of one-and-one-half to two per cent were possible. To achieve the greater operator savings, it was necessary to produce lower quality driver runs (from the union's point of view), even though the runcut did not violate the union contract.

In the meantime, a number of other transit systems started to get involved with RUCUS, but generally these tended to be smaller properties. The earlier experience in smaller properties was quite favourable. Perhaps this can be explained by the fact that smaller transit systems tend to be more adaptable to new techniques. This, in part, is due to the greatly reduced data volume, and to the fact that there is seldom more than one full-time scheduler involved in scheduling the transit service of a small property.

Figure 1

Overall RUCUS Runcutting Logic
of Original System

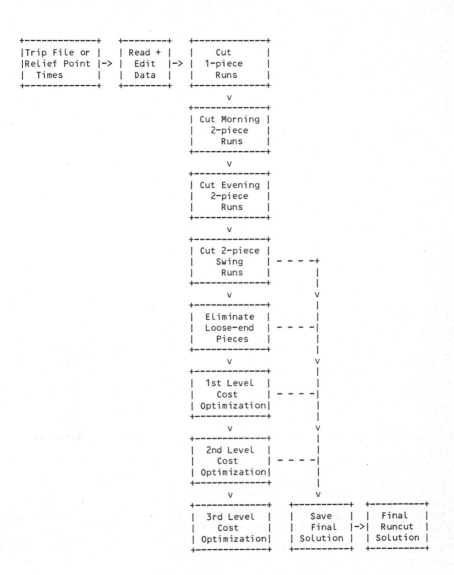

Over the following two years, a number of improvements to the computer programs were made by different consulting firms, and, independently, by a number of transit systems. Better results were obtained, but it became apparent that there was more to implementing computer-assisted run cutting than developing good heuristic algorithms. The human side of the problem was neglected: eventually, a scheduler with no computer background would be expected to use the system as part of his everyday environment.

It was concluded that the original RUCUS system was too difficult for a scheduler to use. Yet the alternative of having the scheduler use an intermediary, a computer 'expert', was considered unacceptable, since it limits the scheduler's ability to produce a high-quality end product.

THE MAJOR PROBLEMS WITH 'RUCUS' RUNCUTTING

To understand why RUCUS was difficult to use, consider what was required to operate the original RUCUS package. Firstly, the input data had to be prepared. It could be in one of two forms: a trip file (TPFILE), or simply the times a vehicle passed a relief point at which a driver could be relieved from the vehicle.

Early users of RUCUS attempted to build and maintain a trip file, since this was easier to prepare from a manual timetable. But, in general, it was found that the effort required to maintain this data was prohibitive. Why? It should be remembered that the first implementations of RUCUS were done in a batch environment, where all the data were keypunched on to cards. Updating a trip file required supplying a number of update cards to a program which would read in an old trip file and generate a new trip file. For a scheduler who was used to the practice of changing a time on a schedule with an eraser and pencil, this hardly seemed like progress!

Consequently, many users gave up computerizing the complete schedule, and simply coded the minimum data required for runcutting - the arrival times at relief points. But even so, this task was still burdensome. Whereas in a manual environment, a scheduler can start runcutting the moment the vehicle blocks are created, in a computerized environment, a significant amount of time is spent getting the vehicle schedule into computerized form before the computerized runcut can be started.

The second, and more important, deficiency of the RUCUS package was the lack of control over the program. The user was required to establish a set of parameters prior to the program execution. There were approximately fifty parameters to control what the program did. Some of these had rather strange names like CRTSPN or ERLSWG. Imagine an experienced scheduler trying to understand names such as these.

There was no capability of putting conditional tests between the runcutting steps to control the execution. Essentially, it was a straight-through process. If the parameters were not set up correctly at the start, then undesirable results would be obtained. So there were really just two choices. Either the user could let the program run right through the whole sequence of steps to the end, and waste computer time if an unsatisfactory result was obtained in the first step, or the user could keep rerunning the program doing one more step each time. Add to this all the complexities of IBM job control language, the problem of remembering what the appropriate input and output files should be, and the turnaround delays in a batch environment, and one very quickly gets an idea of the unacceptability of the basic approach for the average scheduling department.

HOW WERE THE PROBLEMS OVERCOME?

The problem of preparing the runcutting data and enabling the scheduler to cut runs as soon as the vehicle blocks are completed has been solved by the development of the Mini-Scheduler system, described elsewhere (2).

However, it was still necessary to improve the ease of use of computer-assisted runcutting and provide the user with more control. There were a number of attempts to improve matters before satisfactory results were obtained.

The first modifications added even more parameters to the program. Rather than setting up one set of parameters that would apply to all steps of the process, additional parameters were added so that it was possible to constrain the program in different ways for different steps.

Due to the inherent inflexibility of the runcutting logic itself, the cost routine quickly became the favourite place for incorporating additional controls and logic to improve the quality of driver runs. This was done by flagging a run as being illegal when really it was just undesirable or inflating the pay-hours, so the runcutting program would choose a 'cheaper' run in preference to the first choice. Clearly, this was not the most efficient or sensible way of improving the logic of the software. The algorithms were attempting to create many more possibilities than the cost routine could accept.

More logic was built into the cost routine, to provide better control over the end result. Penalties and bonuses were added to allow the user to build a weighting factor into the pay-hours that the optimization routines minimize.

These measures provided some improvement, but still did not give the level of control that most users required. The next development cycle was to break the logic down into discrete steps, and produce a 'step-wise' runcutting system. The step-wise runcutting system allowed the user to modify the parameters prior to each step of the runcutting process. Also, the user could now select the sequence of steps to be performed. For example, the user could cut the evening runs before the morning runs, if so desired.

In the meantime, the use of time-sharing systems had grown considerably from the late 1960s and early 70s. The next natural development, therefore, was to develop an 'interactive batch' environment. The main benefits of this were to eliminate all the job control requirements for executing the runcutting step. By using the features of time-sharing systems, such as IBM's TSO and CMS, it was possible to build relatively sophisticated command procedures that would interrogate the user for information as to the routes that were to be cut, and where the results were to be stored. The command procedures would submit a job to the batch environment. This type of environment was easier for the scheduler to adapt to.

However, the user still had to deal with the same strange step names and parameters. It became clear that, until the user could talk to the system in an English-like language, the acceptance of computerized runcutting would not materialize. In 1978, SAGE developed a command language for runcutting, which was incorporated into the runcutting logic. The command language enables the user to type in a command such as EARLIES BEFORE 700 PAY 600-830 (this statement means: cut the early runs prior to 7:00 with pay-hours between six hours and eight-and-one-half hours).

The most recent developments have been to make the system fully interactive, and use the time-sharing features that have become generally accepted throughout North America. Instead of having to set up a set of punch cards to do a runcut, the user can now go to a screen and type in a number of commands, and interact with the system. Manual capabilities were added so that the scheduler could duplicate the manual process using the computer system to check every stage of the cut.

Another recently added capability is to allow the user to reverse the process at any stage. For example, if the morning straight runs have been cut in a particular way, but the quality of the runs is unsatisfactory, those runs can be undone and cut in a different way, by imposing different constraints.

In general, schedulers feel much more comfortable with this technology. There still remains some reluctance for schedulers to give up the paper and pencil, and use the screen and keyboard for part of their work. The best environment is one where the schedulers have a low-speed printer next to the screen. Then they can interact with the system, obtain a printout of their results and go back to their desks. There they can review the results, and decide what sort of changes might be required before returning to the screen for future changes. In a way, the scheduling system becomes more like a desk calculator. It becomes a tool rather than a black box.

To bring home how computer-assisted runcutting has evolved over the past five years, perhaps it is useful to give a before-and-after comparison of a particular stage of the runcutting process. Figure 2 indicates the type of input and control statements that the user had to construct in 1975 to use the RUCUS runcutting system. Figure 3 indicates a set of commands the user now executes in 1980, using the SAGE interactive runcutting system. As you can see, the ease of use of the system has been improved significantly.

We believe that an interactive environment, together with a natural command language, are important requirements of any computer-assisted scheduling system. Schedulers should feel at ease with the system, and be able to use the system to do what they do manually, in addition to having a number of advanced techniques available to them to simplify their work.

In the past, the computer costs for interactive applications have been considerable. (In North America, time-sharing on a service bureau typically costs about $50 per connect hour when all resource charges have been included.) But mini-computers are already reducing the computer costs of scheduling significantly. For example, all SAGE's scheduling software operates on a relatively cheap Prime mini-computer.

Figure 2

Example of Original RUCUS Runcutting Process

```
//GO EXEC RUCUS,TPIN=TPFILE3,RPIN=RPFILE4,TPOUT=TPFILE4,IDIN=IDFILE2,
//        REGION=570K,TIME=3,LINES=5
//GO.SYSIN DD *
                    TEST OF RUCUS RUNCUTTING SYSTEM
 &PARAM
  STARAM=600,LENAM=200,LENMID=800,LENPM=200,
  ERLYAM=500,LATEPM=2000,ERLYST=400,LATEST=2800,
  MINSTR=700,MAXSTR=900,MINPCE=130,MAXPCE=530,AVGPCE=530,
  MINSWG=30,MAXSWG=500,ERLSWG=0,MINPLT=600,MAXPLT=900,
  MAXSPD=1300,SPAN=300,CRTSPN=530,TRVTME=-1,INITDR=1,
  PRTSPC=0,GARNOD=9999,DELCST=1,DELDRV=1,
  SPDPEN=2,PLTPEN=30,SPLPEN=1000,PCEPEN=2,DSRBON=500,REGBON=500,
  RDCARD=T,INIT=F,ITCOST=F,BKDATA=F,RDSELC=F,INTCUT=T,ELMSPC=T,
  CSTOP1=T,CSTOP2=T,CSTOP3=T,DETAIL=T,SUMRY=T,PUNCH=F,DVPNTR=T,
  MAXPSG=600,MINPSG=30,MINPAY=800,MAXPAY=957,BASPAY=800
 &END
/*
```

Shown above is a typical 'job' that the scheduler was required to prepare and submit to the computer system for a RUCUS runcut.

Figure 3

Example of SAGE Interactive Runcutting Process

```
?
READ ROUTE 27
   13 blocks have been set up.

   Travel times for this data
                        Paid  Desirable
   Garage to Garage =    0        5
   Garage to Rlf. E =   24       29
   Garage to Rlf. W =   24       29
   Rlf. E to Garage =   24       24
   Rlf. E to Rlf. E =    0        0
   Rlf. E to Rlf. W =    0        0
   Rlf. W to Garage =   24       24
   Rlf. W to Rlf. E =    0        0
   Rlf. W to Rlf. W =    0        0
?
PMS PAY 730-930

Run +----Blk---+--On-----Off--+--On-----Off--+--On-----Off--+-Bon-+-Ot-+-Time
  4 |    10- 6|             |*1823  2122+*|*2207+ 0302  |     | 19 | 8:58
  5 |     4- 10|            |*1653+ 2052+*|*2122+ 0058  |     | 10 | 8:30
  6 |     8- 4|             |*1527+ 1937  |*2052+ 0028  |     | 27 | 9:21
  7 |     7- 2|             |*1411+ 1722+*|*1808+ 2314  |     | 31 | 9:33
  Unable to cut block   7
     7                        *        *          V
        ---------------------    ------------
        4:48                 14:11+ 17:22+       22:29
?
HELP
 Enter:
  Carriage return if ok to proceed
  U if to unwind problem block
  P if to relax PAY time
  L if to relax LEAVE time

  R if to find next run

  M if to monitor runs
  Q if to quit cutting
?
U
   1 run undone.

Run +----Blk---+--On-----Off--+--On-----Off--+--On-----Off--+-Bon-+-Ot-+-Time
  7 |     6- 7|             |*1424+ 1733+*|*1805+ 2229  |     |  9 | 8:27
  8 |     9- 2|             |*1427+ 1837+*|*1937+ 2314  |     | 16 | 8:48
  9 |     7- 9|             |*1327+ 1805+*|*1837+ 2214  |     | 30 | 9:30
 10 |     2- 6|             |*1335+ 1634+*|*1733+ 2207+*|   | 21 | 9:04
 11 |     1- 2|             |*1111+ 1534+*|*1634+ 1937+*|   | 18 | 8:54
?
PLOT LEFT AFTER 730P
   Nothing to plot
```

STATUS TODAY

What is the status of computer-assisted runcutting in North America today? It is fair to say that interest in computer-assisted scheduling lessened somewhat in the late 1970s. The interest and enthusiasm which greeted the original RUCUS package when it was first released, diminished when people saw what was involved in implementing the system. It would require changes to the scheduling environment, and extensive retraining of existing scheduling staff. Over the last 24 months, however, interest has increased considerably. We are currently working on computer-assisted runcutting projects in New York, Los Angeles, Chicago, Toronto, Ottawa, Denver, Calgary, Miami, Washington,D.C., Cincinnati, San Antonio, St. Louis and Long Beach. As you can see from that list, most of the largest transit systems in North America are involved in computer-assisted scheduling. Some of these large systems are already using computer technology in a production environment.

At the present time, SAGE Management Consultants is under contract to the U.S. Urban Mass Transportation Administration to develop a second generation version of the RUCUS scheduling system based on the experience and the software developments undertaken by SAGE over the past six years.

THE FUTURE

What do we see happening over the next five years? Firstly, we feel that we have developed a good environment for computer-assisted scheduling with the development of the Mini-Scheduler for trip and vehicle scheduling, and the Interactive Runcutting System. These interactive systems make it possible for the scheduler to interact with the computer in a convenient and productive manner. Only part of our effort has gone into improving the algorithms that lie at the heart of the scheduling systems. We would like to see the research community develop libraries of algorithms that could be incorporated into the interactive scheduling environment that we have developed. There is no point in anyone having to re-solve the 'human engineering problems' that we have been faced with in implementing these systems over the past six years.

Now that computer-assisted scheduling is becoming accepted in the majority of North American transit properties, the major task is to develop better techniques and better algorithms that the user can call upon at various stages of the scheduling process.

We see a new class of users entering the transit system over the next five years. As the older schedulers retire, they will be replaced by younger, better-qualified people with a transit planning background, rather than an operations background. We see the short range planning responsibilities and the scheduling responsibilities becoming more closely related in most North American transit systems, as these new users enter the scheduling area.

On the technical side, we will see increasing use of computer graphics to present the status of the scheduling process to the scheduler in a more concise and graphical way. It is conceivable that the use of light pens might also eliminate much of the need for the keyboard in the schedulers' interaction with the system. They could use the light pen to select from a menu of operations, or touch the screen to indicate pieces of work that they want to be cut, switched or shifted.

Perhaps the most interesting area will be the development of computer-assisted scheduling on microprocessors. If not already, within five years from now, you will see computer-assisted scheduling being done on an Apple home computer. This use of cheap microprocessor technology will open up the computer-assisted scheduling area even further, and make it possible for small transit systems to get involved. Larger transit systems will put a microprocessor on each scheduler's desk. These microprocessors will be connected to centralized data files, so that the final scheduling results are integrated into the total transit information system. The use of microprocessors will have a major impact on reducing the computer requirements for computer-assisted scheduling.

SUMMARY

The past five or six years have seen dramatic changes in computer-assisted scheduling in North America. Five years ago, the scheduler was dealing with inflexible, poorly conceived and difficult to use programs that were executed in a batch environment. Today, schedulers can interact with the application in an environment that is more closely akin to their current manual scheduling environment. Computer-assisted scheduling is becoming a way of life in North America, and the future holds a number of exciting prospects for increasing the flexibility and power of scheduling systems in transit.

REFERENCES

1. Wilhelm, E.B. Overview of the RUCUS package driver run cutting program (RUNS), Workshop on Automated Techniques for Scheduling of Vehicle Operators for Urban Public Transportation Services (Chicago 1975).

2. Keaveny, I. and Burbeck, S. Automatic trip scheduling and optimal vehicle assignments. Appearing in this volume (1981).

Computer Scheduling of Public Transport
A. Wren (ed.)
©*North-Holland Publishing Company, 1981*

TWO APPROACHES
TO COMPUTER CREW SCHEDULING

Margaret E. Parker and Barbara M. Smith

Operational Research Unit
Department of Computer Studies
University of Leeds
Leeds, U.K.

This paper describes two approaches to the production of bus crew schedules by computer. The first, which was a heuristic method, has been used successfully by several public transport operators over a number of years.

The second approach, which is currently being developed, employs the principles of linear programming to derive a schedule. It is thought that this may be more successful than the heuristic approach in some circumstances. The problem of selecting those duties which cover the schedule at minimum cost, from a large number of possible legal duties, is regarded as one of set covering.

1.0 INTRODUCTION

Research into the production of crew schedules by computer has been undertaken over a number of years by staff of the Operational Research Unit, University of Leeds. The techniques developed have been of a heuristic nature, and these have been used successfully for a number of transport organisations.

The process consists of an initial program which produces a legal crew schedule and which may leave some stretches of work uncovered if necessary, and a series of refining programs. These try to reduce the number of such stretches and also try to improve the quality of the final schedule.

The principles behind these processes will be outlined, and selected case histories will be studied.

More recent applications of these techniques have led us to think that the heuristic approach might not be the most appropriate in every case. The search for a suitable alternative has been in the field of linear programming, and it is here that the most recent developments have taken place.

A large number of legal duties are generated and mathematical programming techniques are used to select those duties which cover the work at minimum cost, i.e. the problem is regarded as one of set covering. The main difficulty with this approach is that the total number of legal duties is so large, that it is impracticable to consider all of them. It is necessary therefore to devise a method of restricting the number of duties generated without rejecting those duties which are essential for a good schedule.

The advantage of this type of approach is that it should be possible to produce acceptable crew schedules, without manipulating the program; however good a heuristic can be devised there is generally some 'fine tuning' which must be made, in order to suit the particular requirements of the organisation.

Recent advances with the mathematical programming approach will be described.

2.0 HISTORICAL BACKGROUND

Interest in transport scheduling problems in the University of Leeds dates back to 1959, when the British Transport Commission sponsored a pilot study on the use of computers in transport scheduling. Attention was paid to the fields of rail and bus scheduling and it was in the former of these that computer programs were first developed.

Following attempts by several organisations to investigate the feasibility of using computers to produce bus and crew schedules, the University of Leeds, in 1966, applied to the Science Research Council for funds to mount their own investigations. A grant was awarded in 1967 and enabled the University to engage a research assistant for three years.

Discussions with interested parties from the bus industry were held to decide which of bus or bus-crew scheduling should be studied first, and it was recommended that initial research should be in the field of bus crew scheduling.

In the light of experience it is now felt that more immediate benefits can be gained from bus scheduling, where a bus saved at each peak leads to the saving of up to two crews. This is not to say that computer scheduling of crews is unimportant; it will assist in the speedy overall compilation of schedules, which may be the means by which revisions which save buses can be implemented quickly. However, crew scheduling is a more difficult problem and, had work not been started in 1967, the current state of the art in the United Kingdom would have been less advanced.

During the period 1967 to 1970, the investigation concentrated on the needs of one particular bus company. Discussions were held with several other organisations during this time to ensure that the methods which were being developed were unbiassed. Since 1970, many of the algorithms have changed dramatically, but the basic approach to the problem remains the same. This is to construct an initial schedule which satisfies all the constraints, and to refine this by a series of optimising routines. The wide differences between union agreements are handled both by parameters and by special routines.

It was hoped initially that the optimising techniques which had been developed would be sufficiently powerful to improve a poor initial schedule to one that could be implemented. This approach was seen to be fallible in many cases due to the presence of awkward constraints. Our approach now is to produce as good an initial schedule as possible, although it is important that powerful refining techniques should also be available.

In the search for a good initial algorithm, several different approaches were developed, assessed and rejected. It seems almost ironic that this search started by using the power of the computer to develop a solution rather than the ability of an algorithm to do so, while our most recent efforts have been directed towards algorithms, the use of which are now only becoming effective due to the power of modern computers. This refers to the linear programming approach to crew scheduling, a description of which occupies the second half of this paper.

Since 1970, support for computer crew scheduling has come from several organisations both in the United Kingdom and abroad. This work will be discussed later.

3.0 OUTLINE OF THE APPROACH

The fact that management-union agreements differ very widely from one bus company to another makes the development of a generally applicable program difficult. An initial idea was to construct a set of parameters by which the various processes in the program suite would be controlled. Experience has shown however, that with every new bus company with whom we have worked, we have found at least one constraint which is totally different to any previously known. In some cases we find that new features have to be introduced into the program to deal with particular circumstances. These features are usually to help the initial program produce a good schedule, and we try to ensure that any such modifications are generalised.

In the light of this it was obvious that a wholly parameter-driven program would be quite unsuitable. Our present method of working is therefore to use parameters where possible, but to introduce features into the program to suit individual bus companies as necessary. The approach adopted has been to have the program attempt to form duties according to specified parameters which are sufficiently general so as not to exclude any possible duties. When a duty is found which satisfies the conditions implied by the parameters, a special routine is entered which will validate the duty according to the conditions of the bus company concerned. At a later stage it will be necessary to judge between two possible sets of duties and here again it is appropriate to appeal to a special routine which will assess the cost of any duty (including any 'cost' attributable because the duty includes some undesirable feature).

Thus, in addition to a set of parameters, there are two routines which are written explicitly for a bus company. The first of these, which we call VALID, validates any proposed duty while the second, WAGES, tells us its cost. The coding of these two routines is straightforward; the more difficult task is usually to determine from the operator exactly what is required.

We have found it convenient to classify duties according to the types normally considered by a bus company. For each of these types we have a parameter list consisting of eight entries, namely:

      the earliest time that the crew can sign on;
      the earliest time a crew can take over a bus;
      the latest time the crew can leave the bus;
      the latest time the crew can sign off;
      the maximum length of time worked without a meal break;
      the maximum length of time worked in a duty;
      the maximum spreadover of a duty;
      the minimum time paid for a duty.

Originally we had four types of duty:

1. Early straight duties which normally start before the morning peak and work
    until sometime in the afternoon, with a break (paid or unpaid) as near to the
    minimum as possible;

2. Late straight duties which finish by taking a bus into the depot after about
    2200;

3. Middle straight duties which finish in the earlier part of the evening, having
    started around or before noon;

4. Spreadover duties which cover both peaks and have a long break in the middle.

Later a fifth duty type had to be incorporated to cater for bus companies which
normally had certain stretches of work left out of the schedule. These were
worked as overtime stretches. More recently, a sixth type has been allowed for
one bus company. This is a straight duty which starts around 0800 and finishes
about 1800, and is called a day duty.

In addition to the parameters associated with particular types of duty, there are
certain parameters which govern the number of duties of each type, and other
general features.

The overall approach of the method may therefore be seen as one of constructing
tentative duties according to a set of parameters, and of carrying out further
tests according to some specially written routines. Within this approach we
distinguish a first stage in which we construct a schedule which satisfies all the
constraints of the bus company, from the subsequent stages, in which we try to
improve on this in some way. Before describing the functions of the various
stages, however, it will be appropriate to describe briefly the data requirements.

4.0 INPUT DATA

In addition to the parameters mentioned above, it is necessary to describe the bus
schedule for which the duty schedule is to be constructed, and the time allowances
that must be given to crews at the start or finish of a duty or when changing
buses.

It will be recognised that there are a limited number of points at which a crew
may join or leave a bus; we call these <u>relief points</u>. The garage will always be
a relief point, as will any other point where a bus may be left unattended by a
crew. In addition there will be agreed relief points on every route (but often
only one on any route). It does not follow that because a certain point is the
relief point for one route it will be a relief point for another route that passes
it.

The total work of any bus may be broken down into a number of indivisible units,
in the course of which a crew cannot be relieved. The beginnings and ends of
these units are the times at which the bus passes a relief point applicable to its
route and are known as <u>relief times</u>.

The data includes a list of names of all the relief points used so that the output is easily understood. The points are numbered, and these numbers are used in the data.

Each relief time forms an item of data. The relief times are grouped by bus, and the first time for any bus will normally be the time when it leaves the garage; the exception is where a portion of the bus is covered by a crew from another schedule, in which case that portion is excluded from the data, and the remainder is treated as if it were a separate bus starting on the road. The data associated with particular relief time is as follows:

route number (optional); this is useful where several routes are being scheduled together and there are constraints or preferences affecting the way different routes are treated or mixed;

running board (block) number;

relief time;

relief point number;

It is necessary to know the time which must be allowed at any relief point for a crew to sign on, including any associated travel time if appropriate. Similar information is required for signing off. It is also necessary to know the nearest canteen to each relief point.

Three square tables are necessary with a row and column for each relief point. The first gives the minimum time which must be allowed if a crew is to leave a bus at one point, travel if necessary to another point, and join another bus without a meal break; we call these join-up times. The second table gives similar information for the cases where a meal break is taken; we call these break times. A certain portion of the break may be paid irrespective of whether the whole break is paid, for example where the relief point is far from a canteen, or where other travelling is involved; these paid times are specified in the third table.

5.0 INITIAL STAGE

An initial program constructs a schedule whose duties satisfy all the constraints, leaving some stretches of work for later treatment if necessary. A second program deals in a rudimentary way with these stretches of work which have been left out. (They will be treated more thoroughly in the refining stages). Throughout the description of this initial stage it is to be understood that the program will construct tentative duties, or parts of duties, satifying the broad parameters in the data, and will then use the VALID routine to determine whether these duties would be legal.

The first process in the initial program is to determine, for every bus that leaves the garage before the morning peak, the latest time that the crew which takes the bus out of the garage may leave the bus. To illustrate the different functions of the list of parameters and the VALID routine, we shall explain in some detail how this is done. The relief times for the bus are scanned, starting with the earliest, until one is found which would, according to the parameter list, exceed the maximum length of time without a break for an early duty. The previous relief time is then taken and the VALID routine checks the stretch of work from the time the bus leaves the garage until this time to determine whether

it can be part of an early duty; if it cannot the next earlier time is taken and
so on until a valid stretch is found.

We refer to the set of relief times now formed as <u>marked times</u>. The function of
the marked times is to indicate when a crew should leave or join a bus. They are
not necessarily going to be used since we may ultimately use an earlier time.

```
              500    615    730       900    1030
    Bus 1     I------I------I---------X-------I---


              445   600   715   815   915   1030
    Bus 2     I------I------I-----I-----X------I---


              515    630     745      910     1045
    Bus 3     I------I-------I--------X--------I--


                615 700   800   900    1010  1115
    Bus 4       I----I-----I-----I------X-----I---


              545 630       800   900    1030
    Bus 5     I---I---------I-----X-------I------


                615    730   830  915
    Bus 6       I------I-----I----X
```

X indicates the marked time

(maximum time without a meal break is $4\frac{1}{4}$ hours)

The only cases when we stipulate that a marked time must be used are where the bus
finishes at that time (e.g. the time the bus returns to the garage after the
peak), or, when some duties have been formed, and the time has already been chosen
to start the second part of a duty for another crew. Such a marked time is said
to be <u>fixed</u>. If any buses leave the garage after the end of the morning peak but
before noon their starting times are also marked. The program then checks to see
whether enough of the stretches leading up to marked times would be valid in
spreadover duties (which may have a lower limit on the amount of time in a
stretch). If not it tries to adjust the marks accordingly. The marked times are
then sorted into chronological order.

A similar exercise is performed for buses which work over the evening peak. Where
the bus runs into the late evening, the marked time is set as the earliest time
the crew which takes the bus into the garage may join it (usually some time after
the evening peak). Where the bus returns to the garage immediately after the
evening peak, two times are marked, namely the time it returns to the garage and
the earliest time the last crew must join it, if it is to form the last stretch of
work for the crew. It will be noted that these marked times now indicate where
evening meal breaks might be taken, or where an afternoon break might end on a
middle or spreadover duty. These marked times are now sorted into reverse
chronological order.

The process by which duties are formed will now be described briefly, but it should be appreciated that there are many complexities which space does not allow us to mention.

The program first builds up early duties (although an option to allow it to start with late duties has been incorporated). It takes each marked time in order, and examines it to determine whether it is fixed (i.e. must be used). If it is not fixed, this implies that the bus continues after the marked time and that no crew has yet been allocated to the following portion. Since this is then the earliest marked time following which no crew is yet allocated, an additional crew would have to be assigned to take over the bus at that time. It will usually be best to start this crew as early as possible to provide additional cover over the whole of the peak, and not just over part of it. The marked time is therefore moved as early as possible, without leaving an unreasonably small stretch of work at the start of the bus.

An attempt is now made to form a duty whose first stretch of work is on this bus, finishing at the earlier marked time, and whose second stretch of work takes over another bus at, or before, its marked time. Normally a number of such duties may be possible, and the program will give some preference to taking over the second bus at the marked time since the next duty formed is likely to be relieved later, and may then be too late to take over at this marked time. The program will also, in making its choice, take into account various other preferences affecting the nature of the duty being formed. Having found the 'best' duty using the earlier marked time, the program will move the marked time progressively later until it reaches the original mark, and will choose the best overall duty. It will also consider forming a part-duty which includes a change of bus without a meal break.

Throughout the process of forming early duties, the program ensures that no stretch of work is used to form the first half of an early duty if it is a potential first half of a spreadover duty, unless there are sufficient remaining potential first halves of spreadover duties to make up the desired number. The program will also refrain from forming an early duty if the duty it could form still fails some test of efficiency, for example if the meal break would be longer than some specified limit.

Whenever a duty or part-duty is formed, the program will adjust the list of marked times, fixing those used in the duty, and adding a further marked time to the portion of the bus beyond the time the crew has left it; this indicates the maximum time the next crew can stay on the bus. The list of marked times is then re-sorted, and the next earliest time is investigated. Where a part-duty has been formed, the program will at a later stage consider what should follow the second stretch.

The following example of the construction of early duties is illustrated in Figure 1. It is assumed that two spreadover duties are required, and that they cannot start before 0600, that the maximum time without a meal break is 4½ hours, the maximum time in a duty is eight hours and the minimum meal break is 45 minutes. All relief times are assumed to be at the same point. Each line in the Figure refers to a bus, the relief times being shown. The marked times at the start of the process are shown by means of a ring and the duties ultimately formed are indicated.

1. The earliest marked time is at 0900 on bus 1. This is moved earlier and we shall assume that the earliest reasonable time on that bus is 0730. This is linked to bus 2 at 0815, and the duty formed then works on bus 1 until 0730, and then on bus 2 from 0815 to 1245. The mark on bus 2 is now moved from 0915 and fixed at 0815. The mark on bus 1 is fixed at 0730, and a further mark is put on at 1145, which is the latest time and a crew joining the bus at 0730

can leave it.

2. The earliest mark is now 0815 on bus 2. This is linked to 0910 on bus 3 rather than the earlier time of 0900 on bus 4 because the former is marked. The duty will finish at 1230. The mark at 0910 on bus 3 is now fixed.

3. The mark at 0910 on bus 3 is linked to 1010 on bus 4 - the duty finishing at 1400. The mark at 1010 is fixed.

4. The mark at 0915 on bus 6 (which is already fixed because it is the end of the bus) is linked to 0920 on bus 5 without a break, continuing until 1030. Note that the possibility of joining to bus 5 at 0920 could not be used at the previous stage because the crew starting at 0515 on bus 3 could not have continued until 1030 without a break. The mark on bus 5 at 0920 is now fixed and an additional fixed mark is placed at 1030.

5. The mark at 0920 on bus 5 is linked to 1030, also on bus 5, the duty finishing at 1415.

6. The next mark is at 1010 on bus 4. However, the early work on bus 4 is one of only two portions which start late enough to form part of a spreadover duty (the other is the portion on bus 1 from 0730), and this must be left aside.

7. The next mark is at 1030 on bus 5 and this is linked to 1145 on bus 1, forming a three-part duty which finishes at 1500.

8. The next, and last mark is at 1145 on bus 1, but again this has to be part of a spreadover duty.

We have now formed five early duties and have left aside two portions which can form the first parts of spreadover duties.

A similar process is applied to the evening buses, working backwards into the afternoon. Here care has to be taken when moving marked times later into the evening that no opportunities of using the evening peak part of a bus as the latter part of a spreadover duty are lost.

By this time most early duties, all late duties, and some middle duties will have been formed. There will remain certain work during the peaks and possibly other work during the day. The peak work is now examined to determine which portions can be paired to form spreadover duties, and any stretches of work still unallocated during the morning peak are formed into early duties with, if possible, stretches of midday work.

If by this stage the desired number of duties has been reached or exceeded, the initial program stops; otherwise it will form unassigned work into duties of one stretch, starting with the latest finishing work until the desired number is reached.

A second program, which tries to fit in any unallocated work (possibly as third portions of duties), without rearranging anything already grouped together, is now entered. Any work which still cannot be fitted in is then designated as a duty of the special fifth type. This type is costed very highly in the refining routines.

6.0 REFINING STAGES

The routines used in the refining stages may be broken down into two groups.   The first of these consists of routines designed to try to decrease the number of crews or of unassigned portions of work.   The routines in the second group attempt to reduce the cost of the schedule, including any notional cost contributed by undesirable features.   There is no specific order in which the various routines must be used, and experience shows that some of the routines may be more appropriate for one bus company than another.   However, it is normal to use the first group of routines immediately following the initial stage and then to follow this with some routines from the second group.   A return may be made to a routine from the first group to see whether the number of crews can be reduced further. Some routines may be used several times in the process.

6.1   Routines To Reduce Numbers Of Duties

These routines are concerned only with reducing the numbers of proper duties or unallocated portions of work; they do not take into account the cost of the resultant schedule.   The full process of trying to reduce the number of crews can be very time consuming, and considerable effort has been spent evolving methods which are compromises between searching for all possibilities, however remote, and saving computer time.

6.1.1 <u>Reduce</u> This routine first checks to see whether the target number of duties has been exceeded, and only takes action if this is so. It has been our experience, in some cases, that bus companies prefer to have a solution which uses more crews than the minimum, in order not to increase unduly the average work content of duties, and for this reason we do not reduce the number of duties below this target.   In this routine each duty is considered in turn and an attempt is made to redistribute its work among the other duties.   Sometimes it would be necessary to take a stretch of work out of another duty in order to make room for the redistributed work and this is done if this stretch of work can be absorbed elsewhere.

6.1.2 <u>Maxspread</u> This routine tries to decrease the work in duties of low spreadover by increasing the work in duties of higher spreadover so that gaps are created to help REDUCE.

6.1.3 <u>Only5alter</u> This routine considers only the unassigned work (fifth duty type).   It tries to reduce an unassigned stretch of work as much as possible by putting as many pieces of it on to any other duty or duties which will take them. If all the work cannot be completely removed in this way, the remaining stretch of work is swopped with any other smaller stretch of work on any other duty (other than a type 5 duty).   This swopped stretch is then examined to see if any of the work involved can be removed, and so on until no further reducing can be done.

6.2   Routines To Reduce Cost

The routines in this group appeal to the WAGES routine in order to determine the cost of any revision of duties.   For this purpose, the WAGES routine calculates not only the cost in terms of payments to crews, but also a notional cost associated with any undesirable feature in a duty; the sum of these two costs is the objective which the routines try to minimize.   The formula by which the notional cost is calculated is usually determined after consultations with the schedules department of the bus company.   However, it may be changed if, after inspecting the first computer-produced schedules, some undesirable features are still present.

6.2.1 <u>Halves</u> This routine cuts each duty into two portions at a break point and forms two lists of half duties as follows:-

DUTY TYPE	LIST 1	LIST 2
early	first half	second half
split	first half	second half
middle	first half	second half
late	second half	first half

This grouping has been chosen as that which gives the maximum number of possibilities in pairing members of one list with members of the other. The problem of determining the optimum pairing is an assignment problem but, in order to reduce the amount of computer time needed, the current solution is taken as the starting solution for an optimisation method which is a modification of the standard method for solving the transportation problem. Where there is a restriction on the number of duties of one type, there might be a danger of this routine, which cannot look at overall numbers, producing more duties than required. In order to overcome this problem, the routine is called twice, first with a restriction on the members of list 1 which can be part of this type of duty, then with a similar restriction on the members of list 2.

6.2.2 <u>Recut</u> This takes the work of each bus in turn and considers all the times when crews are changed on that bus. If, by moving one of these changeovers to another relief time, the cost is reduced such a move is made. In some cases this move will actually be to another relief time which is also a changeover time; one of the two crews will then be working for zero time on that bus, and will have the number of portions in the duty reduced by one.

6.2.3 <u>Changends</u> This routine removes a small piece of work around the middle of the day from each duty, and solves the assignment problem of reallocating these in the optimal way. The pieces removed will generally be the last parts of early duties, the first parts of middle or late duties, and some part out of the middle of split duties. Where a duty is currently in three parts, a whole part will be removed if possible; otherwise a piece of work is removed from one portion of work.

6.2.4 <u>Stretchswop</u> This routine tries to level out duties by looking at each duty in turn to determine whether firstly, by removing any stretch and putting the stretch on another duty, or secondly, by exchanging any stretch for any other stretch in another duty, the cost is lowered.

7.0 EXPERIENCE

We now have experience in using the program on behalf of several bus companies with widely differing constraints; in some cases with different constraints in separate areas of one bus company. Typical results for some of these bus companies are displayed in Table 1. The individual experiences will now be discussed.

7.1 Bristol Omnibus Company Ltd.

We examined the Bristol City Services of this organisation, where routes, or groups of routes, are treated individually. In 1972, the program was constructing schedules of approximately comparable wage cost and numbers of duties with the manual schedules. However, it was found necessary to adhere strictly to specified numbers of each type of duty. This caused considerable problems, but eventually satisfactory schedules were produced for the routes which had been used as test data. In Bristol, at that time, a six-day rota was in operation so that the average duty length was six hours forty minutes. This produced some severe constraints on the duties which could be formed.

7.2 Midland Red

The program produced consistently good results for Midland Red, except in certain cases where preferences for certain types of duty had not been made known to us before the computer run. 'Good' results here were taken to mean results which used fewer crews, or were cheaper to operate, or were better in a qualitative sense than those produced by the company. In all cases schedules covered an entire depot. While there was no direct implementation, some features of the computer schedules were later incorporated in manual schedules.

7.3 Cleveland Transit

Here too, an entire depot was treated as a unit. A different sort of manual schedule existed here, in that an average duty was composed of about four stretches of work in order to meet the many limitations on the amount of work that could be covered on an individual route. Further, associated with certain duties were what are called 'attached specials'. These are straight duties of normal length (between 7:36 and 8:25 work content), to which an additional stretch of depot to depot working is attached as an integral part of the duty schedule. This stretch is paid at overtime rates. There are bounds on the number of such duties and there are no split duties as such. The program consistently produced comparable schedules to the manual ones; in many cases they were an improvement. For one depot, the schedules were implemented directly, as the spreadover of all the duties was less than that currently in use.

7.4 West Yorkshire Passenger Transport Executive

Our association with the Leeds District of the West Yorkshire PTE began in 1967 when they supplied a set of data upon which experiments could be tried with different ideas for producing a crew schedule by computer. Their comments on the early computer-produced schedules were invaluable and enabled the foundations of the algorithm to be assessed in a realistic situation.

Dialogue with them has continued intermittently ever since with the result that the initial program has now been finely tuned to their particular requirements. Schedules are currently being produced which are as good as those produced manually and several have been implemented.

It is not possible to describe here all the work which has been accomplished, as much is now of historical interest only; however, two aspects will be recalled in a little detail.

In 1977, we were asked to ascertain the likely effect of imposing EEC drivers' hours regulations on urban bus operation. (It must be explained that these regulations do not apply to routes less than 50km in length, and therefore most city services are excluded. However, it was deemed necessary to know the precise effect of these regulations for all types of bus operation throughout the country, in order that a fuller understanding of them might be gained.) The bus schedule used was that relating to the Monday to Friday working for the whole of one garage as this was felt to be generally representative of the District's operation as a whole.

The drivers' hours regulations may be interpreted in several ways, the fullest of which means a fundamental change of concept in our basic algorithm. It was therefore decided to implement the simplest one and to use the existing Union agreement except in cases of conflict. The results of the exercise may be seen in Table 1. Studying the resultant schedule, the PTE was able to determine the possible effects, in terms of increase in manpower and hours paid, which incorporation of the regulations district-wide would imply, and were therefore able to contribute to nationwide discussions on the topic from a position of some strength.

The second exercise which has recently been undertaken has been the assessment of different types of duty constraints, and this was run jointly as a University-Management-Union project. In the United Kingdom there are regulations laid down by law which must be followed strictly in the compilation of crew duties. However, each public transport company, and even integral units within a company, may negotiate additional constraints with their immediate management, according to the demand of the local workforce.

Starting with the basic legal requirements for the construction of duties, various modifications of these were tried, including variations on the Leeds District union agreement. Several schedules were quickly compiled and this enabled the management and union teams to decide upon the types of constraints which each felt would lead to the most efficient use of resources. Further schedules were produced along the lines suggested by the teams and eventually a set of constraints satisfying both parties was evolved. Although the final schedule based on these constraints was not compiled by computer, its use had been instrumental in rapidly producing schedules based on a number of ideas. This in turn led to a speedy assessment of each stage and allowed the most efficacious set of constraints to be formulated very quickly. In eight weeks, three sets of data (Monday to Friday, Saturday and Sunday) were punched and checked and 32 crew schedules were constructed; each crew schedule being not inconsiderable viz. 150 (approx) crews for weekdays, 115 (approx) crews for Saturday, and 80 (approx) crews for Sunday. This work is reported in greater detail in Parker (3).

7.5 Greater Glasgow Passenger Transport Executive

The work which was undertaken for Greater Glasgow PTE concerned some holiday schedules covering entire depots. Although it was possible to produce schedules comparable to the manual ones in terms of numbers of duties, considerable difficulty was encountered in producing schedules with given numbers of early and late duties. This feature was required for rotation purposes. These difficulties emanated partly from this constrained duty type mix, and partly from some unique situations with regard to the number of very early bus pullouts, for example at

0435. The presence of a low peak to off-peak ratio of buses on the road only served to exacerbate the situation.

7.6 Greater Manchester Passenger Transport Executive

A feasibilty study was conducted for Greater Manchester PTE and involved three schedules each displaying different characteristics. This exercise was conducted in parallel with manual schedulers and by three different computer programs, in order to assess the relative merits of these programs. In many respects the results of the exercise may be regarded as disappointing, in that the computer produced schedules were being compared with schedules upon which much more manual effort than normal had been expended. The main problem areas were demonstrated as follows: the capability of producing a schedule containing a given number of different duty types; the ability to deal with a high proportion of the crew requirement before 0600, during the noon period, and during the intermediate period between noon and the evening peak; the ability to make best use of widely spaced relief opportunities. Computer schedules better than the existing manual schedules were produced in all cases.

7.7 London Transport

Conditions relevant to crew scheduling in London Transport are rather different from those in existence elsewhere in the United Kingdom. This fact was not fully appreciated until it became clear that it was going to be very difficult to produce crew schedules as good as the manual ones for the three routes we had been given to study.

There are a number of possible reasons for this apparent difficulty. The bus schedule for a route in London is often altered manually to suit the needs of the crew schedule, and the duties produced are then usually approximately equal in length, and as full of work as possible within all the constraints. No work is then left out of the schedule for overtime purposes.

As the program is a heuristic, it is unlikely to find exactly the same solution as London Transport, and it seems likely that there will not be many equally good solutions to each problem. Indeed, we believe that in some cases the London Transport schedulers have found the only possible solution with the minimum number of crews, and that they have redesigned the bus schedule specifically to achieve this objective. There is considerable scope for amending the bus schedule in this way since London routes are extremely long, with many turn-back points, and generally with very short headways. Few passengers wish to travel over more than a relatively short portion of any route, and buses can be turned short with impunity to suit the crew schedule, other short trips being run over the remainder of the route if necessary. Most routes are worked by several depots, and individual journeys may be switched from one depot to another if this will help the overall crew schedule.

7.8 Coras Iompair Eireann, Dublin City Services

A feasibility study of three man-months was undertaken for this organisation during which time some problems rather different from those we had encountered in earlier work were revealed. These made it impossible to develop a satisfactory computer program in the time available. In addition, a further three man-months of our own time were devoted to the solution of these problems and an algorithm was produced which could have formed the basis of a revised program specifically designed to deal with these problems. CIE decided, however, not to proceed with further work in this area, though they did supply us with further crew schedules, in addition to the three we were originally given, to use in the evaluation of the new algorithm.

The following are the problems referred to:

7.8.1 Crews were not normally allowed to work on more than two buses, unless the circumstances were exceptional. The initial program will construct a schedule in which there may be many three-part duties; the refining processes would normally reduce these to an acceptable level. Being prohibited from forming three-part duties severely inhibited the programs.

7.8.2 Middle duties have their breaks after the evening peak. Our programs form late duties before middle duties, and then expect to form the latter with breaks before, or occasionally during, the peak.

7.8.3 There is, on weekday schedules, a relatively high midday peak. This forces the duties to be of a rather different nature to those we have usually met.

8.0 BUS CREW SCHEDULING BY MATHEMATICAL PROGRAMMING

8.1 Introduction.

The bus-crew scheduling problem can, in theory, be solved by generating a very large number of possible duties, which together cover all the work in the bus schedule many times over, and then using mathematical programming methods to select from these a set of duties which covers the bus schedule at minimum cost. The main practical difficulty is to restrict the number of duties generated, since even in small problems the total number of legally valid duties is far too large to deal with. Hence, some sensible way of reducing the number of duties produced must be found, bearing in mind also the practical limitations of whatever mathematical programming package is available.

The following Section describes the progress that has been made so far in devising methods to produce suitable sets of duties; it should be borne in mind that this work is continuing and that many areas remain to be investigated. Further, the crew schedules produced so far have all been based on Leeds bus schedules, so that throughout the work, the rules governing the construction of crew schedules are those operating in Leeds.

8.2 Generation Of Sensible Duties.

Several approaches have been investigated in the restriction of the number of duties generated. Manington (1) studied manually-produced crew schedules in order to establish the characteristics of those duties which are most likely to be used. From these he produced a set of rules which 'sensible' duties must satisfy, to be added to the rules based on Union agreements, etc., which define valid duties. These rules may be summarised as follows:-

1. Duties must have either two or three stretches. (A stretch of work here is the period of time spent on one bus.)

2. Various types of stretch (e.g. the first stretch of an early duty) must be at least a specified length. (This contrasts with the maximum length of stretch allowed for valid duties.)

3. There are restrictions on the sign-on and sign-off times of the different types of duty, e.g. late duties must sign off after 1900.

4. There are specified maximum lengths for meal-breaks and join-ups. (A join-up is a short break, only involving travelling time.)

By making these additional rules more or less restrictive, the number of duties generated can be varied at will.

8.3 Next Available Pieces.

An alternative approach is to allow any duty to do only the next available piece of work at any stage, with possible relaxations to allow 2nd and 3rd availables. In this context, a piece of work is the time between successive relief times on the same bus. This approach will be described more fully by Ryan and Foster (2).

8.4 Selected Relief Times.

The method currently being developed uses both of the ideas described above to some extent, but the number of duties is limited mostly by the fact that many of the relief times are not allowed to be used to change crews. The reasoning is that if we can identify those relief times which are most likely to give duties leading to a good schedule, then the quality of the solution will not be greatly affected by banning the remaining times, and the number of duties generated will be reduced to a manageable size. At present, in a typical urban situation with relief times about every half-hour, the majority of relief times are banned.

The basic procedure is to mark certain relief times on each bus which are approximately the maximum stretch length apart: for each bus in turn, it is supposed that a crew starts work when the bus leaves the garage, and the latest time at which the crew may leave the bus is marked. Then the latest finishing time on this bus for another crew taking it over at the marked time is also marked, and so on, until the bus returns to the garage. If crews on this bus are changed only at the marked relief times, then the bus will be covered by the minimum number of stretches of work.

Similarly, relief times can be marked in the other direction, starting when the bus returns to the garage and working backwards in time until it first leaves the garage. If these 'backward' marked times are uses to change crews then, again, the bus will be covered by the minimum number of stretches.

Sometimes the 'forward' and 'backward' marked times coincide, but generally each backward marked time is earlier than the corresponding forward marked time. Each pair of marked times defines a time-band within which crews should be changed over, if each bus is to be covered by the minimum number of stretches. Figure 2 (at the end of the paper) shows the bus graph for a small bus schedule, with all the relief times indicated; Figure 3 shows the backward and forward marked times for the same bus graph.

Example. Suppose a bus leaves the garage at 0700 and returns at 2100, with relief times every hour, and the maximum stretch length is four and a half hours.

```
Forward
 marked   0700         1100         1500         1900  2100
 times:    I----------->------------>------------>----I

Backward
 marked   0700  0900         1300         1700         2100
 times:    I-----<------------<------------<-----------I

Time-     0700         1100         1500         1900  2100
 bands:    I-----<=====>-----<=====>-----<=====>----I
          0700  0900         1300         1700         2100
```

The bus can be covered by 4 stretches of work, but not if any of the relief times at 0800,1200,1600,2000 are used.

This is the basis of the selection procedure, but further refinements are required, firstly because the time-bands may on some buses be so wide that it is not practicable to allow every relief time within them to be used, so that a further selection procedure is necessary. Secondly, there are cases where it is necessary to choose relief times outside the time-bands in order to ensure that all the schedule may be covered. Some of these procedures are described below.

1. The backward and forward times are not allowed to fall within the morning and evening peaks. However, if a bus could be covered in fewer stretches of work by changing crews during the evening peak, suitable relief times are selected.

2. If an early bus carries on after the morning peak, then the first crew should stop for a meal-break, preferably between the first pair of marked times, and there should be another crew ready to take over, following a first stretch of duty on another bus and then a meal-break. In some cases, no such second crew can be found, because the first pair of marked times is too early to allow a crew to fit in a meal-break following the morning peak. The alternative is to allow the second crew to take over following a join-up, and to work on the bus for only a short time before taking a meal-break. In most of these cases, the second crew can stay on the bus beyond the first pair of marked times, so this illustrates the fact that it is sometimes necessary to select relief times outside the time-bands.

3. Potential first and second halves of two-stretch splits are identified, covering the morning and evening peaks respectively. These are matched up so as to minimise the break in the middle of the duty. This shows which relief times are needed for split duties, and indicates how long the break in a

2-stretch split is likely to be.

A split duty must start at the garage on a bus which starts before the morning peak, but late enough to allow it to be covered by a split duty. At this stage, it is assumed that the crew stays on the bus for as long as possible and that if any of these buses can be covered by early duties, they will be the earliest finishing buses. Then each of the remaining first stretches, in order of finishing time is linked with the earliest unallocated 2nd stretch.

The longest break found in constructing these split duties is useful information for the duty-generation phase, because the maximum length must be specified as a parameter to the program.

The selected relief times for the bus-graph of Figure 2 are shown in Figure 4.

8.5 Generation Of Duties

Using the selected relief times only, a set of duties which are both legally valid and sensible is formed. That is, rules similar to Manington's still apply, as well as those which determine whether or not a duty is valid.

At present, the following types of duty are formed:

1. 3-stretch early duties, with a join-up following the first stretch and a meal-break between the 2nd and 3rd stretches.

2. 2-stretch early duties with a meal-break after the morning peak.

3. 2- and 3-stretch split (or spreadover) duties. The first stretch must cover the morning peak and the last stretch must (at least partly) cover the evening peak.

4. 2-stretch lates and middles.

5. 3-stretch lates and middles, with a join-up following the first stretch, before the evening peak.

So far these have proved sufficient for Monday - Friday schedules; if weekend schedules were being considered, it would also be necessary to generate day duties (i.e. starting at about 0900 and finishing about 1700).

The type of duty which has caused most problems is the middle duty. Middle duties start after the morning peak, at 1100 or later, and cover the evening peak, generally finishing later than split duties. They are less well-defined than other types of duty, and their function is sometimes hard to determine; hence, it is difficult to lay down rules for sensible duties of this type.

8.6 Mathematical Programming Formulation.

Having generated a suitable set of duties, the scheduling problem is formulated as a set-covering problem, that is, a sub-set of duties is to be chosen so that each piece of work in the bus schedule is covered at least once, while at the same time the total cost of the duties chosen is minimised.

In this formulation, the constraints correspond to the pieces of work to be covered, and each duty corresponds to a variable which can take the value 0 or 1, depending on whether the duty is or is not included in the crew schedule. First the linear programming problem is solved; here non-integer values are allowed, so that duty-variables can take any value between 0 and 1. Obviously, if any of the duty-variables take fractional values, the solution is not a practicable crew schedule, but it may happen, as described later, that in the solution to the L.P. all the variables have integer values. If not, an integer solution must be found in a further process.

The set-covering formulation allows any piece of work to be covered by more than one duty. Clearly, this cannot be allowed in a practical crew schedule. However, a set-covering formulation is preferable to a set-partitioning formulation (which would cover each piece of work exactly once) because fewer duties need be generated if duties are allowed to overlap slightly rather than meeting exactly. In practice, covering pieces of work more than once is not a problem; if a good schedule has been produced, the overlaps will be minor and can easily be resolved (manually, at present). Conversely, if a schedule contains large overlaps which cannot be easily resolved, the solution generally contains too many duties, and so would be unacceptable for that reason.

It is also possible to leave pieces of work uncovered by, in effect, choosing a 'duty' which covers just one piece of work: these single-piece duties are not formed explicitly in the duty-generation process, but appear in the mathematical programming formulation as slack variables, suitably costed (e.g. at the minimum cost of a duty).

A starting solution is constructed by choosing duties to cover each of a set of nominated pieces of work. These pieces are the first piece on any bus which covers the morning peak, and the last piece on any bus which finishes late in the evening. As each of the nominated pieces is considered, we choose the duty which covers this piece and as much as possible of the uncovered part of the schedule. The starting solution also contains the slack variable for any piece of work which is not covered by any of the selected duties.

8.7 Cost Of Duties.

As each duty is formed, it is assigned a cost, which is the number of minutes for which the bus company has to pay wages. Although this is the cost which the bus company is interested in, for various reasons it is not the best way of calculating the cost for the L.P. At present, the cost of a duty which is used by the L.P. is calculated as:
     cost charged to bus company in minutes
          − no. of minutes of bus schedule covered
               + minimum paid day in minutes
                    + 1000.

Subtracting the work covered from the chargeable cost means that the result is related to the unproductive part of the duty. It avoids having a large number of short duties, which are relatively undesirable, all costed at the length of the minimum paid day and so as cheap as any other duty.

(Chargeable cost) - (work covered) was found to be an unsuitable cost function. This is because (in Leeds) split duties are much more expensive than straight duties, and it then becomes cheaper to choose an extra early duty and an extra late duty to cover the work which should be done by a split duty. Since the set-covering formulation allows work to be covered more than once, it does not matter that the 2nd half of the early duty and the 2nd half of the late duty are redundant.

One way of avoiding this problem is to add a sufficiently large constant to the cost of each duty. The minimum paid day is certainly large enough: it has the slight advantage that the result is of a comparable size to the chargeable cost (and means that the cost of slack variables (single-piece duties), which is also the minimum paid day, does not have to be changed).

Finally, 1000 is added to the cost of every duty, including slacks, in order to put more emphasis on reducing the number of duties selected; it is felt that this should have higher priority than choosing cheap duties.

8.8 Effect Of Selecting Relief Times.

The original intention in allowing only selected relief times to be used in the duty-generation process was to reduce the number of duties formed. Selecting relief times also has a considerable effect on the solution of the L.P. Firstly, each constraint in the L.P. corresponds to a piece of work in the bus schedule, where a piece of work is initially defined as the period between two successive relief times on a bus. However, if a relief time is not used by any duty as a change-over time, the constraints corresponding to the adjacent pieces of work are equivalent. Hence, each distinct constraint in fact corresponds to the the period between successive selected relief times. This reduces the problem size considerably; for instance, a bus schedule with 84 buses (requiring 72 duties) initially contained 695 pieces of work, which were reduced to 249 by the selection process.

A further consequence of selecting relief times is that, in most cases the solution to the linear programming problem is integer, so that it is not often necessary to resort to a branch-and-bound procedure to find an integer solution. It is not yet fully understood why this should be so, or, more importantly, why occasionally it is not so, but it seems reasonable to believe that choosing relatively few relief times, with small groups of relief times separated by long gaps, makes it difficult to form a non-integer solution. As will be seen later, of the 5 data-sets for which schedules have been found so far, 4 gave mostly integer solutions, under a wide variety of conditions, and the remaining one persisted in giving non-integer solutions, except in a few attempts, when the resulting schedule was not acceptable.

8.9 Results.

Because of the reduction in problem size and the fact that the L.P. solution is
in most cases integer, it is possible to solve crew scheduling problems of a
realistic size quite quickly. For instance, the largest schedule solved so far
required 90 duties: between 3500 and 5600 duties were generated and there were
about 250 constraints in the L.P. The time taken to solve the L.P.   was 80-160
secs. (on an Amdahl V7) depending on the number of duties generated, and since
almost all of these solutions were integer, it was not necessary to go any
further.   The selection of relief times and duty-generation takes only a few
seconds.

Equally important, of course, is the quality of the solution, and this can be
judged   by comparing the number of duties in the crew schedule with an estimate of
the number of duties required, produced by the relief-time selection program.
This estimate is derived from the number of buses on the road at various times of
the day, and gives a lower limit to the number of duties of each type required to
cover the schedule.   Only a few problems have been solved so far, but in every
case except one, it has proved possible to produce a solution using the minimum
number of duties. (The exception is also the data-set which produces consistently
non-integer solutions.) For the larger data sets, many attempts were needed before
this solution was found, but it is hoped that as the research progresses, this
will be improved.

A crew schedule for the bus graph of Figure 2 is shown in Figures 5 and 6. It can
be seen that there are a few cases of overlapping duties in the schedule, but only
slight alterations to the duties involved are required to get rid of the overlaps.

Table 2 summarises the best results obtained for each bus schedule dealt with so
far.

9.0 CONCLUSIONS

Bus crew scheduling by computer has been shown to be a viable proposition, but the
very nature of the work, which involves determining precisely the requirements of
a bus company, implies that those organisations with whom we have had a long
association in computer crew scheduling have been able to benefit most from our
research. This is not to say that the contributions from other organisations have
been to no purpose.   Each exercise gives us further insight into the different
scheduling practices in existence, and often reveals new and hitherto unknown
constraints. The pool of knowledge which we have been establishing over the years
is thus increased.

In our work to establish computer methods for producing crew schedules, our
objective is to assist a manual scheduler in his job. It is generally accepted
that the quality of manually-produced schedules is such that often no improvement
can be made.   We seek to relieve the scheduler of much of the routine work
involved in constructing a crew schedule, and to produce a schedule which can be
altered speedily by an experienced scheduler to give the desired quality. This
speed, as has been shown, can be used to revise and test new schedules more
easily.

Our experience has lead us to believe that a mathematical programming formulation may be the best approach in some circumstances, and this aspect is now being investigated. It is too early however, to determine whether this line of research will succeed in those cases where other methods have been unsuccessful.

10.0 ACKNOWLEDGEMENTS

Over the years many members of the Operational Research Unit of the University of Leeds have contributed to this research work, the results of which are reported here. Since its inception, the research has been directed by Mr Anthony Wren to whom all the original ideas and concepts must be attributed. In our most recent work on mathematical programming, Dr David M. Ryan, Department of Theoretical and Applied Mathematics, University of Auckland, New Zealand, has made some valuable suggestions, and has provided the mathematical programming package used in the research (4). We should also like to thank the staff of many bus companies who have taken an interest in our work.

11.0 REFERENCES

1. Manington,P.D. Mathematical & heuristic approaches to road transport scheduling. Ph.D. Thesis, University of Leeds (1977).

2. Ryan,D.M. & Foster,B.A. An integer programming approach to scheduling. Appearing in this volume (1981).

3. Parker,M.E. Different forms of bus crew working agreements and their effects on a bus schedule. Report No. 24, Operational Research Unit, University of Leeds (January 1979).

4. Ryan,D.M. ZIP - a zero-one integer programming package for scheduling. Computer Science and Systems Division, A.E.R.E. Harwell, Oxfordshire (1980).

Table 1. Results of heuristic program.

	No. of Duties	Cost	Unallocated Portions	Cost	E	LE	S	M	L
Bristol									
Manual	39	266:02	1	1:17	13	6	3	5	12
Computer	39	265:21	1	2:00	13	6	3	5	12
Midland Red									
1.(Manual	46	380:50	0	0	13	-	19	4	10
(Computer	46	379:28	0	0	13	-	19	4	10
2.(Manual	18	145:09	0	0	1	-	12	2	3
(Computer	17	142:56	0	0	1	-	12	1	3
Cleveland									
1.(Manual	57	526:17	6	11:22	24	-	-	12	21
(Computer	57	520:55	3	10:14	25	-	-	11	21
2.(Manual	128%	1038:49	22	45:06	52	-	-	31	45
(Computer$	128%	1020:32	14	27:21	51	-		35	42
WYPTE-Leeds									
(Manual	152	1499:02	19	34:38	45	1+	61	8	37
(Computer(EEC)	175	1601:07	0	0	51	6+	57	11	50
(Manual'	56	?	0	0	23	-	5	10	18
(Computer	52	413.23	0	0	22	-	4	8	18
Glasgow									
Manual	79	695:00*	0	0	44	-	-	6	29
Computer	79	706:46*	0	0	41	-	-	9	29
Manchester									
Manual	130	?	?	?	40	-	25	33	32
Computer	125	995:41	2	10:42	37	-	24	32	32
London									
1.(Manual	43	38:03@	0	0	17	-	8	10	8
(Computer	43	34:00@	1	4:16	17	-	8	10	8
2.(Manual	20	14:12@	0	0	8	-	3	2	7
(Computer	20	14:29@	0	0	8	-	3	2	7
3.(Manual	29	2:18@	0	0	15	-	-	5	9
(Computer	29	3:13@	2	7:03	15	-	-	5	9
CIE									
Route 16 Monday-Friday									
(Manual	54	397:05	1	0:48	23	-	8!	7	16
(Computer	54	396:20	0	0	23	-	8!	7	16
Route 20 Monday-Friday									
(Manual	36	266:31	0	0	16	-	4!	6	10
(Computer	36	264:44	1	2:07	16	-	4!	6	10
Route 16 Sunday									
(Manual	40	266:40	0	0	13	-	-	10	17
(Computer	40	266:19	0	0	13	-	-	10	17

NOTES: % This consisted of six different sets of duties
          ranging in number from 10 to 38, each of which
          had to be compiled separately.
        $ Schedule implemented by operator.
        + Day duties (see para 3.0).
        * Comparisons in Glasgow are based on total
          spreadover of all duties.
        @ Comparisons in London are based on penalty
          payments only.
        ! Bogey duties: a duty which may or may not
          cover both peaks.
        ' Holiday schedule.

Table 2. Results.

Data-set	(1)	(2)	(3)	(4)	(5)
No. of buses	20	115	84	41	43
No. of pieces of work	263	715	695	465	230
No. of pieces after selection of relief times	63	252	249	148	83
Estimated no. of duties required	19	90	72	43	31
No. of duties generated	490	4815	5205	3476	1673
Value of L.P. solution	30451	149099	118257	70680.9	51387
No. of iterations	98	2191	2038	831	106
Time in secs.	0.7	141	145	37	2
Integer?	Yes	Yes	Yes	No *	Yes
No. of duties in schedule	19	90	72	44	31
Cost of schedule (in minutes)	11219	53291	42597	25299	18039

    * Acceptable integer solution found by branch-and-bound in 14 sec.: value 70774.

Note: Data-sets (4) and (5) together make up data-set (3).

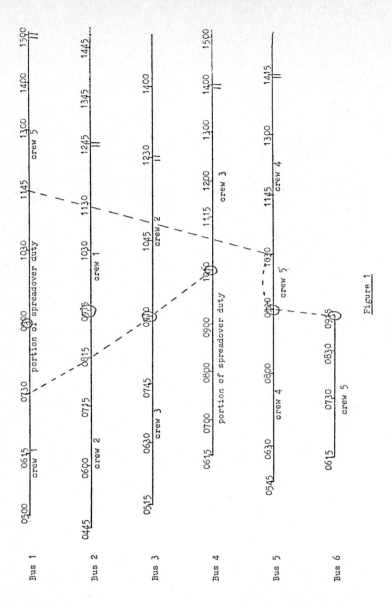

Figure 1

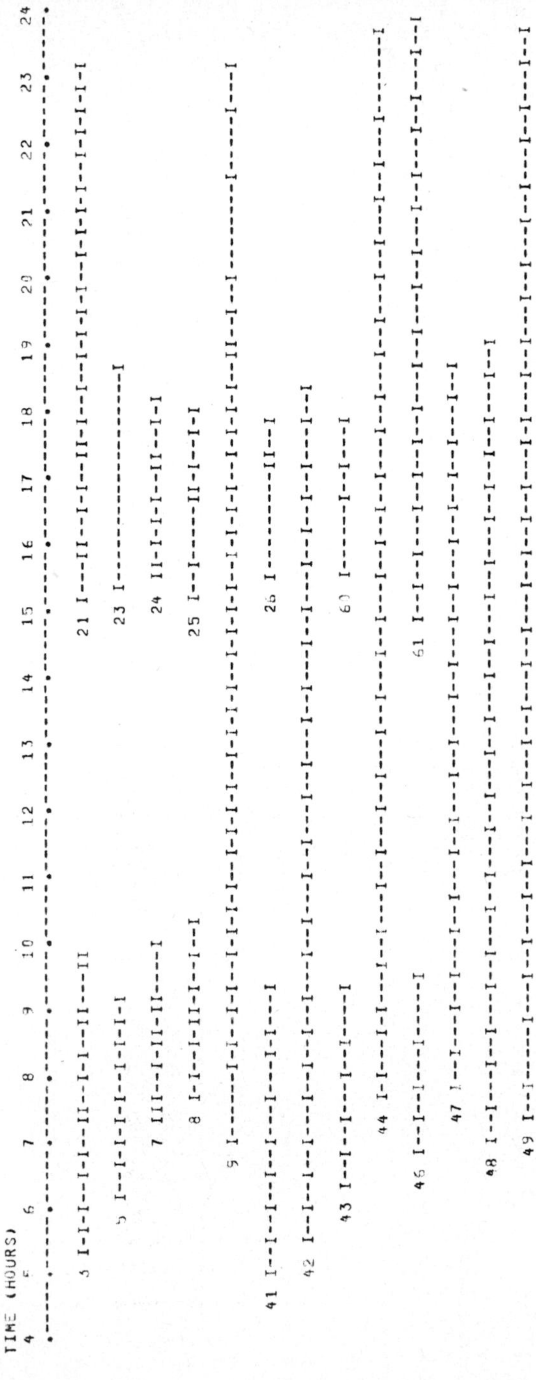

FIGURE 2. BUS GRAPH SHOWING ALL RELIEF TIMES

FIGURE 3.   BUS GRAPH SHOWING PARKED TIMES

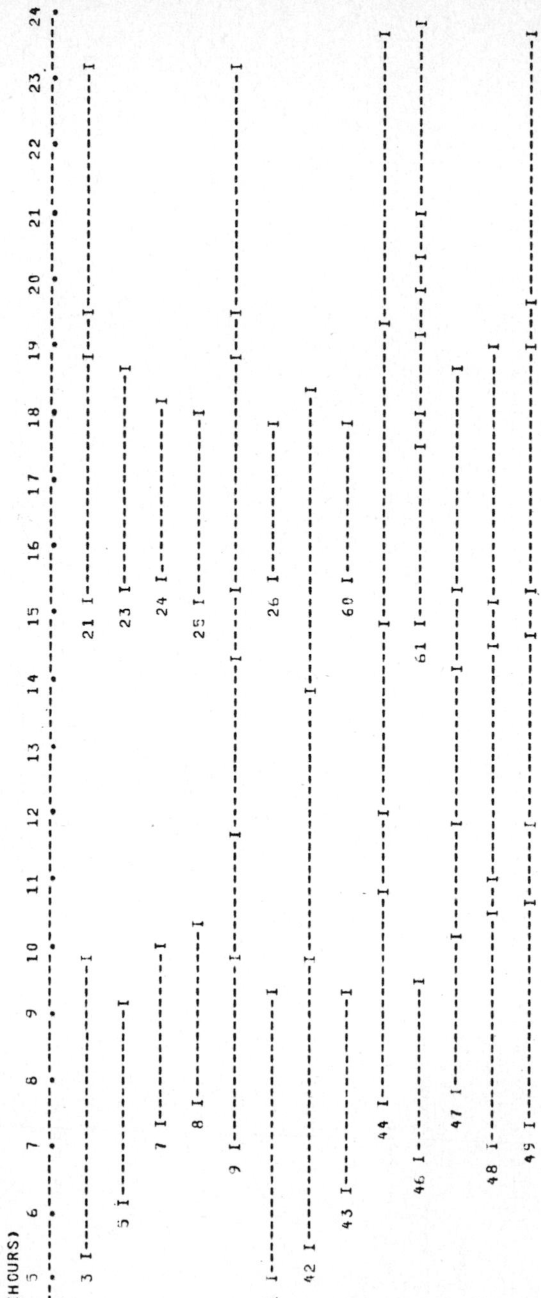

FIGURE 4. BUS GRAPH SHOWING SELECTED RELIEF TIMES

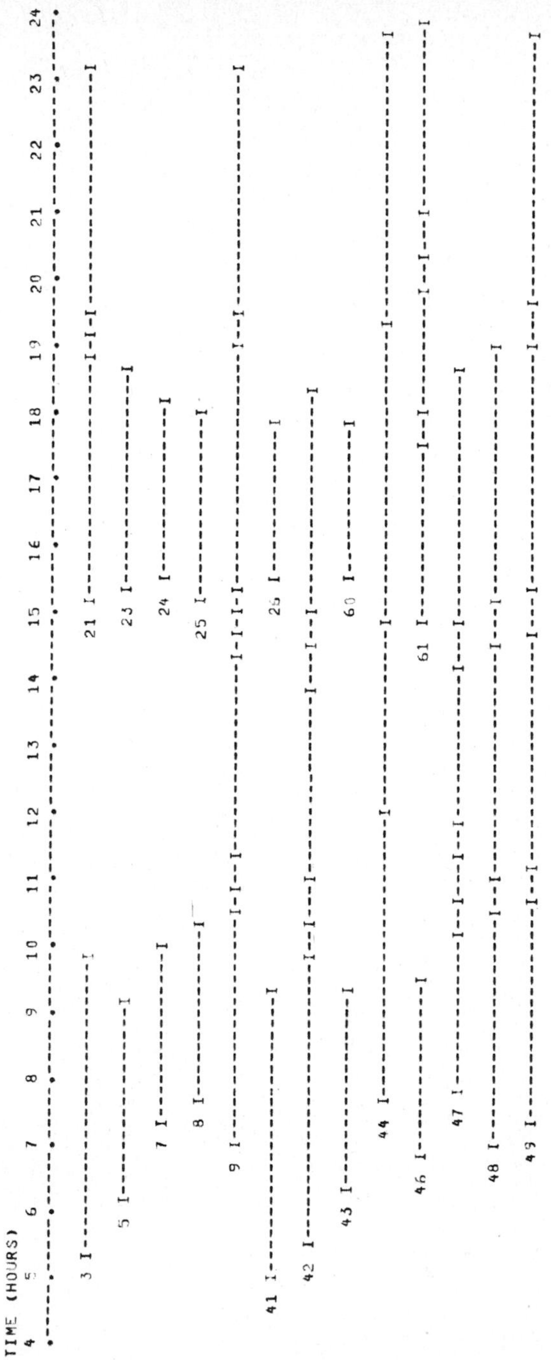

FIGURE 5.   LIST OF DUTIES IN CREW SCHEDULE

DUTY NO.	BUS	FROM	TO	BUS	FROM	TO	BUS	FROM	TO	L.P. COST	TRUE COST	DUTY TYPE
1	43	616	916	48	1030	1434				1494	462	E
2	41	501	916	42	1024	1354				1485	494	E
3	8	741	1022	42	1354	1819				1706	676	S
4	47	747	1154 *	49	1517	1904				1690	708	S
5	46	647	927	47	1414	1839				1819	788	S
6	48	702	1030	48	1434	1859				1757	774	S
7	44	736	1200	23	1520	1837				1691	696	S
8	24	1525	1805	44	1924	2340				1512	472	L
9	26	1525	1749	49	1904	2339				1506	469	L
10	5	612	907	42	950	1024	49	1114	1517	1519	515	E
11	44	1200	1454	61	1732	2100				1623	549	M
12	7	720	959	9	1435	1900				1792	760	S
13	3	517	950	47	1044	1414				1481	508	E
14	49	717	1114	61	1450	1732				1710	653	S
15	42	531	950	9	1045	1435				1481	514	E
16	60	1525	1747	21	1849	2314				1505	456	L
17	9	700	1119	21	1510	1849				1732	754	S
18	44	1454	1924	61	2024	2354				1481	505	L
19	25	1510	1759	9	1900	2314				1491	458	L

TOTAL COST   11211

INDICATES THAT THIS STRETCH IS PARTLY COVERED BY
A STRETCH OF ANOTHER DUTY.

```
FIGURE 6.  BUS GRAPH SHOWING CREW SCHEDULE.
-------------------------------------------

TIME (HOURS)
4    5    6    7    8    9    10   11   12   13   14   15   16   17   18   19   20   21   22   23   24
.----.----.----.----.----.----.----.----.----.----.----.----.----.----.----.----.----.----.----.----.

   3  ----------------------------                              21  -------------------------------------------------
      +13.13.13.13.13.13.13.13.13+                                  +17.17.17.17.17.17.17.+16.16.16.16.16.16.16.16.1+

      5  -------------------                                     23  ---------------------
         +10.10.10.10.10.10+                                         +7.7.7.7.7.7.7.7.7.7+

           7  ----------------                                    24  -----------------
              +12.12.12.12.12.+                                       +8.8.8.8.8.8.8.8+

             8  -----------------                                25  ------------------
                +3.3.3.3.3.3.3.3+                                    +19.19.19.19.19.1+

            9  ---------------------------------------------------------------------------------------------------
                                  +15.15.15.15.15.15.15.1+12.12.12.12.12.12.12.12.1+19.19.19.19.19.19.19.19.+
               +17.17.17.17.17.17.17.17.1+

  41  ---------------------------                                 26  ---------------
      +2.2.2.2.2.2.2.2.2.2.2.2.2+                                     +9.9.9.9.9.9.9+

    42  ------------------------------------------------------------------------------
        +15.15.15.15.15.15.15.15.1+10+2.2.2.2.2.2.2.2.2.2.+3.3.3.3.3.3.3.3.3.3.3.3.3.+

       43  -------------------                                    60  ---------------
           +1.1.1.1.1.1.1.1.1.1+                                      +16.16.16.16.1+

             44  ----------------------------------------------------------------------------------------------------
                 +7.7.7.7.7.7.7.7.7.7.7.7.7.7+11.11.11.11.11.1+18.18.18.18.18.18.18.18.18+8.8.8.8.8.8.8.8.8.8.8.8.8+

          46  ----------------                                  61  ----------------------------------------------------------
              +5.5.5.5.5.5.5.5+                                     +14.14.14.14.14.+11.11.11.11.11.11.11+
                                                                                              +18.18.18.18.18.18.18+

              47  -------------------------------------------------------------------
                  +4.4.4.4.4.4.4.4.4.4.4.4.4.4+        +5.5.5.5.5.5.5.5.5.5.5.5.5.5.+
                                  +13.13.13.13.13.13.13+

           48  --------------------------------------------------------------------------
               +6.6.6.6.6.6.6.6.6.6.+1.1.1.1.1.1.1.1.1.1.1.1+6.6.6.6.6.6.6.6.6.6.6.6.6.+

            49  ----------------------------------------------------------------------------------------------------
                +14.14.14.14.14.14.14.1+10.10.10.10.10.10.10.10.+4.4.4.4.4.4.4.4.4.4.4.4+9.9.9.9.9.9.9.9.9.9.9.9.9.9+
```

Computer Scheduling of Public Transport
A. Wren (ed.)
© *North-Holland Publishing Company, 1981*

PRACTICAL ASPECTS IN
AUTOMATIC CREW SCHEDULING

C. Piccione, A. Cherici, M. Bielli & A. La Bella

A.CO.TRA.L., A.T.A.C., & I.A.S.I.
Rome, Italy

The aim of this paper is to present the experience of the
Public Transport System (A.T.A.C.) in the metropolitan area of
Rome, in using automatic techniques for the operation of the
whole system. The work in progress is to achieve
computer-integrated management of all the functions relating
to the operation of the transport system, from the collection
of data to the evaluation of the service quality. In the
paper, attention is focussed on the structure of the
integrated system of models to be constructed. Moreover, the
model already implemented, of optimal assignment of drivers to
bus routes, is described in detail, taking into account the
constraints posed by the drivers' collective agreement.
Computational problems and results of A.T.A.C.'s experience in
using the above model are discussed.

1. INTRODUCTION

The public transport system in Rome is made up of 235 two-way lines (10 tram-ways
and 225 bus-lines), plus two underground lines. Surface and underground lines are
run by two different publicly-owned companies. In this paper, we are only
concerned with the surface transit system (A.T.A.C.), which covers a network of
1,964 km. with 195 trams and 2,468 buses, which have a daily utilization factor of
about 80%. A.T.A.C. employs about 16,430 workers, and operates about 127 million
km. per year. The number of passengers per year increased from 592 million in
1970, to 1,279 million in 1979.

The main problems that A.T.A.C. faces are:

a) high traffic density due to the high number of private cars (1 car per 3.5
   inhabitants);
b) too few reserved bus lanes (less than 11% of the total mileage);
c) level of service to be increased (buses are, in general, overcrowded, slow and
   not sufficiently frequent, especially during peak hours).

The above problems can only be solved by the intervention of central and local
authority, and are beyond the influence of the transport company. However, given
available resources, the company can try to reduce the consequences by planning
and control aimed at matching service supply and transport demand under all
traffic conditions.

To this end, an operational planning structure must be developed, in order to
ensure the best performance of the system, with the use of data base, real-time
information and optimization techniques.

In this paper, we present the operational planning problems as tackled by A.T.A.C.; after a short discussion of the subject, we illustrate in particular the procedure developed for automatic crew scheduling. Some numerical results are also presented.

2. OPERATIONAL PLANNING IN A PUBLIC TRANSPORT SYSTEM

Operational planning can be defined as the set of operations and procedures aimed at matching service supply and transport demand. A representation of the various activities involved in operational planning is shown in Figure 1, where, for a given structure of the transit network (lines determination), we can distinguish five levels of operation, each characterised by a different time-horizon: vehicle scheduling and assignment to lines and depots, crew scheduling, crew rostering and attendance, centralised control. Obviously, centralised control must operate in real time, crew rostering can be considered a daily operation, whereas vehicle and crew scheduling operate periodically, depending on the dynamics of transport demand.

In order to develop automatic operational planning procedures, it is necessary to design a data collection and management system, able to supply information on transport demand, resource availability and traffic conditions at the required levels of aggregation, accuracy and period of intervention.

The structure shown in Figure 1 is based on a decomposition of the overall operational planning function, and allows for a separate study of the different problems. However, owing to strong interactions between different levels, attention must be drawn to the integration of the various procedures, in order to pursue the global optimum of the performance of the system.

In fact, accuracy of data and the type of model used at each level affect the solution of the next level, and then the global optimum, so that periodic feedback from the real environment is necessary in order to verify the consistency of the operational system. In the following Section, a short description of the state of A.T.A.C. activities will be given.

3. THE PROGRESS OF THE A.T.A.C. PROGRAMME

The computer-integrated management of all the operational planning functions is a very difficult and onerous task; at present, only preliminary studies have been developed by A.T.A.C., and experimental tests have been carried out towards a gradual introduction of automatic procedures. Crew rostering and attendance has been the first automatic procedure introduced by A.T.A.C. The system was developed by Partners in Management Ltd., and its characteristics and performance are described in detail in another paper in the present volume (8).

Data collection is now based on periodic detection on each line; passenger load diagrams with respect to location and time are periodically constructed, and times needed to cover trips under different traffic conditions are detected.

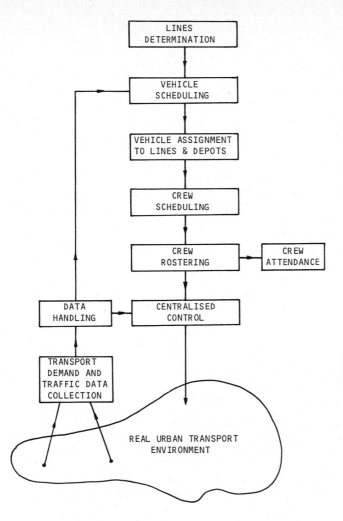

Figure 1. Operational planning structure

A first experiment in automatic data detection on buses, for one line only, started in August, 1979, using a centralised information and on-line data processing system to control the transit service.

This is the basis of the automatic generation of trip times; data handling, however, is still a manual operation, and consists of determining, for each time interval T, in which transport demand and times to cover trips can be considered constant:
- the headway of the line $h = T \times C/P$, where C is the capacity of a standard vehicle, and P is the number of passengers measured at the line section of maximal load;
- the number of vehicles $N = g/h$, where g is the total round trip time, including layovers.

In Table 1, a typical situation for a short journey has been reported, that shows a high variation of parameters in different time intervals.

In constructing a bus schedule, a problem arises in determining an adequate service, with relation to the changing demand and time to cover trips. In particular, when passing from time interval T_1, with given parameters, to time interval T_2, with different parameters (see Figure 2), nine cases are possible, depending on relative values of $N(T_1)$, $N(T_2)$, $h(T_1)$, $H(T_2)$:

$$N(T_1) \gtrless N(T_2)$$

$$h(T_1) \gtrless h(T_2)$$

The heuristic algorithm developed by A.T.A.C. reproduces manual criteria and determines a solution for each case, by introducing or removing vehicles in the transition periods, minimizing layover times under general constraints regarding the numbers of vehicles to be utilised in the given time intervals. The relevant computer program has been tested, but it is not in current use. A new program is now being studied, which should supply an implementable optimal solution to the vehicle scheduling problem.

As far as the assignment of vehicles to lines and depots with the objective of minimizing idle paths is concerned, a classical transportation problem has been formulated and a computer program has been implemented, able to manage 20 depots and a network of 300 nodes.

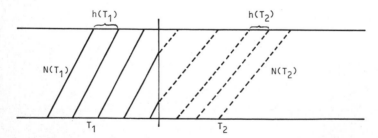

Figure 2.   Trip representation for different time intervals.

Table 1. General Timetable

time interval	number of vehicles	headway (min)	----one-way-----		-----return-----	
			time to cover trip	layover time	time to cover trip	layover time
5.45- 6.30	2	15.0	12	3	12	3
6.31- 7.00	3	10.6	14	2	13	3
7.01- 7.30	7	4.7	14	3	14	2
7.31- 8.45	9	4.2	19	2	15	2
8.46- 9.30	7	5.6	17	2	17	3
9.31-12.30	5	8.0	18	2	18	2
12.31-13.30	7	5.6	16	3	18	2
13.31-15.45	4	8.0	14	2	14	2
15.46-19.00	6	8.0	18	3	24	3
19.01-21.00	7	7.0	19	3	25	2
21.01-22.00	3	11.0	14	2	14	3
22.01-24.00	2	15.0	13	2	13	2

4. CREW SCHEDULING

The crew scheduling problem has been formulated as a set covering or set partitioning problem, but, because of the high number of variables and constraints, the problem in general is not soluble. Usually, the solution is obtained by means of heuristic techniques based on procedures that try to improve a solution in current use. An algorithm that does not need this initial solution has been proposed (1), and other procedures have been developed to satisfy more modest requirements (2).

Our approach uses a set partitioning method (for a general survey of this type of method, see (3)), and solves the problem for each line separately.

Let $P = \{p_i\}$ be the set of pieces of work starting and ending in relief points (the depots or the termini of the line), into which the daily service over a given line can be decomposed. The set P, in its turn, must be decomposed into subsets t_j, in accordance with the regulations of the personnel. The set $T = \{t_j\}$ will be referred to as the set of feasible duties. A schedule is constituted by a subset of T satisfying the conditions:

1. $t_j \cap t_i = 0$ $\forall\ i,j$ $i \neq j$

2. $P = \bigcup t_j$

Letting c_j be the cost of duty t_j, $\forall j$, and

$$a_{ij} = \begin{cases} 1 & \text{if } p_i \in t_j \\ 0 & \text{otherwise,} \end{cases}$$

the problem of finding the optimal crew schedule can be stated as:

$$\min z = \sum_{j \in T} c_j \, x_j \qquad \qquad (i)$$

$$\sum_{j \in T} a_{ij} \, x_j = 1 \qquad \qquad i \in P \qquad \qquad (ii)$$

$$x_j = 0 , 1 \qquad \qquad j \in T \qquad \qquad (iii)$$

where constraints (ii) state that each period p_i belongs to one duty only, and constraints (iii) represent the indivisibility of each duty.

4.1   Algorithm and Constraints Introduced

The conditions previously imposed in (ii) and (iii) involve the techniques of zero-one integer programming, and, as noted, require a high computation time. However, there are algorithms that apply general methods to these specific problems and allow for a noticeable reduction of computation time: among these the algorithm of Garfinkel and Nemhauser (4) has been chosen, which provided a solution to the problem under investigation. However, the computation time was exorbitant if the number of vehicles per line exceeded ten.

The ways that are generally accepted to reduce computation time tend to make use of heuristic algorithms rather than exact ones: for example by the elimination from set P of certain pieces of work belonging to duties t_j, predetermined with techniques similar to the manual ones. This yields usually sub-optimal solutions.

Another possible way, followed here, is that of maintaining the use of exact algorithms and reducing the set of feasible solutions by the addition of new constraints.

In the following we illustrate the functioning of the algorithm and the additional constraints introduced in the problem under consideration.

A. Duty matrix generation

First of all, feasible duties covering the daily work in a general way are generated. This phase requires only a few computer seconds. In order to reduce the set T of all feasible duties, each vehicle is taken separately and cut into duties and trippers. Then the minimal length and the maximal cost of duty for each vehicle is computed: this allows the elimination from the set T of duties falling outside these bounds.

B. Search for a basic solution

A basic solution is generated as the set of optimal duties vehicle by vehicle, providing an initial global cost $z_0 < \infty$, proportional to paid idle time (in the Garfinkel and Nemhauser algorithm, one begins from $z_0 = \infty$.)

As a result of several cases already studied, it is possible to single out, a priori, certain duties that appear to be in the optimal solution (e.g. owing to the characteristics of certain pieces of work with respect to duty length).

The next step is to determine these pre-established duties. It would then be possible to form the set T of all duties, eliminating those containing pieces of work p_i belonging to pre-established duties, and those exceeding maximal cost and minimal length constraints calculated in the basic solution.

In this way one can reduce the set T to an acceptable dimension (not more than 1000 to 1500 elements) with respect to the computation time.

C. Duty matrix reduction

Set T can be decomposed into disjoined subsets T_i characterised by the presence in the first position of each $t_i \in T_i$ of the period p_i. Table 2 shows a test duty matrix in which subset T_1 contains four elements (beginning with period p_1), subset T_2 contains seven elements (beginning with period p_2) etc., and in each subset, duties are ordered according to increasing costs: this allows us to eliminate duties belonging to a given subset T_i in the following optimization phase.

To reduce the duty matrix, the following efficient technique has been developed. Starting from the end of the matrix, one finds duties in which the last piece of work p_n is contained (e.g. p_{44} in Table 2), and other periods p_k, common to all these duties (e.g. p_{31}, p_{34}, p_{36}, p_{38}, p_{40}, p_{42}, p_{43}) are detected.

It is obvious that to guarantee the presence of p_n, one duty containing p_n must appear in the final solution, which necessarily contains the other periods p_k. It is therefore possible to eliminate from the matrix all duties that do not contain p_n and that contain at least one p_k. In the same way, we proceed with periods p_{n-1}, p_{n-2}, etc. In Table 2, duties that can be eliminated with this procedure are distinguished by +++, resulting in a reduction of the number of duties from the original 171 to 58.

4.2 Optimization phase

The technique used is based on the well known Garfinkel and Nemhauser algorithm, and consists of the construction of a partial solution vector, K, containing duties that satisfy constraints (ii) and (iii). To this algorithm we have added some innovations that lead to a substantial reduction of computer time. In the following, we illustrate three of these.

A. Cost control

When adding a duty to vector K, the partial solution cost must satisfy the condition $z < z_o$, where z_o is the cost of the last feasible solution obtained. As previously mentioned, we start with the basic solution cost.

We observe that the search for a duty to add to the current partial solution is limited to the subset T_i, corresponding to the first period p_i missing from K. Since duties are ordered according to increasing cost within each subset, if condition $z < z_o$ does not hold, the search in the corresponding subset can be stopped.

TABLE 2

LINE 37   LIST OF POSSIBLE COMBINATION IN DUTIES

COMB	PERIODS WHICH MAKE UP THE COMBINATION											COST
1	1	2	3	4	7	9	11	13	14	15	16	15
2+++	1	2	3	4	7	9	11	13	14	15	O	16
3	1	2	3	4	7	O	O	O	O	O	O	24
4+++	1	2	3	4	7	9	11	13	14	O	O	119
5	2	3	4	7	9	11	13	14	15	16	O	16
6+++	2	3	4	7	9	11	13	14	15	O	O	17
7	2	3	4	7	9	O	O	O	O	O	O	156
8	2	3	4	7	O	O	O	O	O	O	O	295
9+++	2	3	4	7	9	11	13	14	O	O	O	326
10+++	2	3	4	8	O	O	O	O	O	O	O	415
11+++	2	3	6	8	O	O	O	O	O	O	O	415
12	3	4	7	9	11	13	14	15	16	17	O	16
13	3	4	7	9	11	13	14	15	16	O	O	17
14	3	4	7	9	11	O	O	O	O	O	O	24
15	3	4	7	9	O	O	O	O	O	O	O	160
16+++	3	4	7	9	11	13	14	15	O	O	O	223
17	3	4	7	9	11	13	14	15	16	19	O	321

. . . .

COMB	PERIODS WHICH MAKE UP THE COMBINATION											COST
144	28	29	30	31	34	36	38	40	42	43	44	15
145+++	28	29	30	31	34	36	38	40	42	43	O	16
146+++	28	29	30	31	34	36	38	40	42	O	O	17
147+++	28	29	30	31	34	36	38	40	O	O	O	120
148+++	28	29	30	31	34	36	38	41	O	O	O	446
149+++	28	29	30	31	34	36	39	41	O	O	O	477
150+++	28	29	30	31	34	37	39	41	O	O	O	477
151+++	28	29	30	31	36	37	39	41	O	O	O	477
152	29	30	31	34	36	38	40	42	43	44	O	16
153+++	29	30	31	34	36	38	40	42	43	O	O	17
154+++	29	30	31	34	36	38	40	42	O	O	O	120
155+++	30	31	34	36	O	O	O	O	O	O	O	25
156	30	31	34	36	38	40	42	43	44	O	O	68
157+++	30	31	34	36	38	40	42	43	O	O	O	151
158	31	34	36	38	O	O	O	O	O	O	O	26
159	31	34	36	38	40	42	43	44	O	O	O	480
160	32	33	36	37	39	41	O	O	O	O	O	89
161+++	32	33	35	37	39	O	O	O	O	O	O	329
162+++	32	33	35	37	40	O	O	O	O	O	O	409
163+++	32	33	36	38	40	O	O	O	O	O	O	409
164+++	32	33	35	37	O	O	O	O	O	O	O	430
165+++	33	35	37	39	O	O	O	O	O	O	O	65
166	33	35	37	39	41	O	O	O	O	O	O	223
167+++	34	36	38	40	O	O	O	O	O	O	O	25
168+++	34	36	38	41	O	O	O	O	O	O	O	442
169+++	34	36	39	41	O	O	O	O	O	O	O	482
170+++	34	37	39	41	O	O	O	O	O	O	O	482
171	35	37	39	41	O	O	O	O	O	O	O	362

B. Control of intersections

The addition of a new duty t_h to vector K requires a consistency control of t_h with respect to duties already in K, i.e. one has to check that no piece of work included in t_h is also included in duties t_k already in K.

Given the particular structure of the matrix, one has to repeat this control a number of times with consequent high time consumption. Therefore a suitable vector is used being of the same dimension as T: each time a duty is added or taken away from K one marks, with the number of the duty or with a zero, the positions of duties containing at least one piece of work of t_h.

C. Control of pieces of work assignment

In the duty matrix generation phase one registers in a vector the number in which each piece of work appears for the last time (e.g. duty 159 for period p_{44} in Table 2). In this way by assigning a new piece of work the search for a duty can be stopped on reaching that duty number.

5. COMPUTATIONAL EXPERIENCE

The computer program in Fortran implementing the described procedure can be utilised with a maximum of 300 pieces of work and 2000 duties, requiring about 50 Kbytes. The program at A.T.A.C. runs on a IBM 370/145 computer, and for cases with no more than 10 vehicles per line and 50-100 pieces of work consumes from a few seconds to 15 minutes of computation time.

As an example in Table 3 a timetable for a line with 6 vehicles is considered; in Table 4 the basic solution is reported with the pre-established duties (for vehicles 7,9 and 10) and trippers (distinguished by +); Table 5 shows the optimal solution obtained after 8 iterations of the algorithm. The program shows a noticeable sensitivity to the number and length of the pieces of work considered (from 20 minutes to 2.5 hours) because of their influence on the total number of duties. The program is also quite sensitive to the length of the duties (from 4 to 7 hours) and of trippers (up to 3 hours). Therefore a complete sensitivity analysis was not performed.

Garfinkel and Nemhauser's algorithm gives a much quicker result than the classic branch-and-bound algorithms, but given the size of the problem, requires too much computer time to be accepted. The developed technique discussed here leads to a noticeable computer time reduction making crew scheduling operation feasible.

However, the identification of further constraints to reduce the set of feasible solutions can still improve the performance of the proposed algorithm.

TABLE 3

OUTPUT PROGRAMME ·PICCHE

TIMETABLE OF LINE 37

BUS 2 : RIM 0515; CAP 0630, 0732, 0847, 1000, 1112,
         1228, 1342; RIM 1501; out of service; RIM 1705;
         CAP 1843, 2003, 2126, 2230, 2330; RIM 2439 .

BUS 6 : RIM 0530; CAP 0645, 0753, 0908, 1024, 1136,
         1250, 1407, 1517, 1627, 1907, 2030, 2149;
         RIM 2300 .

BUS 7 : RIM 0636; CAP 0759; RIM 0917; out of service;
         RIM 1737; CAP 1915; RIM 2047 · .

BUS 9 : RIM 0545; CAP 0701, 0809, 0924, 1036, 1148,
         1303; RIM 1428 .

BUS 10: RIM 0644; CAP 0814; RIM 0937; out of service;
         RIM 1136; CAP 1309, 1427, 1537, 1647, 1811,
         1931, 2052; RIM 2214 .

BUS 12: RIM 0600; CAP 0717, 0827, 0954, 1144, 1323,
         1437, 1547, 1657, 1819, 1939, 2103, 2215,
         2315; RIM 2424 .

TABLE 4

OUTPUT PROGRAMME PICCHE   LINE 37

BASIC SOLUTION   COST = 9917

DUTY	VEH.	START		END	
1 +	2	RIM	0515	0732	CAP
2	2	CAP	0732	1228	CAP
3 +	2	CAP	1228	1501	RIM
4 +	2	RIM	1705	1843	CAP
5	2	CAP	1843	2439	RIM
6	6	RIM	0530	1136	CAP
7 +	6	CAP	1136	1407	CAP
8	6	CAP	1407	1907	CAP
9	6	CAP	1907	2300	RIM
10 +	7	RIM	0636	0917	RIM
11 +	7	RIM	1737	2047	RIM
12	9	RIM	0545	1148	CAP
13 +	9	CAP	1148	1428	RIM
14 +	10	RIM	0644	0937	RIM
15	10	RIM	1136	1647	CAP
16	10	CAP	1647	2214	RIM
17 +	12	RIM	0600	0827	CAP
18	12	CAP	0827	1323	CAP
19	12	CAP	1323	1819	CAP
20	12	CAP	1819	2424	RIM

+ trippers
Pre-established duties:
10, 11, 12, 13, 14, 15, 16.

TABLE 5

```
SOLUTION  N. 8              COST = 7985
-----------------------------------------------------------------
DUTY   VEH.      START      END      VEH.   START          END
   1 +   7    RIM 0636   0917 RIM
   2 +   7    RIM 1737   2047 RIM
   3       9    RIM 0545   1148 CAP
   4 +   9    CAP 1148   1428 RIM
   5 +  10   RIM 0644   0937 RIM
   6      10   RIM 1136   1647 CAP
   7      10   CAP 1647   2214 RIM
   8 +   2    RIM 0515   0732 CAP
   9 +   6    RIM 0530   0753 CAP
  10 +  12   RIM 0600   0717 CAP    6  CAP 0753    0908 CAP
  11 +  12   CAP 0717   0954 RIM
  12      2    CAP 0732   1342 CAP
  13      6    CAP 0908   1407 CAP
  14     12   RIM 1144   1657 CAP
  15      2    CAP 1342   1501 RIM   12  CAP 1657   1939 CAP
  16      6    CAP 1407   1907 CAP
  17      2    RIM 1705   1843 CAP    6  CAP 1907   2300 RIM
  18      2    CAP 1843   2439 RIM
  19     12   CAP 1939   2424 RIM
-----------------------------------------------------------------
```

+ 8 trippers   average duration   2.43 hours

11 regular duties   average duration 5.30 hours

REFERENCES

1. Rousseau J.M. et al. The problem of assigning drivers to bus routes in an urban transit system. Publication n.44 Centre de Recherche sur les Transports (Montreal, August 1976)

2. Bodin L.D. and Dial R.B. Hierarchical procedures for determining vehicle and crew requirements for mass transit systems. Workshop on Distribution Management, SOGESTA (Urbino Italy, September 1979).

3. Balas E. and Padberg M.W. Set partitioning — A survey in combinatorial optimization, Edited by N. Christofides, A. Mingozzi, P. Toth, and C. Sandi (J.Wiley & Sons, 1979).

4. Garfinkel, R.S. and Nemhauser, G.L. The set partitioning problem; Set covering with equality constraints, Operations Research 17(5) (1969) 848-856.

5. Piccione, C. Un algoritmo per la determinazione meccanografica degli orari delle linee urbane de trasporto, Ingegneria Ferroviaria 6 (June 1974).

6. Piccione, C. La funzione movimento in un'azienda di trasporto pubblico unbano, Fifth Conference of A.I.R.O. (1975).

7. Cherici, A. and Piccione, C. La determinazione, mediante elaboratore, dei turni di servizio in un'azienda di trasporto pubblico urbano, Ingegneria Ferroviaria 7/8 (July/August 1977).

8. Jachnik, J.K. Attendance and rostering system. Appearing in this volume (1981).

Computer Scheduling of Public Transport
A. Wren (ed.)
© *North-Holland Publishing Company, 1981*

CREW SCHEDULING BY COMPUTER:
A TEST ON THE POSSIBILITY OF DESIGNING DUTIES
FOR A CERTAIN BUS LINE

J.M.J.Borret and A.W.Roes

Amsterdam Urban Transport Company (GVB)
and
Dutch Railways Company (NS)

The managements of five urban transport companies asked the operations research group of the Dutch Railways Company to test their system DIGOS by designing bus drivers' duties by computer for a certain number of bus lines in different cities. This paper describes the tests we made on the design of duties for a large bus line of the Amsterdam Urban Transport Company (Gemeentevervoerbedrijf, GVB), using a method which is based on integer linear programming.

1. INTRODUCTION

To indicate the size of the company we give some figures:

```
Number of employees            : about 4000
Number of bus/tram drivers     : about 2500
Number of duties (per week-day): about 1100
Number of buses and trams      : about  660
```

There are eleven persons concerned with the complete scheduling of duties and rosters.

All activities are carried out manually in practice; computers are only used for recording information.

2. THE OBJECTIVES OF CREW SCHEDULING BY COMPUTER

Manual crew scheduling is time consuming, because of the following reasons:

- the constraints to which the duties and rosters are subject are very complicated;

- twice a year a new timetable is required (Saturday, Sunday, Monday-Friday, special days);

- changes of personnel wishes and Union demands;

- the information needed for a quick design of a new schedule is not computerised. Retrieving information and providing information are bottle-necks in the whole crew scheduling process.

So the main objective of crew scheduling by computer is to accelerate this process, in order to give the needed information with more speed. A system built for crew scheduling should satisfy this objective. The possibility of providing alternatives by using a computer is an added important advantage.

This paper deals only with the design of duties by computer, but it is obvious that, for example, rostering of crews should also be automated to achieve a successful acceleration of the whole process.

3. DESCRIPTION OF THE DIGOS SYSTEM

In order to solve the problems just formulated, we have developed a system called DIGOS (DIensten Genereren en Optimaal Selecteren, viz. the generation of duties and the optimal selection). DIGOS is a method which selects an (optimal) set from a generated set of duties by using mathematical programming.

DIGOS can briefly be described as follows:

A route is selected; the trips of this route are defined by their departure time, point of departure, arrival time and point of arrival. Relief points are defined and trips are connected between which no relief possibility exists. From the remaining set of trips, a number of duties are generated, according to a certain number of rules, where each duty satisfies certain conditions. Next, to each duty costs are assigned, depending on the quality of the duty. By solving an integer linear programming problem which minimises the total cost of all duties needed for covering all trips, an optimal selection of duties is made which satisfies certain constraints on groups of duties, for example not exceeding the average working time. Appendix A describes the full system and model used.

4. THE WORKING CONDITIONS

4.1 Types of duties

Crew scheduling consists in subdividing the vehicle schedule into shifts or duties, corresponding to the conditions of work. A duty is one day's work of a bus crew.

Scheduling the lines into duties, one can discern two types of duty:

- early duties, and

- late duties.

These early duties can be divided into two kinds of duty:

- continuous duties (semi-direct, with a short meal break);

- split duties.

The late duties are continuous duties (direct), without a meal break (time to drink coffee is already supplied in the vehicle schedule).

The different types of duty are: (see chart)

- early duties, subdivided into
  . continuous duties:
    - very early duty (xxx)
    - day duty (xx)
    - middle duty (t)
  . split duties:
    - (normal) split duty (x)
    - late finish split duty, finishing after 17.30 (k/s)
      (kop/staartdienst = head/tail duty)

- late duties
    - (normal) late duty (l)
    - coffee car duty (kw)
      (koffiewagen, duty on a car which enables the late duties to
      have a coffee break during the vehicle run).

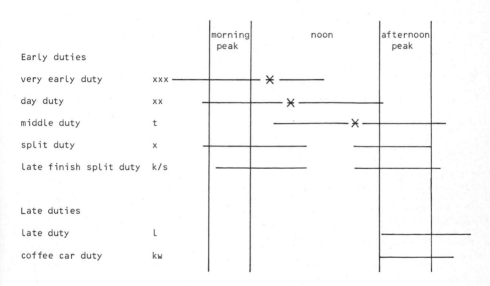

＊ = meal break

4.2 Working conditions

All these duties are subject to working conditions. They can be divided into two
main categories:

- conditions concerning individual duties;
- conditions relating to a group of duties.

Some of the conditions are fixed; others concern values or wishes; others are only valid under certain circumstances. There are also conditions which fall in between the fixed values and those which are merely wishes. In certain cases these different conditions are interdependent.

The conditions concerning individual duties are related to:
- the spread, the time period from the starting time to the finishing time of the duty;
- the working time;
- the time interval of the beginning and ending of duties;
- the departure and arrival points;
- the meal break;
- the working time of the parts of a duty (periods without a break);
- signing on and signing off times;
- bus changes and changing times.

Conditions relating to a group of duties are important for the total quality of the crew schedule. The most important of these conditions are:
- the numbers of duties, split duties, bus changes, and duties with a long meal break should be minimised;
- the average working time should not exceed 7.47 hours;
- the total quality of the crew schedule must be acceptable;
- the very early and middle duties must cover as few trips as possible, other duties as many trips as possible;
- the earliest starting duties should finish first.

The working conditions concerning individual duties are specified in Appendix B.

5. DATA RELATING TO PIECES OF WORK

Route 15, the route which had to be scheduled, is one of the more complicated routes of the Amsterdam Urban Transport Company. The length of one piece of work is about 2 hours on average, which reduces the possibility of combining trips into duties, compared with routes consisting of smaller pieces.

The relief points are:
- the West garage
- the Sloterdijk terminus
- the Kabelweg terminus.

The relief times are given by the starting time at the terminus and the arrival time of a vehicle at the garage.

Walking time between relief points is introduced by using so-called passenger trips within the timetable which have the length of a walking time. These trips do not have to be covered by duties, but when it is useful they can be used.

The following table shows the size of the problem we are dealing with.

NUMBER OF	SATURDAY	SUNDAY	MONDAY/FRIDAY
TRIPS, about:	140	120	300
VEHICLES	15	14	50

6. PREPARING THE GENERATION OF DUTIES

6.1 Connecting trips

Each starting time at a relief point and the arrival time at the garage is a possible relief time. However, in the morning hours, it is not useful to relieve a driver very early after one or two trips, for two reasons:
- the first part of a duty should not be too short;
- the first relief creates the beginning of a new duty.

Consequently, the first relief time must be as late as possible. All relief times before this time can be deleted: these trips are connected.

In the evening hours, late duties should not begin before 16.00. Also the rules apply that late duties do not have meal breaks and that the number of changes are restricted; therefore a lot of trips can be connected.

In this manner, the number of trips to be covered by duties can be reduced from about 140 to 90 trips on Saturday (see Appendix D), from 120 to about 80 on Sunday, and from 300 to about 200 on Monday/Friday.

6.2 Estimation of the number of duties

6.2.1 The total number of duties

Due to the roster with 29 days free in 14 weeks and different time compensations, the average working time for a duty is 7.47 hours. By experience, it is possible to estimate the number of duties necessary for a typical line.

For line 15 on Saturday, 32 duties are estimated. In practice, the real number of duties based on the working conditions can differ from the estimation.

6.2.2 The number of duties per type of duty

Given the specific bus schedule of line 15, it is possible to discern the estimated number of duties for the several types. For line 15 on Saturday, the estimated number of:
- late duties = 13
- early duties= 19   of which   xxx   = 5
                                   t   = 7
                                   xx and x together   = 7
                                   k/s   = 0
- all duties = 32

6.3 Preparing the starting and arrival times of the types of duty

One of the working conditions is that, if possible, the earliest starting duties should finish first. Owing to this, relief times can be marked out as starting or arrival times for a certain type of duty. By doing so, it is possible to avoid generating a great number infeasible duties. As this condition is not fixed, and also the estimation of the number of duties is not exact, a certain margin should be left.

7. DESCRIPTION OF THE TESTS

Using the timetable of '78-'79 for Saturday, route 15, two methods were tried out
in order to design suitable duties by using the developed system. In method 1
nearly all possible duties were generated from which an optimal set was selected
after computing a well-balanced objective function. In method 2 a strategy was
introduced which limited the number of generated duties drastically.

This strategy implied the following measures:

   1) We did not allow changes of bus within the portions of the very early duties
   or within the portions of the middle duties (see diagram), though in practice
   these changes of bus are used.

   2) The total number of split duties generated was reduced by generating mainly
   early and late <u>parts</u> of duties, where any early part could be linked to any
   late part to form a feasible split duty. Not all split duties could be
   constructed in this way; therefore a limited number of complete split duties
   had to be generated in addition. However, the reduction involved was
   considerable. One constraint had to be added to the mathematical model which
   provided the balance between early and late parts of split duties. Because the
   final schedule normally contains only a few split duties, linking these parts
   to split duties is easily done.

8. RESULTS

In the Saturday case the total number of duties generated according to method 1
was 1642. An overview of these duties, distinguished by the types of duties is
shown in Appendix C. Following method 2 only 452 duties were produced by the
generator of duties (including parts of duties, each counting for one duty).
Applied to Saturday, method 1 resulted in a good solution of 32 duties, bus method
2 produced a schedule of poor quality, though the number of duties was correct
(also 32) and the total schedule satisfied the formal conditions.

In Appendix D the solution according to method 1 is described, as an example for
this paper.

No problems were involved in designing the duties for Sunday; a good solution of
30 duties (one less than the manual schedule) was attained after generating nearly
all possible duties (3124) out ot 82 trips, using the experiences of the Saturday
case.

The design of duties for the Monday-Friday schedule on the other hand was very
complicated. According to method 1 about 30,000 duties could be generated out ot
about 200 trips. Therefore method 2 was developed using the strategy described
before.

Only about 2000 duties were left after programming the duty generator with this
strategy. The solutions derived from these duties were of rather good quality,
where the Saturday solution, produced in a comparable way, was poor. They all
consisted of 65 duties.

A very essential part of this test was the construction of the objective function
in the mathematical model. About fifteen criteria influenced the cost of the
duties (though not simultaneously); the costs related to these criteria had to be
well balanced, so that no criterion should dominate too much. A detailed
description of these costs is given in Appendix E.

Some priorities were given to minimisation of: the total number of duties, the number of split duties, the number of duties with meal breaks greater than one hour, the number of duties with bus changes and the number of some particular duties of poor quality. Because of the conflicts between the criteria, the development of an equally balanced objective function was very complicated, but possible.

The advantages of using linear programming instead of some particular standard problem like the set partitioning problem appeared especially as we were asked to produce an alternative solution with at most seven duties with a long break (greater than one hour). The first solution contained fourteen long-break duties. Adding this constraint to the mathematical model gave a new and better solution, containing only seven long-break duties, of course.

The results of the Monday-Friday case proved that the system was able to produce good solutions to problems which are complicated because of the complex constraints, and because of the size of the problem. In this case, technically the problem was solved.

9. IMPLEMENTATION?

Proving the ability of the system to make a good set of good duties was the priority during the test described, not the thought of implementation. Nevertheless, implementation is the final objective and the decision to implement the system depends on:

1. the quality of solutions presented by the system.

2. the goodwill of the (future) users.

3. the costs of using the system compared with the actual situation

4. the benefits of using the system compared with the actual situation

5. the automation of other planning processes within the company.

6. the organising aspects within the company.

The following comments relate to these points:

1. The solutions produced so far are good, but not better than the manual ones, though there is some kind of guarantee of optimality to small problems.

2. The people who design the duties manually are not convinced of the advantages of a computerised system. They like their work of puzzling and sharp thinking, which would be limited.

3. Depending on the way a computer is used the costs of using the system depend on several matters:
    - the initial expense of a new computer,
    - the maintenance of the hardware and software,
    - the education of people in order to use the system well,
    - the computation time and memory needed to design duties.

    It also depends on the automation of other planning processes.

4,5. The main objective of introducing a computer system is the acceleration of the whole planning process, which consists of the planning of the timetable, the bus schedule, the designing of duties and the rostering process. Acceleration can only be achieved if most of these processes are automated, not the design of duties alone. If one process is separated from the others all attention will be directed to that process, with a proportional chance of failure. Short-term implementation must therefore be excluded.

6.   Using computers for the daily work will bring about many changes in the organisation of the company. Specialists will be needed to support this work. Changes within an organisation always give a lot of trouble, so this can be an obstructing factor in implementing the system.

10. COMPUTATIONAL REMARKS

All tests were carried out on an IBM 3031 computer; the programs have been written in FORTRAN.

In order to solve the integer linear programming problem the MPSX/MIP standard package of IBM was used, which in some cases provided a solution very quickly (within one minute) but in other cases needed half an hour CPU time. In general only the first integer solution was obtained to save CPU time, which generally was satisfactory.

The input of MPSX needs a lot of disk memory, e.g. 700 kbytes for a problem of 200 x 2500. Introducing new constraints can consume much CPU time. The CPU time needed seems also to depend strongly on the number of non-integer variables in the continuous solution.

In future a crew scheduling based mathematical programming program should be developed, having the same facilities as MPSX, but being less time consuming.

The method used by Garfinkel and Nemhauser (1) is not satisfactory because of computational reasons. Furthermore, adding constraints to the set partitioning problem is not really possible within this method. The method developed by Marsten (2) seems to offer more possibilities to problems of the size we have met.

Experiences with a heuristic gradient method for solving SPP or SCP like Toyoda (3) have been very disappointing because of the lack of sensitivity to penalties on duties.

11. CONCLUSIONS

We arrive at the following conclusions:

    - the system developed for the design of bus drivers' duties gives good results to a test on a rather complicated large size problem.

    - the system is general; it is not specialised to a certain company. Changes in individual duty constraints can be worked into the (parameters of the) duty generator; changes in group constraints can be translated into formulae in the mathematical model which finds the soluton of the duty problem.

    - essentials for a good result have been:
      . the construction of a good strategy to limit the generating of duties,
      . the balancing of an objective function in the mathematical model.

- a disadvantage of the system is the fact that a duty will not appear in the solution if it is not generated. So too limited a strategy is dangerous, when it relates to the optimality objective.

- when all duties can be generated (this occurs in problems of small size) an optimal solution can be attained.

- when a good strategy and an objective function have been developed, an acceleration of the scheduling process can be achieved. The development of a new strategy or objective function is time consuming and must be avoided. Therefore the system turns out to be used in a batch mode rather than in an interactive way.

- though technically the problem of designing duties can be solved, nevertheless there are a lot of problems which have to be solved before implementation can take place. The expected costs and profits of using the system, the automation of other planning processes and the organising aspects play a great part.

12. REFERENCES

1. Garfinkel,R.S. and Nemhauser,G.L. Integer Programming (Wiley & Sons 1972).

2. Marsten,R.E. An Algorithm for large set partitioning problems, Management Science 20(5) (1974).

3. Senju,S. and Toyoda,Y. An approach to linear programming with 0-1 variables, Management Science 15(4) (1968).

APPENDIX A. DESCRIPTION OF THE DIGOS SYSTEM

Step 1 : Define sets of trips I' and passenger trips P.
Step 2 : Reduce set of trips I' to I.
Step 3 : Define strategy and parameter values for generating duties.
Step 4 : Generate set of duties J,
                 set of early duty parts E $\Big\}$
                 set of late duty parts L $\Big\}$ appropriate for split duties.
Step 5 : Assign costs c_j to each duty.
Step 6 : Solve the following integer linear programming model to select
         an optimal set of duties:

$$\text{minimise} \quad \sum_{j \in U} c_j\, x_j$$

$$\text{subject to} \quad (1) \quad \sum_{j \in U} a_{ij}\, x_j = 1 \quad \forall\, i \in I$$

$$(2) \quad \sum_{j \in E} x_j = \sum_{j \in L} x_j$$

$$(3) \quad \sum_{j \in U} w_j\, x_j \leqslant \overline{w} \sum_{j \in U} x_j$$

$$(4) \quad \sum_{j \in J_k} x_j \; \left. \begin{array}{c} \leqslant \\ = \\ \geqslant \end{array} \right\} \; n_k \quad k = 1,2,\ldots.$$

$$(5) \quad x_j = 0 \text{ or } 1 \quad \forall\, j \in U$$

with: U   = J u E u L = set of all generated duties and duty-parts.

J   = set of all generated complete duties.

E   = set of generated early duty-parts.

L   = set of generated late duty-parts.

J_k = set of generated duties of type k.

I   = set of trips to be covered.

c_j = costs of duty j.

x_j = variable which indicates that duty j is in the solution (x_j=1) or not (x_j=0).

a_{ij} = 1 if duty j contains trip i,

= 0 otherwise.

w_j = working time of duty j.

n_k = maximum/exact/minimum number of duties of type k allowed in the solution.

$\overline{W}$ = maximum average working time.

Meaning of the constraints:

(1) each trip, except passenger trips, must be covered by exactly one duty.

(2) the number of early duty-parts should equal the number of late duty-parts, to get split duties.

(3) the average working time should not exceed $\overline{W}$.

(4) for some well-defined groups of duties, constraints can be formulated on the allowed number.

(5) a duty is either taken into the solution or it is not.

APPENDIX B

Individual working conditions

type of duty	spread max.	break length min.	max.	max. number bus changes (incl. break)	departure time/point	arrival time/point
early duty						
— continuous duty						
. very early (xxx)	10.00	0.30	1.15	2	before morning peak (m.p.) in garage	$\geqslant$ last relief time before 12.00; $\leqslant$ 15.30
. day duty (xx)					before or during m.p. in garage	$\leqslant$ 19.30
. middle (t)					after m.p.	$\leqslant$ 19.30
— split duty						
. split duty (x)	12.00	1.45	—	2	before or during m.p. in garage	$\leqslant$ 17.30
. late finish (k/s)		—	—	1	during m.p. in garage	$>$ 17.30; $\leqslant$ 19.30
late duty						
. late duty (l)	8.45	—	—	—	$\geqslant$ 16.00	$\geqslant$ 24.00 in garage
. coffee car duty (kw)					$\geqslant$ 15.30 in garage; $\geqslant$ 15.30 at terminus	$\geqslant$ 22.30 in garage; $<$ 24.00 in garage

— the signing-on time at the terminus is five minutes and is added to the working time of the duty part;

— a duty part is 1.50 at least (for split duties 2.00) and 5.45 at most;

— walking time is counted as working time and is added to the nearest duty part; walk first, then break;

— a bus change without walking takes five minutes (signing-on time) at least and should not be more than 29 minutes + 5 minutes signing-on time. If a change takes more than 34 minutes, it will be a break;

— the minimum working time is 5.30, the maximum 8.45.

APPENDIX C

Data relating to generated duties and duties in the solution of Saturday.

type of duty	number of bus-changes	number of duties	
		generated	in solution
xxx	⩽ 2	382	5
xx	⩽ 2	83	5
t	⩽ 2	675	7
x	⩽ 2	417	2
1	0	13	13
Total		1642	32

APPENDIX D

Solution Saturday

Lijn 15
Zaterdagen

Wagenuren: 231.16
21: 3.28

	-21-
5	6.28
	8
	10.31 sld.

1	2	3	4	5	6	7	8	9	10	11	12	13	14
6.08	6.22	6.32		6.09	6.21	7.02	GAR 8.51	5.53	6.06		6.05	6.15	8.00
5	19	9	9x	6	7	10		2	4		3	18	11x
8.10	8.20	8.30	GAR 11.51	8.40	8.50	9.00	9.09	9.18	9.26	GAR 11.11	9.35	9.44	9.52
10.01	10.10	10.18	12.09	13	10.36	10.44	10.53	11.02	11.10	13.05	11.19	11.28	11.36
2x	3x	x11	x2	10.27	5	4	12.41	12.49	12.57	11	13.13	13.21	13.29
11.45	11.53	12.01	14.01	12.17	12.25	12.33	x9	18	19	14.57	13	12	14
8x	7x	10x	17	x3	14.17	14.25	14.33	14.41	14.49	16.48	15.05	15.13	15.21
13.37	13.45	13.53	15.53	14.09	x7	x10	16.24	16.32	16.40		16.56	17.04	17.12
15	1	16	17.32	x8	16.08	16.16							
15.29	15.37	15.45	17.43	16.01									
17.20	17.28	17.36		20	21	22	23	24	25	26	27	28	29
30	31	32		22.56	0.39	0.46	0.53	0.33	0.55	0.49	0.56	1.03	1.10
0.15	0.23	0.31											

Explanation:

Each column corresponds to one vehicle.

All vehicles start and finish in the garage, except bus 21/5 which runs to Sld.

All times given are possible relief times.

In the garage, five minutes signing-off time is added to the arrival time.

The number, written by hand in the column, indicates the number of the duty.

A line drawn above the relief time means that at this time the duty terminates, or will be continued later on. For example, duty number 5 starts at 6.08 at car 1, continues at car 1 until 10.01; after a meal break of thirty minutes, and five minutes signing-on time, it continues at car 6 at 10.36 until 14.17; there it terminates.

If an x is put, a bus change takes place within the part of the duty. For example, duty 3 starts at 6.05 at bus 12, gets its break at 9.35 until 10.10 (30 + 5 minutes), continues at bus 2 until 11.53, changes to bus 5 at 12.17 and terminates at 14.09.

* = break
bus trip numbers

Bus trip numbers (per duty, top of table):

805
804
1305
604   405
605 505 401 705 1103 1205 1405 106 306 404
206 402 504 704 603 1403 204 104 304 ... 105 305 403 905 1005
1101* 901* 1201* 1001* 101 102* 501*1492 601 602* 2101 2198* 301 302* 701 702* 1401 303*1102 801 802 803*1304 502 503*1204 902 903*1404 1002 1003* 1302 1303* 1301* 904 201 202*1004
506 606 706 806 906 1006 1104 1206 1306 1406 107 207 307

	1	2	3	4	5	6	7	8	9	10	11	12	13	14	15	16	17	18	19	20	21	22	23	24	25	26	27	28	29	30	31	32
number of trips	3	3	3	4	3	4	4	6	4	4	5	4	4	4	4	5	3	4	1	1	1	1	1	1	1	1	1	1	1	1	1	1
changing/walking/signing-on time	5	29	29	5	5	5	37	37	57	37	31	5	10	10	10	10	10	10	5	5	5	5	5	5	5	5	5	5	5	5	5	5
length of break	35	38	30	113	30	107	112	109	108	112	59	35	51	35	35	35	35	300	242	0	0	0	0	0	0	0	0	0	0	0	0	0
length of 2nd duty part	348	405	404	346	346	342	420	421	433	420	348	348	348	348	348	347	348	348	0	0	0	0	0	0	0	0	0	0	0	0	0	0
length of 1st duty part	154	325	330	320	353	231	415	403	411	342	401	350	342	336	336	343	342	329	348	0	0	0	0	0	0	0	0	0	0	0	0	0
number of bus changes (including break)	1	2	2	1	1	1	2	2	2	2	2	1	1	1	1	1	1	1	0	0	0	0	0	0	0	0	0	0	0	0	0	0
finishing point	2	2	2	2	2	2	2	2	2	2	2	2	2	2	2	2	1	2	1	1	1	1	1	1	1	1	1	1	1	1	1	1
spreadover time	617	808	804	819	809	720	947	933	952	914	848	813	821	759	759	806	804	1017	1018	700	836	835	834	806	820	806	805	804	803	700	700	700
finishing time	1728	1401	1409	1417	1329	1608	1601	1624	1616	1648	1656	1712	1726	1736	1743	1632	1640	2256	2439	2446	2453	2433	2455	2449	2456	2503	2510	2415	2423	2431		
starting time	1111	553	605	606	609	621	628	632	702	800	851	913	921	930	939	615	622	1556	1603	1611	1619	1627	1635	1643	1651	1659	1707	1715	1723	1731		
working time	542	730	734	706	739	613	835	824	802	749	738	730	724	724	731	729	717	736	700	836	835	834	806	820	806	805	804	803	700	700	700	
starting point	1	1	1	1	1	1	1	1	1	1	1	1	2	2	2	2	2	2	1	1	2	2	2	2	2	2	2	2	2	2	2	2
duty number	1	2	3	4	5	6	7	8	9	10	11	12	13	14	15	16	17	18	19	20	21	22	23	24	25	26	27	28	29	30	31	32

APPENDIX E

The objective function in the Monday to Friday case.

		costs
1.	Total number of duties	very high
2.	'Tripduties' (Slacks)	very high
3.	Split duties	very high
4.	Marginal duties	high
5.	Late split duties	high
6.	First part of duty long	high
7.	Second part of duty long	high
8.	Any duty part short	medium
9.	Bus change in part of duty	low
10.	Length of certain duties	low
11.	Breaks longer than an hour	low
12.	Some other criteria	(very) low

very high : 10^6

high   : 10^5, 10^6

medium   : 10^4, 10^5

low   : 10^3, 10^4

very low : 0 , 10^3

Computer Scheduling of Public Transport
A. Wren (ed.)
© *North-Holland Publishing Company, 1981*

HASTUS I:
A MATHEMATICAL PROGRAMMING APPROACH
TO THE BUS DRIVER SCHEDULING PROBLEM

Réjean Lessard, Jean-Marc Rousseau and Daniel Dupuis

Centre de recherche sur les transports,
Université de Montréal
and
Commission des Transports de la Communauté Urbaine de Québec,
(C.T.C.U.Q.)
Canada

In this paper, we first present a mathematical programming formulation of the bus driver scheduling problem in a transit company. Because in general this problem is too large, we introduce a relaxation of the problem and describe a solution strategy. The implementation and results obtained in Québec City are briefly reviewed.

1. THE PROBLEM

The bus driver scheduling (BDS) problem in a transit company involves establishing at minimum cost for each day of the week, a list of workdays which assign a driver to each bus in the timetable and respect all clauses in the union contract. In the approach discussed here it is assumed that the bus schedule is known and that once the list of feasible workdays is established, the problem is solved. In fact, in most North-American companies, the assignment of workdays to drivers is carried out by the drivers themselves and this selection is done on a seniority basis.

The difficulty of the problem arises directly from the kind of service that a transit company must offer and the travel patterns of a population. Figure 1 illustrates the service level by time of day for Québec City.

We note that the number of vehicles in service may be much greater at peak hours than at off-peak hours. This obviously necessitates either part time drivers, or split-shift workdays for full time drivers, or both. In most companies, unions are refusing or severely restricting the part-time driver solution. Several rules have then appeared defining legal split-shift workdays and working conditions which limit the number and/or compensate the drivers for less desirable workdays. These working conditions are described in more detail in several papers (1, 3, 13, 14).

We introduce here the basic terminology and some related rules which characterize the problem.

A <u>block</u> is the itinerary of a vehicle between its departure from and its return to the garage. It includes all deadhead time required to take the bus in and out of the garage and to and from the route(s) it services. There are generally short blocks to cover the peak periods and long blocks for the basic service.

Relief times are the times corresponding to points on the route where a change of drivers is possible. In general the number of such points is small.

A workday is a daily assignment consisting of one or more pieces of work, which must satisfy the union contract rules.

A piece of work (or piece)) refers to the period of time during which a driver works continuously with the same vehicle without a break. Generally the number of pieces of work in a workday is limited (2, 3 or 4) and the pieces must have a limited duration (2-3 hours).

A tripper is a small piece of work which is normally done in overtime by regular drivers or assigned to stand-by drivers. In general the companies hope for a few or no trippers. By extension and simplicity of notation we consider that a tripper is a workday. However we assume that there is no explicit upper bound on the number of trippers thus insuring the existence of a feasible schedule. Moreover, a high penalty is imposed on trippers.

A block partition is a set of pieces of work which covers exactly the block.

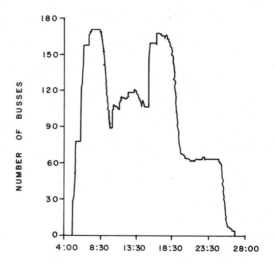

FIG. I — LEVEL OF SERVICE BY TIME OF DAY

The BDS problem has been described in detail and several approximate solution methods have been proposed. The proceedings from the two workshops on the BDS problem provide an excellent set of references (10, 11).

In the next section we present a general mathematical programming formulation of the BDS problem. Because in general this problem is too large we introduce a relaxation of the problem and present a solution approach. The application of the system in Québec City (250 buses) is briefly reviewed. In another paper (5) other alternative solution techniques are explored. The notation used in this paper is similar to the one used in the latter paper. We borrow heavily from that paper in the presentation of the model.

2. THE MODEL

For simplicity of presentation, we now assume that there are at most two pieces of work in a workday. The extension to three or more pieces of work is done later on; in fact in Québec, we use up to three pieces.

The notation for the model is first introduced. By a pair (ij) we denote <u>a piece of work</u> starting at time i and ending at time j. Only feasible pairs (ij) are considered, that is pairs such that i and j correspond to either a starting time, ending time or relief time in a given block. Note that (ij) could be feasible relative to several blocks. In the first part of this paper however we assume that (ij) is feasible relative to only one block (this could easily be done by small perturbations). For practical reasons, we also include in the feasible set of pieces of work the null pieces (OO).

A <u>quadruplet (ijkh) denotes a workday</u> made up with the feasible pairs (ij) and (kh). Only the workdays (ijkh) which are feasible within the union contract and the company regulations are considered. If (ij) or (kh) is a null piece the workday is either without a break or corresponds to a tripper.

In addition, we define:

L : the number of blocks

K : the number of distinct pieces of work

I : the set of feasible quadruplets (ijkh)

$I(ij) \subset I$: the set of feasible quadruplets (mnkh) where one of the pieces is (ij); it includes the quadruplet (ij00)

T_p : the set of all times which are either relief times, the starting time or the ending time for block p

x_{ijkh} : a binary variable taking value 1 if and only if a driver is assigned to workday (ijkh)

x : the vector with component x_{ijkh}, (ijkh)∈I

y_{ij} : a binary variable taking value 1 if the piece (ij) is used to be part of a driver workday. If $y_{ij}=1$, the piece (ij) has been chosen as part of the partition of the given block relative to which it has been defined.

y : the vector with component y_{ij} for <u>all</u> feasible (ij)

c_{ijkh} : the cost of a workday composed of the piece (ij) and the piece (kh) according to the union contract.

The problem can now be formulated as follows:

(2.1) $\text{Min} \sum_I c_{ijkh} \, x_{ijkh}$

s.t. i) $\sum_{I(ij)} x_{mnkh} - y_{ij} = 0$ for all (ij) except (00)

ii) $D \, x \geqslant d$

iii) $\sum_{i \epsilon T_p} y_{ik} - \sum_{j \epsilon T_p} y_{kj} = b_k^p$ for all $k \epsilon T_p$, for all p

where $b_k^p = \begin{cases} -1 & \text{if k is the starting time of block p} \\ +1 & \text{if k is the ending time of block p} \\ 0 & \text{otherwise} \end{cases}$

iv) $x_{ijkh} = 0,1$, $y_{ij} = 0,1.$

The constraints (iii) correspond to the flow formulation used to partition each block p into pieces of work. Figure 2 illustrates the concept. The feasible pieces of work (we are assuming here a minimum length of two hours) are represented by arcs and listed in the figure. We have assumed for simplicity that a relief point exists every hour in this example. The indices k in the constraint formulation correspond to points where a change of driver is feasible and the constraints ensure that a flow of one goes from the origin of the block (7:00) to its end (13:00), using arcs (ij) corresponding to feasible pieces. Constraints (iii) define a flow on an uncapacitated network.

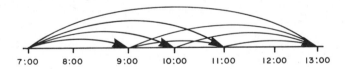

The feasible pieces are

| 7 - 9 | 7 - 11 | 9 - 11 | 10 - 13 |
| 7 - 10 | 7 - 13 | 9 - 13 | 11 - 13 |

Figure 2. The flow formulation for the partition of a block

With constraint (i) we ensure that any feasible piece (ij) used to partition a block will be used in a workday of type (ijkh) or (mnij).

In fact, given the values of the y_{ij}, i.e. the partition of the blocks into pieces of work, constraint (i) with the objective function can be reformulated into a maximum weight matching problem (described in Section 6).

Constraints of type (ii) refer to other constraints of the union contract. Examples of such constraints are:

- a minimum or maximum number of workdays without a break or with a limited break

- a limit on the number of drivers

- a limit on the average length of a workday

- etc.

Unless the problem is small (i.e. the number of blocks is small and thus the number of pieces and workdays is limited), this formulation seems impractical. Given a medium size transit network as in Québec City, we can easily generate over ten thousand pieces of work and five million workday variables without considering the flow variables and the difficulty of determining integer solutions for x_{ijkh}. In fact this formulation is nearly equivalent to the set covering formulation found in Heurgon (8,9). The set covering formulation was used in Paris to solve the problem one route at a time (drivers were not allowed to change route). However, the formulation (2.1) seems to be more amenable to a solution strategy that can handle very large problems.

3. SOLUTION STRATEGY

The chosen strategy is to use the obvious decomposition of the problem into the generation of a partition of each block into pieces of work (constraint (iii)), and the matching problem (constraint (i)) to form workdays. It has to be ensured that constraints (ii) are also satisfied. Three main steps compose this strategy:

Step 1: Using a relaxation of the whole problem we generate a partition of each block into feasible pieces of work that will respect as much as possible the constraint set (ii).

Step 2: Using an assignment algorithm and a heuristic procedure to split the pieces of work into two categories, we solve heuristically the matching problem to obtain a solution to the BDS problem. (Recently, a very fast matching algorithm has been developed by Derigs and communicated by Bodin (4), and it is planned eventually to replace the assignment algorithm by this matching algorithm.)

Step 3: Using a set of heuristic techniques, the solution previously obtained is improved, and it is made sure that constraint set (ii) is respected.

The solutions found in all test cases in Québec City and Montréal were either comparable to, or better than, manual solutions. The process has been implemented in Québec City since March 1979 and is currently being developed into a package for the Montréal transit authority. Each of the steps are described in more detail in the following sections, and results from the use of HASTUS I in Québec City are reported.

4. A RELAXATION OF THE MODEL: THE HASTUS-MACRO APPROACH

Firstly, the integrality of the x variables is relaxed, since several methods exist to derive reasonably good integer solutions when a continuous solution has been found. Secondly, we assume that the starting times, relief times and ending times for the blocks may only occur at predetermined times $t \epsilon T$, for example every 15 or 30 minutes. In the latter case, this means that all bus blocks are approximated to the nearest half-hour, and relief points are possible at some of, or at each, half-hour period. More comlicated schemes could also be devised; for example, one could use different time periods for peak and off-peak times. This relaxation of the problem considerably reduces the number of possible pieces of work (ij); however, it is important to note that a piece (ij) may now be feasible to several blocks, which also means that x_{ijkh} may be greater than 1.0. All i,j,k,h are now in T.

Moreover, the problem is further relaxed by requiring that the workdays selected be sufficient to cover the total requirement of drivers per time period (i.e. from one predetermined time to the next), instead of requiring that they exactly cover all the blocks individually. Using the same notation, this relaxtion problem can be written as follows:

(4.1) $\text{Min} \sum_I c_{ijkh} \, x_{ijkh}$

s.t.   i) $\sum_{I(t)} x_{ijkh} \geqslant N_t$ for all $t \epsilon T$

ii) $Dx \geqslant d$

iii) $\sum_{I(pq)} x_{ijkh} \geqslant Q_{pq}$ for all (pq) such that a small block exists from p to q, $(p,q \in T)$

iv) $\sum_{L(t)} x_{ijkh} \geqslant K_t$ for all $t \epsilon T$

v) $x_{ijkh} \geqslant 0$ (integrality is relaxed), $i,j,k,h \in T$,

where:

T   : the set of predetermined times which could be relief times, starting or ending times of blocks

I(t) : the set of workdays (ijkh)ϵI such that $i \leqslant t < j$ or $k \leqslant t < h$

L(t) : the set of workdays (ijkh)ϵI with a piece starting at time t $(i=t$ or $k=t)$

N_t : the number of buses in operation during time period starting at t

Q_{pq} : the number of blocks from p to q

K_t : the number of blocks starting at t.

The set of constraints (i) ensures that during all periods of the day the number of drivers working is greater than or equal to the number of vehicles in circulation. Constraint (ii) refers to union contract constraints as previously described. In constraint (iii), the number of pieces of work from p to q is at least as large as Q_{pq}, the number of small blocks from p to q. A small block is defined by the user as a block that cannot be partitioned and should be allocated as one piece of work to a driver. This generally corresponds to blocks with a duration of less than twice the minimum duration of a piece of work.

In constraint (iv) the number of pieces of work beginning at t must at least be equal to K_t, the number of blocks starting at t. Finally, x_{ijkh} is a continuous variable that can take any positive value in this relaxation. However, for x_{ijkh} to exist there must be a piece (ij) and a piece (kh), each feasible with respect to at least one block.

The HASTUS-macro approach is independently described in several other papers (1,3,12), and has been used on several occasions to analyse modifications to the drivers' union contract. A package for the utilisation of HASTUS-macro has also been developed (2) and implemented both in Québec City and Montréal and was extensively used by these companies during their last union contract negotiations.

5. PARTITIONING THE BLOCKS

In the present context however, the HASTUS-macro approach is used to help generate a first feasible solution as close as possible to the lower bound it indicates. This is done first by generating an intitial block partition that uses similar types of pieces of work and in approximately the same number as indicated by HASTUS-macro. Until recently, this was achieved by first generating for each block a set of partitions made up of pieces used in workdays corresponding to positive variables x_{ijkh} in the optimal solution of (4.1). A linear programming algorithm was then set up to choose one of the partitions generated for each block in order that the pieces thus chosen correspond as closely as possible to the solution of the HASTUS-macro problem (4.1). However, we recently adapted our work with Gallo, Carraresi and Davini (6), and will shortly implement in Québec City the technique described here which achieves the same purpose more efficiently. The following problem is considered.

$$(5.1) \quad \text{Min } z = \sum_{(ij)} (\sum_{I(ij)} x_{mnkh} - \sum_p {y_{ij}^p}^2 + \sum_p \sum_{(ij)} d_{ij}^p y_{ij}^p$$

$$\text{where} \quad \sum_{i \in T_p} y_{ik}^p - \sum_{j \in T_p} y_{kj}^p = b_k^p \quad \text{for all } k \in T_p, \text{ for all } p$$

$$y_{ij}^p = 0,1; \quad i,j \in T, \quad T_p \subset T$$

$\bar{x}_{mnkh}$ correspond to the optimal continuous solution of (4.1)

y_{ij}^p is a binary variable taking value 1 if piece (ij) is used in the partition of block p

d_{ij}^p is a penalty associated with the use of the piece (ij) on block p; this penalty takes into account the difference between actual relief time in the bus schedule and approximated relief time on which piece (ij) is defines (i,j∈T).

As in problem 2.1, the constraints correspond to the formulation of an uncapacitated flow problem.

This problem can easily be solved with an heuristic procedure. In fact, note that if we consider all the variables not associated with block r fixed, (i.e., y_{ij}^p, p≠r), the objective function is reduced as follows:

$$\sum_{(ij)} (\sum_{I(ij)} \bar{x}_{mnkh} - \sum_{p \ne r} y_{ij}^p - y_{ij}^p)^2 + \sum_{p \ne r} \sum_{(ij)} d_{ij}^p y_{ij}^p + \sum_{(ij)} d_{ij}^r y_{ij}^r$$

$$= \sum_{(ij)} ((\sum_{I(ij)} \bar{x}_{mnkh} - \sum_{p \ne r} y_{ij}^p)^2 - 2 y_{ij}^r (\sum_{I(ij)} \bar{x}_{mnkh} - \sum_{p \ne r} y_{ij}^p) + (y_{ij}^r)^2)$$

$$+ \sum_{p \ne r} \sum_{(ij)} d_{ij}^p y_{ij}^p + \sum_{(ij)} d_{ij}^r y_{ij}^r .$$

Because $y_{ij}^r = 0,1$, $(y_{ij}^r)^2 = y_{ij}^r$, and the previous function can be written as

$$D + \sum_{(ij)} c_{ij}^r y_{ij}^r ,$$

where
$$D = \sum_{(ij)} (\sum_{I(ij)} \bar{x}_{mnkh} - \sum_{p \ne r} y_{ij}^p)^2 + \sum_{p \ne r} \sum_{(ij)} d_{ij}^p y_{ij}^p$$

and
$$c_{ij}^r = -2(\sum_{I(ij)} \bar{x}_{mnkh} - \sum_{p \ne r} y_{ij}^p) + 1 + d_{ij}^r ,$$

and we can define a shortest path problem for block r defined as:

$$P_r: \quad \text{Min} \ \sum_{(ij)} c_{ij}^r y_{ij}^r$$

$$\sum_{i \in T_r} y_{ik}^r - \sum_{j \in T_r} y_{kj}^r = b_k^r \qquad \text{for all } k \in T_r$$

$$y_{ij}^r = 0,1 .$$

The suboptimal algorithm to solve (5.1) can now be summarised as follows:

1. a) Take any feasible solution y_{ij}^p and evaluate z_o, the corresponding value of the objective function;
   b) Set k to 1.

2. a) Solve successively P_r for r = 1,2,...,L; note y_k, the solution attained;
   b) Evaluate z_k, the objective function attained for $y = y_k$.

3. a) If $z_k = z_{k-1}$, stop;
   b) Set k to (k+1); go to 2.

When this algorithm stops, we have a partition of each block into pieces of work defined on periods, closely related to the HASTUS-macro solution. Actual pieces defined on real starting, relief or ending times for the blocks are then cut to correspond as closely as possible to the pieces defined on the periods. We define at this point the set V of feasible pieces of work on real times obtained by this process. The next step consists in building up a first feasible solution.

6. THE MATCHING PROBLEM

A maximum weight matching problem can be set up to generate the best set of workdays with a minimum number of trippers. This problem can be defined as follows:

(6.1)   Max $\sum_{I'} \bar{c}_{ijkh} x_{ijkh}$

$$\sum_{I'(ij)} \bar{x}_{mnkh} \leqslant 1 \qquad (ij) \in V$$

$$x_{ijkh} = 0,1$$

where $\bar{c}_{ijkh} = M - c_{ijkh}$, with

V   : the set of feasible pieces defined on real times resulting from the partitioning of the blocks;

I'   : the set of feasible workdays using pieces from V;

I'(ij) : the set of feasible workdays (mnkh)$\in$I' where one of the pieces is (ij);

M   : a large number; it corresponds to the relative penalty associated with a tripper.

Note that contrary to problem (2.1) only the x_{ijkh} which are feasible and use pieces of work previously generated by the partition algorithm are generated. A matching code can be used for the solution of this problem. However, with the currently available code, and the size of problem generated (500 nodes, 10,000 arcs), it tends to use a great amount of computer time. Until a more rapid matching code becomes available, we approximate the problem (6.1) by an assignment type problem that we solve with a minimum cost flow algorithm.

To do this, the set V of pieces of work is first split into two subsets so that there are only very few matching possibilities within each subset, and a maximum of matching possibilities between the two subsets. This objective is achieved by following the indications of the HASTUS-macro. We put in the first set, A, the pieces which occur either in the morning or the evening, and in set P the remaining afternoon pieces. An afternoon piece in the macro is either the second piece of a workday connected with a morning piece or the first piece of a workday connected with an evening piece. The dummy piece (00) is added to both sets. The cost c_{ijkh} corresponds to the actual cost of the workday (ijkh). If either (ij) or (kh) is the dummy piece (00), c_{ijkh} is the cost of the tripper or the workday without break. The flow problem corresponding to problem (6.1) is described below, and with RNET (7) we are able to solve our problem (500 nodes, 10,000 arcs) in about 15 seconds CPU time on a CDC 173.

The assignment problem can be written as

(6.2)   Min $\sum_{I'} c_{ijkh} x_{ijkh}$

$$\sum_{(kh)\in P} (x_{ijkh} + x_{khij}) = 1 \quad \text{for all } (ij) \in A-(00)$$

$$\sum_{(kh)\in A} (x_{ijkh} + x_{khij}) = 1 \quad \text{for all } (ij) \in P-(00)$$

$$x_{ijkh} = 0,1.$$

The solution obtained uses only feasible workdays; however constraints (ii) of (2.1) may not be respected, and several trippers may remain. The heuristic described in the following section is designed to eliminate further the trippers (between 10 and 20 at this step according to our experience in Québec City) and restore feasibility (very slightly violated).

7. A MARGINAL IMPROVEMENT HEURISTIC

The main process of this heuristic involves marginally replacing each partition of each block by an alternative partition. This is achieved as follows:

> Step 1: For each block generate the set Bp of all (if not too many) partitions that use only pieces (ij) corresponding to a positive x_{ijkh} or x_{khjj} in the optimal solution of HASTUS-macro (4.1). If insufficient partitions are generated, pieces corresponding to null x_{ijkh} with a small reduced cost may be used. (See (1) for more details.)
>
> Step 2: For each block p = 1,2,...,L:
> a) take out first the partition p_o of block p used in the matching problem (either 6.1 or 6.2);
> b) consider the resulting set of trippers R_p (composed of trippers in the preceding matching solution and pieces that were matched to pieces of the partition p_o used for block p);
> c) choose the partition p_k of B_p, which, matched with the trippers of set R_p, produces the least cost solution (trippers being highly penalised) which improves feasibility if violated. Replace p_o by p_k and update the matching solution accordingly (p_k may equal p_o).
>
> Step 3: If the solution has improved (cost is reduced or feasibility improved) after considering alternatively each block, go back to step 2. If not, resolve the matching problem (6.1 or 6.2) and stop.

If after these steps a satisfactory solution is not obtained, the solution may be perturbed in different ways to try to achieve a better solution by reapplying Steps 2 and 3 of the heuristic. For example, we arbitrarily increase the number of trippers in the matching solution (by removing a certain number of matches) and reapply the heuristic.

This perturbation applied repeatedly has proved useful to generate solutions with no trippers. In practice, however, the CTCUQ is generally satisfied with the first solution produced by the heuristic, which may have from three to five remaining trippers.

At this stage, we could also use any other marginal improvement heuristics in the literature.

8. VARIANTS OF THE ALGORITHM

8.1 Algorithm Modifications for Workdays with Three Pieces of Work

In Québec City, workdays with three pieces are permitted and compose in general about ten percent of all workdays. The adaptation of the general strategy described is however straightforward and heuristic in nature. The adaptation of the general formulation (2.1) is direct; variables x_{ijkhmn} are created for such feasible workdays. For the HASTUS-macro formulation, the same comment applies: it is necessary however to limit the number of such variables created, considering only the most probable location in the time-table for such workdays. After the partition of the blocks and before the matching problem, it is necessary to pre-match two of the pieces of any three-piece workday that emerges from the HASTUS-macro solution. These pre-matched pieces are considered as one piece in the matching problem (6.1 or 6.2). In the marginal improvement heuristic, it may be possible to generate additional three-piece workdays to reduce the number of trippers; such a routine exists in the HASTUS program implemented in Québec City.

8.2 Algorithm Modification for Workdays without a Break

The presence of (and in some cases the necessity for) a certain number of workdays without a break in the solution may considerably reduce the flexibility of the problem, and the HASTUS-macro solution may not be as good once these workdays are taken out of the schedule. We have found it useful to proceed as follows:

Step 1: Use HASTUS-macro on the whole problem;

Step 2: Partition the blocks;

Step 3: Remove from the blocks the pieces corresponding to workdays without a break (make sure there are enough);

Step 4: Use HASTUS-macro on the reduced problem;

Step 5: Partition the blocks;

Step 6: Match the pieces;

Step 7: Heuristically improve the solution.

9. RESULTS AND CONCLUSION

This system has been in operation in Québec City Transit Authority (CTCUQ) since March 1979. After a period of test it has been used to generate the assignment of drivers for all schedules (week-days and week-ends). Table 1 shows a continuing reduction of the premium paid by the company since the introduction of HASTUS. Even if HASTUS is still more costly for week-end assignment, a total saving of 0.9%, which represents an annual saving of $125,000, was achieved. This represents 16% of the premiums (which represent the total premium for savings). The CTCUQ is using the system on an IBM 370/148; it takes 45 minutes of CPU time. It has also developed a series of printouts to be used directly by the drivers to sign for their assignments. Other reports are also used for administrative purposes.

	Manual solution	HASTUS solution		
	Oct 79	Dec 79	March 80	June 80
Weekdays	6.03%	5.51%	5.38%	4.79%
Saturday	3.46%	4.65%	4.45%	3.81%
Sunday	3.70%	5.25%	5.45%	4.60%
Weekly average	5.55%	5.40%	5.28%	4.66%

Table 1   Premium paid in percentage of total salary

Note that the system is used even if a sophisticated package is not available. A computer analyst is responsible for the runs of this system and for reporting the results to the scheduler. Occasionally, several runs are necessary, but most of the time one run is enough. The CTCUQ has been very satisfied with this system.

Following these results, the Montréal transit authority (CTCUM) (2,000 buses) has
decided to adopt this approach. However, for this project a more sophisticated
package is currently under development. This package will include several
interactive routines to let the schedulers specify additional constraints and
modify the solution produced. Implementation is scheduled to start in January
1981, and several reports are planned. Other researches have also been undertaken
to study alternative mathematical programming approaches which could improve
further the quality of the solution produced (5).

REFERENCES

1. Blais, J.-Y. et al. The problem of assigning drivers to bus routes in an urban
    transit system. Publication 44, Centre de recherche sur les transports,
    Université de Montréal (1976).

2. Blais, J.-Y. User manual for HASTUS-macro. Publication 93, Centre de recherche
    sur les transports, Université de Montréal (1978).

3. Blais, J.-Y. and Rousseau, J.-M. HASTUS: an evaluation model for drivers'
    union negotiation in transit companies. Publication 163, Centre de recherche
    sur les transports, Université de Montréal (1980).

4. Bodin, L. Private communication (1980).

5. Carraresi, P., Gallo, G. and Rousseau, J.-M. A decomposition approach to large
    scale bus driver scheduling. Presented at Euro IV conference, Cambridge, July
    1980. Publication 172, Centre de recherche sur les transports, Université de
    Montréal (1980).

6. Davini, A. Il problema della formazione dei 'turni-lavoro' per il personale
    viaggeante di una azianda publica di transporti urbani. University of Pisa
    thesis (1980).

7. Gregoriadis, M. and Hsu, T. RNET, The Rutgers minimum cost network flow
    subroutines. User documentation, version 3.5. Department of Computer Science,
    Rutgers University (1979).

8. Heurgon, E. Un problème de recouvrement: L'habillage des horaires d'une ligne
    d'autobus. Revue Francaise d'Automatique, d'Informatique et de Recherche
    Opérationnelle, 6 (1972) 13-29.

9. Heurgon, E. Preparing duty rosters for bus routes by computer. Preprints of
    the Workshop on Automated Technques for Scheduling of Vehicle Operators for
    Urban Public Transportation Services, Chicago (1795).

10. Preprints of the Workshop on Automated Techniques for Scheduling of Vehicle
    Operators for Urban Public Transportation Services, Chicago (1975).

11. This volume (1981).

12. Rousseau, J.-M., Dupuis, D. and Blais, J.-Y. Affectation des chauffeurs avec
    le système HASTUS-macro. Routes et transports, 23 (August 1979).

13. R.A.T.P. Conditions de travail des machinistes européens. Enquête, 1978, RP-2,
    Paris (1979).

14. Sharp, G.P. Constraints for scheduling operators for urban public transport
    systems. Preprints of the Workshop on Automated Techniques for Scheduling of
    Vehicle Operators for Urban Public Transportation Services, Chicago (1975).

Computer Scheduling of Public Transport
A. Wren (ed.)
© *North-Holland Publishing Company, 1981*

AN INTEGER PROGRAMMING APPROACH TO SCHEDULING

D. M. Ryan and B. A. Foster

Department of TAM, University of Auckland, New Zealand,
and Operations Research Group, AERE, Harwell, U.K.

The formulation of crew scheduling as set-partitioning or
set-covering integer programs usually gives rise to I.P.
problems of excessive size and computational complexity. By
imposing sensible additional structure not inherent in the
I.P. model, overconstrained I.P. subproblems can be formed.
Optimal solutions to these subproblems can be found using
reasonable computing resources, since the additional structure
has a strongly integerizing effect on the associated L.P.
model. Some applications of this approach to a New Zealand
metropolitan bus operation are presented.

1.1 INTRODUCTION

Set-partitioning models of mathematical programming and graph theory occur in many
practical applications. Balas and Padberg (1), in an excellent survey paper on the
set-partitioning problem, suggest that in terms of its applications, it would be
more important than its close relation, the set-covering problem, and also the
well-known travelling salesman problem. They give a comprehensive bibliography of
applications, which includes problems of crew scheduling, vehicle routeing and
scheduling, information retrieval, switching circuit design, stock cutting,
portfolio analysis, plant and facility location and political districting.

Our interest in the set-partitioning problem is confined to problems of scheduling
in which the model takes the form

$$\text{SPP: minimize} \quad Z = \underline{c}^T \underline{x}, \qquad \underline{x} \in \mathbb{R}^n \qquad \text{(i)}$$

$$\text{subject to} \quad A\underline{x} = \underline{e}, \qquad \underline{e}^T = (1,1,\ldots,1) \in \mathbb{R}^m \qquad \text{(ii)}$$

$$\text{and} \qquad x_j = 0 \text{ or } 1, \qquad j = 1,\ldots,n \qquad \text{(iii)}$$

where A is an m x n matrix of zeroes and ones, and $\underline{c}$ is the objective coefficient
vector. Each of the columns $\underline{a}_j$, j=1,...,n, of A represents a duty (or schedule)
with an associated cost c_j, and the corresponding variable x_j can be thought of as
the 'probability' that the j-th column is included in a solution. The j-th duty $\underline{a}_j$
has elements

$$a_{ij} = 1 \text{ if duty } j \text{ performs task } i$$

$$= 0 \text{ otherwise.}$$

The constraints (ii) require that each of the m tasks (or resources) is performed
(or covered) exactly once in any solution. (The set-covering model is obtained by

replacing (ii) with the constraint system $A\underline{x} \geqslant \underline{e}$, which requires that each task is performed at least once.) An optimal solution of SPP is given by a subset of duties with $x_j = 1$, which together satisfy (ii) (i.e. perform the tasks) at minimal cost. The zero or one values of the components of $\underline{x}$ thus define a partition of the set of all duties, and a partition of the tasks.

Much research has been undertaken during the past decade, to develop both theoretical results and efficient methods for the solution of SPP, and related models, and, although significant progress has been made (see Balas and Padberg (1)), it is often an expensive, and sometimes prohibitive, task to find optimal solutions. This is especially true in the context of scheduling, where, typically, the total number of possible duties (and therefore variables) is extremely large, even though the number of constraints is relatively small. The usual method for solving the SPP involves the relaxation of the integer restrictions (iii), and their replacement by the weaker bound condition $\underline{x} \geqslant 0$, thus creating a relaxed SPP linear program. In scheduling applications, the solution of this linear program seldom produces a naturally integer solution, and often requires an excessive computational effort, first to solve the L.P., and then to resolve the fractionality. Despite these two problems of computational complexity, which are perhaps more peculiar to scheduling applications, Balas and Padberg (1) argue that the solution of a general SPP can often be found by carefully adding further constraints or cuts, to improve the integer properties of the SPP linear program. In this paper, we explore an alternative approach for overcoming the problems of computational complexity present in scheduling SPPs. We develop an 'optimal heuristic' methodology for reducing scheduling SPP models to realistically-sized near-integer linear programs, by carefully selecting a subset of duties from amongst all possible legal duties.

Because of the extremely large number of variables (i.e. duties) present in scheduling SPPs, it is essential to reduce the dimensionality by selecting a subset of the duties likely to contain the optimal solution (or, equivalently, to discard those duties unlikely to be found in an optimal solution) and solve the resulting reduced SPP. This selection process essentially attacks just the size aspect of the computational problem. If, however, some care is taken in the selection process, it is possible to improve simultaneously the natural integer properties of the reduced SPP linear program, without seriously affecting optimality. In other words, we attempt to construct a small SPP which contains the optimal solution of the full SPP, and which also has a relaxed linear program with a significant number of the vertices (i.e. basic feasible solutions) integral. An application of this methodology is illustrated in Section 1.2, in the context of the vehicle scheduling problem.

In Section 2, we discuss some characterizations of integrality in SPP, and identify those structures or properties of duties which permit the formation or occurrence of fractional solutions in the relaxed linear program. These considerations lead, in Section 3, to a further application of the integerizing selection process discussed above. In this application, we consider a bus crew scheduling problem. We conclude by examining a constraint branching process, which, in the SPP context, provides a more effective branch and bound structure for the resolution of fractional solutions.

1.2 A VEHICLE SCHEDULING SPP

The vehicle scheduling problem has attracted a great deal of attention over the past fifteen years. The problem in its simplest form is to design a set of routes (i.e. duties) from a central depot to service n customers (i.e. perform tasks) at known locations, with a quantity q_i of some commodity such that all customers are visited, and any restrictions on vehicle capacity and route length are observed.

This problem is conveniently represented by the set-partitioning model (i), (ii) and (iii) in which each constraint of (ii) ensures that the corresponding delivery is perfomed, and the duties or columns of A can be thought of as possible or potential vehicle routes, contributing only to those constraints visited by the route. The constraints on vehicle capacity and route length do not appear explicitly in the model, but are used implicitly to determine legal routes (or variables) of the model. In any practical situation, one could expect more than one hundred customers (i.e. constraints) and many, many thousands of possible routes. Because of this obvious problem of computational complexity, most published methods for solving the vehicle scheduling problem (see Mole (10) for a survey of such methods) 'ignore' the set-covering model, and proceed on the basis of some heuristic method. Foster and Ryan (5), in contrast, have developed a method which reduces the complexity of the set-partitioning formulation by imposing further implicit overconstraints. The overconstraints essentially remove many of the variables from the original model, on the grounds that they have a structure which is most unlikely to be present in the routes of an optimal solution. In this way, it can be argued that optimality is unlikely to be seriously affected by solving the smaller problem.

The definition or concept of a good or likely vehicle route is obviously an important factor in the effectiveness of the approach. An examination of routes occurring in the optimal solutions of small test problems led to the identification of petal structure as a particularly attractive attribute of good routes. The petal concept has also been utilized in a number of heuristic methods for the solution of the vehicle scheduling problem (Gillett and Millar (6) and Gillett and Johnson (7)). A route with petal structure can be described as one which visits all customers in a particular sector of the region with centre at the depot. The routes of a petal solution radiate from the depot like petals of a flower, and do not overlap. Besides defining a very much smaller number of variables over which the SPP has to be solved, the petal concept has a further significant property. It has been shown (Foster and Ryan (5)) that all the extreme points of the feasible solution set of the petal SPP occur at integer points (i.e. all components of $\underline{x}$ are either 0 or 1). In other words, the solution of the relaxed petal SPP linear program also satisfies the integer restrictions on the variables. In summary, this approach has simultaneously reduced both aspects of the complexity problem – the number of variables has been reduced dramatically, and the integer restrictions have been removed altogether. The obvious question now concerns the effect on optimality of such a major restiction on the set of variables. It is easy to demonstrate that optimality is affected, and Foster and Ryan discuss ways in which the overconstraints can be relaxed in a controlled manner, to permit desirable non-petal routes, previously banned, to be considered by the L.P. In theory, such non-petal routes also enable fractional solutions to occur, but, in practice, the tendency for the L.P. to generate fractional solutions appears to be very slight. The petal approach of Foster and Ryan can be described as an 'optimal heuristic' in the sense that a heuristically reduced model is solved optimally. The heuristic is designed specifically to reduce complexity.

2. INTEGER STRUCTURES FOR SPP

The mathematical definitions of classes of zero/one matrices with every vertex integral have been discussed by Hoffman and Kruskal (8) (unimodularity), Berge (2) (balanced matrices) and Padberg (11) (perfect matrices). The relative strengths of these conditions are illustrated in Figure 2.1. Both balanced and perfect matrices may be defined in terms of forbidden submatrices which represent structures with fractioning capability.

A balanced matrix is most simply defined as a matrix containing no submatrix of odd order having row and column sums equal to two. The form of such submatrices is illustrated in Figure 2.2. The forbidden submatrices may be interpreted as being formed by a subset of variables, each contributing one link to a closed cycle without chords in the corresponding graph. We can clearly avoid the formation of the forbidden submatrices if we restrict the links (pairs of constraints to which a variable contributes) so as to prevent the closing of the cycle. This observation provides the motivation for a series of simple selection rules that can be used to extract a unimodular or balanced subproblem from the original SPP.

Figure 2.1   Strength of Integrality Conditions

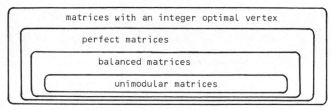

Figure 2.2   Forbidden Submatrices of Balanced Matrices

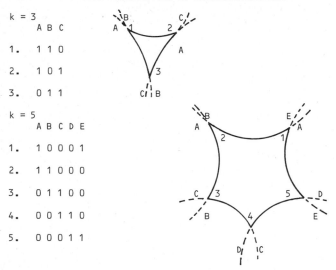

2.1 CONSTRAINT ORDERING (PETAL STRUCTURE)

We associate with each constraint a unique ordering index p_j, j=1,...,m. Variables are only considered as feasible for the SPP subproblem if they appear only in a contiguous subset of the constraints defined by (p_i, i=k,k+1,...,k+e), and appear in every member of such a subset. The reduced constraint matrix now takes the form given in Figure 2.3. Clearly, the closed cycles cannot be formed, the matrix is therefore balanced and all vertices are integral. This form of constraint ordering structure was applied by Foster and Ryan (5) to the vehicle scheduling problem where the ordering index is derived from the geographical radial ordering of the delivery locations around the depot. For the index to be unique, we must also nominate a natural break in the radial ordering (i.e. we must nominate constraint p_1).

Figure 2.3 Constraint Ordering Matrix and Graph Structure

```
      A B C D
1.    1 0 0 0
2.    1 1 0 0
3.    1 1 1 0 etc.
4.    0 1 1 1
5.    0 1 0 1
```

2.2 UNIQUE SUBSEQUENCE/PRECEDENCE

Again, we define a unique ordering of the constraints as p_j, $j=1,\ldots,m$. Further, with each constraint p_j, we associate a unique subsequent constraint $S(p_j)$, where $S(p_j)=p_k$ and $k > j$. Any variable contributing to constraint p_j must contribute to the subsequent constraint $S(p_j)$, or must not contribute to any constraint p_k for $k > j$. The form of the constraint matrix derived from this selection rule is illustrated in Figure 2.4. Again, it is easy to see that no closed cycles can form in the associated graph, and hence the constraint matrix is balanced. The unique subsequence structuring of variables has been applied by Edwards (3,4) to bus crew scheduling, and is discussed in detail in Section 3. The constraints are ordered by the start times of the corresponding trips, and each trip takes the first available subsequent trip to give the unique subsequent constraint.

Unique subsequence is a generalisation of unique ordering, and it has been shown by Edwards that unique subsequence structures are in fact unimodular, as well as balanced. By reversing the constraint ordering, we can also define an equivalent unique precedence selection rule.

Figure 2.4 Unique Subsequence Matrix and Graph Structure

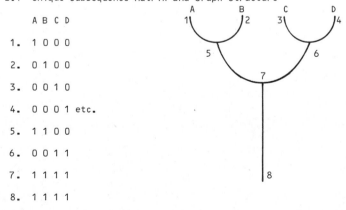

```
      A B C D
1.    1 0 0 0
2.    0 1 0 0
3.    0 0 1 0
4.    0 0 0 1 etc.
5.    1 1 0 0
6.    0 0 1 1
7.    1 1 1 1
8.    1 1 1 1
```

2.3 RELAXATION OF THE SELECTION RULES

These selection rules are far more restrictive than is necessary to satisfy the balanced matrix condition, which in turn is more restrictive than the desired condition of integer optimality. In our computational experience (see also Edwards (3,4)), significant relaxations can be made to these rules without creating many fractional vertices. For any specific problem, the selected variable set could certainly be extended by direct testing against the 'closed cycle without chords' condition. Further, if the constraint matrix can be decomposed into a number of non-interacting submatrices (i.e. a number of unconnected subgraphs), then a different subsequence (or precedence) ordering could be applied to each subgraph.

The formation of a closed cycle without chords in itself merely indicates a capability of producing a fractional vertex. If the constraint matrix also contains a constraint that prevents the formation occurring in a basic set, then the cycle can be permitted. For example, in Figure 2.5, we show part of a simple non-balanced matrix that is nevertheless totally integral because of the existence of constraint 4. A variable appears in constraint 4 if it appears in at least two other constraints. Constraints of this form were explicitly added to the vehicle scheduling SPP of Foster and Ryan, as integer forcing cuts. A generalisation of these cycle-breaking conditions is embodied in the definition of a perfect matrix.

An m x n zero/one matrix is perfect if no k x k submatrix K (k > 3) can be found to satisfy the conditions:

- the row and column sums of K are each equal to b (b ≥ 2)   (1)

and

- there exists no row of the (m-k)xk submatrix formed by the constraints not included in K with a row sum greater than b. (2)

The conditions on the forbidden submatrix can be interpreted as preventing the wider class of cycles of the form (1) indicated in Figure 2.6, unless a constraint of the form (2) is also present.

The perfect matrix definition is more difficult to interpret directly as a set of variable selection rules. However, it can be seen that for problems where each variable must contribute to one, and only one, of a small band of constraints (e.g. each duty must contain one of a small number of evening peak trips), the resulting constraints will tend to be of type (2), and hence prevent the formation of fractioning cycles.

Figure 2.5   Cycle-breaking Cuts

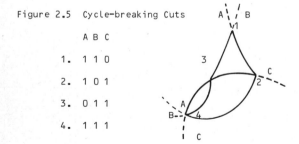

```
       A B C
   1.  1 1 0
   2.  1 0 1
   3.  0 1 1
   4.  1 1 1
```

Figure 2.6 Forbidden Submatrices of Perfect Matrices

k = 5 : b = 3

```
     A B C D E

1.   1 0 0 1 1

2.   1 1 0 0 1

3.   1 1 1 0 0

4.   0 1 1 1 0

5.   0 0 1 1 1
```

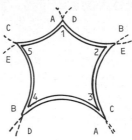

Examination of the graphs associated with fractional optimal solutions occurring in the crew scheduling problem leads us to one final observation. In cases where it is unreasonable to prevent the formation of closed cycles, it is often possible to prevent these cycles being self-contained (i.e. further fractioning of variables is required to satisfy the constraints). If short duties (subsets of other duties) and slack variables are excluded, or discouraged, by high associated objective contributions, then this implies that further fractioning structures must appear elsewhere in the basic set to complete the partition. Clearly, the same completion argument applies to these structures also. We would hypothesise that it is often this difficulty in completing a partition with such fractional structures that causes a high incidence of integer solutions, especially near the optimum, even when the variable selection rule of unique subsequence is only strictly enforced in sections of the duty period.

3. BUS CREW SCHEDULING

The Auckland Regional Authority (ARA), New Zealand, operates a large fleet of buses from a number of garages. Each garage services a particular region of the city, and, within each region, a fixed independent set of <u>trips</u>, specified by starting and finishing times and locations, must be performed. The ARA operation allows the scheduling of the bus and its crew to be performed as one task. This contrasts with the alternative mode of fixed headways on defined routes. Such an approach requires first the construction of a bus graph or schedule to meet the required service levels, and a subsequent task of determining crew schedules to cover the bus graph.

A valid crew duty in the ARA sense consists of a sequence of trips always starting and finishing at the garage, and satisfying union and operating restrictions relating to hours worked, meal-break allowances, etc. The crew scheduling problem consists of finding a minimal set of legal driver duties which covers all the timetabled trips, at minimal total operating cost. In general terms, this is achieved by a roster of approximately uniform driver duties, containing as little unproductive time and performing as many trips as possible. Edwards (3,4) discusses the formulation of a set-partitioning model for the ARA problem, and, by subtracting out the fixed costs of covering the timetable, reduces the optimization objective essentially to a minimization of overheads, which include crew idle-time, bus dead-running and overtime payments. The resulting model is similar in structure to the set-covering model formulated by Manington (9) in the context of fixed headway operations.

The Edwards model exhibits the usual properties of large-scale scheduling SPPs. There are a very large number of valid crew duties, many of which, however, are unlikely to occur in optimal solutions. Typically, such duties will cover few trips of the timetable, or they will involve long periods of crew idle-time or expensive dead-running between the end of one trip and the start of the next trip. The 'cost per unit of cover' of these sorts of duties tends to be relatively high. Following the philosophy developed in the context of vehicle scheduling, we attempt to reduce the complexity of the model by generating a small set of potential duties which is likely to contain the optimal solution (or at least some very good solutions), and which is also likely to increase the frequency of naturally integer solutions (or, equivalently, reduce the potential for fractional solutions) in the SPP linear program.

Edwards (3,4) has developed a method for generation of duties, based on the concept of 'next availables'. For each trip of the timetable, all other trips which could possibly be performed following its completion are ordered, according to their start times, in a set of 'next availables'. The first trip of the next available set for trip p is called the 'first available', since it is the first trip which could be performed on completion of trip p. Second and higher availables are defined in a similar manner. It is obvious that, if possible, a trip should be followed by its 'first available', so as to minimize unproductive crew idle-time between successive trips of the duty. Edwards (4) has shown that, if all duties are constructed so that any component trip either terminates the duty or is followed by its unique first available run, then the SPP linear program is naturally integer in the sense that all basic feasible solutions are integer. This generalizes the vehicle scheduling petal results of Foster and Ryan (5), and forms a particular case of a 'unique subsequence' ordering of the constraints (i.e. trips) as discussed in Section 2. The time ordering of the crew scheduling model is a much more natural ordering than the geographical radial ordering used by Foster and Ryan in defining petal routes, since next availables directly influence the objective contributions of the duties. From a practical and 'local' point of view, a duty with pure first available structure (i.e. each trip either terminates the duty or is followed by its first available) is in a sense optimal, since, given the initial trip, the unproductive idle-time and bus dead-running between successive trips of the duty has been minimized. It is obvious that the first available property is likely to occur in many of the duties of the optimal or any near-optimal solution. Indeed, manually constructed solutions actually operated by the ARA also exhibit this property. Many of the duties in a manual solution appear to have been constructed entirely with first available structure. Most of the remaining duties deviate in just one or two places from first available structure (i.e. second or higher availables are present) and a few remaining duties have a rather bizarre structure, suggesting that they have been constructed simply to cover the timetable.

The pure first available structure for a duty is unrealistically limited in two ways. First, the inclusion of meal-breaks within the first available structure destroys the formal proof of natural integrality, since the trip preceeding the meal-break is unlikely to have a unique subsequent trip in all other duties in which it occurs. In other words, the natural time interval before the first available is unlikely to permit the insertion of a meal-break, and the duty must therefore be continued by the first available <u>following</u> the completion of the meal-break. The formal proof of natural integrality also fails when a break-period is inserted in a broken or split duty. Edwards (3) calls the set of first available duties, including meal-breaks and break-periods, a 'modified first available' set of duties. The lack of formal proof of natural integrality on the set of modified first available duties does not seem to have a very adverse effect on the integer properties of basic feasible solutions of the SPP linear program. Extensive computational experience suggests that fractional bases occur rather infrequently during the convergence of the modifed first available linear program.

This observation can be explained by considering the way in which fractional solutions must be formed, and since the deviations from first available structure are local and restricted, it can be expected that fractional solutions will be rather difficult to construct.

The second and more important limitation of first available structure is apparent in the particularly restricted class of duties which it permits. We have already commented that manual solutions do contain duties that deviate, sometimes significantly, from first available structure. It is also apparent from examination of modified first available solutions that this class of duties alone is unlikely to provide an acceptable overall cover of the timetable. It is clear then that first available structure must be further relaxed and a more general set of duties considered if optimality is not to be seriously compromised.

One extreme form of relaxation could be to permit duties to contain first and second (and even higher) available structure. That is, any trip of a duty could be followed by either the first or second (or higher) available trip. This obviously provides a much larger and more general set of duties but, if taken too far, it also destroys much of the integer structure inherent in first available duties. Instead of such a comprehensive relaxation of first available structure, Edwards (3) has proposed and developed a number of strategies for selected relaxations based on second and higher availables which extend the class of good duties but also tend to preserve integer properties of the SPP linear program.

The first approach permits higher availables for a limited number of specified trips of the timetable. The identification of trips whose higher availables should be permitted can be made in a number of ways. The most obvious situation can be detected from an examination of the timetable. If a particular trip, p say, does not appear as a first available for any other trip, then the only form of first available duty that can contain this trip must start with the trip. For trips early in the timetable, this may not be a serious restriction but for trips later in the timetable, it is clear that the first available restriction should be relaxed on some other trip to permit p as a second or even higher available if necessary. The situation is shown in Figure 3.1.

Figure 3.1 Typical 'next available' Patterns

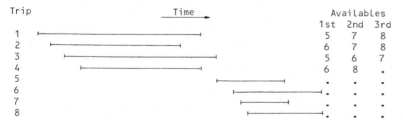

Trip		Availables		
	Time	1st	2nd	3rd
1		5	7	8
2		6	7	8
3		5	6	7
4		6	8	.
5		.	.	.
6		.	.	.
7		.	.	.
8		.	.	.

Notes:

1. Trip 6 cannot follow trip 1, and trip 7 cannot follow trip 4 because the intertrip time intervals will not permit deadrunning.
2. Trips 7 and 8 do not appear as first availables. By relaxing first available restrictions for trips 1 and/or 2 and trip 4, trips 7 and 8 will appear as second availables.

Examination of the set of generated duties and later, the optimal SPP linear program solution, can also be used to identify trips which appear difficult to cover given the current set of duties. A similar relaxation of first available structure can then be permitted to provide some additional duties. The main disadvantage with this approach, apart from the difficulties of correctly identifying where first available structure should be relaxed, is found in the increased potential for fractional solutions of the SPP linear program. In practice, however, provided the relaxations are not too extensive, many of the basic feasible solutions remain naturally integer. The resolving of optimal fractional solutions is readily accomplished by an application of branch and bound as discussed in section 4. One important aspect of the branch and bound process is that it usually produces integer solutions with objective values quite close to the L.P. optimum.

A second strategy for generating selected relaxations of first available structure is provided by a sequential heuristic process. The 'best' duties of the optimal SPP linear program are selected and the trips covered by them are 'removed' from the timetable. A new subproblem, defined on the remaining trips is formulated thus defining a new 'next available' ordering for each remaining trip. The subproblem is solved using the modified first available structure to generate a new duty set for the SPP linear program. These duties, although first available in the subproblem, will include implied higher availables when viewed in the context of the original timetable. It is important to observe that the subproblem is reduced in size and again exhibits strong integer properties making it easy to solve. A composite integer solution is provided by simply combining the optimal solution of the subproblem with the 'best' duties selected from the original solution. The selection process could, of course, be repeated on the subproblem solution so defining yet another smaller problem. A 'bound' for improved integer solutions can be readily computed by reconverging the aggregated linear program in which all duties of the original problem and subsequent subproblems are included. Because of the significant deviations from first available structure, it is unlikely that the bound solution would be naturally integer but from evidence gathered by Edwards, the composite integer objective value is usually quite close to the aggregated linear program optimum.

The method of selecting 'best' duties is clearly one which determines the effectiveness of such an approach. Work is proceeding in this area to evaluate a number of possible strategies but even with naive selection and one subproblem it is usually possible to improve the manual solution. In many ways, the sequential selection process based on modified first available structure has much in common with the manual method of duty construction. It is not unreasonable to imagine the selection process being influenced or even controlled by the scheduler in an interactive manner with the computer being used in its most effective role of quickly identifying an optimal set of good quality duties from which the scheduler can choose. We believe that this sort of approach will enable the scheduler to impose desirable characteristics or personal preferences not implicit in the mathematical model, and it will tend to avoid the unsatisfactory black-box image of many computer optimization packages.

4. A SPP BRANCHING STRATEGY

Fractional solutions produced by the SPP linear program are usually resolved either by cutting plane techniques, as discussed by Balas and Padberg (1), or by branch and bound techniques based on variable branches. The conventional variable branch at a node of the branch and bound tree chooses one component or variable of the fractional solution (say x_j) which satisfies

$$0 < x_j < 1.$$

Two new linear programs are formed, in one of which we impose the restriction $x_j = 0$ (i.e. the 0-branch), and in the other, the restriction $x_j = 1$ (i.e. the 1-branch). In the context of scheduling SPPs, the 0-branch has very little effect on the SPP linear program objective value, even when the variable being forced to zero has a fractional value close to one. This claim, supported by computational experience, can be explained by observing that the removal of one duty can usually be accommodated simply by moving to some other nearby solution with similar objective value. Typically, just one or two dual simplex iterations are required to recover primal feasibility. The 1-branch, in contrast, usually results in a significant change in solution and objective values, and often requires many dual simplex iterations. The uneven variable branch then encourages an unbalanced growth of the branch and bound tree with the objective value almost never being bounded on the zero branch. Because it is expected that the SPP solution objective value is likely to be quite close to that of the SPP linear program, a more direct strategy for increasing the L.P. bound at each branch would seem attractive. We therefore look for a more even branching strategy, in which both sides of the branch result in a significant change in objective value.

A more even branch can be created by observing that in every fractional solution of the SPP linear program, there must exist at least one pair of constraints (say r_1 and r_2), for which

$$0 < \sum_{j \varepsilon J(r_1, r_2)} x_j < 1$$

where $J(r_1, r_2)$ is the set of all variables/duties covering both constraints r_1 and r_2 simultaneously. The remaining fraction of cover for each of the constraints in the pair must therefore be provided by variables/duties which do not cover both constraints r_1 and r_2 simultaneously. An effective 'constraint branch' can then be imposed by requiring that

either
$$\sum_{j \varepsilon J(r_1, r_2)} x_j \leqslant 0 \qquad \text{- 0-branch}$$

or
$$\sum_{j \varepsilon J(r_1, r_2)} x_j \geqslant 1 \qquad \text{- 1-branch}$$

where the 0-branch implies that constraints r_1 and r_2 must not be covered together, while the 1-branch implies that the pair must be covered together. The constraint branch now involves a set of variables $J(r_1, r_2)$ instead of a single variable, and the tree tends to grow in a more balanced manner. The 1-branch of a constraint branch could be imposed as a cut by adding it as a formal constraint. In the equality-constrained SPP, however, the 1-branch can be imposed more conveniently by forcing to zero all variables/duties in the comlementary sets $J(\bar{r}_1, r_2)$ and $J(r_1, \bar{r}_2)$, where $J(\bar{r}_1, r_2)$ is the set of all variables/duties covering constraint r_2, but not constraint r_1. $J(r_1, \bar{r}_2)$ is defined similarly. The only variables/duties remaining in the L.P. which cover r_1 or r_2 are members of $J(r_1, r_2)$.

It is also interesting to observe that if, in the context of the bus crew scheduling problem of Section 3, the fraction has resulted from a trip being associated with both its first and second available trip in the fractional solution, then a constraint branch can be based on the trip and its first available. One side of the branch prevents the first available pairing and the other side of the branch forces the first available pairing. If third and higher available duties are not present, then both sides of the branch are strongly integerizing, at least in a local sense, since each branch defines a unique subsequence ordering of either the first or the second available. Computational experience with the constraint branch suggests that it is indeed more effective than the variable branch and produces a much more balanced tree structure especially when the depths of availability are limited to two or three.

REFERENCES

1. Balas, E. and Padberg, M.W. Set partitioning - a survey. SIAM Review 19 (1976) 710-776. (Reprinted in Combinatorial Optimization, eds. Christofides, N., Mingozzi, A., Toth, P. and Sandi, C. (Wiley,1979)).

2. Berge, C. Balanced matrices, Math.prog. 2 (1972) 19-31.

3. Edwards, G.R. An approach to the crew scheduling problem. NZOR 7 (1979).

4. Edwards, G.R. Ph.D. Thesis, University of Auckland. In preparation.

5. Foster, B.A. and Ryan, D.M. An integer programming approach to the vehicle scheduling problem. Opl.Res.Q. 27 (1976) 367-384.

6. Gillett, B.C. and Miller, L.R. A heuristic algorithm for the vehicle dispatch problem. Op.Res. 22(2) (1974) 340-349.

7. Gillett, B.C. and Johnson, T. Sweep algorithms for the multiple depot vehicle dispatch problem. Paper presented at ORSA/TIMS meeting (San Juan, Puerto Rico, 1974).

8. Hoffman, A.J. and Kruskal, J.B. Integer boundary points of convex polyhedra. Annals of Mathematics Study No. 38 (Princeton University Press, Princeton, 1956) 233-246.

9. Manington, P.D. Mathematical and heuristic approaches to road transport scheduling. Ph.D. Thesis, University of Leeds (1977).

10. Mole, R.H. A survey of local delivery routing methodology. J.Opl.Res.Soc. 30(3) (1979) 245-252.

11. Padberg, M.W. Perfect zero-one matrices, Math.prog. 3 (1973) 199-215.

Computer Scheduling of Public Transport
A. Wren (ed.)
© *North-Holland Publishing Company, 1981*

A COMPUTER BASED CREW SCHEDULING SYSTEM
USING A MATHEMATICAL PROGRAMMING APPROACH

G. Mitra and A.P.G. Welsh

Unicom Consultants Limited,
Brunel University
and
Partners in Management Limited
Richmond, Surrey, UK

Two formulations of the bus crew scheduling problem are first set out. The computational difficulties and the inadequacy of the models are then considered. Some relevant aspects of an 'optimiser' specially developed for this purpose are discussed. Finally, the data input, the commands and the information flow of the overall system are briefly described.

1.0 INTRODUCTION

This paper is concerned with the computational problem of constructing duty schedules for bus crews such that these schedules fit a set of 'bus running boards'. A bus running board defines the bus schedule and the time and location of all relief opportunities. Presented in this light the problem is limited and well defined; all the same it has proven to be computationally difficult. In practice a skilled human scheduler can often compile an optimal or a near optimal schedule within an acceptable time scale. Heuristic methods have been tried to tackle this problem. However, the choice of heuristics for different operators (bus companies) has proven to be fairly unclear and non-uniform; the performance of these heuristics has not been sufficiently encouraging (1).

It has been conjectured (2), (3) that a better approach is to schedule the duties of the crews to match the frequency profiles of passenger demands and then construct the bus running boards around these duties. This idea has not been investigated in depth.

Considered in the context of mathematical programmibng a 'broad brush' description of the problem may be set out as an Integer Linear Program (ILP). In this formulation the difference between the underlying (relaxed) Linear Programming (LP) model and the ILP model is not very significant. Unfortunately, this model, although very valuable in its own right, does not provide a workable schedule. From a strictly practical point of view a complete description of a workable schedule is obtained by a detailed integer programming formulation of the problem, which is best described as a set covering problem with side constraints. Because there are additional constraints, strictly set covering or partitioning algorithms (4), (5) are not directly applicable. Indeed, some of the recommended reduction procedures (7) turn out to be unsuitable because of the computational difficulties. Also for any realistic problem the ILP model may have a large number of columns. By some kind of pre-analysis (6) it may be possible to reduce the number of columns, i.e., potential duties, considered. An LP system which exploits sparsity by a specially compact data structure has been developed to handle this problem. The system uses the Elimination Form of Inverse (EFI) in the simplex iterative steps; it also uses a simple but effective subproblem definition and branch and bound strategy to investigate the ILP model.

In this paper the two formulations of the LP problem are first presented in
Section 2. In Section 3 the computational difficulties involved in obtaining an
optimal solution are discussed, and a few alternative ways of exploring the
mathematical programming models are considered. In Section 4 the relevant aspects
of the LP data structure and some algorithmic procedures of the 'in core' LP
system specially written for this problem are set out. The overall system, its
features and the information flow are outlined in Section 5. An illustrative
schedule constructed for one user is presented and discussed in Section 6. The
input information, the command formats and the output report formats are described
in the Appendix.

2.0 TWO FORMULATIONS OF THE PROBLEM

The broad brush or the aggregated formulation is derived in the following way.
Let the day be divided into m periods. These need not be of equal duration, but
in practice equal quarter hour periods have been used. Let the number of buses on
the road in period $i = 1,2,\ldots,m$, be denoted by b_i. Let there be n possible
duties, which in this model are referred to as 'skeleton' duties since they do not
refer to specific buses to be worked, but only to the appropriate times of start
and finish and of breaks.

Define a matrix $A:(a_{ij})$ such that

$$a_{ij} = 1 \text{ if duty } j \text{ covers period } i \left.\right\} \begin{array}{l} i = 1,2,\ldots,m \\ j = 1,2,\ldots,n \end{array} \qquad (1)$$
$$a_{ij} = 0 \text{ otherwise}$$

Let the (notional) cost of the skeleton duty j be c_j. Then the aggregated (ILP)
formulation may be stated as

$$\text{Minimise} \quad \sum_{j=1}^{n} x_j c_j$$

$$\text{subject to} \quad \sum_{j=1}^{n} x_j a_{ij} \geqslant b_i, \qquad i = 1,2,\ldots,m, \qquad (2)$$

$$x_j \geqslant 0, \text{ and integer}, j = 1,2,\ldots,n.$$

The variable x_j in this formulation indicates the level of the skeleton duty, that
is the number of these duties which should be in the optimal schedule.

Note that the number n could be large, and some preselection of the duties
(columns) by dominance relations is usually essential. In addition, it is often
necessary to preselect on the basis of 'common sense'.

In practice, the above formulation is augmented by constraints on the number of
each duty type and also by constraints representing the need for certain specific
jobs (usually buses on short runs without relief opportunity) which must be manned
by one duty.

In the complete formulation which follows, the intervals of work and the relief
opportunities are considered together to propose workable duties and schedules.

Let there be p different duty types. Define the sets of indices $D_1, D_2, \ldots, D_p$ corresponding to these duty types:

$$D_1 = \{1, 2, \ldots, n_1\},$$
$$D_2 = \{n_1+1, n_1+2, \ldots, n_2\}, \tag{3}$$
$$D_p = \{n_{p-1}+1, n_{p-1}+2, \ldots, n_p\},$$

and $n_1 < n_2 < \ldots < n_p$. Let $\overline{D}$ be the union of these sets of indices:

$$\overline{D} = \bigcup_{k=1}^{p} D_k = \{1, 2, \ldots, n_p\}. \tag{4}$$

Let $i = 1, 2, \ldots, m$ denote the unique number assigned to the interval of work between pairs of relief opportunities. Let these be referred to as bits of work, and define

$$b_i = 1, \quad i = 1, 2, \ldots, m, \tag{5}$$

such that these bits of work can be scheduled independently of the surrounding work.

Define the matrix

$$A:(a_{ij}), \quad i = 1, 2, \ldots, m; \quad j \in \overline{D}$$

such that

$$a_{ij} = 1 \text{ if duty } j \text{ covers bit } i,$$
$$= 0 \text{ otherwise.} \tag{6}$$

Let c_j be the notional cost of duty j,

t_j be the time worked by duty j, $\left. \right\} \ j \in \overline{D}$

v_k be the limit on the average time worked by duty type k,

N_k be the minimum number of duties of type k required in the schedule, $\left. \right\} \ k = 1, 2, \ldots, p$ $\tag{7}$

N be the maximum (target) number of duties in which the schedule must be constructed,

x_j denote the binary decision variable such that

$x_j = 1$ indicates that the jth duty is in the schedule,

$x_j = 0$ otherwise. $\left. \right\} \ j \in \overline{D}$ $\tag{8}$

The complete formulation of the problem may now be stated as

$$\text{Minimise} \quad \sum_{j \in \bar{D}} c_j x_j$$

$$\text{subject to} \quad \sum_{j \in \bar{D}} a_{ij} x_j \geqslant 1, \quad i = 1,2,\ldots,m, \tag{9}$$

$$x_j = 0 \text{ or } 1,$$

and the additional side constraints:

- minimum number of duties of each type

$$\sum_{j \in D_k} x_j \geqslant N_k, \qquad k = 1,2,\ldots,p, \tag{10}$$

- average time constraint for each duty type

$$\sum_{j \in D_k} (t_j - v_k) x_j \leqslant 0, \quad k = 1,2,\ldots,p, \tag{11}$$

- target number of duties in which to construct the schedule

$$\sum_{j \in \bar{D}} x_j \leqslant N \tag{12}$$

Note that in any meaningful problem the inequality, $N \geqslant \sum_{k=1}^{p} N_k$ must be satisfied.

The average time constraint perhaps merits a brief explanation which follows. The average time of duty type k is less than or equal to the limit v_k, that is

$$(\sum_{j \in D_k} t_j x_j) / (\sum_{j \in D_k} x_j) \leqslant v_k. \tag{13}$$

Multiplying both sides by the denominator of the left hand side and rearranging, the constraint (11) is derived.

Note that in a certain sense the set partitioning formulation, in which the constraints given in (9) are changed to equality restrictions, is more appropriate than the set covering one.

In any feasible solution of the above problem, if any bit of work is over-covered then it is possible to remove the over-cover from one or more of the duties on the schedule. Such a procedure does not adversely affect the restrictions set out in (11) and makes the set covering formulation equivalent to the set partitioning formulation as long as the modified duty remains a valid duty in the same duty type.

3.0 DISCUSSION OF THE COMPUTATIONAL DIFFICULTIES

The aggregated model described in the last section is easy to solve and it has at most $24 \times 4 = 96$ rows if the side constraints are ignored. It is, however, of limited use. The complete formulation as described in the last section has been used in France (6) and in the UK (2). The computational problems prove much more severe with operators in this country than in Europe for reasons set out below.

The size and complexity of the problem for a given number of duties depend upon two factors. Firstly the average length of time between relief opportunities directly affects the average number of rows (or bits of work) per duty, and hence the degree of degeneracy in the problem. The ratio of rows to duties can vary from a little over two in a particular case in France (6) to as much as eight in examples used by the authors (2).

The other factor, which tends to make the problems of the UK operator considerably more complex than in other countries, is the requirement for meal and other breaks implied by government legislation and negotiated by unions. The consequence of this is that in the UK any given duty will cover work on at least two buses, and frequently three or even four, while in most other countries the norm is one. This results in a much larger number of columns (i.e., possible duties) and a much greater degree of interaction between these columns.

Because the problem is highly degenerate, and the set $\overline{D}$ of all possible duties is very large, solving the complete problem optimally has proven to be computationally difficult. The experience of the authors as gained from computing a number of experimental schedules may be summarised in the following way.

1. If N, the limit on the number of duties in which a feasible schedule must be found, is greater than the optimal number by around 5% or more, then feasible schedules can be constructed without too much difficulty. However, the search for optimality over the last few percent has proven to be difficult.

2. Often the minimum or target number of duties in which a feasible schedule may be achieved can be specified from other considerations such as the bounds obtained from model 1 in the last section, etc.. If N is set to this value then it is observed that schedules which do not cover a few bits of work, but are otherwise optimal in their total number, may again be constructed without too much computational difficulty.

3. In discussions with the skilled manual schedulers it has been observed that often some of the rules are broken to obtain an optimal schedule, as long as the breaking of the rule is not too 'severe'.

In many senses the crew scheduling system, with its integrated LP and ILP system, does not work in the conventional way. For instance it was considered that it would be computationally advantageous to generate the columns or the duties as and when required. In view of the limitations outlined in (1) and (2) above, and the major weakness of any rigid mathematical model as set out in (3), the authors conjecture that it is perhaps best to investigate alternative heuristics of column (duty) generation which admit the possibility of breaking the rules by some prespecified set of priorities. Unfortunately, the last idea has not been investigated as yet.

4.0 FEATURES OF THE LP SYSTEM

Consider the objective row and the constraints (9),(10),(11) and (12) outlined in Section 2. Any individual column (duty) has at most two nonunit nonzero coefficient values, corresponding to side constraints. This fact has prompted the authors to use a compact data structure to store the columns of the constraint matrix. Display 1 and Table 1 together specify the storage scheme.

ARRAY 4

NEXT = 7	NONZE = 5
IROW = 3	IROW = 5
IROW = 6	IROW = −7
IROW = −1	
RVAL = 3.5	
RVAL = 2.5	
NCOLNO = 100	
NEXT =	

ROWS 3,5,6 have coefficient values = +1;   ROW 7 has coefficient value = 3.5;
ROW 1 has coefficient value = 2.5;   Total number of nonzeros = 5;
Next colums header is offest by 7 (*4) locations;   The column number is 100.

Display 1

Variable	Type	Comments
ARRAY 4	*4 REAL 4 bytes	Large array in which the packed columns of the constraint matrix are stored.
NEXT	*2 INTEGER 2 bytes	Header information pointing to the next column header. It measures the offset by *4 locations to the start of the following header.
NONZE	*2 INTEGER 2 bytes	Indicates total number of nonzeros in the given column.
IROW	*2 INTEGER 2 bytes	Indicates the row positions of the nonzero values. If IROW > 0, the coefficient value is +1. If IROW < 0, the row number is obtained by negating this quantity. The coefficient value is given in the contiguous *4 real locations (RVAL) held in ARRAY 4.
RVAL	*4 REAL 4 bytes	Holds the nonzero coefficient value when this is different from +1.
NCLONO	*4 INTEGER	Contains the column number identifying the present column of the matrix.

Table 1

In a set covering problem corresponding to any prime cover it is possible to associate an involutory basis matrix (7). An involutory matrix is one which is its own inverse and is of lower triangular structure. In the models considered here the basis matrices at intermediate simplex steps are found to be nearly lower triangular. During the last decade considerable progress has taken place in the sparse representation of the inverse of a basis matrix (8), (9), as used in the revised simplex algorithm. At inversion time the basis matrix is restructured to assume an 'optimally block lower triangular structure' (9). The matrix is then suitably factorised into an LU form, and eta vectors are created to obtain an Elimination Form of Inverse (EFI) representation. In the eta vector storage an appropriate scheme of pointers has been devised whereby the basis columns of the original matrix can be used whenever lower triangular etas are unaffected by pivotal updates. The resulting storage scheme appears to be extremely efficient. For instance, it is possible to iterate on 300 row LP problems with around 2,000 basis nonzero coefficients within a data area of 24K bytes. On a Prime 550 computer, around 3,000 iterations could be carried out in about 15 CP minutes.

In the LP/ILP optimiser it is possible to enter the branch and bound tree search algorithm at any stage of the solution of the LP. The LP solution is in Phase 2 or Phase 1 depending on whether strategy (i) or strategy (ii) (see Section 2) is being used for investigating the model. In either case it is possible to enter the branch and bound search for integer solution. Because the underlying problem is a set covering one, it is not necessary to impose the upper bound of unity on the variables: in the LP problem this is naturally satisfied. The variable chosen for branching is the one with a fractional value in the current solution and which provides the largest 'partial cover'. This variable is then set to unity, and in the subproblem this implies that those set covering rows in which the present variable (duty) has a unit coefficient can be made free rows.

For non-set-covering rows, the right hand side values are updated. This strategy more or less determines that a last-in-first-out scheme is being used in the resulting tree search. As in the main LP algorithm, be it Phase 1 or Phase 2, the suboptimisation may be terminated after a prespecified number of iterations. At this point either a satisfactory integer solution is reached or a new variable is chosen for branching and the steps are repeated.

5.0 LAYOUT AND STRUCTURE OF THE SYSTEM

The crew scheduling system is called NUCRU, and is new in relation to an earlier version based on the first model. The system is based on the second (complete) formulation and is designed from the outset to be as general as possible. A wide variety of different types of constraints may be specified and it is easy to use by non computer professionals. A schematic flow diagram of the entire system is set out in Display 2. The input to the system is defined by the BUSDATA and a set of commands (CONTROL DATA) which specify the rules governing the types of duties and a few other parameters of the system. The input program interprets these commands, reads and validates the bus data and prepares the problem for processing. The OPTIMISER then processes this problem file: the OPTIMISER has built into it a column (duty) generation facility. A solution interpreter prints out the results in an intermediate format which is both human and computer readable. The last output may be manually adjusted if this is considered necessary, and a second report writing program validates such amendments and produces a final printed schedule. A restart scheme has also been introduced whereby an intermediate solution from the OPTIMISER, a manually specified solution or a combination of the two may be used as a starting point for reoptimisation. The last two facilities listed above are not yet fully operational.

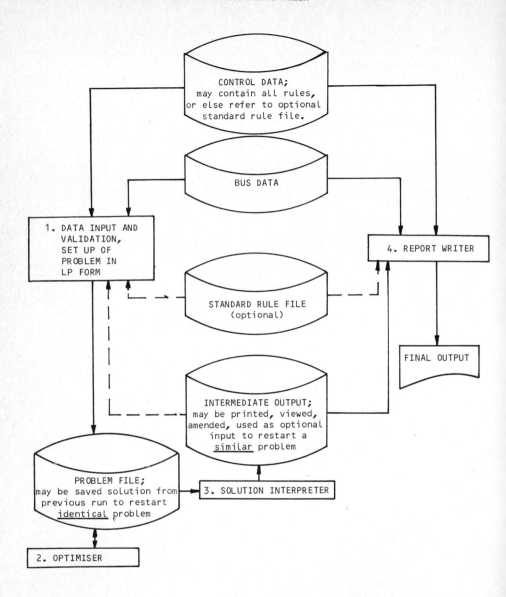

Display 2   Schematic flow diagram of the NUCRU crew scheduling system.   The
              numbers indicate the normal sequence of execution of the four
              programs.

6.0 DISCUSSION OF RESULTS

Most of the authors' recent work has concentrated on four Monday to Friday schedules supplied by C.I.E. of Dublin. The expected number of duties required to man these schedules, and the approximate number of set covering rows (i.e., bits of work) in each problem were as follows:

Problem	Expected Number of Duties	Approximate Number of Set Covering Rows
1	12	60
2	28	190
3	34	230
4	52	325

To date, it has not proved possible to produce automatically a feasible solution to any of the four problems using the expected number of duties. However, on the '12 duty' problem, it has been possible to:

produce a schedule using 13 duties, in 500 LP iterations and 8 ILP iterations;

when constrained to 12 duties, iterate to the point where infeasibility was proven, demonstrating that no 12 duty solution actually exists;

demonstrate by other considerations, to the satisfaction of C.I.E. and the authors, that the problem is indeed infeasible with only 12 duties.

On the '28 duty' schedule, a 29 duty solution has been produced automatically. It was found possible to amend this manually with about one hour's effort to produce an acceptable 28 duty solution.

Little work has been done on the larger two schedules, although trials on the 300 row problem have demonstrated:

the efficiency of the storage method, enabling this problem to be handled within about 24KB of data storage;

the feasibility of iterating on this size problem at acceptable speeds, and of producing feasible solutions with about 2 more duties than believed necessary.

The authors regard these results as encouraging, although clearly further work is required. This will concentrate on the methods used to generate duties for inclusion in the basis. Several ideas are currently under consideration or test, including:

criteria for duty generation which are quite separate from the LP and the shadow prices it generates;

criteria related to the likely level of the selected duty, rather than just its reduced cost, which currently guides the generation process and which can lead to considerable degeneracy problems.

ACKNOWLEDGEMENTS

The authors would like to thank .Mr. B. Fitzgerald, Mr. B. Collins and Mr. R. Eager of C.I.E., and Mr. J. Nixon of West Midlands Passenger Transport Executive for their involvement in the development of the system described in this paper. A substantial amount of computer time had to be expended to carry out the experiments needed to develop the system. Messers Wootton Jeffreys and Partners have been very kind to provide us with most of this computer time on their Prime 550 computer, and their support in this respect is gratefully acknowledged.

REFERENCES

1. Wren, A., and Manington, B. A general computer method for bus crew scheduling. University of Leeds Operational Research Unit Report ULORU 22. (May 1975).

2. Welsh, A.P.G. A progress report on the development of computerised bus duty scheduling, Partners in Management Ltd.. (Richmond, Surrey).

3. Rousseau, J-M. A mathematical programming approach to the bus crew scheduling problem. Presented to the Mathematical Programming Study Group, British Computer Society. (1979).

4. Garfinkel, R.S. and Nemhauser, G.L. The set-partitioning problem: set covering with equality constraints, Operations Research, 17 (5) (September – October 1969).

5. Marsten, R.E. An implicit enumeration algorithm for the set partitioning problem with side constraints, PhD dissertation (UCLA 1972).

6. Heurgon, E. and Delorme, J. Set covering problems by linear programming and branch and bound algorithm, presented to the VIIIth Mathematical Programming Conference (Stanford, USA, August 1973).

7. Garfinkel, R.S. and Nemhauser, G.L. Integer programming (John Wiley and Sons, 1972) 298-322.

8. Mitra, G. Sparse inverse in the factored form and maintaining sparsity during simplex iterations, Software for numerical mathematics, Ed. D.J. Evans (Academic Press, 1974) 85-97.

9. Darby-Dowman, K. and Mitra, G. Investigation of algorithms used in the restructuring of linear programming basis matrices prior to inversion, presented to the Xth International Mathematical Programming Symposium (Montreal, August 1979).

APPENDIX

BUS DATA AND SYSTEMS COMMANDS

The purpose of the bus data file is to specify the pertinent details of the bus running boards for which duty schedules are required.

One file may contain the running boards for all buses on all days of the week, even though these will not be scheduled together. In any particular execution of the scheduling system, the control data will specify which day of the week is to be scheduled, and enables certain services, or groups of services, to be selected.

The bus data file comprises fixed—format 80-column records.   Each running board starts with a new record, the header record, and may be continued on up to 98 continuation records.

The format is as specified in Display A1, and an example is given in Display A2.

Note that:

1. Any relief time and place field may be left entirely blank and will be ignored; this makes editing the file easier;

2. Times must be in ascending sequence within a bus;

3. Times and places may be coded (e.g. for subsequent printing of timetables) even if they do not represent relief opportunities; if the place code does not match one of the relief point codes specified in the rules then' the time and place will be ignored by the duty scheduling system.

4. If a bus is 'parked', i.e., need not be manned, for a period during the day, this may be coded by means of a special place code. By default this code is 'PARK', but the user may use a different code if he specifies this in the rules.

Display A3 shows an example of a control file, used in conjunction with the bus data of Display A2 to produce the 13—duty schedule shown in Display B1.

This is a free—format file, specifying the rules and control parameters for the run, as follows:

1. Select service code 41, for MONDAY

2. Maximum number of jobs per duty is 3 (i.e. not more than 2 breaks)

3. Four district place codes are defined; LAST, AST etc. are pseudonyms

4. Vector 1 gives 4 times, in minutes, to be used in subsequent rules according to which of the four places are relevant (see 7 below)

5. Matrix 1 gives a triangular matrix of times to be used where two places are relevant to a given rule

6. Maximum spread 10 hours, work 8 hours 27 minutes

7. Sign on (off) time to be 5 (15) minutes plus the relevant value from vector 1 (i.e. sign—on at 'DST' is 20 minutes)

8. Minimum meal (gap) 50 (5) minutes plus the relevant value from matrix 1

9. Maximum time in each 'half' of duty (i.e. without meal) is 4 hours 55 minutes

10. Maximum unpaid meal 10 hours (not strictly necessary)

11. Target avarage paid time 7 hours 40 minutes

    All the above apply to all duty types, unless overridden for a specific duty.
    For example:

12. Dutytype P (full name 'PLUM') has a maximum working time of 7 hours, a latest
    finish time of 14.50, may only have 2 jobs (1 break), and there may not be
    more than 2 of these.

All the above is specified in the first 11 lines of the control file;   the   rest
should be self-explanatory.

DISPLAY A1

BUS DATA FORMAT

Character Position	Validity	Meaning and comments
1 - 4	numeric	bus number (-1 to terminate data) must be in ascending sequence
5 - 6	numeric	card number within bus; must be in ascending order from 1 for each bus
8 - 11 @	alphanumeric	service code; used only in respect of certain service-dependent rules
13 - 20 @	alphanumeric	bus identifier; used for output only; need not be unique
22 - 29 @	numeric	zero or one to indicate whether or not bus runs on each of 8 'days of week'; 8th day may be used as a pseudonym for 'Monday to Thursday' or some other group of days
31 - 32	alphanumeric	selection code used to select specified group of bus running boards for duty scheduling
35 - 38	numeric	time of day in hours and minutes *
39 - 42	alphanumeric	place code or park code *

The last two fields are repeated up to four times in positions 44 to 51, 53 to 60, 62 to 69, 71 to 78.

79 - 80	alphanumeric	blank if continuation card expected; any character to indicate end of current running board

@ On continuation records, an additional two times and places can be specified in character positions 17 through 33.

* See notes in text of Appendix.

```
11 1    5413    0111110  54  0743SG   0900LAST  0946EQ    1053LAST 1137EQ
11 2         1242LAST 1327EQ   1428LAST 1514EQ   1619LAST 1705EQ   1818LAST
11 3              1909EQ   2017LAST 2102EQ   2202LAST
11 4                      2423SG                                            *
12 1    5414    0111110  54  0754SG   0916LAST  1003EQ    1104LAST 1150EQ
12 2         1256LAST 1338EQ   1441LAST 1530EQ   1636DST  1741LAST
12 3              1843SG                                                    *
13 1    5407    0111110  54  0658SG   0809DST   0910DST   1017EQ   1122LAST
13 2         1205EQ   1306LAST 1351EQ   1503EQ   1620EQ   1737EQ
13 3              1851SG                                                    *
14 1    5401    0111110  54  0600SG   0739LAST  0828EQ             0943PARK
14 2         1600SG   1655EQ   1805LAST 1855EQ   2003LAST 2047EQ   2148LAST
14 3                      2418SG                                            *
01 1    4103    0111111  41  0635SG   0828LAST  0936PARK 1103LAST 1230LAST
01 2         1408LAST 1528LAST 1655LAST 1835PARK 2147SG            2443SG   *
02 1    4104    0111110  41  0655SG   0858LAST  1020LAST 1148PARK 1200LAST
02 2         1311LAST 1443LAST 1615LAST 1753LAST 1930PARK 1935LAST 2105PARK
02 3              2110LAST 2253SG                                           *
03 1    4104    0000001  41  1130SG   1339LAST  1511LAST 1627PARK 1640LAST
03 2         1829PARK 2127SG          2442SG                                *
04 1    4105    0111111  41  0705SG   0840LAST  1005PARK 1110SG   1252LAST
04 2         1430LAST 1602LAST 1712LAST 1828LAST 2016LAST 2202SG            *
05 1    4102    0111111  41  0622SG   0735LAST  0946PARK 1030SG   1145LAST
05 2         1256PARK 1525SG   1651LAST 1845LAST 2040LAST
05 3              2423SG                                                    *
06 1    4101    0111110  41  0546SG   0645LAST  0745LAST 0845LAST 0950LAST
06 2         1101PARK 1532SG   1725LAST 1903LAST 2036SG                     *
07 1    4101    0000001  41  0546SG   0645LAST  0745LAST 0845LAST 0950LAST
07 2         1101PARK 1150SG   1327PARK 1532SG   1725LAST 1903LAST 2036SG   *
08 1    4106    0111110  41  0714SG   0842LAST  1026PARK 1130SG   1339LAST
08 2         1511LAST 1627PARK 1640LAST 1829PARK 2127SG            2442SG   *
09 1    4106    0000001  41  0704SG   0842LAST  1020LAST 1148LAST 1314LAST
09 2         1446LAST 1618LAST 1756LAST 1935LAST 2105PARK 2110LAST 2253SG   *
-1
```

DISPLAY A2

```
SELECT '41';DAY MONDAY
MAXJOBS 3
PLACE SG;PLACE DST;PLACE EQ;PLACE LAST AST NES PSQE PSQW
VECTOR 1 0 15 14 12;MATRIX 1 10 15 0 14 0 0 12 0 0
MAXSPRD 1000;MAXWORK 827;SIGNON 5 1;SIGNOFF 15 1;MINMEAL 50 1
MINGAP 5;MAXH1,,455;MAXH1S,,455;MAXH2,,455;MAXH2S,,455
MAXMEAL 1000
TARGET 7 HRS 40
DUTYTYPE P PLUM;MAXWORK 700;LFINISH 1450
MAXJOBS 2
TARGET 2
DUTYTYPE E EARLY;LFINISH,,1605;MAXWORK 806;ESTART,,635
MAXJOBS 2
TARGET 4
TARGET 7 HRS 30
DUTYTYPE B BOGEY;ESTART,,715;MAXSPRD 1200
TARGET 2
TARGET 7 HRS 40
DUTYTYPE M MIDDLE;ESTART 1150;LFINISH,,2202
TARGET 8 HRS 10
DUTYTYPE L LATE; ESTART 1420;LSMEAL,,2100
EFMEAL,,1855
TARGET 4
TARGET 8 HRS 10
END
```

DISPLAY A3

```
NUCRU VERSION 1.1 APRIL 1979 - DUTY SCHEDULE        (OVERCOVER & SER.)

   10   1 P    546  745 4101    ML          546   745  231    0
   20   1 P    858 1148 4104                858  1148  231    0
   30   1 P   1200 1311 4104               1200  1311  231    0

   40   2 P    622  946 4102    ML          622   946  265    0
   50   2 P   1110 1252 4105               1110  1252  265    0

   60   3 E    635  936 4103    ML          635   936    3    1
   70   3 E   1103 1528 4103               1103  1528    3    1

   80   4 E    655  858 4104    ML          655   858  236    0
   90   4 E   1030 1256 4102               1030  1256  236    0

  100   5 E    705 1005 4105    ML          705  1005  237    0
  110   5 E   1130 1511 4106               1130  1511  237    0

  120   6 B    714 1026 4106    ML          714  1026   88    0
  130   6 B   1511 1627 4106               1511  1627   88    0
  140   6 B   1640 1829 4106               1640  1829   88    0

  150   7 B    745 1101 4101    ML          745  1101  198    0
  160   7 B   1712 1828 4105               1430  1828  198    0

  170   8 M   1252 1712 4105    ML         1252  1712   14    0
  180   8 M   1828 2202 4105               1828  2202   14    0

  190   9 M   1311 1753 4104    ML         1311  1753  112    0
  200   9 M   1845 2040 4102               1845  2040  112    0

  210  10 L   1525 1845 4102    ML         1525  1845   76    0
  220  10 L   1935 2105 4104               1935  2105   76    0
  230  10 L   2110 2253 4104               2110  2253   76    0

  240  11 L   1528 1835 4103    ML         1528  1835   20    0
  250  11 L   2127 2442 4106               2127  2442   20    0

  260  12 L   1532 2016 4101    ML         1532  2016   22    0
  270  12 L   2147 2443 4103               2147  2443   22    0

  280  13 L   1753 1930 4104    ML         1753  1930  131    0
  290  13 L   2040 2423 4102               2040  2423  131    0

NUCRU VERSION 1.1 APRIL 1979 - UNCOVERED WORK


NORMAL END OF JOB
```

DISPLAY B1

CIE TEST CN SERVICE 16/16A   JANUARY 1979

DAY 2, RUN 0, PAGE 9

LATE   DUTIES

DUTY NUMBER	BUS NO. AND NAME	STARTING TIME AND PLACE	FINISHING TIME AND PLACE	SIGA ON/OFF	REPORT TIMES	BREAK LENGTH	PART DUTY	PAID TIME	SPREAD		
301	17 1501 23 1619	1506 PARNELL SQ WEST 2018 PARNELL SQ EAST	1916 SUMMERHILL GGE 2344 SUMMERHILL GGE	17 0 0 15	1449 1916 2018 2359	62	427 341	820	910		242/ 34 243/ 125
302	18 1521 26 1606	1509 PARNELL SQ WEST 2026 PARNELL SQ EAST	1924 SUMMERHILL GGE 2346 SUMMERHILL GGE	17 0 0 15	1452 1924 2026 2401	62	432 335	819	909		260/ 48 261/ 176
303	21 1605 34 1622	1521 PARNELL SQ WEST 2107 PARNELL SQ EAST	2010 PARNELL SQ EAST 2351 SUMMERHILL GGE	17 0 0 15	1506 2010 2107 2406	57	506 259	805	902	NB	224/ 90 225/ 310
304	36 1613 37 1617	1523 PARNELL SQ EAST 2036 PARNELL SQ WEST	1933 SUMMERHILL GGE 2355 SUMMERHILL GGE	17 0 0 15	1506 1933 2036 2414	63	427 338	817	908		248/ 346 249/ 360
305	22 1626 27 1634	1526 PARNELL SQ WEST 2034 PARNELL SQ EAST	1732 PARNELL SQ EAST 2403 SUMMERHILL GGE	17 0 0 15	1509 1932 2034 2418	62	423 344	819	909		284/ 110 285/ 195
306	38 1623 30 1615	1530 PARNELL SQ EAST 1557 PARNELL SQ EAST	1852 PARNELL SQ WEST 2420 SUMMERHILL GGE	17 0 0 15	1513 1852 1957 2435	65	339 438	817	922		230/ 373 231/ 251
307	24 1607 38 1623	1532 PARNELL SQ WEST 2122 PARNELL SQ EAST	2021 SUMMERHILL GGE 2406 SUMMERHILL GGE	17 0 0 15	1515 2021 2122 2421	61	506 259	817	906	NB	272/ 143 273/ 373
308	25 1610 31 1627	1537 PARNELL SQ WEST 2059 PARNELL SQ EAST	1947 SUMMERHILL GGE 2343 SUMMERHILL GGE	17 0 0 15	1520 1947 2059 2358	72	427 259	738	838		290/ 160 291/ 270
309	26 1606 24 1607	1543 PARNELL SQ WEST 2158 SUMMERHILL GGE	2326 PARNELL SQ EAST 2349 SUMMERHILL GGE	17 0 0 15	1526 2026 2158 2404	92	500 206	718	838	NB	308/ 176 309/ 143
310	16 1614 21 1605	1545 PARNELL SQ EAST 2010 PARNELL SQ WEST	1910 PARNELL SQ WEST 2431 SUMMERHILL GGE	17 0 0 15	1528 1910 2010 2446	60	342 436	718	918		266/ 17 267/ 90
311	30 1616 47 1602	1601 SUMMERHILL GGE 2050 PARNELL SQ EAST	1557 PARNELL SQ EAST 2413 SUMMERHILL GGE	5 0 0 15	1556 1957 2050 2428	53	401 338	739	832		254/ 251 255/ 435
312	23 1619 16 1614	1610 SUMMERHILL GGE 2130 PARNELL SQ EAST	2013 PARNELL SQ EAST 2414 SUMMERHILL GGE	5 0 0 15	1605 2018 2130 2429	72	413 259	712	824		278/ 125 279/ 17

DISPLAY B2

Computer Scheduling of Public Transport
A. Wren (ed.)
© *North-Holland Publishing Company, 1981*

A PROBLEM DECOMPOSITION APPROACH TO SCHEDULING
THE DRIVERS AND CREWS OF MASS TRANSIT SYSTEMS

Richard E. Ward, Philip A. Durant and A.B. Hallman

West Virginia University,
ATE Management and Service Company, Virginia,
and Dept. of Transportation, Washington D.C.,
U.S.A.

A mathematical programming approach to bus operator scheduling
is presented, in which the total problem is decomposed into
tractable components. The first component consists of
scheduling the late and middle duties. This approach has been
applied to three very different test cases, which are
presented, and the late and middle duties obtained are shown
to compare favorably with manual and other computer solutions.
The next stage will be to investigate the remaining components
and to combine the results.

BACKGROUND

The approach described in this paper to generate solutions to the bus operator
scheduling problem stems from the combined experiences of its authors of some 20
years. The earliest published account of this experience was by Ward in 1968 (10).
Benefiting largely from the leadership of Elias, a pioneer in the field of bus
operator scheduling (1,2), Ward constructed heuristic algorithms which refined
(reduced the cost of) operator schedules produced by Elias' heuristic scheduling
methodology.

Additional work by Ward was documented in 1968 (11), by which time the heuristic
methodology of Elias was abandoned in favor of new heuristic approaches which
sequentially constructed an initial schedule, one duty at a time. The previously
mentioned refinement algorithms were then adapted for use with these initial
schedules. Although testing of these new algorithms met with some success while
Ward was at the New York City Transit Authority, progress beyond this point was
slow, if not stalled at times, due to a personal career shift to automated
transport systems. It is worth noting at this point that it has since become
apparent that portions of the RUCUS Code (8), which had its beginning in the early
seventies, incorporated features taken from this early development work at the New
York City Transit Authority.

Work by Ward did continue, however, and in 1972, Ward and Deibel published a
summary accounting of the earlier progress, and documented new advances in the
area of refinement algorithms (12). At the same time, the work of Wren was
progressing in Great Britain (7, 13, 14, 15). While the work of Wren and Ward was
similar, in that they both used sequential heuristic algorithms to construct
initial schedules, and they both used refinement algorithms to optimize or improve
on the costs of the initial schedules, they differed noticeably in their
philosophy as to what constituted an initial schedule. While Wren was pursuing
ways of constructing the best possible initial schedule, Ward felt that almost any
'quick and dirty' initial schedule would work, so long as it was valid according
to contract stipulations or work rules. He believed that the key was in the
refinement algorithms and that if properly written, they could significantly

improve even poorly constructed schedules.

Influenced by Wren, along with much experimentation, the concept of the best possible initial schedule eventually dominated all future development work. In 1975, with the sponsorship of the British Science Research Council, Ward and Wren joined forces in Great Britain for a year of collaborative research. Durant already had a year of tutorship under Wren, and joined the collaborative effort. Hallman had been in place at UMTA, facilitating the development and deployment of RUCUS.

Part of the year 1975-76 was spent in developing a new refinement algorithm which extended the idea of recutting small pieces of work off the ends of valid stretches of work and reallocating them (12). Subsequent testing found this particular refinement algorithm to be instrumental in making some previously unacceptable computerized schedules acceptable.

The greatest part of 1975-76 was focused on improving Wren's algorithms for constructing initial schedules. Wren, even before the advent of RUCUS, sought to generalize the algorithm, thus making it easier to adapt to any property and to almost any conditions. The key was a highly parameterized model, with the parameters under the control of the user. It was found, however, that even the best laid plans would eventually be undone by the vastly varying conditions and work rules between properties, a fact which, over the years, has probably been the main reason behind the bus industry's slow movement into computerized scheduling.

Frustrations over not being able to produce acceptable schedules, at least not without substantial manual intervention into what was supposed to be an automated process, led to the quest for yet another way to approach the problem. The particular condition being faced at the time was a bus property whose union specified that no more than a given number of duties, called 'middles', may finish between the hours of 8pm and 10pm, and that meal breaks off the bus were mandatory on all duties (i.e. two and three piece duties). The sequential heuristic algorithm, for very good reason, could not produce the required maximum number of middles, and extra duties were inevitably created in order to get adequate meal breaks for the remaining 'late' duties, the latter finishing anywhere from 10pm until the last bus pulled into the depot. The main reason for this problem had to be the scarcity of, and temporal location of, relief points falling during this critical region (i.e. post pm-peak period, but before 10pm). Such a condition meant that there were only a very few combinations of ways the work could be cut and combined into duties working through or ending in this time period while still meeting the maximum 'middles' requirement. The sequential method of creating duties was not capable of hitting on the right combination. Moreover, the refinement routines could not rectify the problem..

Other data sets exhibited similar problems and constraints, and therefore there was ample cause to consider the alternatives.

ALTERNATIVES TO SEQUENTIAL HEURISTICS

The only alternative being given any serious attention by others researching the bus operator scheduling problem was to employ some form of mathematical programming, with the most promising formulation being set partitioning (herein after called SP). The SP problem may be stated generally as:

$$\text{Min} \sum_{j=1}^{n} c_j x_j, \qquad \text{with } c_j > 0,$$

$$\text{and } x_j = 0,1 \ (j=1,\ldots,n)$$

Subject to $\displaystyle\sum_{j=1}^{n} a_{ij}\, x_j = 1$ for $i = 1,\ldots,m$
                           with $a_{ij} = 0,1 \; \forall \; i,j$

The bus operator and other crew scheduling problems are innately zero-one integer programs; that is according to the assumption that only one operator is assigned to a bus at any particular time. Application of the above formulation presupposes prior generation of all possible duties which can be used to cover the work set forth in the bus schedule. The number of duties generated is equivalent to the number of variables. The objective of the set partitioning program is to select a subset of duties from all the variables so as to minimize the cost of covering the work.

Furthermore, it is assumed that the total work to be covered in the bus schedule can be expressed as a number of shorter increments of work. An increment of work is defined as the work between two adjacent relief points on a single block. With this understanding, the following conventions apply.

x_j equals 1 if duty j is retained in the solution, otherwise it equals 0.
c_j is the cost of duty j taking into account the time spent on a bus plus any allowances and bonuses for such things as overtime. For dummy duties, to be described later, c_j is a large number used to restrict the number of dummy duties formed.
a_{ij} equals 1 if duty j covers increment of work i, otherwise it equals 0. Therefore, there is one constraint row in the program for every increment of work.

It is clear that unless the problems to be solved are sufficiently small, in terms of the number of buses and number of driver duties required, or unless steps are taken somehow to make them seem smaller than they were, that SP would not be feasible because of the enormous number of rows and columns in the mathematical formulation. For the cases where SP was used, apparently with some success (4,5), the following characteristics were noted: (i) driver meal reliefs were taken on the bus, and therefore multi-piece duties were not a part of the problem, resulting in a much simpler problem to solve; and (ii) the number of available relief points in the bus 'blocks' or 'running boards' was reduced, a priori, by heuristic decision rules in order to reduce both the number of rows and the number of columns in the resulting SP problem formulation. Given that the authors do not wish to prejudge relief points to the point of excluding them from entering the solution, and that multi-piece duties are to be very much a part of the problem, another way of capitalizing on the solution potential of SP was required.

The SP approach to be described in this paper departs from the previous proposals for its use in that its application is based on the hypothesis that the original problem can be decomposed to a number of smaller problems, that SP can be used with little or no difficulty to solve the subproblems, and that the resulting solution can then be combined to form the total solution, which, if not optimal in the global sense, will be a very good solution. Moreover, it is felt that such an approach offers a way of circumventing problems of duty selection which prove difficult for the popular heuristic methods, which sequentially cut duties away from the bus schedules in some prescribed order. While post-optimization of a completed schedule of duties ultimately might be necessary, it is argued that the extent of such post-optimization would be less than might otherwise be required.

IDENTIFYING SUBPROBLEMS

A profile of bus service usually implies a natural pattern of duty-types which will be required to cover the work. Such a pattern is illustrated in Figure 1. In fact, most labor-management agreements even specify their duties by type, according to a particular time of day when they start and finish work. Moreover, some agreements even specify the minimum and/or maximum number of a given type which are permissible in the final operator schedule, which was the case for the problem with the 'middles', cited earlier.

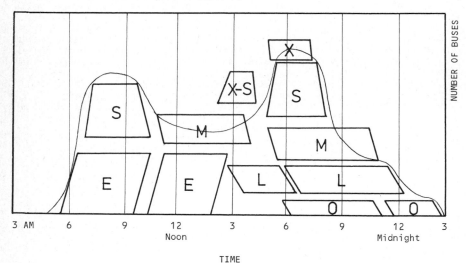

Key to duty types: E - Early straights
                     L - Late straights
                     M - Middle straights
                     O - Owls (late late straights)
                     S - Spread or split duties
                     X - Extra pieces (for use as Trippers or the
                         3rd piece of work on a straight duty)

Figure 1.   Illustration of bus service profile and the way in which buses
            may be covered by a combination of duty types.

Manual schedulers for a company will normally prepare a schedule very much in the manner of most sequential heuristics; that is, one peak, then the other, then all remaining work. In terms of the duties mentioned above, this could be redefined as scheduling all the early straights first, then all the owl and late and middle straights, and finally the split duties.

The manual schedulers are thus attempting to construct the best manual schedule for each duty type. However, it is obvious that for very large problems, the overview of a scheduler is as limited as a heuristic, although manual schedulers do develop considerable instincts for what is a bad cut, for example.

Exploiting the duty-type structure imposed on this problem by labor contracts and the general pattern of bus service, this paper describes attempts to decompose the problem to a number of smaller problems, each dealing with a specific duty-type.

Previous research has depended heavily on routines which took an initial solution and massaged this into a good solution. Experience has since shown that this can do very little to alter bad cuts already made and can also be exhausting and computationally expensive. It is believed that the method described in this paper has the potential of producing an automatic by-pass to this step by having a more global perspective, at least within each duty-type, than an initial heuristic cut. Furthermore, by working with smaller subproblems, it is expected that computational problems posed by a more global SP formulation of the problem will not be experienced.

To gain initial computational experience, the general problem was decomposed to the point of dealing only with buses running through and beyond the evening peak, and optimal assignments made only for owls, lates and middle straights where these existed. It is not expected that extending the approach to deal with the morning peak should cause any considerable variance in the method of solution. In fact, work is now in progress to do just that.

One reason for dealing only with the evening buses in the initial stage of research is that, traditionally, manual schedulers and heuristics have mainly attempted to solve the morning peak first, and then proceeded to the evening peak. The viewpoint taken in this study is that better schedules are ultimately constructed when the work in the evening period is covered first and the number of middle duties held to a minimum, since the number of all other duty-types is usually determined by the bus service profile. It is believed this result is achieved when none of the possible work is covered in the total schedule before the late duties are constructed. While this aspect of the problem is addressed, little conclusive evidence will be offered, since complete solutions to work covering the entire day have not yet been attempted.

It is, however, conceivable that when the program is extended in the future to deal with both peaks, the modular nature of the algorithm will allow quick and easy comparisons of the order in which the various duty types are constructed. For example, one schedule would be cut in the order owls, lates, middles, earlies, spreads; and yet another cut earlies, owls, lates, middles, spreads and so on. This would give the schedule director considerable latitude in the selection of a schedule.

The principal objectives of the study being reported therefore were as follows:

1. To decompose the bus operator scheduling problem to deal specifically with independent subproblems defined by different duty-types.
2. To attempt solutions to independent subproblems for owl, late and middle duties, using an SP program approach.
3. To set the objective of the SP program at any one stage to minimize the total pay-hours for the duty-type being considered.
4. To gain computational experience with the proposed methodology using three test data sets aquired from three different bus properties.
5. To assess the feasibility of the proposed methodology in terms of actually achieving integer solutions to the SP programs, and in terms of the quality of the resulting duties.

With solutions to only part of the problem it would obviously be difficult to make rigid comparisons with a total schedule produced either manually or by RUCUS type heuristics. However, it is possible to look at the productivity of the partial schedules and to use this dimensionless quantity of work produced, as well as how this productivity compares with that in an overall schedule.

Moreover, it is also possible to look at the work left uncovered and to see if
difficult problems were produced at any stage. In any event, for each data set
tested, comparisons will be made with duties of the same type produced by other
methods, and computational experience will be discussed in terms of computer
resources utilized as a function of problem size.

MORE ON SUBPROBLEMS

One prerequisite to the decomposition is having some advance knowledge or estimate
of the desired number of duties, by type. This might be provided by an experienced
schedule maker, or it might be derived from a pre-analysis of the bus schedule and
the work which must be covered.

The following discussion outlines a pre-analysis step used in guiding the choice
of subproblems in the study. Also discussed is the method employed to generate the
large set of duties (variables) which are used as input to the SP program.

As an example of the pre-analysis, consider the sample of bus schedules, or blocks
of work, shown in Figure 2. Assume that the example bus company has established,
through its labor contract, that any duty which finishes work after 10pm at night
is a late duty. Therefore, assuming that this company has no buses running later
than those shown in Figure 2, the maximum number of lates in an efficient schedule
would be four. Assume that the company has also agreed with labor that split or
spread duties must finish work before 6:15 in the evening. Therefore, the minimum
number of middle duties, finishing before 10pm, would be five (the total number of
buses out after 6:15, being nine in this case, minus four, the number of lates).

A similar analysis can also be made for early duties covering only the morning
peak. However, this study has chosen to work only with the evening buses at this
point in investigating the SP approach. The reason for focusing on the duties
covering the evening buses is the belief that this is the period in the day where
the greatest difficulty often lies in selecting the correct relief points to make
cuts for the purpose of forming duties, a problem which it is felt SP can
overcome. In the example given in Figure 2, it would be a crucial point to good
scheduling that the minimum estimate for middle duties be achieved if make-up time
is not to be excessive. The minimum nunber of late and early duties is almost
always achievable.

To comprehend fully the dicussion on generating variables and constraints, a
minimum number of definitions must be made. As was mentioned earlier, duties are
typified by the time of day operators start and finish work, the number of breaks
occurring, and the length in time of these breaks for relief or meals. However, it
can be surmised from Figure 1 that duties are normally made up of one or more
pieces of work. A duty with two pieces of work will be cut from different vehicle
blocks. The terminology used to define a two piece run is as follows:

A POINT — the beginning point of the first (earlier) piece of work

B POINT — the ending point of the first piece of work

C POINT — the beginning point of the second (later) piece of work

D POINT — the ending point of the second piece of work.

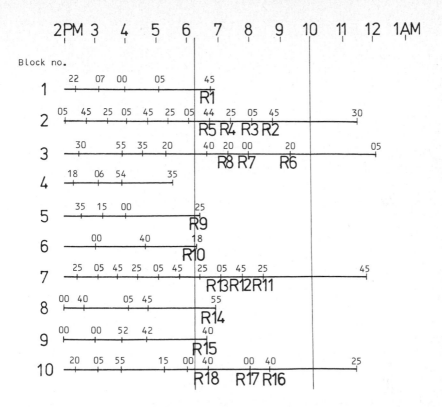

Key: The number above the hash mark + designates minutes
     past the hour: i.e. the first hash mark on Block
     No. 1 indicates that a relief point on Bus 1 occurs
     at 2:22 p.m.

     R= – Designates a row number for the associated
         linear program.

FIGURE 2.   Illustration of the generation of rows for a linear program
            to select late duties from an example of 10 buses which were
            extracted from a larger data set.

With this in mind, an explanation of the method used to generate variables and constraints is made much easier.

Each subproblem, one for each duty-type, will have its own set of variables and constraints. A parameter-driven program was written expressly for the purpose of generating the variables and constraints of each subproblem.

At the start of each subproblem all relief points for the given schedule of buses are used as input to the generator, as are the values for key parameters (contractual specifications) pertinent to the duty-type being considered. An example of such a parameter is the minimum length of a piece of work.

Recall that each relief point, or rather the work between adjacent relief points, forms a constraint (row) in the SP program, thus ensuring that each increment of work is covered once and only once in the final solution. However, for a given duty-type, it is necessary to extract only those relief points which will somehow figure into the duty-type being considered, as potential A,B,C, or D points. This is to be illustrated using Figure 2. The generator makes this selection based on the parameters and rules governing the formation of the duty-type.

Further assisting in the extraction of relief points is that all applicable vehicle blocks are one of two types. Since this study considered only those duties which cover work occurring in the evening and early morning, one of these duty-types will be used to illustrate what is meant by two types of vehicle block.

Assume that the subproblem for late duties is to be used as the example. A late duty is any duty finishing after a stipulated time. In the case of the example in Figure 2, the stipulated cut-off time was 10pm. Therefore, any vehicle block running past this point is considered for the purposes of this example to be a type 1 block, and every relief point on these blocks which constitutes a feasible C point for the late duties to work this bus is extracted and used as a constraint (row). The pull-in time for each of these blocks will form a D point for a late duty.

All vehicle blocks finishing before the cut-off time for middle duties, and whose finishing time could potentially form a valid B point, are considered type 2 blocks. Only the final relief point (pull-in time) of type 2 blocks is likewise extracted and used as a constraint.

In generating the complete set of potential late duties, every possible C point on every type 1 block is linked with every valid B point on every other type 1 and type 2 block. Then, for every D,C and B point which is so chosen, an A point of least cost is chosen. The resulting duty is used as a variable in the SP program. This process is repeated until every possible combination (duty) is found. So, for example, the late duties for Block 2 in Figure 2 might read:

1. Link R2 with R7, the duty to start at 3:55. The stretches are 3:55 to 8:00 on bus 3, and 8:45 to 11:30 on bus 2.

2. Link R2 with R12, the duty to start at 3:45. The stretches here are 3:45 to 7:45 on bus 7, and 8:45 to 11:30 on bus 2.
    .
    .
    .
    .
n. Link R4 with R1, the duty to start at 3:07. The stretches are 3:07 to 6:45 on bus 1 and 7:25 to 11:30 on bus 2.

To be realistic in these examples, allowances should be added in before the duty stretches are finally determined.

Such an exhaustive enumeration is deemed feasible because the problem has been decomposed to deal with only one duty-type at a time. It is pointed out that there is nothing unique about the generator, as it is only that, a generator of duties, and no attempt is made at this stage to limit the number of duties to be generated.

Focusing again on Figure 2, an example is provided for generating a complete data set consisting of rows and columns of the SP program. Assume that the maximum work without a break, including all allowances, is four hours forty-five minutes; that the sign off allowance at a garage is 15 minutes; lates are all duties finishing after 10 at night; that split or spread duties must finish by 6:15; and finally meal breaks be between 30 and 60 minutes. The subproblem to be solved is generated in the following manner. It should be pointed out that the assumptions made here are actual contractual agreements at present in force for the data illustrated in Figure 2.

As described previously, the number of late buses was four and the total number of late and middle buses was nine. Using the definitions for type 1 and type 2 blocks just given, it is now possible to generate the inputs to the generator as follows.

In this example for scheduling lates, type 1 blocks are lates and type 2 blocks are middles. For each type 1 block, each relief point which could form a valid stretch of work is given a number to correspond to a row number in the binary matrix for SP. So for example, using the restriction of a stretch length of four hours forty-five minutes, block number 2 in Figure 2 generates 3 possible stretches of valid work or 3 C points.

The type 2 blocks form only valid B points so only their final relief point is used as a row in the constraint matrix. The numbers R1, R2, and so on correspond to the row numbers in the constraint matrix for the SP program.

Bus number 4 does not figure at this point because it does not qualify as an exclusive possible piece of work for either a late or middle duty; it could in fact qualify as a split or spread duty.

A sample valid duty to serve for a variable in the binary constraint matrix would cover rows 18, 4, 3, and 2, and all such duties for each data set would be generated.

The final inputs required to drive the sequence are the costs of each variable generated as described in the above example. Herein lies the first quality-sensitive point of the analysis. Each relief point of type 1 or type 2 block is first set up as a dummy variable and given a very high cost. The explanation is that every type 1 bus must be in the final solution but that exclusion of a relief point from a real variable means an extra duty will be created to cover this work. Some of these may be left out because of the nature of the problem, but this high cost is an attempt to restrict the number of such extra duties created.

Each real variable or duty is costed in this study according to contractual rules for:

1. travel time and report and clear allowances

2. work content or platform time

3. make-up and overtime allowances

4. excessive spread costs.

Also, one can use some subjective costs to restrict the duties selected in the final solution to one form or another. The subjective cost used in the study was a measure of productivity expressed as the ratio of total pay time to actual work time. While no other subjective costs were used in this study, there is really no limit to what one might wish to specify.

SENSITIVITY ANALYSIS

As was stated previously, many of the earlier integer programming formulations were found not to be practical, because the global approach taxed available computer resources. This study was undertaken because it was believed that this problem would be circumvented by decomposing the bus operator scheduling problem. However, even using this approach, a subproblem, although within the bounds of computational feasibility, can still be quite large, of the order of several thousand variables.

The question is raised as to just how large the data set of potential duties (number of variables) needs to be. Moreover, it was felt that more than likely the totally enumerated set of duties would not be necessary to obtain the optimal solution.

Part of the plan of this study, therefore, was to investigate the sensitivity of the final solution as a function of the size of the input data set, or number of variables. Specifically, it was hoped that the minimum data set could be determined which causes a discernible change in the optimum solution. If this were possible, the computational effort could be reduced significantly.

TEST CASES

Computational experience with the methods described in the preceding chapter was gained by using data acquired from three different bus properties. In each case, the properties supplying data had already experimented with computerized run-cutting. In fact two of the properties were experimenting with a version of the Vehicle Scheduling and Driver Run Cutting (RUCUS) computer package developed under the sponsorship of the Urban Mass Transportation Administration (UMTA).

The participating properties, for the purposes of this study, will be referred to as Property A, Property B, and Property C. A description of each data set follows.

Property A made available the data set for the largest of its scheduling divisions. It was expected that this would be the data set which would tend to test the proposed methodology to the maximum limits set.

Property A operates out of this depot as a single garage, multi-route, multi-relief point division. With 234 buses operating during the evening peak, it exhibits most of the characteristics required for test data.

The maximum stretch length without a break is five hours 30 minutes, except for owl duties, when this may be extended to six hours. Owl duties are the only duties which may be a single stretch of work up to the six-hour maximum. There is no established minimum stretch.

On this property, the ratio of straight duties (duties working only one peak) to spread duties (duties normally working both peaks) cannot be less than 1.0.

As was stated, the division is a multi-route, multi-relief point garage, with 234 evening peak runs. In addition, it has 241 morning peak runs and a peak-to-base ratio of about 3 to 1, which can be considered very high. The higher this ratio, the greater the number of spread duties which will be required.

From the profile of bus workings, it is possible to isolate 34 runs as late straights, 31 runs as middle straights and 12 owls. Given the restriction of the number of straight duties to the number of spread duties, and assuming that a schedule is normally at its most effective when meals are prohibited in the peaks, the total of 241 morning peaks and 234 evening peaks, and 12 owls working neither peak, shows that at peak times, 487 driver duties are needed to cover the day's work. Spread duties are, however, duplicated in the peaks and if the minimum 1:1 ratio for total straights to total spread duties is taken, it would be expected that at least 158 spread duties cover both peaks with 83 straights working the morning peak and 76 straights working the evening peak. The minimum number of duties given the minimum 1:1 straight/spread relationship is 317 peak and 12 owls. Any increase in the ratio of straight to spread duties would result in a greater number of duties being formed.

Using the estimate of 329 duties, an estimate for the average platform time (time working on a bus) of a driver can be made. Property A has a total platform time of 2318 hours and 56 minutes, giving an estimated average of 7 hours and 20 minutes. Although arguably the above method is non-rigorous, in the absence of more sophisticated pre-analysis techniques, it gives some guidelines as to the anticipated results, and the figure of 440 minutes was used to cost the productivity of any duty produced as well as to estimate how much over the minimum the final solution might be.

Property B is much like Property A in that it has most of the duty-types encountered: owls, lates, middays, morning straights and spreads. However, it was selected because of its manifest differences from Property A. Property A schedules all its labor by division, while Property B takes the more restricted approach of run-cutting according to route. As a result, the problem is a small example compared to that expected from Property A, but worthwhile to look at so as to test the methodology's performance for a variety of different circumstances.

Property B is also different from Property A in that its owls are unbroken duties and no actual meal relief is made. The driver always remains with the bus.

The route for which data was provided had 17 morning peak buses, 23 evening buses, and 3 owls not working either peak. Of the evening peak buses, 8 were exclusively late and 4 were middles. By the rules, these had to be 12 straight runs. This leaves 11 spread duties. However, the same conclusion can be reached by following a similar analysis to that used for property A. Letting X be the number of runs covering both peaks, being no more than 40 per cent of the total in this case, then it follows that 3X/2 must be the minimum number of straight runs. Furthermore, if the total number of buses over both peaks must be covered by the spreads (counted twice) plus the straights, then:

$$X + X + 3X/2 = 40, \text{ and}$$

$$X = 11 \text{ spreads, rounded down.}$$

So the number of duties to cover the schedule at a minimum would be 11 spreads + 6 morning peaks + 12 evening peaks + 3 owls, for a total of 32. The present manual and computer schedules use 35 duties. With 32 duties, the average platform time for the total work of 260 hours and 43 minutes is 8 hours and 9 minutes, implying that with a surplus of labor more duties could be created, and with a shortage of labor, overtime over the basic 8 hours would be paid.

Property C provided a data set with no owl duties, unlike Property A or Property B, but is of a size midway between the two. The schedule profile shows 35 evening peak buses and 33 morning peak buses.

Because of the restriction that no spread duties can finish after 6:15 in the evening, the profile shows that 30 of the evening peak buses must be straights, and only five spread duties work the evening peak. Without much analysis, the minimum number of duties is then 30 + 5 + 28 for a total of 63 duties. The present manual schedule shows 66 duties. Using 63 as a minimum, the efficient average platform content of a duty is 6 hours 55 minutes. It should be pointed out again that these figures only supply a rough estimate and are not to be taken as precise. They are used only as a guide to listing the duties to be generated by the methodology.

In summary, the data sets were selected because of the fact that some computerized run-cutting had been attempted for these data sets. It was further felt that these data sets had the qualities to provide realistic testing for the approach to be taken. Moreover, the data from Property C was the very problem referred to earlier which instigated this study in the first place.

RESULTS

Based on other reports regarding methods of achieving solutions to SP problems, a variety of approaches had been planned. Code developed by Salkin (6,9) was initially thought to be the best approach, particularly since it was reported to be successful with formulations having a sparse matrix. However, unanticipated problems were experienced with the code, which could not be solved, and therefore it was abandoned for the time being in favour of the alternatives.

There was reason to believe that using a conventional linear programming code would work in most cases (i.e. producing total 0-1 solutions). This alternative was then adopted. In the event of partial continuous solutions, a variation of the Garfinkel-Nemhauser code (3) was to be employed to completely integerize the incomplete solutions produced from conventional LP code. The inspiration to take this latter course was gained from the work reported by Heurgon (4,5).

Once testing got under way, it was found that the conventional LP code did in fact produce complete integer solutions for every test made, and it was never necessary to fall back on the modified, curtailed branch and bound code. The computational results of these tests are presented in Table 1, and are representative of results one could expect on an IBM 360/75 computer using IBM's MPSX linear programming code.

In one case, shown in Table 1, the size of the problem generated and the size of the problem solved were different, the latter being smaller. The reason for this was simply to reduce the computational time required to arrive at a solution. However, in none of the cases did this affect the objective cost of the solution.

Table 1. Computational results for the three properties used as test cases.

Prop.	Duty Type	No. of Duties	Size of problem generated (rowsxcols)	CPS time (secs)	Size of problem submitted (rowsxcols)	CPU time (secs)	Models used to achieve integer solution
A	Owls	12	116 x 572	11.55	116 x 572	22.71	MPSX
	Lates	34	230 x 4433	43.95	230 x 1071	68.24	MPSX
	Middles	31	476 x 1819	24.90	476 x 1819	155.53	MPSX
B	Lates	8	45 x 130	3.79	45 x 130	4.84	MPSX
	Middles	4	50 x 62	3.15	50 x 62	3.27	MPSX
C	Lates	21	99 x 971	9.09	99 x 971	48.54	MPSX
	Middles	9	36 x 117	2.91	36 x 117	4.22	MPSX

The idea of doing this stemmed from initial experimentation where it was found that regardless of the size of the problem submitted, the final solution never used more than the tenth cheapest duty covering the same bus, from among all the duties (variables) generated.

Since this could not be assumed to be true in all cases, it was decided to begin the experimentation with the three test properties using no more than the 25 least-cost duties covering the same work on the same bus. The final results showed that the 12 cheapest duties would always yield the least costly solution.

From the previous discussion, it appears that the method is computationally feasible. It is, however, not sufficient to obtain a theoretical solution. The real question in real world terms is: is it a schedule acceptable to worker and management alike? The remaining discussion presents what it is believed are quality partial solutions for the three data sets provided.

The schedule results for the data sets of Properties A, B, and C are presented in Table 2. Since this research restricted all tests to the evening peak buses only, it can be argued that no real comparisons can be made at this point with actual schedules now being produced by the bus property. While this is a fair argument, one should not totally ignore an analysis of the duties formed as a product of this research. Such an analysis would entail comparing the number of duties required to cover similar working hours by the alternative run-cutting methods, and the productivity of the partial schedules in terms of the ratio of work hours to actual paid hours. The decision as to whether the methodology being investigated appears to be on track is likely to be quite clear from the above comparisons.

One final observation needs to be made. The schedules provided by Properties A, B, and C, against which the results of this research are compared, are the product of many refinements and iterations, which at times seemed to border on computer assisted manual run-cutting. By comparison, no manual intervention was required in order to arrive at solutions using the methodology of this study, nor were the final solutions refined in any way. Moreover, it is anticipated that much of the effort of solution refinement, which is now an important part of current run-cutting methods (e.g. RUCUS), will be minimized with the use of run-cutting methods similar to that which is outlined in this paper. However, it is not realistic to expect that the combining of many partial optimal solutions would create an optimal solution to the total problem. The optimal solution for a problem of this set is unknown. Therefore, it would probably be necessary to refine the combined solution, but not to the massive extent of present methods, where what is actually done is a near-complete resplit of bus runs.

The results for the three properties are given in Table 2, and are compared therein to the schedules provided by the three properties.

The data set provided for Property B was such a small data set that going from a manual to a heuristic (RUCUS) to an optimizing algorithm was not likely to produce startling improvements, because with a small number of options, it is possible for even a manual cut to be fairly exhaustive. This was not totally reflected in the results shown in Table 2. Although the manual schedule was acceptable and worked (there being no alternative), the heuristic improved on even this small data set, and the productivity of the SP approach appears to be even better. Property C was a reasonably complicated data set because unlike Property B, the options are not so obvious, and the effect of an initial bad cut is likely to cause some considerable effect on the final schedule. This was in fact manifested in the manual schedule with an extra duty being produced to cover the work (over the actual number of buses on the road), thus generating obvious idle time on the other duties. By comparison, the SP approach produced no more duties than there were buses on the road, with no decrease in productivity.

There is one apparent discrepancy in this solution. The manual method appears to cover more platform hours than the SP approach. This is in fact misleading, for the duty generator, as set up, has no access to work not in the evening peak and will not, at this point, be able to add make-up work to build duties up to closer to 8 hours. This work could be added, if necessary, when the partial optimal solutions (for different duty-types) are being combined.

Although results were not available from previous heuristic computer solutions for Property C, it was known that the computer could produce no fewer than 12 middle duties. In this case, the union would not accept a schedule with more than 10 middle duties. The results from the SP approach had been a most encouraging show of precision and quality duties.

CONCLUSIONS

The results of this study overall are encouraging, and work is scheduled to continue in the near future. Plans outlined include extending the methodology to cover all duty types and to combine the solutions to form a completed schedule. Also planned is an investigation into the requirements for integrating this methodology into the heuristic, step-wise approaches to automated schedule generation discussed by others active in the field.

The number of persons actively investigating this problem is heartening. This fact, coupled with the advent of mini and micro computers and their possible role in solving such problems, along with the really untapped methods of interactive schedule generation, means that the future will undoubtedly see a more rapid industry shift to computerized operator scheduling.

Table 2. Comparison of duties for three properties from different methods of run cutting.

	Property A		Property B			Property C	
	SP	Rucus	SP	Rucus	Manual	SP	Manual
Number of duties							
Owls	12	12					
Lates	34	32	8	8	8	21	21
Middles	31	34	4	4	4	9	10
Platform hours							
Owls	92.3	98.6					
Lates	260.76	283.05	61.35	61.43	61.93	141.68	144.53
Middles	246.8	232.0	30.31	29.73	29.05	64.2	68.65
Pay hours							
Owls	105.34	113.01					
Lates	283.05	278.60	67.2	67.9	71.8	157.68	160.65
Middles	270.57	263.06	35.1	34.4	33.4	72.7	78.23
Productivity ratio							
Owls	1.141	1.147					
Lates	1.085	1.132	1.095	1.105	1.159	1.113	1.112
Middles	1.096	1.133	1.158	1.157	1.150	1.132	1.140
Combined	1.097	1.135	1.116	1.122	1.156	1.119	1.121

REFERENCES

1. Elias, S.E.G., The use of digital computers in the economic scheduling for both man and machine in public transportation, Special Report No. 49, Kansas Engineering Experiment Station, Manhattan, Kansas.

2. Elias, S.E.G., A mathematical model for optimizing the assignment of man and machines, Research Bulletin No. 81, West Virginia University Engineering Experiment Station, Morgantown (1966).

3. Garfinkel, R.S. and Nemhauser, G.L., The set-partitioning problem; set covering with equality constraints, Operations Research, (Sept-Oct 1969) 848-856.

4. Heurgon, E. and Hervillard, R., Preparing duty rosters for bus routes by computer, UITP Revue 1 (1975) 33-37.

5. Heurgon, E., Preparing duty rosters for bus routes by computer, Proceedings of Workshop on Automated Techniques for Scheduling of Vehicle Operators for Urban Public Transportation Services, (Chicago, 1975).

6. Lemke, C.E., Salkin, H.M. and Spielberg, K., Set covering by single-branch enumeration with linear programming subproblems, Operations Research 19(4) (1971) 998-1022.

7. Manington, B. and Wren, A., Leeds University - N.B.C. - I.C.L. Bus crew scheduling, Proceedings of the Annual Seminar for Operational Research in the Bus Industry, The University of Leeds (1972) 93-96.

8. Mitre Corporation, Vehicle scheduling and driver run cutting: RUCUS package user documentation, MTR-6678 (1974).

9. Salkin, H.M., Integer programming (Addison-Wesley, 1975).

10. Ward, R.E., Heuristic programming and transit manpower scheduling, M.S. thesis, West Virginia University, Morgantown (1968).

11. Ward, R.E., Computerized run-cutting, Unpublished report, New York City Transit Authority, New York (1969).

12. Ward, R.E. and Deibel, L.E., The advancement of computerized assignment of transit operators to vehicles through programming techniques, Invited paper presented at the Joint National Meeting of the Operations Research Society of America, Atlantic City, New Jersey (1972).

13. Weaver, A. and Wren, A., Bus and crew scheduling, University of Leeds Operational Research Unit Report (1970).

14. Wren, A., Computer scheduling of buses and crews: A review, Proceedings of the Annual Seminar for Operational Research in the Bus Industry, The University of Leeds (1974).

15. Wren, A., Bus crew scheduling, Proceedings of the Annual Seminar for Operational Research in the Bus Industry, The University of Leeds (1975).

16. Wren, A. and Manington, B., A general computer method for bus and crew scheduling, Proceedings of Workshop on Automated Techniques for Scheduling of Vehicle Operators for Urban Public Transportation Services, (Chicago, 1975).

Computer Scheduling of Public Transport
A. Wren (ed.)
© *North-Holland Publishing Company, 1981*

EXPERIMENTATION WITH A COMPUTERIZED SYSTEM
FOR SCHEDULING MASS TRANSIT VEHICLES AND CREWS

Michael O. Ball, Lawrence D. Bodin and Robert Dial

University of Maryland and
U.S. Department of Transportation
U.S.A.

An interactive model is proposed for simultaneous solution of
the vehicle and driver scheduling problems. A non-interactive
version has been programmed and has achieved results which
compare favorably on test data with those achieved by manual
methods. The model uses a network representation of the
problem, and schedules are built up from the network using a
series of matching processes.

1. INTRODUCTION

Typically, today, mass transit crews are scheduled manually. Computer aided
procedures, such as modified versions of RUCUS (10), have received limited use.
Seasonal variations and changes in demand patterns require that new schedules be
produced several times a year. It takes schedulers and planners a significant
amount of time to produce a new set of crew and vehicle schedules. Consequently,
it is impossible to alter the schedules on short notice and to perform a variety
of planning functions without a computerized procedure. In addition, lack of
computerization makes it virtually impossible to determine crew and vehicle costs
as a function of changes in work rules, to determine the sensitivity of crew and
vehicle costs to changes in routes and to determine the effects of system growth
on operating costs. It is generally believed that proficient schedulers produce
cost effective schedules; however, several years of experience are usually
required before a scheduler becomes truly expert.

The principal value of the system we describe in this paper is that it eliminates
many of the problems mentioned above. In particular, the automation of the
scheduling process should give schedulers much more flexibility and allow planners
to evaluate quickly and accurately the effect of changes in system specifications.
In addition, the overhead associated with training schedulers should be reduced.

Our system uses optimization algorithms to generate a low cost set of crew and
vehicle schedules. At the same time, it allows a planner or scheduler to alter
dynamically the transit systems being produced and to derive crew and vehicle
schedules quickly and efficiently. The specifications for the system were
developed based on a review of documentation on existing systems
((2),(8),(9),(10),(12),(13),(14)).

The system will work as follows. A scheduler will sit at a terminal while the
algorithms generate schedules on the computer. At various break points, the
algorithms will report their progress to the scheduler. The scheduler then may
alter the schedules currently generated, freeze or free up some of these schedules
or alter the costs and constraints. Thus, constraints, such as the limitations on
the amount of interlining, may be imposed without being stated explicitly ahead of

time and the scheduler's insight into the structure of good schedules may be used dynamically by the algorithm.

The software development of a non-interactive version of the system has been completed and is being refined through testing on a variety of problems. Concurrently, development has begun on the interactive portion of the system. Naturally this development will draw on experience with the test problems on the non-interactive system. A flow chart of the entire system is presented later in this paper (Figure 6).

2. PROBLEM DEFINITION

An urban mass transit system may be considered from three viewpoints: the passenger, the crew and the vehicle. Routes and schedules may be defined for all three of these entities. The purpose of the mass transit system is to provide service to passengers. Thus, the driving forces of the system are lines and line schedules that define the service to the passenger. A <u>line</u> is defined to be a specification of a start location, an end location and intermediate stop locations, over which service is to be provided. A <u>line schedule (headway sheet)</u> is defined to be the time schedule for a line including the travel times between stops on the line and the frequency with which the line is traversed (headway). Travel times and headways may vary with time of day.

The problem considered is to find crew and vehicle schedules that will service the line schedules at minimum costs. Typically a vehicle will start at a garage in the morning, travel to the start location of the line, traverse it several times, travel to the start location of another line, traverse it several times and continue in this manner until it finally returns to the garage. Because of peaking in the morning and afternoon, the vehicle could return to the garage during the day and reappear on the streets later in the day. A crew on the other hand, might stay with one vehicle for a piece of work, and get off the vehicle at a designated relief point, where another crew would take over. The first crew would take a lunch break or return to the garage. Later in the day the crew would relieve another crew at another relief point and carry on in a similar manner. Our investigation of existing transit systems has shown that this process could continue for as many as four work segments during the day.

In the remainder of this report, the following definitions will be used to describe precisely the solution of the scheduling problem posed above.

<u>relief point</u>: a location along a line where one crew can go on break and a second crew can begin service on the same vehicle.
<u>trip</u>: a single one-way traversal of a line.
<u>round-trip</u>: a single two-way traversal of a line.
<u>d-trip</u>: the portion of a trip or combination of trips that must be traversed by the same driver and vehicle. By defining d-trips a scheduler may incorporate a variety of constraints into the model.
<u>piece</u>: the segment of a crew schedule in which the crew remains on the same vehicle. (Note that d-trips are part of the problem specification input into the model, whereas pieces are a portion of the output of the model).
<u>run</u>: the combination of pieces that make up a crew schedule.
<u>k-piece run</u>: a run consisting of k pieces.
<u>tripper</u>: a run consisting of one short piece (trippers usually incur heavy cost penalties and are considered undesirable).
<u>break time</u>: the length of the break in a run. Most runs will contain a specified rest or lunch break between the end of one piece and the beginning of the next piece. Typically union rules constrain the length of this break and its location in a run.

straight shift: a run with a break time sufficient to allow the crew a local lunch break (usually no more than one hour).
split shift: a run with a break time sufficient to allow the crew to go home and return to work (usually three to five hours).
spread time: time between start of first piece and end of last piece on a run.
platform time: time during a run that the crew is on the vehicle.
block: a vehicle schedule.
deadhead time: time during which a vehicle is travelling but is not involved in revenue producing service, i.e. not traversing a line.
dead time: time during which a vehicle is not involved in revenue producing service, i.e. deadhead time plus idle time.

3. NON-QUANTIFIABLE ISSUES

The problem of scheduling crews and vehicles is very complex. Consequently, it is unlikely that there exists a compact statement of the problem for which an efficient exact solution procedure exists. Our approach has been to examine characteristics of the problem and pitfalls of existing procedures, such as the RUCUS system and its variations ((2),(8),(9),(10)) and then judiciously to make tradeoffs in the design of the system to obtain a computationally tractable solution procedure.

Scheduling constraints can vary significantly from municipality to municipality. Probably the single greatest difficulty with the RUCUS system is its inflexibility. The following is a list of examples where greater flexibility is required.

(1) Union contracts in some cities prohibit three and four piece runs while in others they are allowed. RUCUS generates only one and two piece runs (RUCUS has been modified in Baltimore to treat three and four piece runs).

(2) Most municipalities assume a vehicle always makes a round trip over a line and never only a one-way trip. RUCUS assumes vehicles make one-way trips and then may make the return trip or may go to another line.

(3) Restrictions on the allowable proportion of straight shifts to split shifts vary widely from city to city.

(4) Many cities have restrictions on the degree to which a vehicle can transfer from one line to another (interlining). RUCUS has no way of restricting these transfers.

A second related difficulty involves the degree to which the human scheduler has control over the schedules output by the computer. No matter how the schedules are generated, before they are finally implemented they must be approved by the scheduler who is responsible for them. Before giving this approval, the scheduler must have the ability to alter schedules. The types of alterations required would probably arise from many of the issues discussed above as well as less tangible political issues.

We believe that consideration of the two problems just described is essential to the development of a successful system. Our approach to their solution is an interactive procedure; that is, a procedure in which a human can exercise control over the solution, not only by adjusting it at the end but also by actively taking part in its generation. The interaction we envision between man and computer was described briefly in Section 1 of this report.

Flexibility is not only handled through interactive processing but also through the design of problem parameters and data structures. For example, the concept of a d-trip allows the scheduler to specify that a particular driver and vehicle must remain on a particular line.

A third issue that significantly influenced our design was that crew costs are generally significantly greater than vehicle costs. Consequently, in our procedure crew scheduling is performed concurrently with vehicle scheduling. The traditional view is that vehicles are scheduled first, which implies that vehicle schedules put constraints on crew schedules. We hope that by emphasizing crew schedules, and consequently crew costs, a more cost effective solution can be achieved.

4. PROBLEM FORMULATION

In this section we give a formulation of the crew/vehicle scheduling problem. This formulation is a partitioning problem on an acyclic graph. Dantzig and Fulkerson pioneered the use of this type of formulation in their solution of the tanker scheduling problem (3). More recently variations and extensions on it have been used to solve a wide class of routeing and scheduling problems (see for example (11)).

The model requires a timetable as input. For each trip in the timetable a start time, end time, start location, end location and the location of the relief points are provided.

A graph is generated as follows. A vertex represents a part of a trip or combination of trips that a crew/vehicle is to service (d-trip). A vertex is characterized by a start time, start location, end time, and end location. An edge is directed from one vertex to another if it possible for a crew and vehicle or simply a crew to service the d-trip associated with the first vertex and subsequently the d-trip associated with the second. Thus edges are of two types, those which indicate that a crew and vehicle proceed from one d-trip to another, and those which indicate that only the crew proceeds from one d-trip to another. In addition, there are two vertices, s and t, representing the garage. There is an edge pointing from vertex s into all vertices except vertex t and an edge pointing out of all vertices except vertex s into vertex t. The crew/vehicle scheduling problem is to partition this graph into a set of paths from s to t, where each path has a variety of restrictions placed on it. Each path represents a crew schedule. As such, its associated platform time is restricted, e.g. between 6 and 9 hours, each path must contain an arc representing a break whose break time is within the appropriate limits etc. The solution to this problem gives both vehicle and crew schedules and with the choice of appropriate costs it gives a least-cost crew/vehicle schedule.

Figure 1 illustrates the types of vertices and edges in the graph. It represents a possible decomposition of a trip into d-trips. In this example each vertex corresponds to part of a trip, e.g. vertex 1 corresponds to the part of the trip from 10:00 to 10:13. The trip represents a one-way traversal of a line which has two intermediate relief points. It is decomposed into three d-trips. The first starts at the beginning of the trip, and goes to the first relief point, the second goes from the first relief point to the second, and the third goes from the second relief point to the end of the trip. It is assumed that the vehicle may deadhead from the end of any other line to the beginning of this one and from the end of this line to the beginning of any other. Seven types of edges are possible. They are numbered 1 through 7 and are described below.

Edge Type 1. represents crew and vehicle travelling from the garage to the beginning of the trip.

Edge Type 2. represents crew and vehicle travelling from the end of one trip to
              the beginning of another.
Edge Type 3. represents the end of a run, i.e. a crew proceeds from this break
              point to the garage via public transportation.
Edge Type 4. represents a crew break, i.e. the specified break (lunch break)
              within the run or a shorter break between pieces on a three and four
              piece runs.
Edge Type 5. represents a crew continuing with the vehicle and trip that it is
              already traversing.
Edge Type 6. · represents start of a crew day; crew proceeds from garage to relief
              point via public transportation.
Edge Type 7. represents crew and vehicle travelling from end of trip to garage.

This model can handle a variety of special cases. Two important cases are when a
relief point and the end or beginning of a trip coincide and when several
traversals of a line are required before deadheading to another line is allowed.
When the end of a trip and a relief point coincide, two vertices are formed. This
is illustrated in Figure 2. The first vertex corresponds to the relief point and
the second to the end of the trip. For the end of trip vertex the start time and
the end time are the same and start location and end location are the same.

When only two-way traversals of a trip are allowed the d-trip wraps around the end
of a trip. This is illustrated in Figure 3. In this case, the vertex corresponding
to the end of the first trip and the beginning of the return trip are merged.

Any run (crew schedule) can be represented as an (s,t)-path in this graph (see
Figure 4). If the vertices of the graph are partitioned into a set of (s,t)-paths,
each of which represents a run, then both crew and vehicle schedules will have
been determined (see Figure 5). The number of paths will equal the number of crews
and the number of paths containing type (1) arcs will equal the number of times a
vehicle leaves the garage. The maximum number of vehicles out of the garage at any
time will be the number of vehicles required. If an appropriate costing structure
is used the minimum cost partition will yield a minimum cost crew/vehicle
schedule.

The cost structure associated with crew/vehicle schedules using the above
formulation is very complex. For example, a run might have an associated fixed
cost, a cost per hour for each hour under 8 hours, a higher cost per hour for each
hour over 8 hours, and a penalty cost for split shifts.

Although this section has given a compact statement of the problem, no known 'one
pass' algorithms exist to solve this problem. The algorithm we propose in the next
section decomposes the problem into separate sub-problems and gives solution
algorithms for each of these. In addition, the overall process makes widespread
use of man-machine interaction. The formulation outlined in this section is useful
in analyzing the performance of this algorithm and in structuring its procedures.
In addition, this formulation is allowing us to develop lower bounds on the value
of an optimal solution. The lower bounds allow us to measure how far a particular
solution generated by our procedure is from optimality.

5. SOLUTION PROCEDURE

Figure 6 traces the flow of our solution procedure. Interactive computing is
utilized in three locations in this procedure. First, in blocks I and III,
interactive computing is used to verify and adjust the input data and network
definition to ensure that all special restrictions are included. Second,
interactive computing is used in block IV concurrently with an optimization
algorithm to guide the progress of the algorithm. Here the user can eliminate

infeasible configurations or encourage those that are likely to be in an optimal solution. Third, in blocks V, VII and VIII interactive computing is used to refine the solution generated by an optimization algorithm. Again, changes are made to eliminate infeasible configurations or to include more cost effective ones.

The primary non-interactive optimization performed by the algorithm takes place in blocks IV and VI. The solution procedure is decomposed into two parts: the first part generates a set of pieces whose time duration is less than some constant T (e.g. 4½ hours). The second part merges into runs. The procedure that generates pieces simultaneously generates vehicle schedules. This decomposition is accomplished by deleting all type 3, 4 and 6 edges from the graph and then finding a 'good' set of pieces (block IV). The feasible type 3 or 4 edges out of the last vertex in a piece and the feasible type 4 or 6 edges into the first vertex in a piece are then added to the graph and a least cost set of runs is found (block VI).

6. NON-INTERACTIVE VERSION OF ALGORITHM

We have implemented a non-interactive version of the algorithm and tested it on a data base from the city of Baltimore. This algorithm is described in this section. Several non-interactive procedures replaced blocks I, II and III shown in Figure 6. These used standard RUCUS input files to generate a modified version of the graph described in Section 4. The input files required were the trip-file, the id-file, the deadhead file, the relief point file and the inter-relief point travel time file. These files are described in detail in (8). Blocks VII and VIII were not included in the non-interactive version of the algorithm. Non-interactive versions of blocks IV, V and VI were designed, as follows:

IV: GENERATE PIECES

    A: Partition vertices of graph into set of levels
    B: For each level L starting with L=1
        B1: Expand all partial pieces whose weight > T'
        B2: Form matching graph using expanded partial pieces and vertices on level L
        B3: Find min. cost matching
        B4: Shrink edges in matching to form new set of partial pieces

V: OPTIMIZE PIECES

    A: For each pair of pieces, determine the feasibility of a combination/split
    B: Using pieces as vertices and combination/split costs as edge costs, form matching graph
    C: Find min. cost matching
    D: Determine new piece set based on solution to matching problem

VI: GENERATE RUNS

    A: (Generate partial 3-piece runs)
        A1: Form matching graph whose vertices are pieces and whose edges indicate that a pair of pieces will be used together in a 3-piece run
        A2: Find min. cost matching
        A3: Determine partial 3-piece runs based on solution to matching problem
    B: (Generate runs)
        B1: Form matching graph whose vertices are pieces and partial 3-piece runs and whose edges represent runs

> B2:   Find min. cost matching
> B3:   Determine final set of runs based on solution to matching problem

Several of the procedures involve the solution of a matching problem. The Appendix describes the matching problem.

Block IV, the piece generation algorithm, starts by partitioning the vertices in the graph into a set of levels. The level of a vertex equals the length of the longest path from vertex s to the vertex where the length of a path is defined as the number of edges the path contains (see Figure 7). The algorithm interactively generates larger and larger pieces. At each iteration, it adds the vertices on the next higher numbered level to the graph and attempts to merge these vertices into the 'partial pieces' already generated. If a vertex cannot be merged into a partial piece, it becomes the beginning of a new piece.

The problem of finding the optimal set of merges may be formulated and solved as a matching problem. Figure 8 illustrates this subproblem for iteration k. The vertices in the matching graph are the partial pieces and the vertices on level k. A vertex corresponding to a partial piece is adjacent to a vertex corresponding to a vertex on level k if there exists an edge in the original graph pointing out of the last vertex in the partial piece to the vertex on level k and if, when the vertex and edge are added to the partial piece, its duration does not exceed T. If we assign costs of one to all edges and vertices the minimum cost matching will merge vertices into partial pieces in a way that minimizes the number of new pieces generated.

The efficiency of the algorithm is enhanced by allowing the 'tops' of pieces to vary when the piece length gets close to T. Figure 9 illustrates this process. When the duration of a partial piece goes above a lower limit T' (a number less than T but fairly close to T), the first vertex in the partial piece is expanded. That is, it is no longer fixed as member of a partial piece, but may become a member of any partial piece to which it is adjacent. At the same time the partial piece is allowed to expand by adding a vertex to its bottom. No vertex additions will be allowed unless the new duration of the partial piece is less than T. However, the duration is now measured without including the top vertex which has been freed. In this manner the algorithm exchanges a new bottom vertex for a top vertex, if this process improves the solution. As Figure 9 illustrates, the exchange may be performed using the matching algorithm.

The non-interactive version of V initially considers combining and then possibly resplitting every pair of pieces (refer to Figure 10). A value is associated with this combining/splitting operation for each pair of pieces. We include in this value function components that minimize dead time, minimize trips to the garage (blocks), minimize the number of pieces and minimize the number of short pieces. The problem of determining the best set of combinations/splits can be solved as a matching problem. The vertices are the pieces and the edge costs are the costs of combining/splitting the corresponding pairs of vertices.

The final procedure of the non-interactive algorithm (block VI) combines the pieces into runs. Generating runs from pieces involves fixing crew-only arcs (types 3, 4 and 6). A two step procedure is used. The first step combines pairs of short pieces into partial 3-piece runs. The second step combines pairs of longer pieces or pieces and partial 3-piece runs into 2 and 3-piece runs. Again the matching algorithm is used. For the final step the cost function is the actual crew costs specified by the union contract.

7. COMPUTATIONAL RESULTS

We implemented the non-interactive algorithm in FORTRAN on an IBM 370/158. The matching subproblems were solved using a code developed by Georg Kazakidis, which is based on a method due to U. Derigs (4). We tested our algorithm on a data base for the Hartford Division of the Baltimore MTA bus system. The data base contained close to 1000 trips which produced 1602 d-trips. The d-trips were generated by splitting trips at relief points. Thus, no restrictions were placed on interlining. In practice interlining is allowed but the schedulers try to restrict its use.

The Baltimore MTA has a rather complex cost structure. Some notable features include time and a half paid for trippers with a minimum of two hours of paid time. Regular shifts must be paid a minimum of eight hours with time and a half for overtime. Spread time over ten and one half hours is paid at the rate of time and a half and spread over twelve hours is paid at a rate of double time. Time during a second break on three piece runs is paid for. In addition, the number of straight shifts must be at least as great as the number of split shifts.

If the constraints on the ratio of straight shifts to split shifts were explicitly included, the final problem would no longer be a 'pure' matching problem. We handled this constraint in true Lagrangean fashion (7). That is, we included in the objective function a penalty for violating this constraint.

Table 1 compares the solution we obtained with the solution currently in use which was generated manually by the schedulers in Baltimore. The total time required by both solutions is very close, with our solution being about 1% less. The structures of the two solutions are somewhat different. In particular, our solution requires more trippers but has fewer 3-piece runs. The larger number of trippers increases total time, due to tripper penalties; however, fewer 3-piece runs decreases total time, due to the paid second breaks and time required to travel between relief points.

	Solution Used by MTA	Solution Generated by Algorithm
No. of Crews	133	139
No. of Straights	53	52
No. of Splits	50	52
No. of Trippers	30	35
No. of 3-Piece	34	20
Total Paid Time	1041 hours	1030 hours

Table 1.

These results show that this automated procedure can produce results competitive with those obtained by manual scheduling. In addition, we feel that significant cost savings will be achieved by future implementations. In particular, time and space limitations precluded us from including all edges in the final matching graph. With a matching code better suited for our needs we would be able to include more, if not all, feasible edges in the matching graph and consequently generate a lower cost solution. Secondly, and more importantly, we believe the inclusion of the interactive features in the code will greatly enhance its effectiveness.

8. CONCLUSIONS

We have presented a model for formulating and solving the mass transit crew/vehicle scheduling problem. This model offers a large degree of flexibility due to its use of man/machine interaction. In particular, it allows the human scheduler to involve constraints and to guide the algorithm dynamically as it searches for a low cost solution.

We have presented computational results for a non-interactive version of the algorithm on a data base from the city of Baltimore. These results show that our model provides a viable approach to the problem. The non-interactive algorithm is distinguished from previous approaches in several ways. In particular, traditional approaches first generate vehicle schedules and then 'cut' runs from these schedules. We initially emphasize the crew scheduling component by first generating a set of pieces and then combining these pieces into runs. We feel this approach is particularly appropriate due to the dominance of crew costs over vehicle costs in the economics of this problem.

9. ACKNOWLEDGEMENTS

We wish to thank Roger Mitchell of ATE Management Inc. for providing us with data for the Baltimore problem and Moshe Dror of the University of Maryland for assisting with some of the data manipulation. In addition, we are grateful to Ulrich Derigs for providing us with his matching code.

APPENDIX

The matching problem is a set partitioning problem with no more than two ones per column. That is, it is an integer linear program of the following form:

$$\text{Minimize} \sum_{j=1}^{m} c_j \, x_j$$

$$\text{s.t.} \sum_{j=1}^{m} \bar{a}_j \, x_j = \bar{1}$$

$$x_j = 0,1 \text{ for all } j$$

where $\bar{a}_j$ is an n x 1 (0,1) column vector containing no more than two ones per column, and $\bar{1}$ is an n x 1 vector of ones.

Alternatively, it can be viewed as a problem on graphs. The inputs are a graph with costs associated with edge and vertex. The output is a set of edges and vertices that cover each vertex exactly once and that has minimum total cost. In this case, m = no. of edges plus the number of nodes, and n = no. of nodes (see Figure 11).

The matching problem is one of the few genuine integer programming problems for which an efficient solution procedure is known. Although efficient solution procedures are known for network flow problems, they can not be considered genuine integer programs. This is so because their underlying constraint matrices are totally unimodular and consequently linear programming techniques can be used directly to solve them. It should be noted that no efficient method is known for reducing a matching problem to a network flow problem.

The first solution to the matching problem involved an elegant theory in polyhedral combinatorics developed by Jack Edmonds (5). Several codes have been developed based on this theory. An early version of our crew/vehicle scheduling code used the BLOSSOMI code developed by Edmonds, Johnson and Lockhart (6). Recently, Ulrich Derigs (4) developed a solution procedure based on the use of shortest augmenting paths. The most recent version of our code made use of the Derigs code.

REFERENCES

1. Bodin, L. and Dial, R. Hierarchical procedures for determining vehicle and crew requirements for mass transit systems (or You only get what you pay for – at most) (Manuscript, January 1979).

2. Bennington, G.E. and Rebibo, K.K. Overview of RUCUS vehicle scheduling program (BLOCKS), in Bergmann, D.R. and Bodin, L.D. (eds.) Preprints: Workshop on automated techniques for scheduling of vehicle operators for urban public transportation services (Chicago 1975).

3. Dantzig, G.B. and Fulkerson, D.R. Minimizing the number of tankers to meet a fixed schedule, Naval Research Logistics Quarterly 1 (1954) 217-222.

4. Derigs, U. A shortest augmenting path method for solving minimal perfect matching problems, Report 79-06, Mathematisches Institut der Universitat zu Koln (1979).

5. Edmonds, J. Paths, trees and flowers, Canadian Journal of Mathematics 17 (1965) 440-467.

6. Edmonds, J., Johnson, E.L. and Lockhart, S.C. Blossom I: A computer code for the matching problem.

7. Geoffrion, A. Lagrangian relaxation for integer programming, Mathematical Programming Study 2 (1974) 82-114.

8. The MITRE Corporation, Vehicle scheduling and driver run cutting RUCUS package user documentation, Report MTR-6678 (1974).

9. The MITRE Corporation, Overview of RUCUS package driver run cutting program – RUNS, Report MTR-6803 (1974).

10. The MITRE Corporation, Vehicle scheduling and driver run cutting, Report M71-58 (1973).

11. Orloff, C.S. Route constrained fleet scheduling, Transportation Science 10 (1976) 149-168.

12. SAGE Management Consultants, Automated transit scheduling improvements study for the Ontario Ministry of Transportation and Communications (1977).

13. Ward, R.E. and Durant, P. Feasibility of a complementary solution to the bus operator scheduling problem, Report No. 795620R001REW, U.S. Dept. of Transportation (December 1979).

14. Wilbur Smith and Associates, The London Transport Executive, Main Lafrentz and Company, Allen T. Eaton, Identification of bus scheduling procedures and scheduling by computers, Memorandum Report 21 (1974).

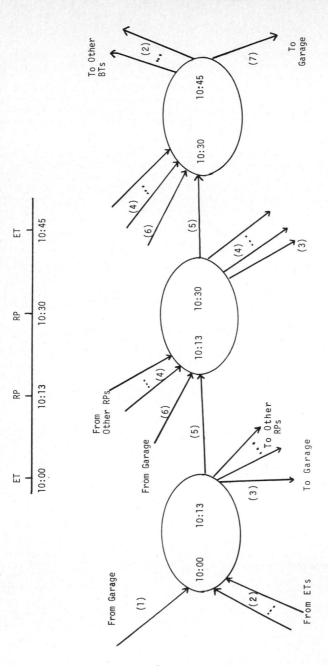

Figure 1: Crew/Vehicle Scheduling Graph

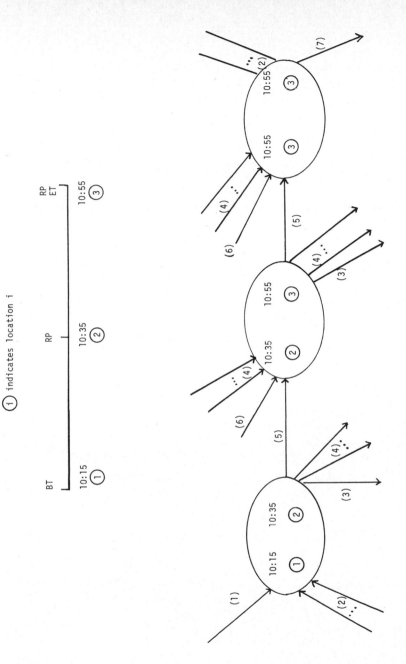

Figure 2: Graph Structure When Relief Point and End of Trip Coincide

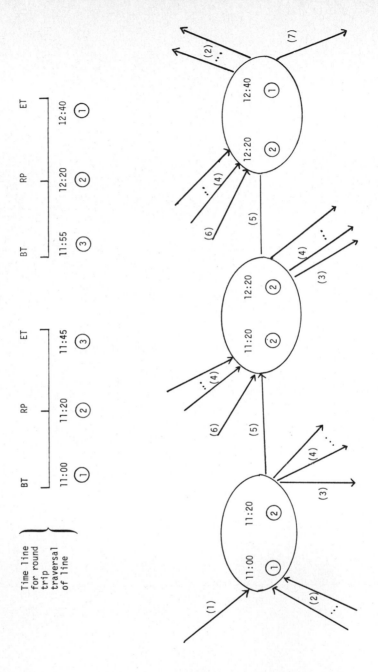

Figure 3: Network Structure When Round Trip Traversal of Line Required

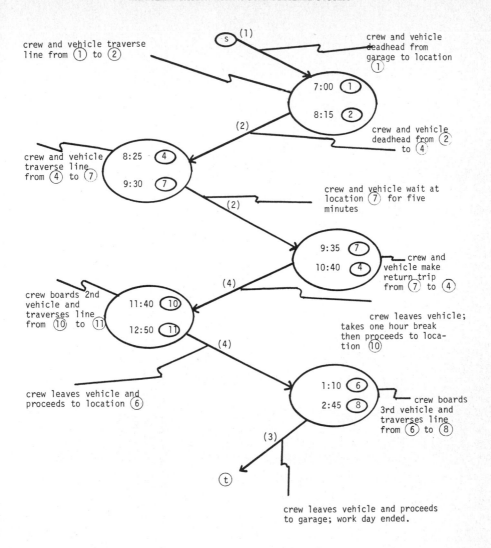

crew and vehicle traverse line from ① to ②

crew and vehicle deadhead from garage to location ①

7:00 ①
8:15 ②

crew and vehicle deadhead from ② to ④

crew and vehicle traverse line from ④ to ⑦

8:25 ④
9:30 ⑦

crew and vehicle wait at location ⑦ for five minutes

9:35 ⑦
10:40 ④

crew and vehicle make return trip from ⑦ to ④

crew boards 2nd vehicle and traverses line from ⑩ to ⑪

11:40 ⑩
12:50 ⑪

crew leaves vehicle; takes one hour break then proceeds to location ⑩

crew leaves vehicle and proceeds to location ⑥

1:10 ⑥
2:45 ⑧

crew boards 3rd vehicle and traverses line from ⑥ to ⑧

crew leaves vehicle and proceeds to garage; work day ended.

Figure 4: Correspondence between Path and Run

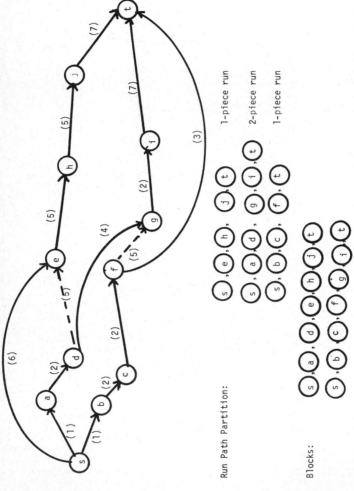

Run Path Partition:

(s , a , d , e , h , j , t)   1-piece run

(s , a , d , g , i , t)   2-piece run

(s , b , c , f , t)   1-piece run

Blocks:

(s , a , d , e , h , j , t)

(s , b , c , f , g , i , t)

If a type (5) edge leaves a vertex, a vehicle always follows it. Consequently, the blocks (vehicle schedules) can be found from the run path partition by deleting all type (3), (4), and (6) edges and adding all type (5) edges not used.

Figure 5:   Runs from (s,t)-Path Partition

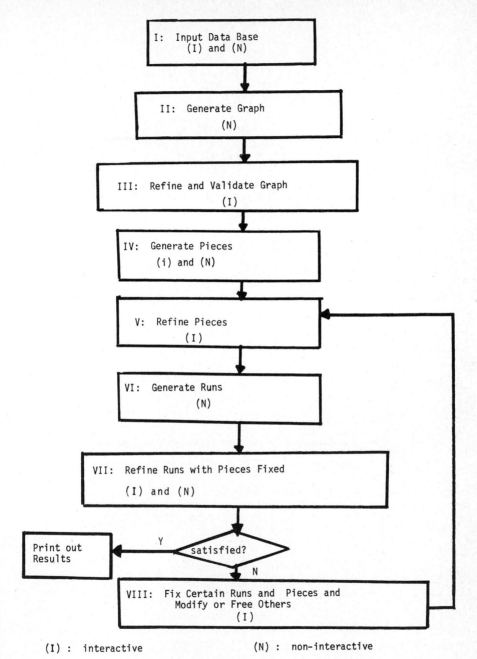

I: Input Data Base
(I) and (N)

II: Generate Graph
(N)

III: Refine and Validate Graph
(I)

IV: Generate Pieces
(i) and (N)

V: Refine Pieces
(I)

VI: Generate Runs
(N)

VII: Refine Runs with Pieces Fixed
(I) and (N)

satisfied?

Y

Print out Results

N

VIII: Fix Certain Runs and Pieces and Modify or Free Others
(I)

(I) : interactive   (N) : non-interactive

Figure 6: Diagram of Solution Procedure

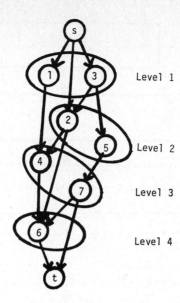

Figure 7: Partition of Vertices into Levels

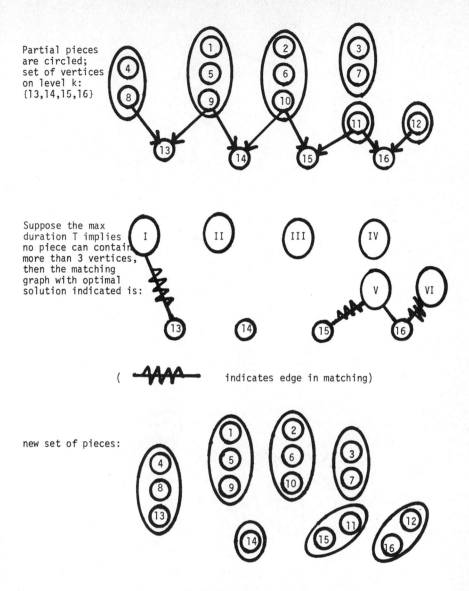

Partial pieces are circled; set of vertices on level k: {13,14,15,16}

Suppose the max duration T implies no piece can contain more than 3 vertices, then the matching graph with optimal solution indicated is:

(⟋⟋⟋⟋ indicates edge in matching)

new set of pieces:

Figure 8: Matching Problem at Iteration k

Using graph from
Figure 9 when tops
of pieces whose
length is greater
than 2 nodes are
expanded the new
graph is:

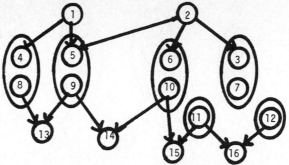

The matching
graph with optimal
solution is:

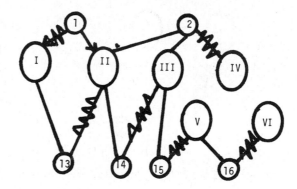

New set of Pieces:

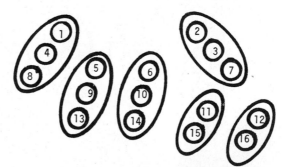

Figure 9: Matching Problem with Expansion
of Tops and Pieces

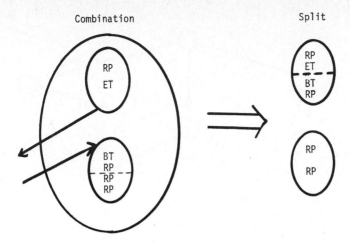

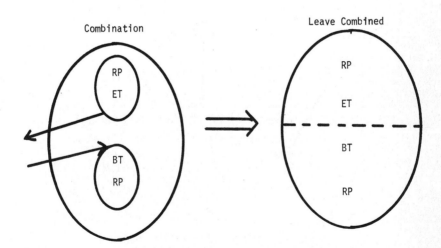

Figure 10A: Combination/Split Eliminates Trips to and from Garage

Figure 10B: Combination Eliminates Piece and Trips to and
From the Garage

Figure 10

Graph with Vertex and Edge Costs:

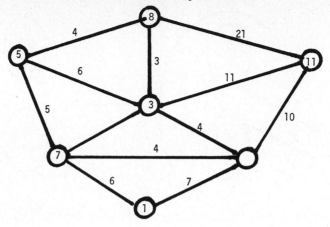

Min Cost Matching:

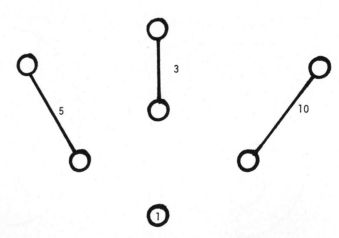

Total Cost = 19

Figure 11

Miscellaneous Papers

Computer Scheduling of Public Transport
A. Wren (ed.)
© *North-Holland Publishing Company, 1981*

ATTENDANCE AND ROSTERING SYSTEM

J.K.Jachnik

Partners in Management Ltd.,
Richmond
Surrey, U.K.

A system to allocate duties automatically to bus crews on a daily basis is described. The system is designed to give an even distribution of the amount of work and types of work done by each crew member. It is currently being operated by the Rome bus company.

INTRODUCTION

In the majority of large cities in Italy the method of organising the bus services poses different problems from those faced by English bus companies. In general, they require that crews work on only one bus in one day. This constraint is applied because of the unpredictability of traffic conditions which necessitates a long idle time between bus changes in order to guarantee that the crew will be available to change buses on time. As a result of this, the crew scheduling problem is greatly simplfied. There is, however, an entirely different problem in creating rosters, caused by the fact that the unions insist that bus crews should, as far as possible, work on different routes each day so that the job does not become too monotonous. This requirement is reversed in Milan because foggy weather conditions make driving hazardous and so it is preferred to have drivers who know their routes well. The purpose of this paper is to discuss the problems of rostering in view of the requirement to change routes each day, and how a computer solution to the problem is being used by Azienda Tramvie ed Autobus delle Comune di Roma (A.T.A.C.), the organisation which operates all of the urban bus and tram services within the city of Rome.

The normal solution to the rostering problem is to take a set of duties which cover certain routes operating from a particular garage and create a rota. The rota is constructed in such a way as to ensure that rest days occur at regular intervals, there is a minimum interval between consecutive day's duties, and duties are allocated so that weeks of early duties and late duties are alternated. A typical rota in England would contain in the region of 100 duties for each day. In Rome, because of the requirement to change routes each day, all of the duties operated from one garage are put into the rota. Thus the rotas typically contain in the region of 600 daily duties. The men working in the garage simply rotate through all of the duties on the rota so that after doing one cycle of the rota, all of the men have, in theory, done the same amount of work. In practice, absenteeism causes considerable unevenness in the distribution of work. In addition, the introduction of new schedules and consequently new rotas causes even more disruption to the work pattern, although new rotas are usually designed to keep this to a minimum. The effects of uneven distribution of work are much more complicated to control when large rotas are being handled, and so A.T.A.C. sought a computer solution to the problem.

The computer solution to the rostering problem is required to perform the function
of a rota, but to compensate automatically for uneven work distribution caused by
absenteeism and changes to schedules. Each day the system has to work out which
staff are available for work and what work has to be done. The two sets are then
matched according to the criteria that would apply to rotas, also taking into
account the even distribution of work. Because a rota enables staff to see well in
advance what duties they are to work, the computer system produces a provisional
roster eight days ahead of when the work is required to be done. The roster is
updated seven days later in order to compensate for changes due to absenteeism. As
the computer system contains information on absenteeism and work done, except for
the minor changes carried out on the day of work, the system also provides the
means of recording attendance and work records which are required for payroll
purposes and for legal purposes (in Italy a government body, INAIL, requires to be
able to inspect records of work done by all drivers of public service vehicles).

Within the garages of Rome, there are many types of duty which are done by
selected groups of staff. These special groups of duties were handled in the
manual system by creating separate rotas which contained the groups of special
duties. Any uncovered duties in these rotas, caused by absenteeism or
understaffing in the group, were covered by taking staff from the group working on
the main rota. Within the computer system it was decided to put all of the duties
operated from one garage for one day into a single large group and match them
against all of the available staff. This considerably increased the size of the
problem being handled on the computer, as the amount of work involved increases in
proportion to the square of the number of duties to be covered and the total
number of duties to be done each day varies from about 600 in the smallest garage
to about 1,100 in the largest, with a typical figure of about 800. It has,
however, proved to be very useful, despite the extra computing overhead, as in
consequence the system is sufficiently flexible to have allowed considerable
changes to the configuration of the special groups of duties with no change to the
system.

DESCRIPTION OF THE SYSTEM

The daily working of the system is now described in chronological order, day N
being the day on which the work is carried out by the bus drivers. Following this
are descriptions of the monthly processing of the system, ad hoc reports which may
be produced, system hardware and extensions to the system.

Prior to day N-8

The traffic department must ensure that any changes to services for day N have
been put into the duty library. The duty library is the means of telling the
rostering system which duties are to be run on day N. It contains a description of
each of the possible duties, details of when each duty may be suppressed in the
event of staff shortage, and information stating the days of the week on which the
duty is to be run and the dates between which it is to be run, so that the
rostering system can pick out all the duties to be run on day N.

The depot must notify the system of all staff expected to be absent on day N for
reasons other than normal rest days, by appropriate entries in the expected
absences file. The expected absences file contains the dates and reasons for
expected periods of absence for each member of staff.

In addition, the depot must make any changes to the staff file which may affect the work to be done on day N, for the staff file contains information on the type of work each member of staff may do, the days each member of staff has a rest day and other information required for the payroll.

Day N-8

The duty library is searched and all the duties to be run on day N are added to the daily duty file. This latter file holds the data organised by days, so that all the duties for day N are grouped together under the date of day N. It contains the description of each duty and its suppression details.

For each member of staff in the staff file a daily staff record is created and added to the daily staff file. The daily staff file holds the data organised by days so that all the staff for day N are grouped together under the date of day N. The daily staff record contains all the information required for the attendance system, i.e. information on work done or absences, etc. At this stage the daily record is blank unless the staff member is expected to be absent on day N or he is resting on day N, in which case the appropriate absence code would have been inserted from the expected absences file or put as RS if he is resting.

For each member of staff available for work at this stage a rostering record is created. This contains the information on the type of work he may do, the time of day at which he may work, the time of finishing work the previous day and the discrepancies from the average as obtained from the averages file.

The averages file is the file which maintains a record of the discrepancy from the average of the work of each member of staff, so that each man may be given an equitable amount of work and types of work. As well as evening out the duration of work done, it is also desired to even out the proportion of one-man operated bus duties, reserved duties and so on, as would have happened on a perfect rota.

The number of staff available for work on day N is counted up and compared to the number of duties to be run on day N. If there are too many duties, then some of the duties are suppressed according to the suppression details indicated on each duty. If there are too many staff then some dummy variation duties are invented by the system. A variation duty is a duty which is only provisionally assigned at this stage.

Not all the staff should be rostered at this stage because a number of staff must remain available as substitutes for those staff who, having been given a duty, become unavailable in the period up to day N: a number of duties are therefore flagged as variation duties. These duties are all the suppressable duties which have not so far been suppressed.

Having now sorted out which staff are to work and which duties are to be worked, each man may be assigned a duty. This is done by calculating a notional cost for each man to do each duty, ie. a measure of how good or bad it would be to give man M duty D, so if man M were working mornings then the cost of doing the duty D would be very high if duty D were in the afternoon, and much lower if in the morning, provided it was suitable in other respects. Many factors go into the calculation of cost, including time of day, duration of the duty, type of duty, when it was last worked, and so on.

Initially each man is given the cheapest duty (i.e. with the lowest cost) of the duties which so far have not been allocated to another man. This is fine for the first man because he will be given the duty best suited to him, but the last man has to take what is left, and this is probably not suitable. So, once a preliminary allocation has been made, the system will swap the men's duties in order to try and reduce the total cost of the allocation. For example, if man M has been given duty D and man N has been given duty E with costs as follows:

	M	N			M	N
D	$\boxed{0}$	100		D	0	$\boxed{100}$
E	100	$\boxed{1000}$		E	$\boxed{100}$	1000

then the total cost of the allocation can be reduced by swapping these duties. The increase in cost (the decrease in suitability of the job) in giving M duty E instead of duty D is less serious than the decrease in cost (the improvement in suitability of the job) achieved by giving man N duty D instead of duty E.

In this manner the system ultimately arrives at the best compromise that it can make between giving some men ideal duties and other men impossible ones.

It must be added that in practice it is not possible to reach the optimum solution to the problem. The cost matrix can be up to 1,200 square and as it is not sparse it actually occupies nearly 1.5 megabytes of storage. The machine being used only has .5 megabytes of real storage available in total, leaving only about 300k bytes to store the cost matrix, and so time constraints require that only that part of the matrix held within real storage is scanned for possible swaps of duties. The results obtained are, however, quite acceptable.

In addition the swapping algorithm outlined does not necessarily produce an optimum solution. It is possible to construct situations where a three-way swap can improve the situation where no two-way swap would do so. To solve the problem and guarantee an optimum solution would require treating the problem as a linear programming assignment problem. This would involve unwarranted complexity in this case.

Having decided upon an allocation of men to the ordinary duties, the system then performs a similar allocation of overtime volunteers to overtime duties, bearing in mind the main duty allocated.

The details of the duties allocated are now put into the staff record for day N and a listing of the staff roster for day N is produced. This shows either the reason for absence, the details of the duty assigned, or 'variazione', if a variation duty has been assigned to the member of staff. In addition, the man's average record is updated with the appropriate details of the duty which has been assigned to him.

Finally, a listing of the duty roster and the uncovered duties for the day N is produced followed by a print-out of the averages file.

The staff roster listing is now posted up in the depot so that the staff may see which duties they have been allocated for day N.

From Day N-7 to N-2

The depot must notify the system of all changes to the absences expected on day N by appropriate entries in the expected absences file.

The daily staff record for day N is now made accessible to the depot so that changes to the duties allocated by the system can be made by the depot staff if desired. The staff member may be given a specific alternative duty or a request for a change may be entered into the change request record for day N. In the latter case the staff member may request that no overtime is done, he does not drive a bus, that he works at a specific time of day, or that he is given a day's leave if there is a surplus of staff. The system will then try as far as possible to meet the request, it being mandatory to satisfy the first two types of request.

Day N-1

The daily staff record for day N is compared with the expected absences file entry for the member of staff. If a member of staff who was assigned a duty at day N-8 is now expected to be absent then the details of the duty he had been allocated would be removed from his record and the appropriate absence details inserted. If the staff member was expected to be absent and is now available for work, then the absence details would be removed from his record. The system will now assign duties to those member of staff who are shown as still available for work.

The staff who are not expected to be absent are split into two groups: those who have already had a duty assigned to them and those who have not. The duties for day N can then be split into two groups: those that have been allocated and those that have not. Then the staff with no duty as yet, can be allocated a duty from those which have not been allocated, in exactly the same manner as at day N-8, except that now no variation duties exist.

The details of the work allocated are then put into the staff records for day N and a new staff roster is produced. In addition, a shorter staff roster is produced showing only those members of staff whose work was changed or whose absence was changed, since day N-8. This variations roster is made available for transmission to the terminal at the depot so that the depot may receive it as early as possible on day N-1.

A duty roster is also produced for use by the despatcher on day N and a list of the duties so far uncovered is made available for transmission to the terminal at the depot.

The depot, having printed the variations roster and the uncovered duties list on their terminal, now make any necessary adjustments to the lists before posting them up in the depot.

Day N and Day N+1 up to 9.00 a.m.

As the duties are being worked the despatcher writes any changes made to the schedule onto the duty roster, as they happen during the day. These arise from unexpected absences, late arrival of staff, buses being held up in traffic and so on. These changes are then written onto the staff roster and communicated to the computer system via the terminal at the depot, so that by 9.00 a.m. on day N+1 the system has a complete record of all the work that was carried out on day N.

Day N+1 from 9.00 a.m.

The system reads through the daily staff records for day N and amends the corresponding average record where necessary. This is so that the man's average record should reflect the work he has actually done, rather than that which he was supposed to do, and in turn this will then affect the duty that the man may be given by the system in the future.

The system also produces a report on the apparent mistakes which have been made by the depot in writing in the changes on the staff roster.

The work done on day N is analysed by the system and a report is produced of the number and type of duties run and the number of staff working, etc.

After Day N+1

The system ceases to process the daily staff record on an individual daily basis as from day N+1. However, the daily record may be accessed via the terminal until the 16th day of the following month.

Confirmation of absences

So that the staff member receives the correct pay at the end of the month, certain reasons for absence need to be confirmed by the personnel department. A report is produced three times each month showing the days and reasons for absence which are to be confirmed. A copy of this report is held as a file within the system and the personnel department can confirm or change a reason for absence by an appropriate entry beneath the corresponding day.

The INAIL Report

On the 16th day of each month all the daily staff records and daily duty records for the whole of the previous month are removed from the system and consolidated into the INAIL report for each member of staff. This report lists the work done each day, reasons for absence, overtime pay, night bonuses, etc., for each day of the month, and summarises the whole month's work, so that pay can be calculated. The details on this report are written to tape, to be archived by the system.

Ideally, the personnel department should have confirmed all the absences that need to be confirmed prior to the INAIL report being produced. As this is not always possible, any unconfirmed absences are provisionally paid and the personnel department have a further two months to confirm the absences. At the end of two months the INAIL tape is read through and corrected and a new INAIL report is produced when changes have been made. Any absences still unconfirmed are assumed to be arbitrary unpaid absences. For each absence which was provisionally paid but which should have been unpaid, a correction record is brought forward to the current INAIL report.

An additional confirmation of absence report is produced when the INAIL report is created. This shows only those absences still unconfirmed when the INAIL report is produced.

Ad Hoc Reports

The following reports may be produced as required:

The duty library may be printed in full for any particular garage

The agents file may be printed in full for any particular garage

The averages file may be printed in full for any particular garage

A list of staff can be produced in descending sequence of holiday points. This enables the depot to decide which staff can be given the day off on a feast day

The INAIL reports may be re-printed from the INAIL tape, either individually or by garage

The confirmation of absences report file may be printed in full

A report showing the occurrence of rest days for each of the possible rest day codes in the staff file

Duty and staff rosters may be printed for any particular day, showing the actual status of the file.

Hardware of the system

The system is currently being run on an IBM 370/138 with 512k bytes of storage running under DOS/VS. Direct access to the data within the system is provided under control of the IBM real-time monitor CICS/VS. IBM 3270 visual display and printer terminals are situated in each garage, in the traffic department, and the personnel department. These terminals permit access to all of the data within the system so that the data may be interrogated and updated as required and reports may be printed locally. The rostering programs currently take about about 2½ hours of dedicated machine time to produce the rosters covering four depots. There is an additional half hour of processing required each day with another two hours on a monthly basis, but these take place under multiprogramming.

Extensions to the system

The system described above became operational at one garage of about 1,000 staff in October 1978. Since then it has been extended to another three garages, two of which are of similar size and one of which has about 1,500 staff. Ultimately it is planned to extend the system to all twelve of the A.T.A.C. garages. Currently work is being done to devise a system which balances the levels of service given by each garage by automatically detaching staff to work on duties operated by other garages. The system is also being extended to record daily utilisation of buses, so that statistics on mileage, breakdowns and maintenance can be produced.

Computer Scheduling of Public Transport
A. Wren (ed.)
© *North-Holland Publishing Company, 1981*

AUTOMATING EXTRABOARD ASSIGNMENTS AND
COACH OPERATOR TIMEKEEPING

James W. Schmidt and R. James Fennessy

SAGE Management Consultants
San Francisco, California
U.S.A.

A well-designed, modular software systems approach streamlines
the entire scheduling, bidding, daily dispatch, operator
timekeeping and control process of a transit property.
Significant economies and improved management efficiency and
control are realised with computer assistance for these
several functions. This paper resents an overview of the
conceptual approach, with features of the applications
software, and describes three key modules and their linkages;
the bidding, timekeeping, and extraboard rostering and
dispatching systems.

INTRODUCTION

The advent of computer-assisted runcutting and its broad implementation in North
America has spawned interest in further extension of the basic outputs. One such
area has been the development of relatively sophisticated exception timekeeping
systems for capturing payroll data for coach operators. At most transit
authorities, the operators select or 'bid' for their work runs on the basis of
seniority. Bidding typically occurs three or four times a year. Since the payhours
composition of regular runs is known in advance, and the bidding process defines
which particular operator will work each work assignment each day of the week, it
is possible to predetermine payroll information - provided that the work is
carried out as scheduled. Thus, only deviations from planned operations need to be
treated in the exception processing concept. Such methods are in relatively
widespread use in North America.

Further extensions of computer assistance in rostering crews and daily timekeeping
exercises are being made. Two examples are on-line computer assistance to manage
the work run selection process (bidding) and on-line runcutting to prepare daily
extraboard assignments. Computer bidding management streamlines the processing and
automates report preparation at the conclusion of the bidding. Interactive
runcutting software has been developed for several large North American transit
authorities. The interactive capability has also been adopted for the extraboard
tripper assignment problem and extraboard working conditions. Although working
rules and specific assignment techniques vary from property to property, the basic
problem statement is consistent - extraboard rotation and tripper assignment must
be done on a daily basis (often within a very short time period); then the
resulting assignments must be posted as the daily duty roster for the extraboard
operators, and the assignments must be passed to the accounting department daily
for payroll processing.

A well designed, modular software systems approach streamlines the entire
scheduling, bidding, daily dispatch, operator timekeeping and transportation
control process. Significant economies and improved management efficiency and
control are realized with computer assistance for these several functions. This

paper presents an overview of the conceptual approach and features of the applications software.

Three key modules are described in the following sections. These are the bidding system, the timekeeping system and the daily extraboard rostering and dispatching system. The linkages between these components can be readily seen.

OPERATOR BIDDING SYSTEM

The SAGE Bidding System is an interactive procedure to enable operator sign-up for run assignments in seniority sequence. It is designed to greatly reduce the time and cost of the typical operator bidding process and to avoid the errors which occur frequently in manual bidding methods.

The logic of the SAGE Bidding System is simple: prior to bidding, operators may enter multiple work run choices into a 'choice' file which is scanned and automatically applied in the signup. If an operator's choices have been depleted by others of higher seniority, a warning is given that allows time to contact the operator. Upon completion of the bidding process, alphabetic lists and seven-day work schedules by line are printed.

HOW DOES IT WORK?

Choice selection

Prior to bidding, the available work runs are posted for review by the operators. Following their scrutiny of the possible work assignments, operators select several preferred run choices and indicate their preference priority for each; their selections (straight runs, extra board, special trips) are then entered into the computer via a video display terminal. The entries are stored by operator and by bid (i.e., operators who signed up for a run), thus giving cross reference capabilities. Prior choice entry may be limited to operators whose work assignment overlaps with their scheduled bid time, but it is advantageous to use the system entirely based on the proxy concept, i.e., operators place their choices in the proxy file and the computer applies the choices to establish the sign-up. The advantage of this approach is the removal of time delay factors from the bid process, since the operators may report their choices any time during their day of selection.

Initialization

At the start of a sign-up a simple initialization procedure must be performed which sets up the seniority order and temporary storage for bids (so it would not interfere with the current bid still in effect).

Sign-up Procedure

Displaying the runs' status aids the operators in their selection. The display reflects each run already taken, by giving only a summary of available runs.

The operators are processed in seniority order by displaying their choice priorities in sequence. When a chosen work run is open, their employee number is entered to assign that operator to the run and the run is removed from the available list.

The screen shows the last operator signed up and the next one according to seniority. If a bid is entered out of sequence, a warning is displayed and supervisory approval is requested.

After each bid the proxy file is searched for the selections of the upcoming operator. When a choice is placed, the system will delete that choice for the remaining operators who entered that run as one of their choices. When the last selection is removed from an operator's choice list, a second warning message is given which allows the dispatcher to contact the operator well in advance of his scheduled sign-up time slot.

Roll-Back Feature

Sign-up procedures may be invalidated for various reasons following a given operator action. The supervisor/dispatcher can erase all bids past that point (saving a significant portion of the ·sign-up), and restart bidding for the remaining operators.

Concluding the Bidding Process

At the end of the bid, the program scans the file and flags any runs not taken or operators not signed up.

Reports

Two reports are printed on completion of the sign-up:

-   Alphabetic list of operators and their run assignments.

-   Five-day work schedule by line.

Corrections and Modifications

Changes to the sign-up can be entered at any time following the sign-up to reflect changes in the personnel file (retirement, new employees, and sick leave, etc.).

Loading the Sign-up File

The new sign-up will remain in a temporary file until the effective date when it is transferred to the permenant sign-up record. This allows early start of the bid without interfering with the current period timekeeping procedures.

OPERATOR TIMEROLL SYSTEM

The SAGE TIMEROLL system is a computer software package for transit operator timekeeping and payroll accounting. It is an 'exception reporting' system, requiring daily entry only for changes to the driver work assignments.

The TIMEROLL system has many features which make it cost effective and convenient:

-   Is fully interactive rather than batch mode for maximum convenience.

-   Detects errors at the point of data entry for immediate resolution.

-   Greatly reduces clerical effort while improving speed and accuracy.

- Is quickly learned and easily used without prior computer experience.

- Will connect to any payroll system.

- Runs on minicomputers, small business computers or mainframe hardware.

- Exception data entry of timekeeping information.

- Modular design with automated interface to computer run cutting module, operator bidding module, transportation dispatch module and gross-to-net payroll module.

- On-line entry, upate and display of personnel, bids, work assignemnts files.

- Automated handling of school day/non-school day assignments, days off, regular runs, relief runs, vacations and holidays, vacation bids and alternate operator assignments.

- Automatic handling of within-period pay rate changes, multiple step pay rates, standard vs. premium pay rules of labor agreement.

- Security protection against unauthorized system access, user password control, and information display-only or update capabilities.

- Allows advance-entering of future work assignments/operator bids prior to implementation date.

- Transaction log of all system entries for control and audit purposes.

- Full audit-trail records including reporting of work run changes, unassigned work, duplicated work, non-assigned operators, and balancing control totals.

- Repertoire of reports including operators' work assignments (alphabetically and chronologically), master lists of operators and work assignments, daily audit reports, management summaries (e.g., manpower utilization, cost analysis, etc.), payroll input master log.

- Maintains operator pay history file for retroactive pay, labor analysis (e.g., absenteeism, extra board costs, labor negotiation evaluations, etc.).

HOW DOES IT WORK?

The SAGE TIMEROLL is an interactive system, allowing the user to create, file, retrieve and alter timekeeping records quickly and easily via a simple video display terminal. Bid data is entered either automatically from the SAGE Bidding System module or by manual keyboard entry. Work run assignments and associated payhours detail is manually or automatically entered directly from the Runcutting System. A timekeeping clerk enters day-by-day exceptions to the scheduled work in only a few minutes each day for a moderate size property. And the dispatcher can use the system to get instant information on such things as bid assignments and unassigned work.

After each day's entries, the system automatically performs audit checks for inconsistencies in the run assignments such as missing or duplicate run assignments and then does the daily balance function. The timeroll records are thereby current after each day's transactions and immediately ready at the end of the payroll period for payroll system processing.

The SAGE TIMEROLL system also provides

-   capture of detailed labor distribution items for operator's time and wages.

-   operator labor utilization and related personnel management reports.

-   route cost analysis reports.

-   hard copy payroll input detail report.

System Processing Description

The SAGE on-line Exception Timeroll Reporting System for transit operators captures daily work assignments and pay hours data for each operator, processes the information for daily control, and passes summary information to the Payroll System.

The Operator Timekeeping System enables major streamlining of the daily recording of operator time for payroll accounting input, and significantly reduces the level of effort required for operator timekeeping. It is highly generalized and easily adaptable to local labor agreement, payroll requirements and timekeeping conditions. The system can accept input from either manually-prepared operator work assignments or from computer-generated (RUCUS) schedules. Moreover, the timekeeping module can automatically link with bidding management and/or daily dispatch modules. The system produces operator utilization and route analysis reports which are valuable for management control, route performance management control, and route performance evaluations.

Timekeeping System Processing Overview

The operator timekeeping system uses three basic sources of information to generate time records for the driver workforce:

Work Run Assignment File - which contains all of the work assignments scheduled to be operated each day of the pay period. This inforation is captured for each operator bid period either manually or on an automated basis using RUCUS. Modifications to the schedule records can easily be made via video display terminals to account for changes in regular runs, relief runs, extraboard slots, or any other special work assignments. The schedule records include regular paytime and its elements (platform, report time, travel, pull-in, etc.), and overtime (overtime premium, spread premium, shift premium). In case of two (or three) piece runs, it shows each piece with its time details, as well as start and end clock times. Regular operator, relief operator according to the signup, and today's operator according to exception entries, are included in the run record. So is the vehicle number operating on the run. The record shows the schedule number, effective date and the date of the last modification.

Personnel File - which contains operator personnel data, as well as bid information, vacation selection, and floating holiday or birthday if appropriate. This file also has on-line update capabilities. In addition, outline procedures for new bid entry are provided. Upon completion of the new bid entry, alphabetic and five-day work schedules can be printed.

Daily Work Exceptions - any variations in regular work assignments, as well as assignments for the extraboard operators, are registered by the dispatcher on his daily dispatcher sheets. These entries constitute daily exceptions which are entered for the affected operators via the on-line video terminal.

At the beginning of each pay period (Pay Period Initialization), a time record is generated from the schedule and personnel files for each operator and each day of the pay period. The time record reflects the work assignments which each operator has bid, and the details of the pay hours pertaining to the work bid for each day of the period, or the reason for not working (day off, vacation, holiday, leave, birthday, etc.).

As daily time records are generated, any pay rate changes during the pay period or legal holidays are automatically accounted for. At the end of this cycle, report listings are output showing the generated time records by day sequence and by operator sequence.

Daily Processing — is performed to account for exceptions registered by the dispatcher. They are easily entered through a video terminal. Transactions are logged and a daily transaction report is printed for supervisory control and monitoring. In addition, a daily audit and balance function is performed immediately after the day's exceptions have been entered to reconcile scheduled and unscheduled pay hours against independent controls (the schedule file plus dispatcher's sheet totals).

Security and Backup

The time records are protected by a carefully devised security system which permits only certain personnel to access the timekeeping records or to initiate any modifications to them. Three levels of security effectively control who may activate a terminal, who may access the time record update program, and who is permitted to enter any modifications.

In addition, daily backup procedures (combined with the transaction log) allow for automatic recapture of data or restart in the event it is needed.

Outputs

At pay period end, the system transmits the operator time records to the Payroll System and produces the following reports (System Outputs) for the current period, and year-to-date:

(1) operator timeroll report

(2) manpower utilization report

(3) labor distribution detail report

(4) line cost analysis report

In addition, a gross earnings file is transmitted to the payroll system that shows the pay hours(regular, or premium), leave records (sick, vacation, etc.), and accounting information.

The daily time records are accumulated on a history file and can be restored for retroactive pay, absenteeism studies, labor negotiation analysis, and for other reasons.

EXTRABOARD ROSTERING AND DISPATCH SYSTEM

Regularly scheduled operator work is determined during the run picking (bidding) process at each signup. Signups occur periodically, which may be intra-divisional or systemwide, or when schedules are changed significantly between the periodic signups. However, extraboard operators must be assigned daily. This system manages that activity.

Extra Board Rostering

All transit properties have extra (or spare) boards, which perform unassigned scheduled work, special services, substitute work,d cover work.

Unassigned scheduled work is usually unbid tripper runs and/or work which could not be rostered into weekly assignments for regular operators. Special service includes charters (although some properties have a charter board as well), special event service, etc. Substitute work is work which is temporarily unassigned because of regular operator birthdays, floating holidays, sick leave, jury duty, suspensions, extended illness, early retirement, etc.

Cover work is work performed on an exception basis because of late operators, no-shows,replacement service for breakdowns or accidents, supplemental service, etc. Cover work is usually performed by a subset of the extra board operators. Because their assignments are tentative, no advance rostering of their time is possible, and they play a waiting game until needed.

Most North American properties rotate the extra board on a daily basis, although some are rotated weekly. At the start of a new service period after a pick, the most senior man is at the top of the list, and others ordered by decreasing seniority. At the end of the day the top man is rotated to the bottom of the list, and a new work list is prepared for the next day (usually ordered by start time so that the top operator is first out).

Extra board rostering or mark-up is generally done manually and, with its complexities and short time frame, is extremely error-prone. As part of an automated dispatch system enhancement to its Exception Timeroll System. SAGE has developed an interactive Extra Board Roster and Dispatch System. The Extra Board Roster and Dispatch System has four components or modules - operator module, work module, assignment module and check-in module.

Operator Module

The Operator Module has two basic functions: initialization and daily operation. The initialization step accepts the operator bid file and extracts the operators who have selected the extra board or have been assigned to it. Seniority is ascertained by verifying badge number with the personnel file, and the initial order of the extra board list generated, with days off noted. The daily step rotates the top operator to the bottom, moves the other operators up one notch, and generates an operator file with the days-off operators 'deactivated', but holding position.

Work Module

The Work Module accepts all open work on two basic files: unassigned scheduled work, and another file containing other miscellaneous open work ascertained on a daily basis. This latter file is prepared by the dispatcher and is usually based upon the same file for the previous day.

Runs are constructed by an extraboard version of the SAGE Interactive RUNCUTTER. With the building of work, all extra board runs are checked for legality, optimized to minimize payhours, and costed out for payroll calculations. A run report is generated, as well as a work file for input to the Assignment Module.

Assignment Module

This mosule orders the runs, and assigns the operators to the extra board runs and cover work. Adjustments are automatically made if an assignment would not allow enough off time required by the labor agreement between runs for any operator. An extra board roster report is generated for posting in each garage.

Check-In Module

This final module accepts an Assigned Work file from the previous module and keeps track of operator notification. Operators at the garage scan the extra board roster and contact the dispatcher, who enters their respective badge numbers into the module. At a specified time, a list of uninformed operators, if any, is generated and they are contacted by the dispatcher. If any operator cannot be contacted, the dispatcher may make a substitution. The output of this module is a Final Work Assignment file for the extra board, which may be automatically input to the Exception Timeroll System for payhours timekeeping.

CONCLUSION

Computer-assisted scheduling innovations, together with computer technology advances, are the springboard for the software application extensions described above. Each of these application extensions depends on a work run file derived from the runcutting system. The expanding use of computer-assisted runcutting in North America has been a direct catalyst for the bidding, timekeeping, and extraboard daily rostering systems described above.

An integrated scheduling-operations dispatch-payroll processing linkage is emerging from this work. This will yield better quality control and data integrity, fewer labor hours required for these steps, more timely reports and information, and direct cost savings. These positive results will be welcomed to offset inflation, spiralling fuel costs and general cost escalation pressures.

Computer Scheduling of Public Transport
A. Wren (ed.)
© *North-Holland Publishing Company, 1981*

A GLOSSARY OF TERMS
IN BUS AND CREW SCHEDULING

Trevor Hartley

Operational Research Unit
Department of Computer Studies
University of Leeds
Leeds, U.K.

Apart from the need to define the terms used in scheduling, the British and American words for the same process are frequently different. Less often, the same word has different meanings in British and American contexts. Therefore, when a term has an exclusive meaning on one side of the Atlantic, this is indicated by the addition of (U.K.) or (U.S.) after the term. Terms peculiar to other countries are shown by (N) Netherlands, (Can.) Canada.

Expressions relating to mathematics or computing have been excluded from this survey, as there is little confusion between British and American usage.

ALLOWANCES   Additions to a CREW'S basic pay on top of PLATFORM TIME, including SIGNING-ON and -OFF allowances (REPORT and CLEAR (U.S.)), MAKE-UP, OVERTIME and SPREAD PENALTY.

ARC (U.S.)   A possible connection or HOOK between the end of one TRIP in service and the start of another. As LINK (U.K.).

BIDDING (U.S.)   The process in which CREWS choose or PICK the DUTY they wish to work. This is an alternative procedure to ROSTERING.

BLOCK (U.S.)   A sequence of TRIPS assigned to one bus for a day's work, beginning with a PULL-OUT and ending with a PULL-IN. As RUNNING BOARD, BUS SCHEDULE (U.K.).

BLOCKING (U.S.)   The allocation of buses to work a known set of TRIPS. As BUS SCHEDULING (U.K.).

BLOCK PARTITION (U.S.)   A set of PIECES OF WORK which exactly covers the BLOCK.

BOARD (U.K.)   Abbreviation of RUNNING BOARD.

BUS SCHEDULE (U.K.)   A set of RUNNING BOARDS or BLOCKS.

BUS SCHEDULING (U.K.) As BLOCKING (U.S.).

CHANGEOVER (U.K.)   The substitution of one CREW for another at a RELIEF POINT.

CLEAR TIME (U.S.)   The time allowed for a CREW to complete sign-off procedures
                        at the end of a DUTY. As SIGNING-OFF TIME (U.K.).

COFFEE CAR DUTY (N)   A LATE DUTY which includes IDLE TIME to permit a short
                        coffee break during the DUTY.

COMPILATION   The building up of PIECES OF WORK from one or more RUNNING
                        BOARDS   to   form   DUTIES.   As CREW SCHEDULING, DRIVER
                        ASSIGNMENT, OPERATOR ASSIGNMENT, RUN CUTTING.

COMPILER   The person who carries out the COMPILATION.

CONTINUOUS DUTY OR RUN   A day's work for a CREW where they will be paid for the
                        whole time from the start to the finish of the DUTY. The
                        term has been used to imply a DUTY with no MEAL BREAK off
                        the bus by some authors; others use it to mean any duty
                        other than a SPLIT DUTY, even if there is a paid MEAL BREAK.
                        As STRAIGHT DUTY.

COVER MEN (U.S.)   Reserve CREWS needed to replace scheduled CREWS who fail to
                        report for work, or to work EXTRA BOARDS. As SPARE MEN.

CREW (U.K.)   One or more persons who operate a bus.

CREW SCHEDULING   As COMPILATION.

CROSSOVER TIME (U.S.)   The time allowed within a DUTY for a CREW to travel between
                        the DEPOT and a RELIEF POINT, or between different RELIEF
                        POINTS when INTERWORKING. As JOIN-UP TIME, TRAVEL TIME
                        (U.S.).

DAY DUTY (U.K.)   A CONTINUOUS DUTY starting during, or just after, the
                        morning PEAK.

DEAD MILEAGE   The distance travelled by a bus not in revenue earning
                        service.

DEAD RUNNING TIME (U.K.)   The time taken for a bus to travel between two TIMING
                        POINTS out of service. As DEADHEAD TIME (U.S.).

DEADHEAD TIME (U.S.)   As DEAD RUNNING TIME (U.K.).

DEPOT   The place where buses are stored when not required for
                        service. As GARAGE, STATION (U.S.).

DEPOT SUPERINTENDENT   (U.K.) The person responsible for assigning buses to
                        RUNNING BOARDS, supervising the movement of buses to and
                        from the depot, and the SIGNING-ON and -OFF of CREWS. As
                        DISPATCHER (U.S.)

DISPATCHER (U.S.)   As DEPOT SUPERINTENDENT (U.K.).

DIVISION (U.S.)   A group of LINES that operate from a common DEPOT.

DRIVER ASSIGNMENT   As COMPILATION.

DRIVER'S MANIFEST (U.S.)   Daily working instructions for a driver. As PADDLE.

DUTY   The work to be performed by a CREW in one day. As SHIFT,
                            TURN, RUN (U.S.), WORKDAY (Can.).

DUTY SCHEDULE   As CREW SCHEDULE.

DUTY SHEET (U.K.)   A document showing details of each DUTY to the CREWS.

EARLY DUTY OR RUN   A CONTINUOUS DUTY which starts before the morning PEAK, and
                            finishes before the evening PEAK.

EXTRA BOARD   A short PIECE OF WORK not included in a DUTY, which is
                            worked by OVERTIME or by SPARE MEN. As TRIPPER, OVERTIME
                            PORTION.

FLEET   The total number of buses owned by a bus company.

FREQUENCY   The number of TRIPS (usually per hour) that are operated on
                            a route. This equals 60 / HEADWAY.

GARAGE   As DEPOT.

HEADWAY   The time between successive buses on a route.
                            This equals 60 / FREQUENCY (minutes).

HEADWAY SHEET (U.S.)   A document showing TERMINAL POINT times, MAXIMUM LOAD POINT
                            times, HEADWAYS etc. for a LINE. As TIMETABLE (U.K.),   LINE
                            SCHEDULE (U.S.).

HOOK (U.S.)   The association of one revenue TRIP to another in forming
                            the BLOCK.

IDLE TIME   The time allowed between the end of one TRIP and the start
                            of another in the same BLOCK, excluding the LAYOVER. As
                            SLACK TIME.

INCREMENT OF WORK (U.S.)   The portion of work between two adjacent RELIEF TIMES.

INTERLINING (U.S.)   The working by a CREW on two or more LINES during one DUTY.
                            As INTERWORKING (U.K.).

INTERWORKING (U.K.)   As INTERLINING (U.S.).

JOIN-UP TIME   As CROSSOVER TIME.

JOURNEY   A one-way movement of a bus along a ROUTE between two
                            TERMINAL POINTS. As TRIP.

LATE DUTY OR RUN   A CONTINUOUS DUTY starting before the evening PEAK, and
                            finishing around midnight.

LAYOVER   The time allowed at the end of a TRIP before further work
                            may start (sometimes called post-layover); or the time
                            before a TRIP that a bus must stand at a TERMINAL POINT
                            (sometimes   called   pre-layover).   As   RECOVERY   TIME
                            (post-layover), TURN-AROUND TIME.

LINE (U.S.)   A series of TIMING POINTS in order starting and finishing
                           with a TERMINAL POINT, between which buses run in service.
                           As ROUTE.

LINE SCHEDULE (U.S.)   As HEADWAY SHEET (U.S.).

LINK (U.K.)   As ARC (U.S.).

LIVE RUNNING TIME   The time taken for a bus to travel between two TIMING POINTS
                           in service.

MAKE-UP TIME (U.S.)   The difference between the guaranteed minimum daily payment
                           (typically eight hours pay) and the paid time in a DUTY,
                           where this is less than that minimum.

MAXIMUM LOAD POINT (U.S.)   The TIMING POINT on a LINE at which the passenger
                           volume is the greatest.

MEAL BREAK   A rest period off the bus during a DUTY to allow the CREW to
                           have a meal, for which payment may be made.

MIDDLE DUTY OR RUN   A CONTINUOUS DUTY starting in the late morning or early
                           afternoon, covering the evening PEAK, and finishing in the
                           early evening.

MULTIPLE PIECE RUN (U.S.)   A RUN consisting of three or more PIECES OF WORK.

NETWORK   The whole ROUTE structure provided by an OPERATOR (U.K.), or
                           PROPERTY (U.S.).

ONE PIECE RUN (U.S.)   A RUN where the CREW stays on one bus with no MEAL BREAK.

OPERATOR (U.K.)   The owner or the management of a bus company. As PROPERTY
                           (U.S.).

OPERATOR (U.S.)   The bus driver.

OPERATOR ASSIGNMENT (U.S.)   As COMPILATION.

OVERTIME   Payment for work exceeding the normal daily or weekly agreed
                           limit.

OVERTIME PORTION (U.K.)   As EXTRA BOARD.

OWL RUN (U.S.)   A LATE RUN starting after the evening PEAK and finishing the
                           following morning around 05.00.

PADDLE (U.S.)   A DRIVER'S MANIFEST when applied to a CREW; a BLOCK when
                           applied to a bus.

PASSENGER SCHEDULE (U.S.)   A survey of passengers at the MAXIMUM LOAD POINT used
                           to construct the HEADWAY SHEET.

PAYHOUR COST (U.S.)   The total cost of a DUTY including PLATFORM TIME and all
                           ALLOWANCES.

PEAK HOUR (U.K.)   The time(s) of maximum passenger demand on the NETWORK
                           during the day, usually at around 07.00 - 09.00 and 16.00 -
                           18.00 as the morning and evening peaks respectively.

PICKING (U.S.)   As BIDDING.

PIECE OF WORK   Part of a DUTY, composed of one or more INCREMENTS OF WORK from a single BLOCK or BOARD. Some authors use this as INCREMENT OF WORK.

PLATFORM TIME   The total time spent working on the bus in a DUTY.

PROPERTY (U.S.)   As OPERATOR (U.K.).

PUBLIC TRANSPORT (U.K.)   Transport services which are generally available, including bus, rail, air, ferry etc. As TRANSIT (U.S.).

PULL-IN   The time a bus returns to the DEPOT at the end of its scheduled work.

PULL-OUT   The time a bus leaves the DEPOT at the beginning of its scheduled work.

RECOVERY TIME   As LAYOVER (in the sense of post-layover).

RELIEF POINT   A TIMING POINT along a ROUTE where a CREW may leave a bus at the end of their DUTY, or for a MEAL BREAK, or to join another bus. Another CREW takes over the bus as the start of their DUTY, or after a MEAL BREAK, or from another bus, and the bus continues in service.

RELIEF TIME   A time during the day when a bus passes a RELIEF POINT.

REPORT TIME (U.S.)   The time allowed for a CREW to sign-on and prepare for work at the start of a DUTY. As SIGNING-ON TIME (U.K.).

ROSTER (U.K.)   A cycle of daily DUTIES for a week or longer which a CREW works in sequence. This is an alternative process to BIDDING. As ROTA SHEET.

ROTA SHEET (U.K.)   As ROSTER.

ROUTE   As LINE.

RUN (U.K.)   As JOURNEY, may be either LIVE or DEAD.

RUN (U.S.)   As DUTY.

RUN CUTTING (U.S.)   As COMPILATION.

RUN TIME (U.S.)   As LIVE RUNNING TIME.

RUNNING BOARD (U.K.) As BLOCK (U.S.).

RUSH HOUR   As PEAK HOUR.

SERVICE (U.K.)   As ROUTE.

SERVICE (U.S.)   The type of schedule e.g. weekday, Sunday etc.

SHIFT   As DUTY.

SHORT WORKING (U.K.)   A TRIP which starts after the usual initial TERMINAL POINT
                        or stops short of the usual final TERMINAL POINT, or both.

SIGNING-OFF TIME (U.K.)   As CLEAR TIME (U.S.).

SIGNING-ON TIME (U.K.)   As REPORT TIME (U.S.).

SLACK TIME   As IDLE TIME.

SPARE MEN   As COVER MEN.

SPLIT DUTY OR RUN   A DUTY which usually covers both PEAKS and has a long MEAL
                         BREAK between the PEAKS that may be unpaid.

SPREAD (U.S.)   Abbreviation of SPREAD TIME.

SPREAD PENALTY   A payment to be made when the SPREAD TIME of a DUTY exceeds
                         an agreed limit.

SPREAD RUN (U.S.)   As SPLIT RUN.

SPREAD TIME (U.S.)   The total time between the start and finish of a DUTY. As
                         SPREADOVER (U.K.).

SPREADOVER (U.K.)   As SPREAD TIME (U.S.).

SPREADOVER DUTY (U.K.)   As SPLIT DUTY.

STATION (U.S.)   As DEPOT.

STRAIGHT DUTY OR RUN   As CONTINUOUS DUTY.

STRETCH (U.K.)   The time from the start of a DUTY to the MEAL BREAK; or from
                         the end of the MEAL BREAK to the end of the DUTY. The
                         authors who use PIECE OF WORK to mean INCREMENT OF WORK use
                         STRETCH to mean PIECE OF WORK.

SWING RUN (U.S.)   As SPLIT RUN.

TAKE-OVER POINT (U.K.)   As RELIEF POINT.

TERMINAL POINT   The starting or finishing TIMING POINT of a ROUTE. As
                         TERMINUS.

TERMINUS   As TERMINAL POINT.

TIMETABLE   As HEADWAY SHEET.

TIMING POINT   A point along a ROUTE at which the times a bus passes are
                         measured.

TRAIN (U.S.)   As BLOCK.

TRANSIT (U.S.)   As PUBLIC TRANSPORT (U.K.), but normally refers to bus
                         services.

TRAVEL TIME   As LIVE RUNNING TIME in BUS SCHEDULING; as CROSSOVER TIME in
                    CREW SCHEDULING.

TRIP   As JOURNEY.

TRIP SCHEDULING (U.S.)   Building up the HEADWAY SHEET from the PASSENGER
                    SCHEDULE.

TRIPPER (U.S.)   As EXTRA BOARD.

TURN (U.K.)   As DUTY.

TURN-AROUND TIME (U.S.)   As LAYOVER.

TWO PIECE RUN (U.S.)   A DUTY with a MEAL BREAK between STRETCHES of work. The
                    STRETCHES may be on different BLOCKS and ROUTES according to
                    local agreements.

VEHICLE SCHEDULE   As BLOCK.

WORKDAY (Can.)   As DUTY.